STEPHEN SCHWARTZ

THE TWO FACES OF ISLAM

Stephen Schwartz is an author and journalist who has been Washington bureau chief for the Jewish *Forward* and an editorial writer for the Voice of America. Prior to that he was an interfaith activist in Bosnia-Hercegovina and Kosovo. His previous books include studies of the Spanish Civil War, the radical culture of California, and the Kosovo War. He lives in Washington, D.C.

ALSO BY STEPHEN SCHWARTZ

Spanish Marxism vs. Soviet Communism:
A History of the POUM
(with Víctor Alba)

From West to East:
California and the Making of the American Mind

Kosovo: Background to a War

THE TWO FACES
OF ISLAM

Saudi Fundamentalism and

Its Role in Terrorism

STEPHEN SCHWARTZ

ANCHOR BOOKS

A Division of Random House, Inc. • *New York*

To the memory of

Myhedin Shehu

Beloved shaykh of the Halveti-Karabashi Sufis

of Rahovec, Kosovo

Murdered July 19, 1998

Fatiha

FIRST ANCHOR BOOKS EDITION, SEPTEMBER 2003

Copyright © 2002, 2003 by Stephen Schwartz

Several of the names and identifying characteristics of the individuals depicted in this book have been changed to protect their privacy.

The Library of Congress has cataloged the Doubleday edition as follows:
Schwartz, Stephen, 1948–
The two faces of Islam: the house of Sa'ud from
tradition to terror / Stephen Schwartz.
1st ed.
New York : Doubleday, 2003.
p. cm.
Includes bibliographical references and index.
1. Islam—History—20th century. 2. Islamic renewal—History—20th century.
3. Islamic fundamentalism—History—20th century.
4. Wahh ab iyah—Saudi Arabia. 5. Islam and state—Saudi Arabia.
6. Islam and state—Islamic countries—20th century.
BP60 .S36 2003
297.8'14—dc21

Anchor ISBN: 1-4000-3045-5

Author photograph © Lorenzo Casanova

www.anchorbooks.com

Printed in the United States of America
10 9 8 7 6 5 4 3 2

The world is no barrier to God;
  He is visible in all that exists.
Remove yourself from between yourself and Him;
  Let Him speak to you as to Moses, from the burning bush.
                              — MEHMED ESAD DEDE

Turmoil filled the skies like the fall of night;
  And spreading, it nearly covered the whole world.
                    — AL-SAYYID ABD AL-RAHMAN AL-AHSA'I

Islam is the best, but we Muslims are not the best. The West is neither corrupted nor degenerate. It is strong, well-educated, and organized. Their schools are better than ours. Their cities are cleaner than
ours. The level of respect for human rights in the West is higher, and
the care for the poor and less capable is better organized. Westerners
are usually responsible and accurate in their words. Instead of hat-
ing the West, let us proclaim cooperation instead of confrontation.
                    — BOSNIAN PRESIDENT ALIJA IZETBEGOVIĆ

CONTENTS

PREFACE

In the aftermath of the terrorist attacks of September 11, 2001, people of goodwill on both sides of the divide between the Judeo-Christian and Muslim worlds were filled with deep anxieties. For Westerners, it seemed that a dreadful clash of civilizations had become imminent and unavoidable. For Muslims, it was clear that serious injury had been done to the most powerful nation on earth—a wound that could only call forth a terrible retaliation. Many Jews and Christians seized on the belief that something feral and evil in the faith of Muhammad had made September 11 inevitable. Many Muslims feared that a new "crusade" against Islam would ensue, expressing deeply ingrained impulses in the West.

After almost one and a half millennia of Islamic civilization, the Judeo-Christian West remains extraordinarily confused and ignorant about this major development in the history of monotheistic religion. It seems absurd to realize that after 14 centuries of contact between the two, mutual comprehension was deferred until a hideous terrorist crime killed thousands in the world's greatest city. Islam is viewed by most people in the West as a monolith, even though a single opinion may no more be ascribed to its adherents than to those of Judaism or Christianity. But in the wake of September 11, Islam has been identified more than ever, in the Western mind, with violence, intolerance, and fanaticism. To many Americans, the face of Islam is seen in Arab celebrations of the twin tower massacres, the malevolent smirk of Osama bin Laden, the images of the

19 hijackers, and suicide bombings in Israel. That face is identified, above all, with maniacal hatred of the United States.

And while the face of Islam appeared, after the attacks on America, to be uniformly menacing, a Babel of ignorant non- and anti-Muslim voices assailed frightened Westerners. Competing explanations for "Muslim hatred" emerged rapidly and on all sides. Some commentators bemoaned the abuses of Western imperialism; others pointed to the problem of Israel. Self-styled experts claimed to have found the proof of deep flaws in Islam itself, in the text of *Qur'an* and the long history of Christendom and Muslim civilization in military conflict. These essayists and columnists sketched the image of an Islam that is intrinsically aggressive, contemptuous of modernity and the West, fearful of women, and hateful of reason and individuality. Conservative ideologues attempted to rouse American opinion by reviving the archaic vocabulary of Christian civilization under attack. Paul Johnson, in a widely read essay, rejected the idea that Islam is "a religion of 'peace.'" This is untrue, he wrote: "Islam means 'submission,' a very different matter, and one of the functions of Islam, in its more militant aspect, is to obtain that submission from all, if necessary by force. Islam is an imperialist religion."

Islamophobic writers proliferated like mushrooms in the Western media, reciting clichés about the alleged forcible conversion of Jewish and Christian populations, a supposed ban on Christian churches in all Islamic societies, and the ostensible prevalence of customs like female genital mutilation in Muslim lands. In Europe, extremist politicians like Jean-Marie Le Pen accumulated votes by manipulating the specter of Muslim immigrants, like marauding pirates with knives between their teeth. Before his assassination the Dutch politician Pim Fortuyn called, in so many words, for his fellow citizens to vote for or against Islam.

Nobody in Western Europe would have dreamed of suggesting a political referendum on Judaism; but Islam was now viewed as the fearsome and implacable Other. It was as if the lessons of the Holocaust, in which Europe had allowed the wholesale massacre of a non-Christian people that had lived for centuries on its territory, strictly because of their faith, had been completely forgotten. Other smears involved charges of wholesale cultural destruction, of the type advanced by V. S. Naipaul, who claimed that India had only become impoverished because of Muslim power. Among the Christian Slavs and their apologists, there had long been talk of a Muslim demographic threat to Europe.

President George W. Bush at first seemed to echo this rhetoric when he clumsily designated the war on the Osama bin Laden/Taliban terror alliance a "crusade," perhaps the worst word that may be used in such a context. Such terminology was a gift to bin Laden; the Western war to liberate the Muslims of Afghanistan might better have been called an authentic and righteous *jihad*.

But none of these views of Islam represented an accurate accounting of its essence. A journey to the authentic heart of Islam sets one at odds with a great deal of erroneous common wisdom in the West—a situation Islamic extremists have exploited to advance their own agenda. The lack of a central religious authority in Islam contributes to the problem; for outsiders it is difficult to distinguish between the margins and the mainstream.

Westerners until now have known almost nothing about the deep conflict that presently rages over the soul of Islam, a struggle to determine its future which is, at the same time, a controversy over its past. Knowledge of this split, and the nature of its protagonists, constitutes a "secret history" comparable to the hidden archival record of Soviet Communism. But it is a confrontation we cannot ignore and from which we cannot stand aloof.

When President Bush and other Western leaders assured their publics that terrorism is at odds with true Islam, and were echoed by the Islamic establishments in many Muslim and non-Muslim countries, they were both right and wrong. The strain of Islam that encouraged bin Laden and his followers represents neither a majority of Muslims nor traditional Islamic values. But nor is it a matter of a simple hijacking of the faith. The extremist face of Islam, which justifies violence and stirs hatred, reflects rich and powerful interests. That face is possessed by the ideology known as Wahhabism, a "death cult" that is the official religious dispensation of the Saudi kingdom and which the Saudis, utilizing the financial power they have derived from their vast oil revenues, have spent decades—and billions of dollars—exporting to the rest of the world, from Pakistan and India to the Balkans, the Philippines, Western Europe, and America itself.

Despite the proliferation of terrorist groups with diverse-sounding names and backers, the real source of our problem is the perversion of Islamic teachings by the fascistic Wahhabi cult that resides at the heart of the Saudi establishment, our putative friends in the region. As is well known to the rest of the world's one billion Muslims, most of whom are not Wahhabi, and who resist its imposition on their societies, this cult has flourished for decades, ironically enough under Western protection. We have nurtured this serpent in our very bosom. Yet no history of the Wahhabi cult has been written for a general audience; it is high time to correct this omission.

Until September 11, we typically saw and heard only two kinds of Muslims in our media: rich oil princes and unemployed ranters in the streets of Arab cities. Even after the atrocities in New York, Washington, and Pennsylvania, old habits persist. The common wisdom is that we must listen to the Arab street, because, we are told, its voice shapes political consciousness in those societies. Nothing could be further from the truth: In the highly stratified Arab and Muslim nations, the street counts for nothing, which is the main reason people often crowd it yelling hateful slogans. The time has come to look beyond the Arab street to the antifundamentalist, anti-Wahhabi traditions in Islam.

The petroleum princes and the shouting street are the two extremes in an environment that is a great deal more educated and diverse than we have led ourselves to believe. America has a lot to learn about Islam. Journalists, academics, and diplomats urgently need to find out whom to listen to, if we are to improve our relations with the Muslim world and prevent the worsening of the so-called clash of civilizations.

With this book I have tried to present a fresh view of Islam, challenging the hegemony of Saudi-backed extremism in the Muslim world but equally rejecting the simplistic, "crusader" polemics widely seen in Western intellectual life today. Mainstream Islam restored to its past power, traditional and pluralistic, will generate new, fruitful contributions to humanity. It will draw on the hidden history the West should have learned long ago, but to which it has been blinded by prejudice, myth, and fear. The war against the terror axis may last a decade, or many decades. It may continue as long as the Cold War did, or longer. It is imperative that we find reliable Muslim allies in this war; that we learn their languages, and understand their cultural differences as well as their similarities.

I do not believe anything in Islam led intrinsically or inevitably to September 11. If Islam had been an unrelievedly violent and aggressive religion, it would have disappeared long ago, like numerous pagan cults. I base this view on my own experience as a journalist and writer on the Balkan wars of the 1990s, during which I encountered the other face of Islam—pluralist, spiritual, and committed to coexistence with the earlier Abrahamic revelations, Judaism and Christianity.

Westerners, terrified of the prospect of an Islamicized West, seem unable to recall that there was once a viable option for a Europeanized Islam. Obsessed with a narrative centered on conflicts, invasions, misunderstandings, and competitions for domination, we have forgotten that there were also long periods of commercial and cultural interchange, in Spain and elsewhere in the Mediterranean, above all in the Ottoman Balkans, whose society was uniquely European *and* Islamic. My review of this history offers an alternative to the concept of an inevitable clash of civilizations.

Many readers may find this assertion counterintuitive, because the Balkan nightmare of the 1990s revived the image of that region as a cauldron of interreligious hatred and savagery, which many presume was derived from a past of Turkish oppression, and where controls on deep-rooted violence disappeared with the end of Communism. Of course, it is inarguable that in the late 18th and 19th centuries, as partially described in this book, the Muslim Balkans fell into decline, their economy far surpassed in development by Western Europe, and inevitably into ethnic and political wars. Nevertheless, during their period of highest prosperity and stability, from the middle of the 15th to the middle of the 18th centuries, the Ottoman Balkans were by far the most forward-looking region in the Islamic world, thanks to their inextricable involvement with the rest of Europe. The West has much to learn from the long Balkan experience of multifaith cooperation and civility: It embodies the other face of Islam, the one we must cultivate and support if we are to help the Muslim world conquer its own destructive demons—its version of fascist and Communist totalitarianism—and thereby help ourselves.

I was first drawn to the Balkans—Albania, the former Yugoslavia, and Romania, in particular—by a linguistic and literary interest in the culture of the Sephardic Jews who once numbered in the hundreds of thousands in the region. These Jews descended from those expelled by the Christian monarchs of Spain and Portugal at the end of the 15th century. Welcomed to the Ottoman domains, they settled as far north as the banks of the Danube, in virtually every city in the Balkans and Turkey: Dubrovnik, Split, Sarajevo, Belgrade, Bucharest, Shkodra, Skopje, Sofia, Vlora, Adrianople, Constantinople, Smyrna. Their "capital" was Salonika in Greek Macedonia, an Ottoman city-state of 100,000, a "Hebraic republic" of which as many as 80 percent were Jewish. There they maintained their own language, which became known as Judeo-Spanish and Ladino. They trained rabbis, wrote commentaries on the *Torah*, taught the mystical secrets of the *Kabbalah*, disputed for leadership of world Jewry, and printed thousands of copies of religious and secular books in Hebrew, Aramaic, and Judeo-Spanish, supplemented, later, by newspapers and magazines. They married, fostered families, wrote poetry and balladry, traded and traveled, and recited the prayers and observed the festivals of their faith in their numerous synagogues. They constituted a whole Jewish civilization.

The Balkan Sephardim struck deep roots in the lands between the Adriatic and the Black seas. They included one of the great pioneers of Zionism, Yehudah Alkalay (1798–1878), who was born in Sarajevo and served as a rabbi in Zemun, across the Sava River from Belgrade. The Sephardim who supported Zionism saw it less as a solution to the problem of anti-Jewish prejudice than as a mystical fulfillment of the messianic Covenant, and those among them who went to the Holy Land typically did so more for spiritual than ideological or political reasons. Many were also drawn into the socialist and other revolutionary movements. But except for those who resided in Turkey and Bulgaria, and small remnants elsewhere in the Balkans, they were wiped out in the Holocaust. Their literary and religious traditions were almost entirely destroyed with them. Sephardic girls facing death in the Nazi concentration camps of Poland comforted each other by singing the Spanish love lyrics with which they had grown up.

I am a child of California, bilingual in English and Spanish; I had worked in Latin America and Spain, and had published volumes on the history of Hispanic culture and the Spanish civil war. I was deeply attracted by the idea that some part of this Judeo-Spanish world might have survived in Bosnia-Hercegovina, its farthest northern extension. As a staff writer for the *San Francisco Chronicle* and a correspondent for the Jewish *Forward*, I first went to the region in 1990, as Yugoslavia was collapsing. I attended Jewish services, photographed synagogues and graveyards, and listened, for the first time, to Sephardic melodies sung by the surviving speakers of the Judeo-Spanish idiom. I was deeply moved, on my first visit to Sarajevo, to find a monument to local volunteers who died while serving in the Spanish Republican Army—all of whom bore Sephardic, i.e., Spanish names. Iberia's long-lost Hebrew children had returned to its soil to sacrifice their lives in the cause of its freedom.

I formed strong friendships in the Jewish communities of Croatia and Bosnia-Hercegovina. But I also encountered there the native European Islam of the Balkans, and the fascinating traditions of the Albanians. And soon I observed the emergence of a new, valiant, desperate, and cruel struggle for liberty, as the Bosnian Muslims, and then the Albanians, came under brutal attack.

From 1991 to 1995, I was active in the work of the Daniel Dajani, S.J., Albanian Catholic Institute, a unique forum for the study of European Islam and its relations with Christians and Jews, located in San Francisco. The Institute was mainly involved in the reconstruction of Catholic life in Albania, Kosovo, and Macedonia, after the long martyrdom imposed by Communism. Thanks to my work there, I gained a detailed knowledge of Albanian linguistics, literature, history, and religion. My literary interest in the Balkans had become historical, then turned in a spiritual direction. In the Jewish realm, I assembled a large personal library, including such Balkan Sephardic classics as the famous *MeAm Lo'ez* (In Foreign Tongues), a *Torah* encyclopedia published in Judeo-Spanish, beginning in the 18th century, in Constantinople and Salonika. But at the same time I read the works of the Albanian and Bosnian Franciscans and Muslims, and encountered the strong local traditions of the Sufi orders. Much of what I found reproduced ideas and concepts I had discovered long before, in the 1960s, as a typical San Francisco student of mysticism, and reaffirmed lessons I had learned in the streets of Narbonne in Provence, Barcelona, and Palma de Mallorca, from the history of Islamic Spain and its relations with Jewish and Christian culture.

I also took up a matter that has become extremely controversial in recent times: the *dhimma*, or contract governing the relations of Muslim rulers with People of the Book, i.e., Christians and Jews. Researching community and ecclesiastical histories, I examined the reality of the Ottoman *dhimma* as it applied to the Balkan Sephardim, and the Bosnian and Albanian Catholics. Unfortunately, the Islamic *dhimma* has lately become a pretext for a prejudicial attitude among some Jews, one that apes the "crusader" mentality by which Islamophobia is justified as a defense of the Christian West. Basing themselves on pseudoscholarship, even respectable authors like the Israeli historian Benny Morris, known for his sympathetic account of the expulsion of Palestinians in 1948, have put forward the claim that Jewish life under Islamic rule was universally and unrelievedly oppressive.

Such claims about the *dhimma*, and an allegedly permanent and unavoidable Jewish-Muslim conflict, may only be sustained by writing the Sephardim in Turkey and the Balkans completely out of Jewish chronicles. It is charged that the Jews were "second-class citizens" under Ottoman rule; but the very concept of citizenship existed nowhere in the world before the late 18th century, and the status of the Jews under the Turkish sultans was unquestionably superior to that in the Christian domains, where Jews were subject to wholesale violence.

Around 1454, Rabbi Isaac Sarfatti of Adrianople gives substance to this view of Jewish life under Muslim rule in a letter to the German Jews, in which he declared,

> I have heard of the afflictions, more bitter than death, that have befallen our brethren in Germany; of the tyrannical laws, the compulsory baptisms and the banishments, which are of daily occurrence. I am told that when they flee from one place a yet harder fate befalls them in another . . . On all sides I learn of anguish of soul and torment of body; of daily exactions levied by merciless oppressors. The clergy and the monks, false priests that

they are, rise up against the unhappy people of God . . . for this reason they have made a law that every Jew found upon a Christian ship bound for the East shall be flung into the sea. Alas! How evilly are the people of God in Germany treated; how sadly is their strength departed! They are driven hither and thither, and they are pursued even unto death . . . Brothers and teachers, friends and acquaintances! I, Isaac Sarfatti, though I spring from a French stock, yet I was born in Germany, and sat there at the feet of my esteemed teachers. I proclaim to you that Turkey is a land wherein nothing is lacking, and where, if you will, all shall yet be well with you. The way to the Holy Land lies open to you through Turkey. Is it not better for you to live under Muslims than under Christians? Here every man may dwell at peace under his own vine and fig tree. Here you are allowed to wear the most precious garments. In Christendom, on the contrary, you dare not even venture to clothe your children in red or in blue, according to our taste, without exposing them to the insult of being beaten black and blue, or kicked green and red, and therefore are ye condemned to go about meanly clad in sad-colored raiment . . . And now, seeing all these things, O Israel, wherefore sleepest thou? Arise! And leave this accursed land forever!

To uphold the image of Muslims as implacable enemies of the Jews over whom they ruled one must further purge from history the "revolution" in Jewish life caused by the 17th-century Cossack massacres in the Ukraine, during which hundreds of thousands of innocents were killed, and when refugees from Eastern Europe looked to the Turkish Sultan to protect and even avenge them.

A valuable truth about the *dhimma* and its consequences emerges from a topic seldom discussed in this context: Jewish printing. The first book printed by Western technique in Asia was a Jewish legal code, the *Arba Turim* or *Four Rows*, authored by Rabbi Yakov Ben Asher of Toledo (c. 1270–c. 1343). This exquisitely designed typographical gem was issued in Constantinople in 1493. (Turkish-language printing did not come into existence for another century, which is no reflection on the Muslims; they had a much larger "guild" of scribes and calligraphers, who long kept the production of manuscript texts as an individual craft.) The first book printed in the continent of Africa was an edition of *Abudarham*, a collection of laws and commentaries on prayer, written in 1340 by Rabbi David Ben Yosef of Sevilla. This volume was produced in the Moroccan city of Fez in 1516. Both of these books, and hundreds more after them, were produced under Muslim rulers.

Although the first printed Hebrew book (Rashi's *Torah* commentary) appeared in Rome in 1470, and Jewish printing proliferated in Italy, then elsewhere in Christendom, issuance of Jewish books was closely monitored, and at times seriously repressed. And while Jewish books were burned in Italy, Jews, Jewish converts to Christianity, and their descendants were burned alive in Spain and elsewhere in Christian Europe. No such immolation ever seems to have occurred in the Ottoman domains. The Turkish Sultans simply did not worry about the books printed by their Jewish subjects. Nor did they subject these men and women to persecution, much less death, for their loyalty to the Covenant of Abraham, Isaac, and Jacob. There is no history of physical attacks on Jews by Muslims in Turkey or the Balkans, notwithstanding the "blood libels" hurled at them, at the instance of local Christians, during the 18th and 19th centuries. These historical facts do not exonerate the Arabs and Persians from brutalities against Jews; but Turkey, as the greatest Islamic power in history, should have pride of place as an example.

George Orwell did not learn about the nature of Stalinism by going to Moscow; rather, he went to Barcelona, where he witnessed the Communist secret police at work undermining the Spanish left. Similarly, I did not need to go to Riyadh to understand the malign activities of the Wahhabis, because I learned about them in Sarajevo, where Saudi-backed extremists actively sought to subvert the legitimate cause of the Bosnian Muslims. I first heard the term "Wahhabi" in a Balkan context at the beginning of the 1990s; and I personally witnessed the struggle between local Muslims and Wahhabis again, in Kosovo, at the end of the century.

My understanding of this phenomenon equipped me to better comprehend both the attacks of September 11 and the perplexing behavior of the Saudi regime in their aftermath. The Saudi attitude remains profoundly puzzling to most Americans; they have assured us none of the cooperation we expect from a major ally in the war against terrorism, and the established Western view of the Saudi kingdom as a moderate force in the Arab and Muslim world has been called into question—rightly so, as it turns out, and in a manner that is long overdue.

In 1999, I retired from the *San Francisco Chronicle* and went to live and work in Bosnia-Hercegovina and Kosovo. There I was honored by the opportunity to collaborate with Jews, Franciscans, scholars and Sufis of Sunni and Shi'a inspiration, and Serbian Orthodox religious leaders in efforts for interfaith cooperation—the most rewarding experiences of my entire life. From Balkan believers and mystics, I have learned much— about Judaism, Christianity, and Islam—but above all, about Islamic spirituality. In Sarajevo, known as the "little Jerusalem of the Balkans," a city that has seen great evil, a solution to the "clash of civilizations" is to be found. A great tearing of the human fabric occurred in the former Yugoslavia, and it could be that an equally great healing could begin there as well. Religion can unite and heal as well as divide. There may be, then, only one solution to the present global crisis—a religious one, based on Abrahamic solidarity.

In the Ashkenazi synagogue of Sarajevo, built exactly a century ago, a bare *minyan*, or quorum of 10 confirmed male Jews, meets to hear the cantor or *chazzan* David Kamhi lead the Sabbath service in the style of the synagogues of Istanbul. He sings the famous kabbalistic Sabbath anthem, *Leha dodi* or "Come my friend," written in Ottoman Palestine half a millennium ago. It includes the lines *Itoreri itoreri, ki va oreh kumi ori*—"Arise, arise, for light has come . . ." In the synagogue, the bells of the Christian churches are heard . . . and the Muslim call to prayer or *adhan*, the evening call known as *aksham*, is heard, and heard again, and again, from the many mosques of Sarajevo. God is great! God is great! The words of the *aksham*, marking the end of the day for Muslim, Christian, Jew, and atheist alike in Sarajevo, filter through the minds of the pious Bosnian Jews. And then the Jews of Sarajevo, the sons of Abraham, Isaac, and Jacob, file out of their synagogue, to the streets of their city, a city no less theirs than the Muslims', where the divine law of the sons of Abraham, Ishmael, and Isaac is tested.

"Arise, arise, for light has come . . ." At the end of the night of hatred, war, and oppression, dawn must appear. Imagine *this* dawn: In a mountainous country, where you have spent the night as a guest in a tiny stone house, you are wakened by the floating, gently piercing predawn call to Muslim prayer, from the minaret of a nearby mosque. You walk to a narrow window and view all of God's creation at its most beautiful: in the black velvet of night, under the brightest stars and a brilliant moon. The predawn call to prayer includes an extra line: "Prayer is better than sleep." And when you stand at the window in the mountains and watch and listen alone you understand those words. You breathe to yourself the blessed and omnipotent words: love, unity, God. And after you have prayed, and serenity has descended upon you, come thin strands of light, then the slow lifting of the veil of darkness: dawn.

This is how their acolytes view the wisdom of the Sufis, and especially the greatest poet among them: Ibn Arabi, *Shaykh ul-Akbar*. Shaykh Muhammad Hisham Kabbani of the Naqshbandi Sufi order has called on President George W. Bush to support a global summit of traditional Muslim leaders, which would consult with Western intellectual and political figures in the beginning of a new Abrahamic dialogue. A "conversation of civilizations," rather than the much-heralded clash between them, could also contribute to a resolution of the Israeli-Arab conflict. But it cannot be posed as a political or diplomatic project. It must rather encompass a mission of Abrahamic reconciliation, emphasizing the common legacy of Jews, Christians, and Muslims, and a common responsibility for the future of humanity.

The United States must take a historic initiative to welcome traditional, pluralist, mainstream Islam into the common spiritual and intellectual discourse throughout the world. This cannot be done merely by embracing Muslims as another flavor in the multicultural buffet. A meaningful effort to counterpose traditional Islam to Wahhabi extremism must also be supported by the West, including measures to induce the Saudis to cease funding its global expansion. The Saudis' apparent desire for a more significant involvement in resolving the Israel-Palestine conflict cannot be viewed with confidence so long as Saudi activities supporting theological extremism and terrorism go unchallenged.

A shift in Islam away from the Wahhabi-Saudi promotion of terror to the mainstream Muslim commitment to mercy and compassion would not only ease tensions between the Western and Islamic worlds but could also make a "believers' peace" possible in Israel. This means taking the Middle East conundrum out of the hands of the politicians on both sides who have a vested interest in the conflict—equally symbolized by Yasir Arafat and Ariel Sharon—and abandoning a peace process based on delusions. Instead, it means encouraging rabbis, *imams*, Christian clerics, Sufi shaykhs, and ayatollahs to enter upon a regional and global "faith-based initative" for peace.

A yawning abyss between the West and Islam is not the only probable future for the world. Even after September 11, Americans, and our allies, which already include many Muslims, are determined and hopeful of victory. In beating the Islamofascism of the Wahhabis, the West can rally traditional Muslims in a way that contributes to a new pluralism and stability in the Islamic global community. Islam may thus fulfill its destiny as a positive force for all humanity—in the name of God, the compassionate, the merciful.

Sarajevo–Washington
2001–2002

THE TWO FACES OF ISLAM

© 2002 Jeffrey L. Ward

CHAPTER 1

Snow in the Desert

MUHAMMAD AND THE MESSAGE OF ISLAM

Islam came to humanity as the third great expression of the monotheistic vision that had begun with Abraham, after Judaism and Christianity. But as we consider its history, we may also see a difference between Islam and the revelations of the One God that preceded it.

Judaism is based on the lives of Prophets separated from modern Jews by thousands of years, who are honored although their historical existence cannot be verified. Many Jews and other Westerners today view the Hebrew Prophets as mythical or symbolic creations of a literary imagination. Christianity centers on the life and works of a gentle rabbi, Jesus, who was incapable of deceit or violence. But no document proves whether or not there was a historical Jesus.

By contrast, Muhammad was a figure whose existence is undoubted except by the most extreme skeptics. Further, Muhammad's life is much closer to that of an ordinary individual, living at any time or place, than those of Moses and Jesus. Nor are accounts of Muhammad dominated by the otherworldly, supernatural aspects that suffuse Jesus' life. Muslims say that Moses was a mighty Prophet but did not see the Promised Land, while Jesus was a great Prophet but was raised up to heaven almost at the beginning of his mission (Muslims believe Judas was crucified in Jesus' place). Muhammad, however, became a ruler of men and women.

Unfortunately, Muhammad has an evil reputation among Westerners that also sets him apart from Moses and Jesus. Jews and Christians reject Muhammad as the apostle of a religion they fear. Jews deny that Jesus was Messiah, but many among them have come to recognize him as a great religious teacher. Little such respect has been accorded to Muhammad. Rather, the Arabian Prophet has been treated with contempt, both by Jews, who have tended to ignore him, and by Christians, who load his name with insults. Islam is considered by most Westerners a hideous, bloodthirsty, intolerant, and aggressive cult, and Muhammad himself has been widely portrayed by non-Muslims as devious, brutal, and perverted. Jews carried away by outrage have fostered bestial images of Muslims. Equally biased Christians have denied that the God worshipped by Muhammad and his followers is the same as the God of Jews and Christians.

Those who ascribe such qualities to Islam and its Prophet often posit their own religions as honorable, kind, and loving alternatives. To do so, they must not only remain ignorant of authentic Islam, but also overlook uncomfortable and inconvenient aspects of their own religious histories. Ancient Judaism was deeply intolerant of idol-worshippers as well as those who resisted its rule over the land of Israel. Thus the *Torah* describes Moses' destruction of the Midianites, even though that nation sheltered him when he fled Egypt, and he had married one of their women. Notwithstanding the preaching of peace by Jesus, Christian rulers were brutal in the imposition of their faith, as well as in their treatment of Jews and Muslims. With the European conquest of the New World, the Christianization of the Caribbean islands and Central and South America encompassed the massacre of whole peoples.

But conversion at swordpoint to the faith of Jesus did not begin with the age of Columbus. At the end of the first Christian millennium, Germans, Nordics, Slavs, and Baltic peoples were forcibly baptized and given new names by order of their rulers. Those who resisted were murdered or driven to flight. The persecutions and expulsions of Spanish and Portuguese Jews and Muslims were notable examples of Christian intolerance, including public burnings of alleged heretics and secret Jews and Muslims. Rage at the Jewish refusal of Jesus produced centuries of bloodshed and enduring bitterness between the two older branches of the Abrahamic tradition.

Fundamentalist Muslims—by no means the majority in the world, notwithstanding rhetoric on both sides of the divide after the terrorist attacks of September 11, 2001—may despise Jews and Christians, but they do not denigrate the Prophets of the *Torah* and Jesus. Rather, they honor them volubly, and many Muslims sincerely believe they understand the essence of Moses' heroic deeds and Jesus' sweet discourses as well as or better than the majority of Jews and Christians. Muhammad's message included warnings not to ignore the righteous among the Jews and Christians, who are collectively known to Muslims as People of the Book. Islam, from its beginnings, banned compulsion in matters of faith and mandated the protection of Jews, Christians, and other religious believers. Yet Muslims are accused, largely falsely, of a savage forced Islamization of subject peoples, supposedly inspired by the narrow, fanatical, and ignorant Muhammad. The Prophet of Islam is typically described as a desert bandit who claimed to have invented a new religion on his own.

Where do these false Western images come from? The aftermath of September 11 shows that when civilizations come into contention, mutual understanding tends to vanish, at least in the short term. But while Islam existed for 1,400 years before the assaults on New York and Washington, little real knowledge of it has ever penetrated the non-Muslim world. Moreover, modern Westerners have inherited deep anxieties about Islam. The Western horror of Islam began with its early, rapid expansion, which seemed irresistible, and its terrifying reputation was strengthened by the later victories of Islamic arms during the Crusades, the Arab conquest and Christian reconquest of Spain, the Ottoman invasions of the Balkans and Central Europe, and maritime conflicts between Christian states and Muslim navies from Morocco to Cyprus.

These conflicts summoned a specter of a bloodthirsty Islamic enemy at the gates of Western civilization, bent on physical destruction and religious devastation. Each of these convulsions produced, on both sides, atrocities and atrocity stories, legends, ballads, and, behind the curtain of combat, cultural exchanges and borrowings that are often overlooked or forgotten but that sometimes changed the course of human history. The situation did not improve in the 20th century, with the collapse of the Ottoman Empire, wars and revolutions in the main Islamic states, and establishment of the state of Israel. In 2002, after 14 centuries, Islam remains enigmatic and frightening to the West.

Nevertheless, when we examine the life of Muhammad, we discover a different reality altogether. Muhammad's career includes militant preaching, the founding of a new religious community, battles with unbelievers, and severe decisions and judgments. But overall, the Prophet's personality reveals a profound commitment to compassion and mercy—the qualities Muslims mainly ascribe, among many attributes, to God, praised in Islam as "Compassionate and Merciful."

Muslims find many more practical lessons in the incidents and details of Muhammad's biography. Because of his humanity, the force of his message, and his benevolent personality, the life of Muhammad, or *Sirah*, has been a model for emulation by Muslims throughout history. Together, the *Sirah* and the *Hadith*,[1] comprising Muhammad's oral commentaries, remarks, and teachings, make up the *Sunna*, or "example," provided by the Prophet. From the *Sunna* is derived the essential body of faith, morals, and doctrine on which Islam is based.

The Prophet's full name was Muhammad ibn Abdallah ibn Abd al-Muttalib. He was born in the year 570. The place was the city of Mecca in southwestern Arabia. His mother was named Aminah. His father had died not long before Muhammad's birth. But as the delivery of Aminah's child approached she felt happy, after her time mourning for her husband.

Aminah is said by the early chronicler Ibn Ishaq to have perceived a light within her as she awaited childbirth. It was so bright that one day she could see as far as Syria. A voice spoke to her. It said, "You carry in your womb the lord of this people, and when he is born, say, 'I place him under the shelter of the One God, from the evil of any envious person'; and so, name him Muhammad." His name means "the glorified."

Muhammad was born into an environment of tribal paganism, in a Middle East that had long been a vessel of religious ferment. Many faiths flourished there at the time of Muhammad's birth, including Christianity, Judaism, and various forms of idol worship. Zoroastrianism thrived in Persia, with remnants of other religions, largely forgotten today, including Gnosticism and Neoplatonism. But the Red Sea had, by then, become encircled by an expanding, militant monotheism. Though small in numbers, Jews and Christians had established colonies in Arabia. Ethiopia, a Christian domain, was fairly close to Mecca and ruled over Yemen, the southwestern part of the Arabian Peninsula.

The Christian Byzantine or Eastern Roman Empire had become the leading power in much of the Middle East. Churches and monasteries proliferated. But the early Christians were troubled by conflicting interpretations that divided their many communities. Syria, to the north of Muhammad's territory, was a land in which Christianity had made a deep impression and Jews were well established. In much of Christendom at that time, Hebrews labored under heavy restrictions, but Alexandria in Egypt, as well as Iraq and Persia, had long sheltered Jews. When Muhammad was born, the center of world Jewry was to be found in Babylon. Wherever the Jews went, they brought their Book, the *Torah*, and celebrated their holidays, dedicated to their Covenant with the One God.

Mecca, now the center of Islamic worship, is the site of the Ka'bah, a stone temple traditionally dedicated to the worship of the One God. Muslims believe it was built by Adam and reconstructed by Abraham, or Ibrahim, and his firstborn son, Ishmael, or Ismail. (The Arabs believe they are descended from Ishmael—an ancestry also affirmed by Jewish religious tradition.) In one of its walls Abraham is said to have placed the Black Stone, a rock that had fallen from the sky. Muhammad traced his own ancestry to Ismail, and soon after he was born Muhammad's grandfather Abd al-Muttalib, caretaker of the Ka'bah, took the child there and gave a prayer of thanks.

Muhammad's people, despite being city-dwellers, were essentially desert folk, and following custom, he was sent away from Mecca as an infant to be raised by a foster mother. Muhammad's early childhood was filled with signs and wonders. He later recalled that when he was small, two angels came to him carrying a golden cup filled with snow. They opened up his heart and removed a black blood clot from it. Muslims interpret this as a reference to the place in every person's heart through which Satan comes and goes. They washed his heart in the snow. Soon after he was returned to his mother in Mecca, but Aminah died when he was six.

Islam, emerging from a desert culture in which water was rare and precious, exalts cleanliness and bathing above all other customs. Muslims cannot pray unless they have cleansed themselves, and the water of ablutions gives the body a sensation of freshness at prayer. Islam values water as evidence of God's grace, and in countries they conquered, like Spain, the Muslims worked wonders of irrigation on dry, barren lands. The cup of snow borne by the angels who cleansed Muhammad's heart may thus be Islam's most powerful metaphor.

Mecca is a city in a green belt near the sea, which makes it a different place from the desert interior of Arabia. But it had little fresh water or arable land and was not a settled, agricultural community—its economy was limited to the caravan trade with Syria and Yemen. Muslims describe their pre-Islamic forebears as existing in "the time of ignorance." The One God worshipped in the Ka'bah bears the name Al-Lah in Arabic, nearly identical to Elohim in Hebrew. In addition, the Arabs, like the Jews, circumcise their sons. However, by the time of Muhammad the original monotheistic worship reputedly founded by Abraham had been diluted by paganism—chiefly the cult of Hubal, an idol brought from the land of Moab. Consequently, the Arab society of Muhammad's day was chaotic and violent.

Muhammad belonged to an Arab tribe called the Quraysh, and a clan called the Banu Hashim. Many of the Quraysh lived without law. Theft and murder were daily activities and topics for boasting. Torture was common. Personal differences led to long feuds and tribal wars. Men accumulated wives, and on their deaths, the eldest son received them, except for his own mother, as an inheritance—thus marrying his stepmothers. The murder of female children was an established custom, one that provoked deep disgust in the heart of Muhammad. He perceived that tribal lawlessness must fall before God's law.

The idol worship of the Quraysh was a primitive affair, unlike the elaborate rituals and temples found in Egypt, Babylon, Greece, and Rome. The desert Arabs were not known for fear of the dead, which was often a source of pagan belief. Indeed, many were doubtful about Islam, when it was offered to them, because of its preaching that the dead would be resurrected. Nor were they obsessed with natural forces: Their physical environment was static. Moreover, as traders their economic life was much less regulated by the passage of the seasons—the foundation of the pagan religions—than that of peoples more dependent on agriculture, such as the Egyptians, the Sumerians, and the gigantic, sedentary societies of India and the Far East.

From the age of 10, Muhammad had accompanied his uncle Abu Talib on the well-traveled caravan route, journeying north to Syria and Egypt in summer and south to Yemen in winter. By the time he was 20 he was himself leading caravans, and was known as a camel whisperer who could calm animals by kindly handling, stroking, and speaking to them. In his profession of merchant, Muhammad earned respect as a righteous person, and was nicknamed "the trustworthy," or "al-Amin."

When he was 25 a rich woman of Mecca named Khadijah hired him to take her goods to Syria. She was distantly related to Muhammad's clan, and she also had a Christian cousin named Waraqa ibn Nawfal, who was literate—a rare achievement in that time and place. Fifteen years older than Muhammad, she was attractive and had been pursued by many men, all of whom she rebuffed. But she fell in love with the young Muhammad, and thanks to a woman friend of hers, a marriage was contracted. Eventually they would have six children: two sons who died young and four daughters who survived to adulthood. Traditional Muslims honor the family of Muhammad, and in their prayers and blessings they invoke 11 wives and a concubine, their children, Muhammad's nephew Ali ibn Abi Talib, and Ali's sons, whom we shall meet. In addition, traditionalists believe that although the parents of Muhammad died before the advent of Islam, they are rewarded in heaven.

Muhammad was viewed as a conciliator within his tribe, as shown by the most significant event recorded about his life before he received his divine message. When he was 35 the Quraysh reconstructed the Ka'bah. The temple of the One God had been defiled by the introduction of idols. Its roof was gone, and a snake had taken possession of its walls, coming out in the sun and frightening people away from the structure. Nothing could more dramatically symbolize the decay of Abraham's religion among the Arabs than the presence of a serpent in the Ka'bah. The snake was the epitome of human temptation, as revealed in the story of Adam and Eve. It was also an object of pagan worship. The Quraysh dithered, deterred from their mission by the reptile. Then, one day, an eagle descended from the heavens and seized the snake in its claws, flying away with it.[2]

The Ka'bah was rebuilt by the Meccans, and Muhammad, respected for his fairness, was asked to be first to enter it. He was to decide which of the competing clans of Quraysh should have the honor of restoring the Black Stone to its position in the structure's walls. Muhammad laid a cloak on the ground and ordered the Black Stone set on it. He then summoned one man from each clan to take a corner of the cloak, that the sacred responsibility be shared. Together they carried the Black Stone into the refurbished structure and placed it in the wall.

This minor event shows Muhammad avoiding disruption and extremes among his people. He was deeply opposed to the idolatry that had infected his community, but he was not a merciless fanatic. Throughout his life, Muhammad advocated peace and the avoidance of conflict. During his struggle to establish the community of Islam, he suffered much at the hands of his relatives and neighbors, the tribe of Quraysh, and the residents of Mecca. But seeking reconciliation and civility even with these, he recited a verse that has since stood as a credo of traditional Islam: "Say: 'Unbelievers, I do not worship what you worship, nor do you worship what I worship. I shall never worship what you worship, nor will you ever worship what I worship. You have your own religion, and I have mine.'"[3]

Muhammad was swept to his core by the revelations he received. He was possessed by the mission of bringing the message of an undiluted worship of One God to his people. But he was not, by nature, a preacher. He was judicious in both word and deed, and that was the basis of his great personal authority.

The sharp difference between the sensible, calm, humble, and kind conception of Muhammad held by traditional Muslims and the fanatical, rigid, overbearing, and puritanical manner adopted by Islamic fundamentalists today presents us with the two faces of Islam—moderation, equanimity, patience, and fairness versus separatism, supremacism, frenzy, and aggression. Traditional Muslims honor the Prophet as a pleasant and positive human being. A poem in his praise by *Imam* Ibrahim al-Bajuri, which was a major Muslim devotional text for centuries, ascribed to him these attributes:

> *A form like the soft lilies and the full moon in splendor,*
> *A character like the ocean in generosity and time in endeavors,*
> *Seeming, due to his majesty, even when you met him alone, to*
> 　*head an army or a large company,*
> *As if the very pearl concealed inside the shell were formed in the*
> 　*two molds of his speech and his smile.*

In contrast with this appealing description, Islamic extremists seek to remove Muhammad from Islam altogether. To Westerners, this seems impossible. But it is true: Islamic fundamentalists ignore the personality of the Prophet and oppose traditional Muslims' love and admiration of his quest for compassion. As we will see, a wholesale purge of the Prophet's personality from Islamic religion has been an essential goal of the "end time" cult of Wahhabism, which has made a serious attempt to reshape Islam in its intolerant image.

In the year 610, when he was 40, Muhammad began receiving divine revelations. Like most Arabs, Muhammad was illiterate, and the instruction embodied in Islam came to him orally. This discourse, imparted (according to Islamic belief) by the angel Gabriel or Jibril, is called The Recitation, or *Qur'an*. The essence of these teachings was and would remain simple and direct: God or Allah is the Sole All-Powerful Creator. God is limitlessly Compassionate and Merciful. And humanity must submit completely to the Divine Will.

The eloquence of Muhammad's prophecy was so great that it swept millions upon millions of people, generation after generation, into the worship of God. Muslims say *There Is No god but God*. That affirmation has had the power of a cosmic explosion: Like the messages given the Jews and Christians, it created a new civilization.

Muhammad first heard the Angel during a retreat into spiritual solitude. He had gone to a cave on Mount Hira close to Mecca, near the end of the month of Ramadan. According to Muslims, Gabriel said to him, "Read!" Muhammad replied, "I am not one of they who can read." The Angel embraced him, insisting, "Read!" Muhammad again answered, "I am not one of they who can read." The Angel again embraced him, and the exchange was repeated again. After the third embrace, the Angel said,

> *Read in the name of your Lord, who created—*
> *created man from a clot of blood.*
> *Read! Your Lord is the Most Bountiful One, who by the pen*
> *taught man what he did not know.*[4]

Muhammad repeated the Angel's words and recalled, "It was as if the words were impressed on my heart." But the experience frightened him, and he fled the cave. As he left, he heard the Angel's voice saying, "O Muhammad, you are God's messenger, and I am Gabriel."

Muhammad rushed back to his home, terrified by this experience. His wife Khadijah comforted him, wrapping him in a blanket. Her Christian relative, Waraqa, assured them that Muhammad had experienced divine revelation, and as he trembled at her side, Khadijah further reassured him. She told him the One God would not betray him, "because you are kind to relatives, you speak only the truth, you help the poor, the orphan, and the needy, and you are an honest man."

These angelic communications continued for two years before the Prophet began sharing them widely. At first he spoke of them only to

Khadijah and some friends, swearing them to secrecy, until he was shown by the Angel how to pray and taught to say *Allahu Akbar* (God is Great) and the salute *As-salaamu alaikum* (Peace be with you). Khadijah was the first to accept the revelation of Islam. After her, Muhammad's earliest adherents were his friend Abu Bakr, his former slave, Zayd, whom he had freed and adopted as a son, and his 10-year-old nephew, Ali ibn Abi Talib. Ali's innocent enthusiasm greatly pleased the Prophet.

The first individuals to accept Islam were city-dwellers like Muhammad, not desert nomads, and their commitment to a revival of monotheism had the unifying élan of an urban enterprise. They were offspring of Mecca and would set themselves apart from the ordinary life of the city, but not in a separatist way. Rather, they would seek to open the hearts of their neighbors by their positive behavior. They knew their advocacy would be tested in the marketplace of ideas and argument because Mecca was precisely that—a marketplace. A more emphatic, disciplined commitment to the One God represented a grave and dramatic challenge to the marketplace of idols that Mecca had become, and it would either be rewarded or rejected by those to whom it was offered—the community in which the Prophet had grown up and where he had every right to expect appreciation and assistance.

A stream of fresh arrivals soon joined the new community of Muslims. One was Uthman ibn Affan, who had heard a voice in the desert pronouncing: "Sleepers Awake!" The voice heralded the arrival of "the most glorified" (Ahmad, another form of Muhammad) in Mecca.

But the Quraysh, Muhammad's own tribe, and most of the other Arabs of Mecca did not at first accept his prophecy. Muhammad had begun preaching in secrecy, and he continually acquired new followers; but as his revival of religion became public, he and his Companions were vilified, assaulted, and tortured.

Why did the Quraysh reject Muhammad? The Quraysh believed intensely in the benefits of their idols, and would not consider giving them up. They thought that to do so would bring down their utter destruction. They also gained considerable income from annual pilgrimages to the Ka'bah by people throughout Arabia, and accordingly they had encouraged more and more idols to be brought to the temple. A religious revelation directed against such practices could not but frighten and offend them.

Muhammad's preaching against the worshippers of idols might convince many pilgrims never to return to Mecca. It might also undermine the authority of the Meccans, which was based on their guardianship of the Kab'ah, and affect their caravan trade. Finally, the idol-worshippers feared that the revival of strict monotheism would break up families— a serious threat in a society based on tribal and clan loyalties. During the season of pilgrimage, the Quraysh posted guards along the roads into Mecca, to inform every visitor that Muhammad was a dangerous sorcerer who did not speak for his neighbors or tribespeople, and should be shunned.

The ranks of Muhammad's followers grew, but so did harassment and violence against them by the Quraysh. A group of Muslims therefore decided to leave for Ethiopia, a Christian kingdom. Though he remained behind, Muhammad supported this venture, which marked the first instance of a recurrent motif in Islam: the emigration of believers to escape persecution. It is here that in the Prophet's own life, the two faces of Islam were first seen: separation, which would inevitably encourage purism and extremism, versus entry into the world, even under difficult conditions, leading to pluralism and tolerance.

From the beginning, a separatist trend sought collective retreat from the company of unbelievers, a kind of "utopian" temptation. This tendency reflected Islamic identification with Abraham, who followed God's commands and "went out" of Chaldea, and with Moses, who "led His people out" of Egypt. But Muslims did not have a national identity, like the Jews, to sustain their Covenant. Because there was no line of ethnic separation between them and nonbelievers, they were often tempted to draw a nonethnic one. Throughout Islamic history this tension remains visible, between separatism and the perseverance of Muslims living alongside others who hew to unbelief. Because traditional Islam accepts the concept of religiously mixed societies, purist separatism, more frequently than aggressive expansionism, underlies Islamic extremism, especially in recent times.

Muslims cannot renounce their faith: They must bear witness to it.[5] Because of this imperative—the coming of Islam as a "mercy to the world," in the vocabulary of Islamic theology, occasionally expressed in a drive to convert others—separatism did not prevail in Islam, at least not for many centuries. The ideal of the traditional Muslim is to attain purification in the world, not to escape it. But the impulse to sustain virtue through flight from a corrupt social order has always been present among Muslims. Traditional Muslims have sought to maintain balance between a dialogue with the world and withdrawal from it, but have not always succeeded.

In Ethiopia, these seeming contradictions were resolved with remarkable ease. The Quraysh sent emissaries to incite the country's Christian ruler against the Muslims, but he had satisfied himself that their respect for Jesus and Mary was sincere, and they were granted sanctuary in the Christian land—a generous act too often forgotten by extremist Muslims today. The Quraysh for their part were displeased by the welcome given the refugees. Back in Mecca, they redoubled their aggression against Muhammad and his Companions.

A decade after his first revelation, Muhammad's wife Khadijah and his uncle Abu Talib died. He entered a year of grief, as he contended with his loss and sudden solitude. Soon afterward, he had an intense supernatural experience known as the Night Journey, a mystical flight from the Ka'bah in which he saw himself astride a winged animal called Buraq, guided by the Angel Gabriel.

The beast conveyed him to the location of the former Temple of the Jews in Jerusalem, where Muhammad was introduced to the great Prophets of the past, including Abraham, Moses, and Jesus, who prayed with him. From a rock at the site, he saw himself rising to the limits of the knowable heavens, and divine radiance descending upon him. Along his way, the unity of the prophetic revelations was reaffirmed to him, and the counsel of Moses led to the fixing of the daily prayers required of Muslims to five.

The Night Journey has become a matter of worldwide attention in recent times, because of its role in Arab-Israeli controversies over the Temple Mount, known to Muslims as the Furthest Mosque. Jews and Christians assume that the Night Journey gives Jerusalem its Muslim importance, but for Muslims the relationship is exactly the opposite: The Night Journey is significant because Jerusalem was the place Muhammad was taken. In the flight to the devastated Jewish Temple, the Night Journey demonstrates the Muslim continuity with the original Abrahamic revelation. With the Temple destroyed and the Jews dispersed throughout the world, the Night Journey shows that Muhammad will rescue and redeem the fallen banner of the One God.

The Night Journey did not merely confirm Muhammad's intimacy with God, it also reaffirmed the content of his message and the urgency of his mission. In his meeting with Abraham, Moses, and Jesus, Muhammad found within himself the qualities identified with them, and magnified through him: the unwavering belief of Abraham, the heroism of Moses in confronting the powerful unbelievers, the loving personality of Jesus. Muslims believe Muhammad to be a peer of Moses and Jesus in the constellation of Prophets, while he is also the Chief of Prophets, their Seal and Crown. It is in support of this standing that Islam reinforces the message of the earlier Prophets, that it be concentrated and focused through Muhammad.

Muhammad's account of his out-of-body flight to his townsmen at Mecca only aggravated his troubles with them. But at the same time, an interest in Muhammad's activities had emerged among the populace of Yathrib, a farming village north of Mecca that was the home of some of his relatives. Yathrib included a Jewish community, and monotheistic ideas were viewed favorably there. Eventually a group of its folk, some of them Jews, invited Muhammad and his followers to assume the governorship of the town.

Why did the people of Yathrib do this? Islamic tradition holds that the Jews of Yathrib had warned their Arab neighbors that a Prophet would come from among them, and, with the support of the Jews, would punish the idolaters. Muslims believe that the Jews had migrated to Yathrib 1,000 years before in anticipation of the appearance of a distinguished Prophet as foretold in their own Scriptures. However, Yathrib was also in deep crisis: Local feuds and immorality had nearly destroyed the town, and the

Yathribites yearned for the coming of a righteous figure who could reduce conflict among them.

Muhammad led a group of Muslims to live in Yathrib, telling his Companions he had seen it in a vision: "I have been shown the place of your emigration: I saw a well-watered land, rich in date palms, between two tracts of black stones." Many left Mecca, and many Yathribites became Muslims. Muhammad accepted the responsibility of ruling over Yathrib, which became Medina — "city of the Prophet" or al-Madinat an-Nabi — an ideal Islamic community. Muhammad departed Mecca with an assassination plot by the Quraysh close on his heels. The year was 622 of the common era, and is marked by Muslims as the beginning of the Islamic calendar.

There is no indication that, before the invitation to Yathrib, Muhammad had ever imagined he would govern others. He seems never to have thought in utopian terms, or wanted to become a "philosopher-king." The option of creating a new city along Islamic lines presented itself when the Prophet's followers were exhausted and disheartened by their bad treatment at the hands of the Meccans. Muhammad also grew disappointed in Medina when he realized that some in the new city would embrace Islam hypocritically, to gain favor with the Prophet's faction. But he was not a politician. His only interest was in offering divine law to his relatives, friends, and neighbors.

In Medina under Muhammad, preaching and prayer were joined, in the sacred space of the mosque, with the public debate and decision-making of the populace. All residents, whatever their religion, were equal beneficiaries of a peace secured by the Muslims. This was embodied in a formal treaty drawn up by the Prophet that obligated the city's tribes to support and defend each other. It was affirmed by the Prophet's supporters (the Emigrants who had come from Mecca, plus the Helpers, the inhabitants of Yathrib who invited him to settle there), and by the Jewish and other tribes then living in the city.

In founding a new city, as well as a new kind of city, Muhammad demonstrated his engagement with the world and his embrace of human life as it exists. He did not accept the evils of the world; he sought to free the world from evil. He was dismayed by the prevalence of unbelief and idolatry among his people and had been deeply hurt by the rejection of the Meccans. But his pain did not lead him to withdraw into a purist refuge. Nor was this the character of mainstream Islam.

If Muhammad had been a separatist and purist and Islam an extremist sect, as imagined by today's fundamentalists, it would never have become a global civilization. By taking responsibility for Medina, Muhammad expressed an essential principle of traditional Islam: That conflicts between people may be settled by peaceful means. God does not negotiate, but people are called upon by God to resolve their differences by negotiation. Fundamentalists have wiped this concept out of Islam just as they have purged Muhammad himself from the faith. But it remains true: The Islamic city is a city based on mutual obligations, arbitration, and mediation. Muslims argue that the agreement Muhammad made in founding Medina was the first written constitution. Islam is viewed by Westerners today as essentially hostile to modernity, but traditional Islam is a religion of *contract*, which is the foundation of modern society.

Although there is almost nothing in Islamic scripture that specifically describes such a social order, it remains a major feature of Muslim theology. Mecca, because of the presence of the Ka'bah, is the original Sacred City of Islam. But Medina represents something else of extraordinary significance. The unity of Medina, embodied in its constitutional treaty, is seen as paralleling the uniqueness of God. The Bosnian Muslim writer and political leader Alija Izetbegović has insightfully placed such a political state—later incarnated in a worldwide Islamic order, the caliphate—midway between the City of God as conceived of by Christian philosophers and the City of the Sun imagined by utopian reformers.

It is therefore incorrect to refer to "political Islam" as distinct from Islam as a faith; all Islam is political. Unfortunately, the original experiment in an Islamic state led by Muhammad in Medina was opposed by more and worse armed conflict with the enraged Quraysh. A new rivalry between Mecca and Medina replaced internal wars among the inhabitants of Yathrib. One would think the Meccans would have been happy to see Muhammad and his followers leave their city for Medina. But the appearance of the new city simply increased the hatred of the Quraysh for the Muslims.

Why was this? One reason was that the Muslims who had come to Medina from Mecca considered themselves righteous refugees, driven from their homes for their faith in God. They believed that this made it legitimate to fight the Meccans by raiding their caravans. Muhammad approved of these activities. But his relationship with the city of his youth remained complicated. When he went to Yathrib, he had left some of his immediate family behind, including his married daughter Zainab. Many of his own kin were among the most determined enemies of Islam. Such postures fostered further family divisions, as children and other close relatives of some of the Prophet's fiercest opponents became Muslims. The Prophet came to understand that friendship and affection would not soften the hearts of those dedicated to idol-worship. Yet his response was tolerant and patient; he would let them find their own path. We read in *Qur'an*, "You cannot guide whomever you please; it is God who guides whom He will."[6]

The bitterness of rejection by so many of his relatives naturally stimulated in Muhammad a greater fondness for those who were loyal to him. Throughout his marriage with Khadijah, he remained faithful to her, and after her death he stayed single for several years, even though he had children to care for. Later, he was reproached by his third and youngest wife, Aisha, for his constant praise of the deceased Khadijah. Aisha asked jealously, "Was she not old? Did God not provide you with a better wife?" The Prophet replied angrily, "No, by God, he did not. She believed in me when no others did. She trusted me when all others called me a liar. She showered me with her wealth when I was poor. She gave me children when no others did."

Muhammad did not remarry until he was past the age of 55. Throughout his life he had 11 wives and four daughters who survived to adulthood. He called on his followers to honor his family and to treat them with a respect equal to that they granted him. At the same time, he demanded that his wives accept the discomforts imposed on them, as members of a family held to a unique standard of morality. He was especially concerned that they not become accustomed to special favors from his followers. Eventually, he gave his wives the choice of remaining with him and sharing his privations, or accepting a worthy compensation and departing his household. He first presented this option to Aisha, telling her she should consult with her parents before making a decision. She was an eloquent young woman, known for composing and reciting verse; she answered that she had no need to talk with her parents. She chose to remain with the Prophet. The rest of his wives agreed with her.

Muhammad's 10th wife was a Jewish woman, Safiyya, who had been taken captive in war. Her family was wealthy, and her father and husband had died fighting the Muslims. Muhammad gave her an opportunity to return to her own people, but she fell deeply in love with him. Aisha and the Prophet's fourth wife, Hafsa, teased her for her Jewish origin, reducing her to tears. Muhammad said to her, "If they say this again, tell them, 'My father is the Prophet Aaron, my uncle is the Prophet Moses, and my husband is, as you know, the Prophet Muhammad.' What more could anyone boast of?"

Qur'an, the revelation Muhammad received, has become problematical in the contemporary world. Before and after September 11, quranic verses were presented out of context both by Islamic extremists and by non-Muslim enemies of the religion in an attempt to show that Islam is not "a religion of peace" but of fanatical intolerance and bloodshed. The misuse of these citations impedes the present, difficult dialogue of the faiths, in which Jew, Christian, and Muslim are separated by fear and hatred.

Westerners believe *Qur'an* preaches violence, forced conversion, and, in general, an aggressive mentality. *Qur'an* is a Book, one among four sacred Scriptures known in Islam, along with *Torah*, the *Psalms of David*, and the *Gospels*. But because it lacks a linear structure *Qur'an* is often described by Westerners who attempt a superficial reading of it as prolix, repetitive, and incomprehensible. Although it includes stories, it is not based in a historical narrative, as *Torah* and the *Gospels* are. In the end, with no offense meant to Muslims or anybody else, it may be more useful to compare *Qur'an* and its 114 chapters, some long and some very short, with the *Psalms* than with *Torah* or the *Gospels*. It is a kind of extended lyrical poem and personal appeal to humanity, from the mouth of God.

Qur'an is without doubt the greatest Arabic literary work, although *Qur'an* specifically disclaims any literary intent, denying that Muhammad, who received the text, could be a poet. In anticipation and defiance of the urge some would have to relegate Muhammad to mere authorship, the text warns, in the chapter "Ya Sin," known as the heart of *Qur'an*, and recited in full as a Muslim memorial to the dead, "We have taught him[7] no poetry, nor does it become him to be a poet. This is but a warning: an eloquent *Qur'an* to exhort the living and to pass judgment on the unbelievers."[8]

Further, the text declares of Muhammad, in a passage that could stand for all of Islamic tradition:

> Do they say, "He is but a poet: we are waiting for some misfortune to befall him"? Say, "Wait if you will, I too am waiting."
>
> Does their reason prompt them to say this? Or is it merely that they are wicked men?
>
> Do they say, "He has invented it[9] himself"? Indeed, they have no faith. Let them produce a Scripture like it, if what they say be true!
>
> Were they created out of the void? Or were they their own creators? Did they create the heavens and the earth? Surely they have no faith!
>
> Do they hold the treasures of your Lord, or have control over them? Have they a ladder by means of which they overhear Him? Let their eavesdropper bring a positive proof!"[10]

Qur'an remains today the touchstone of Islamic faith, more like *Torah* for believing Jews than the *Bible* for Christians. It is a source of legal wisdom and a guide to conduct. But certain verses from *Qur'an* are controversial. These fall into two categories: those dealing with other religions, and those relevant to *jihad*, or sacred struggle against unbelievers. Although *Qur'an* and the *Hadith* express criticism and even condemnation of Jews and Christians, *Qur'an* also honors them as People of the

Book. Muslims are commanded to fight unbelievers, but also to respect treaties with them. And Muslims are required to grant a special protection, a permanent treaty with a higher significance and authority, to Jews and Christians.

One of the most debated verses reads, "Believers, take neither Jews nor Christians for your friends. They are friends with one another. Whoever of you seeks their friendship shall become one of their number."[11] This recommendation has been interpreted by fundamentalists as justifying separatism and the rejection of mixed societies, while being taken by Islamophobes as proof that Muhammad's followers view non-Muslims as implacable enemies. Such claims are belied by the history of Islam in places as diverse as Arab Spain and the Ottoman Empire, where Jews and Christians attained great cultural and religious achievements under Islamic rule.

But mendacious views of this verse are also counterposed by other parts of *Qur'an*. A restatement of it appears: "Believers, do not seek the friendship of the infidels and those who were given the Book before you, [if they] have made of your religion a jest." Further,

> If they observe the *Torah* and the *Gospel* and what is revealed to them from their Lord, they shall enjoy abundance from above and from beneath. There are some among them who are righteous men . . .
>
> Say, "People of the Book, you will attain nothing until you observe the *Torah* and the *Gospel* and that which is revealed to you from your Lord" . . . Believers, Jews, Sabaeans, and Christians—whoever believes in God and the Last Day and does what is right—shall have nothing to fear or to regret."[12]

The following statement applies to Muslim relations with members of any other faith: "God does not forbid you to be kind and equitable to those who have neither made war on your religion nor driven you from your homes. God loves the equitable."[13] In one of the most famous verses, we find a specific repudiation of the use of force in religious matters: "Let there be no compulsion in religion. Truth stands forth from falsehood."[14]

Qur'an includes explicit commands to respect Jews and Christians, including: "Be courteous when you argue with the People of the Book, except with those among them who do evil. Say, 'We believe in that which is revealed to us and which was revealed to you. Our God and your God is one. To Him we surrender ourselves.'"[15]

But other issues arise from the relation between Islam and the People of the Book. *Qur'an* recognizes that Jews would be most resistant to acceptance of its sacred character. It therefore states, "Nearest in affection to them[16] are those who say 'We are Christians.' That is because there are priests and monks among them, and they are free from pride."[17] This is not an expression of hostility, but an accurate perception: Jews cannot alter the essence of their revelation, which is their Covenant as a nation among nations. Both Christians and Muslims have desired to win over the Jews to later revelations. Christians have harbored an aggravated anger at the Jews for failing to recognize Jesus as Messiah. But Muhammad evinced a deeper and more vulnerable sensibility about the Jews. He clearly desired their favor. Failing to receive it, he was dismayed, but he did not, in the end, respond with hatred. Rather, he sought, but did not always obtain, a compromise with Jews that would allow them to continue in their way, while Islam followed its own course.

Indeed, *Qur'an* possesses a feature that is delightfully problematical for today's extremist and fundamentalist Muslims, Jews, and Christians, whose ill intentions stimulate them to foster contempt for each other's faiths: It includes verses clearly assigning the Land of Israel to the Jews and affirming the role Jewish possession of it would play in the Last Days. We read, "[God] said to the Israelites, 'Dwell in this land. When the promise of the hereafter comes to be fulfilled, We shall assemble you all together.'"[18]

Islamic extremists do not offer their own analysis of these verses and their meaning. Rather they attempt to remove them from the consciousness of Muslims. The fundamentalists—essentially, the powerful and fabulously rich Wahhabi cult based in Saudi Arabia—have been overtaken by an apocalyptic belief that the last days are approaching and that Muslims must take up arms against "unbelievers." To do this they focus attention on the *jihad* verses of *Qur'an*, to which they give their own brutalizing emphasis.

One of the verses most frequently cited by Islamophobes to justify their fears and prejudices reads, "Slay the idolators wherever you find them. Arrest them, besiege them, and lie in ambush everywhere for them." This is the epitome of a citation ripped out of context. It is preceded, "Proclaim a woeful punishment to the unbelievers, except for those idolators who have honored their treaties with you. With these keep faith, until their treaties have run their term. God loves the righteous."

The command to "slay the idolators" is also followed by these words: "If they repent and take to prayer and render the alms levy, allow them to go their way. God is forgiving and merciful. If an idolator seeks asylum with you, give him protection so that he may hear the Word of God, and then convey him to safety."[19]

Muhammad's conception of war would be tested in a series of conflicts between Mecca and Medina. Several bloody encounters occurred, including the battles of Badr, Uhud, and the Trench. In reviewing these events, we must depend on Muslim tradition rather than written records; but the battles are considered historical in a way that such biblical incidents as the siege of Jericho are not.

The battle of Badr took place two years after the establishment of Medina, pitting the Quraysh against the Muslims. The irreconcilable pagans among the Quraysh were anxious to do away with the Muslims in any event, but tensions were inflamed by rumors that the Muslims planned to raid their caravan traffic. The forces of the Quraysh numbered around 1,000 infantry—three times the strength of Muslim troops. The Quraysh also commanded 100 men on horses; the Muslims had only two. In addition, the Quraysh campaign was well financed while the Muslims were poor and lacked provisions. Moreover, Muhammad and his Companions found many of their own relatives, with plentiful armor and weapons, arrayed against them. Abu Bakr, Muhammad's old friend and an early Muslim, had to fight his own son. One of the commanders among the idolaters also had a son on the opposing side. And the husband of one of Muhammad's daughters fought with the Quraysh against the army of the Prophet.

Learning of an imminent attack, Muhammad consulted with his Companions. Abu Bakr assured him he and others were prepared to fight.

Muhammad then turned to his supporters among the people of Medina. The guarantees exchanged between them and the Muslims at the founding of the city had exempted the Medinites from war unless the city itself was directly assaulted. Muhammad now asked diplomatically, "Men, what should be done?" One of them replied, "By God, if you ask us, we will follow you into the sea." The courage of the Medinite Helpers made them eternal heroes in Islam. Of the 313 Muslim warriors at Badr, 253 were Medinites.

Badr is a village to the west of Medina on the coastal route from Syria to Mecca. When the Muslims marched from Medina, the young were sent back to the city, since the fighting was expected to be brutal. As the time for combat neared, Muhammad did two things demonstrating his hatred of violence. First, he did not take part in the fighting, since he did not want to shed blood by his own hand. He had also learned that two of his men had been stopped on the way to Badr by unbelievers. To save their lives, the pair had promised not to join battle for the Muslims. Muhammad told them that their word was more important than their presence in the front lines and that he required only God's aid. Muhammad prayed continuously through the battle, moving his Companions to tears.

The battle of Badr fell on March 17, 623, by the modern Christian calendar. It began with duels between leaders, but the fighting was indeed vicious. The left arm of a Muslim named Mu'adh was sliced almost completely through at the shoulder and hung by a bit of flesh. Mu'adh placed his dangling left hand under his foot and tore off the mutilated limb, leaving him free to fight on. But valor was also present in the ranks of the idolaters. Muhammad knew that many of the Quraysh had been drafted to fight against their will, and he even knew their names. He told his men to call out to them that they would be spared. One of them, Abu al-Bakhtari, asked if his fighting comrade could also gain the Muslims' protection. Receiving a negative reply, he refused to abandon his companion and was slain with a war song of the Quraysh on his lips.

The Muslims won the battle, even though they were outnumbered and had no horsemen. They lost only 14 combatants. Unsurprisingly, Muslims view the battle of Badr as a major event in human history and believe Muhammad's forces were favored by divine assistance, including the help of angels. But a biographer of the Prophet, Allama Shibli Nu'mani, observes other details that contributed to the Muslim victory: "The Quraysh were a disunited horde," he notes. Their commander was unenthusiastic and some of their troops had withdrawn before the battle. Heavy rains left the Quraysh camp muddy. In addition, the Quraysh were frightened and believed the Muslims had double their numbers. The Quraysh fought in a disorderly manner, while Muhammad assigned his men to disciplined lines. Finally, the Quraysh were nervous and could not get any rest, but the Muslims were confident and slept well the night before the fighting.

Two Quraysh leaders were executed and about 70 were taken prisoner. Many relatives of Muhammad and his Companions were among them. It is hard to imagine a more affecting symbol of the rejection of the Prophet by his townsmen. His own relatives and neighbors had declared war on his beliefs. In the Muslim mind, nothing but an extraordinary and perverse dedication to unbelief could have impelled them to such an act. Small wonder that Qur'an and Hadith are severe against them! But Muhammad ordered that the prisoners be sheltered and fed, even if the Muslims had to eat nothing but dates, and he forbade any ill treatment of the captives. On their return to Medina, the Companions disagreed on how the Qurayshite prisoners should be dealt with. Abu Bakr pointed out that most of them were relatives of Muslims, and some could be expected to become believers sooner or later. He called for their release after payment of a ransom by their families. Another Companion, Umar, argued that family was nothing compared with Islam and called for their execution, each by a Muslim relative. Two faces of Islam were again exposed: compassion and mercy versus purism and extremism.

The disposition of the captives has given rise to extensive Islamic commentaries. Muhammad decided with Abu Bakr that the prisoners should be ransomed and released. The Prophet then received a revelation expressing divine disapproval: "Had there not been a previous sanction from God, you would have been sternly punished for what you have taken."[20] Muhammad and Abu Bakr are said to have burst into tears, fearing they had done something wrong. But the basis of the divine caution is unclear: Was it a warning against the practice of demanding ransom for a life, or against the taking of spoils in war, or against letting the captives live at all? Traditional authorities hold that it reflected disapproval of the demand for ransom, but Nu'mani wrote delicately, "Generally this verse has been misconstrued, and the displeasure ascribed to having spared the lives of the prisoners."

Finally, families that could afford the ransom paid the money, and their men were freed. Prisoners too poor were released without paying. Literate captives were asked to teach reading and writing to 10 Muslim children in lieu of payment for their liberty. Muhammad's son-in-law Abu al-'As, who had fought for the Quraysh, asked the Prophet's daughter Zainab to provide for his ransom. When the payment arrived it included a necklace given to her by the Prophet's first wife, Khadijah. Muhammad wept when he saw the necklace and obtained the Companions' permission to send it back to his daughter, along with her husband.

For Muslims, the victory at Badr recalls the triumph of Moses over Pharaoh. The Quraysh were deeply humiliated, and public mourning was forbidden in Mecca. Muhammad was personally transformed by the experience, and it is from this period that some major aspects of Islam emerged. The Prophet ordered that the direction of Muslim prayer or *qibla* be changed—previously facing Jerusalem, Muslims would now turn to Mecca. At Badr the Prophet also exhorted his troops by promising direct entry into Paradise for martyrs on the battlefield. Their reward was to include the company of eternal servants and "dark-eyed" or "large-eyed" girls. These virginal lovers are described in *Qur'an* as "immortal youths with bowls and ewers and a cup of purest wine (that will neither pain their heads nor take away their reason); with fruits of their own choice and flesh of fowls that they relish . . . the dark-eyed houris, chaste as hidden pearls."[21]

A further opportunity for martyrdom in combat came a year after the clash at Badr. The Meccans again prepared an army and sent it against Medina. This time numbering 3,000, the Meccan army marched as far as Mount Uhud, a high position in a lava bed about five miles from the Prophet's city. Muhammad, commanding only 700 fighters, again ordered the younger males to leave the ranks, lest they be killed. The ensuing combat was fiercer than at Badr, and Muhammad himself fired arrows with other archers in a detachment that included two women. He was struck down by a sword blow, but, wearing chain mail, was not seriously injured. Nevertheless, the Quraysh cried out triumphantly that Muhammad was dead and shouted praise of their idols Uzzah and Hubal.

A tremor of shock rolled across the battlefield. The Quraysh advance relaxed. Some Muslims fled in dismay; others decided they would die as the Prophet had perished. One who returned to combat shouted that he could smell breezes from the gardens of Paradise, blowing where men were martyred. Believing their Prophet had died, men rushed to follow him into death's outstretched arms, that the virgins of Paradise might delight in granting them their favors. But Muhammad regained his footing and led his detachment to safety on the heights of Mount Uhud. The Quraysh had won the contest of arms, but the survival of the Prophet had turned defeat into a moral victory for the Muslims.

A Quraysh commander shouted, "In Badr you will meet us again next year!" His followers had mutilated the corpses of the Muslim dead. But when the Muslims came to recover the bodies they found a number of surprises. A man who had always rejected Islam had decided to accept it at the moment of the battle and fought in the Muslim ranks. It is said he died and entered Paradise without ever making a profession of faith or saying a Muslim prayer. Another man found among the dead Muslims was at first unrecognized. It was Mukhayriq, a distinguished rabbi of the Jewish clan of Tha'labah, and the owner of rich date groves. He had called on his compatriots to join the Muslims in fighting the worshippers of idols. Before his death, he willed that his groves should be inherited by Muhammad.

Soon after the defeat of Uhud, two Jewish tribes aligned with Mecca, Qaynuqah and Nadir, were driven out of Medina. In 627, Muslim power was again victorious over Mecca at the battle of the Trench, after which the men of the Jewish tribe of Qurayzah, which had also sided with Mecca, were executed. The men of Qurayzah were offered mercy if they accepted Islam, but they were willing to die rather than surrender their faith.

Muhammad's treatment of these groups has led some modern critics to accuse him of anti-Jewish prejudice. However, he was fighting a religious war in a part of the world still without law, leading men whose minds were illuminated with the truth of the One God, and he had against him his own kin and townsmen. Ambiguities in loyalty could no longer be tolerated. But it has also been observed that Muhammad fought people over their attitudes, not their beliefs.

Success at the battle of the Trench drew many Arabs to Islam, and Muhammad undertook to negotiate a truce between Mecca and Medina. The resulting Treaty of Hudaybiyyah was accepted by both warring cities, even though many of the Prophet's Companions deemed it humiliating. A 10-year peace was envisioned, based on a promise of noninterference of the two communities in each others' affairs, and secured by clauses guaranteeing safe conduct for visitors from Medina to Mecca and provisions for peaceful settling of differences. This conciliating work attracted yet more Arabs to the banner of the Prophet. But the treaty remained in force only until the end of 629, when it was violated by Mecca. Now, once and for all, Meccan defiance was to be overcome.

Muhammad raised an army that marched to the city's gates. Mecca capitulated and welcomed its Prophet. Mecca had "opened," in the Muslim vocabulary. Muhammad took control of the town that had so long been his home. Trembling in the shadow of the Ka'bah, the Quraysh gathered, expecting to hear dire judgment passed on them. They anticipated reprisals for the evil they had meted out to Muhammad and his adherents.

But the Prophet said, "O People of Quraysh! What do you expect from me today?"

They replied, "Only the best from a noble brother and the son of a noble brother."

This was a rather cynical attitude for the Quraysh to assume, considering the extent to which they had rejected, persecuted, and made war upon their son and brother. But Muhammad replied, "Depart, for today you are all free!"

No requirement of acceptance of Islam was imposed. However, 360 idols were removed from the Ka'bah, and it was reconsecrated to the One God.

The drama of the "Meccan opening" epitomized the Prophet's compassion, for many other men in such a situation—including Moses— might have ordered the Qurayshites put to the sword. But had the Meccans not rejected him, Islam might never have become more than a tiny sect in their obscure city.

These events in a little-known part of the world were beginning to be known abroad. In the year before his last confrontation with Mecca, Muhammad had written to the rulers of Yemen, Ethiopia, Persia, and the Byzantine Empire announcing the message of Islam and inviting them to accept it. The revelation of Muhammad, and the religion of Islam, were offered to humanity as a restored and purified worship of the One God. This marked the beginning of a stunning expansion of Islam, and its transformation into a great civilization, over the next 10 centuries.

CHAPTER 2

Fortresses and Mountain Paths

1,000 YEARS OF ISLAMIC EXPANSION

Muhammad died in 632 at the age of 63, by the Islamic lunar calendar, leaving behind an *ummah*, or community of believers, based on *Qur'an*. Muslims express their faith through five essential affirmations or "pillars." These are the declaration of belief in One God, daily prayer at five set times, the giving of charity, fasting in the month of Ramadan, and the *hajj* pilgrimage to the Ka'bah for those who can afford it.

Leadership of the *ummah* passed to the lifelong friend of Muhammad, his caliph or successor, Abu Bakr, chosen by the Prophet. Abu Bakr and the three rulers who came after him, all from among the Prophet's Companions, are known as the four rightly guided caliphs. They had been among the most intimate with the Prophet, sharing the essential experiences in the formation of Islam. They presided over the first 30 years of the great Islamic expansion into the world.

By the time of Muhammad's death, nearly all of Arabia had been united under Islamic rule. But the ensuing decades also saw the rise of conflict among Muslims. Specifically, the *ummah* was challenged by the first serious outbreak of purist fundamentalism, represented by a violent faction known as the Khawarij or "rebels." Conflict between the Islamic mainstream and the Khawarij has, ever since, defined the two faces of Islam as those of tolerance and extremism.

The Prophet's Companions numbered in the hundreds and came from many places, including Africa and Persia. They were a collegial group, with no formal relationship that would set them apart from the rest of the faithful. But with the Prophet's death all of Islam faced the challenge of maintaining authority in the absence of the religion's charismatic founder. Had a son of the Prophet survived, leadership might have passed to him. Many of the Companions favored Ali ibn Abi Talib, who had been the youngest to enter Islam and was married to the Prophet's daughter Fatima. Ali eventually became the fourth of the rightly guided caliphs. The Muslims did not want to adopt the imperial hierarchy seen in the Christian churches, nor did they wish to emulate the anarchy of the Jewish rabbis. They groped, step by step, between the Christian and Jewish models, for an appropriate religious structure.

During this period, Islamic history has gaps caused by the confusion of the Muslims as they struggled to find their way forward. Indeed, with the Prophet's passing Islam fell into a chaos that Muslims thereafter viewed with horror. No sane Muslim wanted such painful rivalries, betrayals, and clashes to ever be repeated. The lesson was that Islam had to be ruled by a worthy consensus rather than by personal ambitions. But such a consensus could never be fundamentalist. This reality contrasts strongly with the violent and arbitrary picture Westerners have of Islamic governance.

The early period of the *ummah* remains alive to all Muslims, because it represents a sacred drama, and in this sense Islamic history has never been drained of its holy significance. Muslims feel that they participate collectively and individually in the consequences of past events, in a way largely absent from Christianity (but more present in Judaism).

This period of war within the *ummah* also produced a historic split between a majority, embodied in Sunni Islam, and a minority, known as Shi'a. Shi'ism would introduce enduring issues into Islam, culminating in the explosion of the Iranian clerical movement led by Ayatollah Ruhollah Khomeini at the end of the 1970s.

Abu Bakr told the people of Medina, at the beginning of his rulership, "I am not the best of you . . . The weak among you shall be strong with me until I have secured your rights. The strong among you shall be weak with me until I have gained the rights of others. Obey me so long as I obey God and his Messenger." Abu Bakr oversaw the consolidation of Islamic authority in Arabia. The rule of Islam led to the diminishing of banditry in the Peninsula, since Muslims are required to keep peace with each other.

Abu Bakr was called on to render decisions on Muslim conduct. On one notable occasion, he pondered how to punish a Muslim who drank alcohol. The man claimed he did not know that intoxicating drinks were prohibited in Islam. Abu Bakr consulted with Ali, the son-in-law of the Prophet, who told him to question two of the Emigrants and the Helpers as to whether the man had been properly warned. If he had been instructed in the ban, he should be sanctioned; if not, he should be called on to refrain from drink and allowed to go his way. Abu Bakr investigated and learned that the man had never been cautioned, so he let him go. This just and tolerant attitude constituted the essence of traditional Islam.

Muhammad himself had argued that the demands of men could not override the compassion and mercy of the Creator. This principle is reflected in the language of an important doctrinal summation, dating from the third Islamic century, known as *Al'-Aqida Al-Tahawiyya*: "We do not consider any of the people of our faith to be unbelievers because of any wrong action they have done, as long as they do not consider that action to have been lawful." As shown in the example of Abu Bakr and the drinker, a sinner cannot be excluded from the community of the saved unless he or she believes that sinful behavior is acceptable for Muslims, i.e., is not sinful. The same summation declares, "Nor do we say that the wrong action of a man who has belief does not have a harmful effect on him." Thus, sin has consequences in people's lives, but if the sinner repents and seeks forgiveness, God's mercy is assured. Muhammad taught the prayer, "O God, Indeed You are forgiving, Generous, You love forgiveness, so forgive us."

Abu Bakr's caliphate lasted only two years, when he died of natural causes.

Umar ibn al-Khattab succeeded him as second caliph in 634 and assumed the title Commander of the Faithful. When he took office, he told the Muslims,

> Brothers, it has come to my attention that people fear me. They saw that when the Prophet was alive, Umar was harsh . . . During the caliphate of Abu Bakr, Umar was hard and stern. Now that he has become caliph himself, God knows how hard he will be. Whoever has said this was not wrong . . . Now that the whole responsibility has come to me, you will feel a change in me . . . For those who practice tyranny and deprive others of their rights, I will be harsh and stern, but for those who follow the law, and are devoted to religion, I will be soft and tender.

Umar established the Islamic calendar, dating from Muhammad's emigration to Medina. It is said that children ran after him in the streets of Medina, calling out "Father, father!" Like Abu Bakr, Umar was a man of balance, who asked Ali to guide him in making judgments. Umar is said to have discovered a couple engaging in adulterous sex. The stated punishment for such behavior was death by stoning. But Ali reminded Umar that no fewer than four witnesses are required to certify guilt for such an accusation, and that if he acted without such testimony, he himself would sin. Umar followed Ali's advice and refrained from punishing them.

At the same time, under Umar's leadership the Muslims of Arabia began raiding their neighbors. They met with spectacular success: A Muslim force defeated the armies of the Persian empire in 636. The Persians were mainly Zoroastrians, holding to a faith that believed in an eternal conflict between natural forces of good and evil, light and darkness. A wealthy and ancient society, they were the second great nation, after the Arabs, to enter Islam.

But the cultural heritage of the Persians was far weightier than the Arabs', and their role in the development of Muslim civilization was immense. They brought to it theologians, philosophers, mystics, poets, artists, scientists, mathematicians, a great architectural style, geographers, and great ruling dynasties. Persian influence in Islam would also manifest itself in other ways. The Iranians had long traditions of spirituality that linked them to the shamanism of the Central Asian steppes and the Buddhism of South Asia. Persian Islam would always have a particularly mystical and even an ecstatic nature.

· The triumph over the Persians was followed by the conquest of Syria and Egypt. These were Roman and Christian lands. Egypt had retained much of its ancient wisdom under a thin layer of Greek culture. Syria, which included today's Lebanon, Israel, Palestine, and Jordan, was a rich and powerful province. A year after the fall of the Persians, Jerusalem passed from Byzantine to Muslim control. Ali told Umar that Jerusalem must be considered sacred to Muslims as well as Jews and Christians and recommended that the caliph personally accept the city's surrender.

Umar met the Christian Patriarch of the city and his retinue. The caliph wore coarse Arab dress, although the dignitaries receiving him were richly costumed. The caliph asked the citizens of Jerusalem to take him to a sacred place where he could deliver a prayer of gratitude to God. He declined to pray in a church, fearing such an act would lead the Muslims to expropriate the building for use as a mosque. Instead, he went to the hill known to the Jews as the Temple Mount and prayed at a spot associated with David, King of Israel. Later, in the same precinct, Umar founded the Mosque of Umar, near the Dome of the Rock, which would shelter the stone identified with Muhammad's ascent to Heaven in the Night Journey. The Dome of the Rock was the earliest major example of Islamic sacred architecture.

A treaty for the governance of Jerusalem had previously been drawn up at Umar's direction, providing for the protection of the holy sites of the People of the Book. A cruel suppression imposed by the Byzantines on the Jews, who had founded the city, was immediately lifted. Synagogues long closed were opened. In addition, Umar delivered an address to the Muslims who had secured the city's conquest. He said, "All men are equal. Do not flatter those in authority. Do not seek favors from others. By such acts you demean yourselves . . . God has for the time being made me your ruler. But I am one of you. No special privileges belong to rulers."

The conquest of Syria led Umar to compose one of the most significant canons of Islamic law. This was a pact with the large local Christian populace. The agreement, known as the *dhimma*, would govern Muslim relations with both Christians and Jews for centuries. Later it would be applied to other non-Muslim subjects. The contract mandates protection of those who received God's revelations before Muhammad; indeed its aim was to assure security for the preaching of Islam, not its imposition. Thus under Muslim rule, Hindus were permitted to maintain a religion based on a multitude of idols. Somewhat surprisingly, the contract of Umar obtains in present-day Iran and is generally propounded by advocates of an Islamic legal regime.

However, the provisions of the *dhimma* are restrictive in some ways. They include a bar on the construction of new religious structures, whether monasteries, convents, churches, or synagogues. In some Muslim dominions, this regulation was not strictly enforced. For example, after the Jews were expelled from Christian Spain and Portugal in the 15th century, they were welcomed into Morocco and the Ottoman Empire. Many new synagogues were then established in the Islamic world. However, public manifestations of faiths other than Islam were typically restricted, and solicitation of conversion forbidden. Crosses and Christian holy books could not be displayed on the roads or in the markets controlled by Muslims. Non-Muslims could not be buried in close proximity to the Muslim dead. Many of these regulations had a political flavor. The granting of sanctuary to spies or other enemies of the Muslims was naturally forbidden.

The contract also required Jews and Christians to show respect for Muslims by standing in their presence and to refrain from dressing or parting their hair in the manner of Muslims. They could not ride horses, carry arms, or lift their hands to threaten Muslims. They were forbidden to use Arabic calligraphy on their seals, sell fermented beverages, or build houses higher than those of Muslims. Nor could they employ Muslims as servants. At the same time, the People of the Book maintained order within their communities, settling their own disputes so long as Muslims were not parties to the disagreement. Islamic law, or *Shariah*, was considered to apply only to Muslims. Because the protected communities were defined religiously, their clergy had the right to tax them for their collective needs. Their chief divines—Christian bishops and Jewish rabbis—were functionaries of the Islamic state.

In return for the protection of the Muslim order, and exemption from military service, the People of the Book paid a poll tax, also collected by the priests and rabbis. Acceptance of Islam by members of the protected communities would free them from this burden. Under the contract, the People of the Book could not dissuade their kinfolk from entering Islam, in which case as new Muslims they would cease to be protected and would assume ordinary rights and duties. But numerous Islamic rulers, however intense their devotion to the faith, found it convenient to encourage the Jews and Christians to remain outside Islam, as a financial resource. This historical fact contradicts common Christian legendry claiming that multitudes were forcibly converted to the faith of Muhammad.

Certain non-Muslim commentators have criticized the contract for protection of the People of the Book, on the grounds that it imposed second-class citizenship on Jews and Christians. These critics seldom note that until the 18th century, Jews had no citizenship in Christendom, even in such enlightened societies as Holland, which welcomed Jews as residents but maintained legal curbs on them. Until the 19th century no Muslims had liberties of any kind, including residence, in Christian Europe, except as diplomats and others possessing a safe-conduct. Indeed, as this book is written, restrictions on minority religious rights are a significant problem in Sudan and the Arabian Peninsula, but are by no means found only in Muslim lands: Catholics have very limited rights in Orthodox Russia.

One clause in the contract of Umar discouraged the imposition of walled Jewish urban quarters, or ghettoes, in the Islamic world, by requiring that the gates of the protected communities be always left open. Umar also decreed the expulsion of non-Muslims from the vicinity of the Holy Places in the Arabian Peninsula. But this stricture was not completely enforced before the 18th century, and even then inconsistently. Christians stayed in Mecca and Medina, and Jews in the southern city of Najran, until the final triumph of Wahhabism in the 1920s.

After 10 years as caliph, Umar was assassinated by a Persian slave, Abu'l Lu'lu Firuz, disgruntled that Umar had refused to reduce the levy he was paying his master. He was succeeded by Uthman ibn Affan, third of the rightly guided caliphs. Uthman provided for compilation of an authoritative text of *Qur'an*, and oversaw other achievements. Under his leadership, Islam spread to the island of Cyprus, ruled by the Byzantines, Libya, and eastward to Afghanistan and western India. Muslim rule was also solidified in Persia. Uthman's rule lasted for a dozen years, until he was murdered by soldiers dissatisfied with his policy of favoring his own family, the Umayyads, over that of the Prophet, the Hashimites, in political appointments. His death was a harbinger of further ugly developments: His killers threw stones at his funeral procession.

Uthman had contributed much to the glory of the *ummah*, but his rule was also seriously flawed by his nepotism toward the Umayyads. He did this because he thought it would strengthen control and stability in the *ummah*, but he was mistaken: Its effect was to increase dissension. The Umayyads remained in power but were challenged by supporters of Ali ibn Abi Talib, who was married to the Prophet's daughter Fatima. Ali was the fourth of the rightly guided caliphs, and second of the supreme personalities in Islamic tradition. Some of his supporters were blamed for the killing of Uthman. The nepotism of Uthman and the Umayyads, which seemed based only on family advantage, ran strongly against the feelings of the Muslims of Medina. They responded by supporting what they considered a legitimate form of nepotism in which authority would be reserved for the sacred lineage of Muhammad. The majority of Muslims acclaimed Ali as the new caliph, but he at first declined, recommending they choose someone else. Ali seems to have understood that the growing hatreds and rivalries that had killed Umar and Uthman also threatened him. Further, he was modest and distrusted the passions of the populace. A position of leadership would be valuable to him only as a means to establish God's law; power in itself meant nothing. But crowds gathered in Medina, insisting that he accept the responsibility.

Ali was a model of piety and valor, as shown by his predecessors' habit of deferring to his counsel. The caliph Umar had told him, "God save me from living in a community from which you are absent." The Companion who had entered Islam at the age of 10, he was one of the earliest adherents of Muhammad, of whom he was also a nephew and son-in-law. The Prophet himself had said, "I am the city of knowledge, and Ali is its gate." Some Muslims would have preferred that Ali assume the title of caliph on Muhammad's death.

When he finally agreed to become caliph in the year 656, Ali warned the Muslims that having been among the Emigrants and the Helpers would not earn merit with him—their only reward would be granted by God in the afterlife. Wealth would be distributed to all Muslims, to prevent believers from currying political favor. The caliph Ali was a true and idealistic reformer, bent on rooting out the venality and love of power for which the Umayyads were reproached.

But from the moment of his induction the *ummah* was wracked by civil war. Ali, "soldier, scholar, sage, and saint," was an indecisive ruler who failed to organize an effective defense of his power and seemed incapable of acting with firmness against his opponents. Umayyad-ruled Syria, under the governorship of Muawiya, a relative of Uthman, rose against him following an attempt at mediation to which Ali acceded, but which caused another rebellion against his rule, by the Khawarij, who declared him an unbeliever. Muawiya invaded Iraq, which was Ali's main power base, and also seized Jerusalem from Ali's partisans. The Meccans, meanwhile, were divided between supporters of Ali and of the Umayyads.

The fundamentalists known as the Khawarij emerged from the ranks of Ali's supporters during his conflict with the Umayyads. The Umayyads sought to increase their power over the Muslims, while the followers of Ali desired an egalitarian Islam inclusive of differences. The Khawarij aimed at a dictatorship of the seemingly virtuous, although they hid behind demands for equality. In this, they foreshadowed the extremist ideological regimes of modern times, but especially the Wahhabi phenomenon that emerged in central Arabia in the 18th century, and which gained immense influence over the *ummah* thanks to the proclamation of the Saudi state and the discovery of oil in the Arabian Peninsula.

The trauma of the Khawarij upheaval was so great that their history is obscured; it is as if the *ummah* had tried to forget them, for it knows them today mainly from the commentaries of their opponents. Little may be said of their leaders, their writings, and other aspects of their origins. Among them, the tendencies of separatism, purism, and fundamentalism were fully expressed for the first time, reflecting the difficulties created by the rapid expansion of Islamic power, and stimulated by the crisis of the *ummah* after the Prophet's passing. The Khawarij declared that the errors

Ali reflected a lack of Muslim faith rather than human
these two caliphs were declared traitors and unbelievers.
argued that only the most punctilious observant Muslim,
with religion rather than statecraft, would be fit to lead the
um. At the same time, they rejected everything in the religion of
Muhammad with which they disagreed and ignored Islamic precedents,
inventing their own justifications for their beliefs. Finally, they believed
that *jihad* to impose Islam should be made an obligation of all Muslims.

The Khawarij illustrate a permanent tension between the principle of
consensus, based on the benevolent personality of the Prophet, which
facilitated the expansion of Islam into new territories, and a reactionary
purist conception. This kind of fanaticism reappeared many times in the
history of Islam, but was always defeated, until the time of the Wahhabis.

The claim of exalted moral purity and love of war among the Khawarij
foreshadowed later events, culminating in modern Islamic terrorism.
Their attitudes and actions deeply troubled the *ummah*, and condemnation of them is a major topic in Islamic theology. Some extremely severe
Ahadith of the Prophet are cited as applying to them and to their later
counterparts:

> They recite Qur'an *and consider it in their favor but it is*
>   *against them.*
> They transpose the quranic verses meant to refer to unbelievers
>   and make them refer to the believers.
> What I fear most in my ummah *is a man who interprets verses of*
>   Qur'an *out of context.*
> They will pass through Islam as an arrow passes through its
>   quarry. Wherever you meet them, kill them!
> The one who kills them or who is killed by them is blessed.
> They are the dogs of the people of hell.

The 19th-century Iraqi scholar and poet al-Zahawi emphasized that
the Khawarij had, absurdly, declared Ali as well as the Umayyads unbelievers. The Khawarij proclaimed it lawful for the blood of Muslims they
opposed to be shed—along with that of their associates and families—and

their property seized. In one of the most important expressions of the sep-aratist impulse in Islamic fundamentalism, the Khawarij divided the world between the "house of war," to which they consigned Ali, and the "house of peace" or "house of Islam," which they alone claimed to inhabit.

Ali triumphed over the Khawarij at al-Nahrwan in Iraq in 659, but they proved extremely resistant, continuing to trouble the *ummah* for genera-tions, relaunching their violence and always encountering defeat. Ali told them, "We do not start out killing you nor are you kept out of the mosques of God in which you mention his name. We do not rescind the rights of protection with respect to your life and property afforded you by Islam as long as your hand is with us." The Companions preferred to win the Khawarij back to the right path by debate. They had some success with individuals, but not enough to prevent the death of the great-hearted Ali.

Ali fought and largely defeated the Khawarij, but was assassinated by one of them, becoming the first Muslim ruler to suffer because of indeci-sion in the face of a fundamentalist and terrorist mentality. The two faces of Islam thus came into focus, represented by the Khawarij and their vic-tim, Ali. A Shi'a scholar, Shaykh Muhammad Mahdi Shams al-Din, com-ments that Ali "was compelled to struggle in order to preserve the unity of the Muslims by the peaceful means which his opponents refused to respond to . . . Ali ibn Abi Talib struggled for a long time to attain a frame-work which would preserve the unity of the Muslims and enable him to realize his dream of building a just state. He failed, however, because of his opponents' persistence in their separatist attitude."

After the murder of Ali the Umayyads consolidated their regime in Syria, moving the Islamic capital from Medina to Damascus. Meanwhile the Muslims of Iraq remained loyal to Ali even after his death and became known as the Followers of Ali, or the Shi'at 'Ali. Thus was Shi'ism born as the most enduring and significant of the sects that make up the Islamic world community. Shi'a Muslims identify Ali and a series of successors as spiritual chiefs or *imams*—some recognize seven, others twelve. The Shi'a thus departed from the rest of the *ummah*, which is known as Sunni, after the *Sunna*. But their dissidence generally assumed pluralist rather than fundamentalist attitudes.

The drama of this schism increased in 680, almost 20 years after Ali's death, when his son and the grandson of Muhammad, Husayn, the Third *Imam* of Shi'ism, was convinced by a group of discontented Iraqi Muslims to back them against the arbitrary rule and family favoritism of the Umayyads. Husayn had departed Medina for Mecca, after communications asking his support reached him from Kufah, the capital of Ali's supporters. However, as described by Shaykh Shams al-Din, two of his relatives, who were pious men, warned him of the danger. "Abd Allah ibn 'Abbas told Husayn, 'I have learnt that you are setting out for Iraq. They are treacherous people and are only calling you to war. Do not hurry. If you refuse any other course but to fight against the Umayyad tyrant and yet are unwilling to stay in Mecca, then go to Yemen. Write to your supporters in Kufah and in Iraq that they should drive out their governor. If they do not do that, you should remain in Yemen until God sends His commandment, for there, there are fortresses and mountain paths.'"

Husayn disregarded this advice. He supported the dissidents, but none of them rallied to him. He and some 70 adherents, all from Mecca, were slain by Umayyad forces at Karbala in Iraq, on the 10th day of the month of Muharram. Husayn was killed with his infant son in his arms, and the heads of the victims were displayed in public. The Umayyad commander, 'Ubayd Allah ibn Ziyad, stuck his cane in Husayn's mouth, knocking out his teeth, and a supporter of Husayn named Zayd ibn Arqam began weeping. Ibn Ziyad threatened him, but Zayd ibn Arqam declared, "O people . . . you will be slaves after today. You have killed the son of Fatima . . . By God, the best of your men have been killed, and the worst of them have become masters. May God destroy those who consent to humiliation and shame!"

The murder of Ali and the battle of Karbala were among the most traumatic events in the early history of Islam. Although traditional Sunni Muslims honor Ali and Husayn, the grief of Shi'a Muslims at their deaths is a vivid reality even today. Shi'as express penitence over the failure of the people of Kufah to rally to Husayn. Karbala itself is a symbol of the cosmic conflict between good and evil, and the site became a major shrine and place of pilgrimage. In mourning for the tragedy that occurred there, the Shi'a calendar of observance begins with the first 10 days of Muharram. Shi'as mark each of these days with a commemoration of the Prophets,

Husayn and his supporters, and events in the life of Ali, "a martyr in the path of justice." On the 10th night narratives of the battle of Karbala are recited.

There are many poems on the horror of Karbala. One Persian classic begins:

> *What is raining? Blood.*
> *Who? The eyes.*
> *How? Day and night.*
> *Why? From grief.*
> *Grief for whom?*
> *Grief for the king of Karbala.*

A Turkish poet wrote:

> *The inhabitants of heaven and earth shed black tears today.*
> *And have become confused like your hair, O Husayn.*
> *Dawn sheds its blood out of sadness for Husayn,*
> *And the red tulips wallow in blood*
> *And carry the marks of his grief on their hearts . . .*

The 18th-century Persian-language poet Muhammad Muhsin, living in a part of today's Pakistan, wrote eloquently,

> *The boat of Mustafa's [Muhammad's] family has been drowned*
>   *in blood;*
> *The black cloud of unbelief has waylaid the sun;*
> *The candle of the Prophet was extinguished by the breeze of the*
>   *Kufans.*[1]

(It is interesting to note that a Shi'a scholar has sought to correlate the 10th of Muharram with the Jewish Yom Kippur or Day of Atonement.)

Ali's reforming conscience and Husayn's unhesitating solidarity with a protest movement left profound marks on Shi'a Muslims, who would be known for their strong sense of social justice, their sympathy for victims, and their appeal to the oppressed and excluded. Shaykh Shams al-Din wrote of Ali and Husayn, "Their lives were a continuous chain of sacrifices for the public good. They were only overcome by their Umayyad rivals in the political battles because, in their dealings with the *ummah*, with their rivals and with their supporters, they always followed principles and standards which rose out of their feelings of Islamic responsibility."

The Shi'a also exhibit belief in the coming of millennial change and hope for the advent of a redeemer. Husayn's movement is considered by the Iranian Shi'as of modern times as a revolution within Islam. But Shi'ism, though often radical, generally does not preach that the "end times" have already begun, as some Islamic fundamentalists do. Conflicts between Shi'as and other Muslims would be reflected in 20th-century clashes between Iranian Muslims and the apocalyptic Wahhabi cult in Arabia, and would later impel Iraq, ruled by the dictator Saddam Husayn, to go to war with the Iranians.

Despite their cruelty to Ali and Husayn, or perhaps because of it, the Umayyad caliphs, having overcome the Shi'as, ruled during the great wave of Arab conquests, lasting until the middle of the 8th century, and are associated with major cultural achievements, especially in art and architecture. Existing Mediterranean, Byzantine, and Persian styles were transformed by Islamic conceptions. Some churches, such as that dedicated to St. John the Baptist in Damascus, were turned into mosques. At the same time, the former Byzantine and Persian state bureaucracies were Islamized and Arabized. Byzantine minting of money was supplanted by Islamic coinage. The Umayyad capital, Damascus, became a great world city. In Jerusalem, the Dome of the Rock was completed in 691, under the Umayyad caliph Abd al-Malik.

Another major event of the Umayyad era was the Muslim invasion of Spain in 711. The body of water separating Africa and Europe became known as the Strait of Gibraltar, after a large rock on the Spanish coast named for the Umayyad general who crossed into Europe, *Jebel ul-Tarik* or the Mountain of Tarik. By then the descendants of Abraham and Ismail had brought the whole southern coast of the Mediterranean under their control.

The Muslims gained their first significant European foothold in Spain and began pressing northward. Although it made little impression on the Muslim world, in 732 the French king Charles Martel defeated a Muslim raiding party at the battle of Poitiers, ending their farthest advance into Western Europe. But the extraordinary success of the Muslim armies, emerging from unknown Arabia to reach the interior of Christendom within a century after Muhammad's death, changed European history completely. The next 1,000 years was a millennium of Christian resistance, fear, and insecurity no less than of Muslim conquest, pride, and self-confidence.

The Umayyads imposed a political organization on their conquests that consolidated Islamic society from the Atlantic to the Indian oceans. But the Khawarij did not disappear from the collective life of the Muslims (an Islamic legal tradition derived from them, known as Ibadhism, is today the official sect in the Gulf state of Oman). Nor were they the last group to seek to redefine the standard of Muslim faith and conduct. One group of scholars, the Qadariyya, produced two contradictory positions, one that argued for complete human free will, the other claiming that all actions are foreordained and that unbelievers cannot change. A more important strain of thought was represented by the Mu'tazila, considered predecessors of rationalism by modern historians of religion. Another group, the Murji'a, declared that faith resides in conscience rather than in deeds.

From the ranks of the Murji'a came an individual who would bring a new direction to the Muslim intellect. Abu Hanifah, living in Iraq at the time of the Arab penetration of Western Europe, was the effective founder of Islamic jurisprudence. Prior to Abu Hanifah, each region had its circles or schools of Companions of the Prophet, followed by "the Successors," scholars of faith whose company was sought by the studious. Westerners view Islamic law—*Shariah*—as extreme and intolerant, brutal and relentless in its punishments. But Islamic legal practice, even before Abu Hanifah, was permeated with the spirit of compassion and mercy visible in the previously noted counsels of Ali to Abu Bakr and Umar.

The purpose of systematizing Islamic law, to which Abu Hanifah committed himself, was to derive and codify rulings concerning five categories of human action: the forbidden, the disapproved or disliked, the permitted, the *Sunna* or voluntarily virtuous, and the obligatory. Legal arguments between scholars, before a judge (*qadi*), or in obtaining *fatwas* as to what is permitted or prohibited, rested on the fundamental texts of Islam: *Qur'an*, the *Hadith*, and the lives of the Prophet and his Companions. These were supplemented by analogies drawn from a similar or parallel example of human conduct in *Qur'an* or the *Hadith*. Jurists also drew on consensus, based on debate among the scholars. Here we see a major parallel between Islam and Judaism. Unlike Christian authorities, Muslims followed the Jewish example in seeking to generate a body of law that would merge the religious and civil elements in society.

The *Hanafi* school of jurisprudence created by Abu Hanifah is considered the most tolerant of differences in opinion. It is also by far the most influential of the several schools of legal thought in the Muslim world today, dominating Turkey, the Balkans, Central Asia, Chinese Turkestan, Afghanistan, Pakistan, and India. However, three other schools emerged in the generations following Abu Hanifah that also became standard in Sunni Islam and are considered of equal validity. Each has its own emphasis.

The *Malikis*, centered on customary and legal practices in Medina, are named for Malik Ibn Anas, a Medinite. This tradition struck deep roots in Muslim Spain and in North and West Africa, where it remains the most important Islamic legal school.

The *Shafi'is*, who follow Muhammad ibn al-Shafii, based their thinking on the *Hadith* as well as the use of analogy. The founder of this tradition began as a student of Ibn Anas. Its area of influence presently includes Egypt, the Arab states of the Middle East, the Kurds, and Muslims in the Indian Ocean and Southeast Asia.

The mentor of the *Hanbalis* was Ahmad ibn Hanbal, a vigorous foe of the Mu'tazila and a pioneer of fundamentalist theology in Islam. His school stressed the use of authentic *Hadith* in preference to analogy. It now dominates the Arabian Peninsula.

Shariah, or Islamic law, is the sum of all these systems. (Most Shi'as follow yet another school called the *Jaf'aris*.) An example of the differences between the four schools involves the question of when the holy month of Ramadan begins. It is agreed that Ramadan commences after the new moon, in its crescent form, is sighted. The Hanafis believe that on a clear night, the testimony of two Muslim men, or one man and two women, of good morals, who have observed the new moon, is enough to confirm the start of Ramadan. If clouds obscure the sky, one such witness suffices. Malikis say only that two Muslims of good morals, regardless of their sex, must have seen the moon. For the Shafi'i only one honorable Muslim man is necessary as a witness. In the Hanbali school, one sane, moral, adult Muslim, man or woman, must have seen the new moon; if the sky is cloudy, the month should be considered to have begun the next day without a lunar observance.

In a *Hadith*, the Prophet himself compared the illumination of Muslim scholars to the heavenly bodies in the night sky. He said, "The simile of the scholars of knowledge on the earth is the stars in the sky by which one is guided in the darkness of the land and the sea." In a similar *Hadith*, he said, "My Companions are equivalent to the stars in the sky; whichever of them you point to, you will be guided, and the differences among my Companions are a mercy to you." This benign view of controversies in law is essential to traditional Islam.

Punishments vary considerably not only by school but by region. If *Shariah* punishments seem excessive to Westerners, they were counterbalanced by extremely high standards of evidence, and in later periods *Shariah* has been applied in Muslim countries alongside legal codes derived from pre-Islamic, communal traditions, as well as European sources. While most Westerners are under the mistaken impression that all Muslim countries apply *Shariah* uniformly and without exception, this is an absurd misapprehension. European and American law have influenced today's *Shariah*. Former European colonies throughout the Islamic world, from Morocco and Nigeria to Malaysia, still apply imperial civil and criminal codes. Bosnia-Hercegovina and the Albanian lands maintain *Shariah* and European law together. Central Asian states seek to preserve elements of Russian law. Only Gulf states maintain *Shariah* exclusively.

The universal applicability of exclusive *Shariah*, in its letter rather than its spirit, is a sensitive issue. The Islamic dedication to consensus often, under the later Islamic empires such as the Ottomans, led to the adoption of local customary law. Through the counsel of scholars, Muslim statesmen found ways to combine the spirit of Islamic law with recognition of local conditions. The rapid spread of Islam required the adaptation of Muslim governance to such cultural habits.

Many subjects of the new rulers became Muslims, but many others did not, especially in Spain. For the next 1,000 years, pluralism within Islam and civility between Islam and other faiths under its rule characterized the *ummah*. The choice remained between withdrawal into a narrow, sectarian universe suitable for isolated colonies of desert nomads, or expansion into the world. Engagement with the rest of humanity through conquest and power would elevate the Muslims. Those who opted for fundamentalism might attain great virtue and piety but would never be able to govern large numbers effectively; no society can long be managed as the dominion of an extremist cult.

Islamic history reflects this permanent contradiction between consensus and fundamentalism. The rise of the Khawarij with their penchant for declaring their foes unbelievers whether they are professing Muslims or not remains the essential example of the latter. Al-Zahawi, as we have seen, expressed the traditional reluctance of Muslims to accuse one another of unbelief. But beginning in the time of Muhammad himself, a related issue drove Muslims apart, having to do with the means to salvation. Consensus maintained that belief, however imperfectly an individual might adhere to it, must not be questioned; they argued that belief alone is sufficient for salvation, while fundamentalists declared that faith must be judged in terms of outward conduct. Keepers of the Consensus recognized that human beings are unpredictable in their deeds and may better be judged by their intentions. The fundamentalists became puritan fanatics, treating all who strayed from their norms as unbelievers worthy of extinction.

Islam, in extending its secular sway, came to reflect a necessary openness. The expansion of the Islamic order brought more contact with the knowledge preserved in Christendom and produced new trends in philosophy, science, and spirituality.

A significant shift in sensibilities occurred in 749 when the Umayyads were overthrown by the Abbasids, a Shi'a faction that became Sunni once it attained power. The Abbasids founded the city of Baghdad and moved the center of the Islamic world there from Damascus. They established the first truly great Islamic culture, symbolized by the founding of a university. Under the sponsorship of the Abbasids, Baghdad became a center for the translation of Hebrew, Persian, Sanskrit, and Greek texts into Arabic. The translated works ranged through medicine, mathematics, chemistry, and metallurgy, as well as philosophy.

Fifty years after the Muslim conquest of Spain, a youth named Abd al-Rahman, the only survivor of the overthrow of the Umayyads, established an independent emirate at the old Roman town of Córdoba in Andalusia. After two centuries Córdoba became a separate caliphate. The glory of Islamic Spain exceeded that of the Abbasids: It lasted much longer and included the transformation of Roman and Phoenician towns like Córdoba, Granada, and Sevilla into beautiful cities. But most important, Muslim rule in Spain produced a brilliant cultural dialogue with Jews and Christians. The Arabs made bony, stony Spain, whose lands had been worked out by the Romans, green again, through their mastery of waterworks and irrigation. It is often repeated that "the Arabs brought the fountain to Spain." Arab restoration of the Spanish soil included the introduction of orange and other fruit orchards, sugar, and rice. They created an agricultural band across Andalusia that survives today. Trade between Muslim Spain and Christian France and Italy made the Iberian Peninsula even richer.

The most enduring legacy of this period is the formal development of Islamic mysticism or purification of the self—in Arabic, *tasawwuf*. The first Muslim to speak eloquently of divine love, one of the chief elements of Islamic mysticism, was a woman, Rabiya al-Adawiyya. Rabiya died some 180 years after the founding of Medina. She committed her life to spiritual devotion, declaring that we are compelled to love God as the Creator. The passion of Rabiya for God was profound and fecund. She produced great poetry in which she celebrated her love for the Lord of the

Universe. She wrote, "I have never worshipped God so that I would be rewarded; nor have I prayed to be saved. If I did I should be an ordinary servant. I pray only because I love God with all my soul. To weep and cry out for God's mercy would be for nothing; for all I want is to approach God and dissolve my inner self in Him." These lines could be taken as a summary of all *tasawwuf*, as well as major themes in Jewish and Christian mysticism. The writings of Rabiya and those who came after her strongly parallel parts of the *Song of Songs* ascribed to Solomon.

The first major figure after Rabiya, Husayn bin Mansur al Hallaj (858–922), expounded ecstatically on annihilation of one's being in the Divine Will. He wrote several volumes with such alluring titles as *The Book of Invented and Eternal Letters*, *The Book of Roots and Branches*, and *The Book of Justice and Unity*. He declared "I am both the lover and the beloved," that is, both God and the worshipper. But Hallaj came in conflict as a provocative Sufi, and a religious opinion or *fatwa* was issued calling for his arrest and imprisonment. After an escape and capture, he was jailed for eight years in Baghdad before he was executed. The scholars of his time were split over this terrible deed. His opponents accused him of total unbelief or atheism. His defenders were the pioneers of Islamic spirituality as an organized and disciplined movement, or Sufism. The Sufis would become guardians of tradition and spirituality in Islam; their teachings, gentle in spirit but fostering courage in resistance, would be especially hated by the fundamentalist Wahhabis, who, since their emergence in the 18th century, have sought to wipe them out of existence.

The word "Sufi" derives from the Arabic word for wool (*suf*), denoting the rough clothing worn by the self-denying seekers of truth. Sufis are also known as dervishes. Hallaj means "tanner" in Arabic, and the mystic earned his living in this difficult and unpleasant trade early in his life. Some modern Muslim commentary identifies Hallaj as a saint of the poor, traces the rise of Sufism to protests against the corruptions of wealth and shows a fracture running through Islamic history between the mystics, who are pluralists and lovers, and the legalists, who are hunters of heresy and haters. But one present-day figure, Shaykh Muhammad Hisham Kabbani, offers a clearer definition of Sufism:

Through slow evolution and as a reaction against the increasing worldliness of the social environment, Muslims flocked to . . . saints and their followers until their regimen ended up as a school of practical thought and moral action endowed with its own structure of rules and principles. This became the basis used by Sufi scholars to direct people on the Right Path. As a result, the world soon witnessed the development of a variety of schools of purification . . . Sufi thought, as it spread everywhere, served as a dynamic force behind the growth and fabric of Islamic education.

As described by the scholar and Sufi Abdul Qadri Jilani, "Hallaj spoke the words 'I am God' with the intoxicated language of the heart, a voice unknown to the people." The charge that he had spoken this phrase led to Hallaj's death—some say the actual wording was "I am the Truth," using the word *haqq* or "truth as a manifestation of God." The 13th-century Persian poet and dervish Jalal-ad-din Rumi, whose works have become enormously popular among British and American readers, argued, "Often saints, in a dreamlike state, speak such words. However, when they awake they seek forgiveness. Such were the words of Hallaj."

Hallaj declared that in essence all religions are one, seeking union with the same God that alone decides which faith men and women choose. There should thus be no conflict between creeds. We may see in Hallaj and his executioners the two faces of Islam; but it may seem ironic that a figure identified in the Western mind with Islamic extremism, Ayatollah Khomeini, was also a highly unorthodox mystic who wrote poetry in which he said, "I forget myself and proclaim, 'I am the truth'; and like Mansur Hallaj I give myself up for execution." This verse is interpreted as praising the Sufi surrender to God, while describing Khomeini's own view of himself as suffering for God.

Sufism embodies certain basic elements: the principle of divine love; the search for spiritual union in contemplation of the divine; and the social mission of studying and absorbing other, earlier esoteric beliefs. Ancient traditions were assimilated into Islam from the large populations that came under Muslim domination from Persia through Central Asia. Some of these were Zoroastrian, some were involved in Gnostic cults or Asiatic

Christianity (Nestorianism), some were Buddhist, some followed shamans. The dervishes provided their greatest service to Muslim rulers as agents of goodwill between adherents of the ruling faith and those of the ruled. But this syncretism has always been suspect to Islamic fundamentalists.

While Hallaj was a master of the secret of divine love, spiritual union with God is also identified with the greatest of the mystics, whom many consider the outstanding theologian in the history of Islam. Abu Hamid al-Ghazali (1058–1111) was a Persian who lived in Baghdad between journeys as a wandering ascetic. He is known as the Proof of Islam, and in Western literature as Algazel. Al-Ghazali authored a massive work, *The Revival of the Religious Sciences*, widely read by Jews as well as Muslims. The effect of his teaching was to dampen the rivalry between the mystics and their enemies.

An exemplar of the assimilation of local, earlier mystical traditions to Sufism is Shihab ad-Din Suhrawardi. Born in Iran, Suhrawardi lived from 1153 to 1191 and was also executed at the instance of fundamentalists, before the age of 40. His death is complicated by charges that he had sought to create a philosophical kingdom with himself at its head. Author of *The Science of Illumination*, Suhrawardi dedicated his extensive writings to a merging of the Zoroastrian thought that had so long ruled his native land with Platonic philosophy and Islam. As others have said, Suhrawardi saw light out of the East, where dawn appears.

The contradiction between the two faces of Islam, fundamentalism and pluralism, permeates the lives of three representative Spanish Muslim thinkers. These are Ibn Hazm (994–1064) and Ibn Rushd (1126–1198, known as Averroes)—both sons of Córdoba—and Muhyiddin Ibn Arabi (1165–1240), who was born in Murcia. In the first, we have a personality who brought together within himself, though in discord rather than unity, the conflicting aspects of the Islamic mentality. The second is one of the greatest Islamic philosophers, widely read in the West. In the third, we find the finest of the Sufi poets, known as Shaykh ul-Akbar, the supremely wise.

Ibn Hazm is at the same time one of the most and least appealing figures in Islam. A child of the Córdoba elite, he authored, among a great many medical, religious, and literary works, *The Dove's Neck-Ring*, perhaps the best essay ever written on physical love, in which he included samples of his own verse. The text shows much in common with the concept of courtly love that soon emerged from Languedoc and Provence, parts of the Christian world close to the Spanish Muslim frontier. The principles enunciated in Ibn Hazm's book include the transformation of the lover by love—making him a better and nobler person, relentless desire, and penetrating grief at its lack of fulfilment. True love becomes a kind of illness, causing depression, insomnia, rage, insanity, and even death. Flirtation, conspiracy, and manipulation in pursuit of the desired one are acceptable. The ultimate principle, however, is that of the lover's utter subordination, even prostration before the beloved, whose social status is irrelevant. One may love a slave or an aristocrat with equal intensity.

Ibn Hazm possessed great comprehension of the ordeal of human passion. But he was neither pleasant company nor wise in his views on religion and law. Indeed he was one of the most extreme and irrational fundamentalists in Islamic history, as a follower of Dhahiri or literalist jurisprudence, which is not considered an orthodox Sunni school. Three commentators from the end of the 13th century said, "Even those who greeted Ibn Hazm hated him. They disliked his ideas. They all agreed that he was a heretic. They could not speak well of him. They warned the rulers to beware of him. They told Muslims to keep away from him." Still more interesting are the observations of the 21st-century historian of Islam G. F. Haddad, who notes the following example of Ibn Hazm's extreme literalism in interpreting the *Sunna*.

Muhammad said, quite sensibly, "Let no one urinate in still, non-running water then use it to bathe." From this, Haddad writes, Ibn Hazm "stated the following absurd inferences:

> *The interdiction to bathe applied only to the one who urinated;*
>   *thus, anyone other than him may use that water to bathe.*
> *It applied only if one urinated into the water. He and anyone*
>   *else might therefore use the water to bathe if the urine reached*
>   *the water indirectly, for example after falling on high or*
>   *nearby ground first, or being poured in it from a container.*
> *It applied only if one urinated in it, not defecated in it."*

It would be difficult to imagine a more ridiculous expression of fundamentalist rigidity.

The dean of Western historians of the Middle East, Bernard Lewis, has pointed out another unattractive aspect of Ibn Hazm. Author of a major comparative work on religion, Ibn Hazm also composed a violent pamphlet against Judaism. Lewis notes, "It is surely significant that it is the only known book of its kind," i.e., a Muslim polemic of the classic era against Judaism as a faith. Ibn Hazm seems to have been motivated mainly by jealousy toward a competing Andalusian poet who was a Jew. He was also a ferocious bigot against the Shi'as.

Averroes was outstanding among a number of medieval Muslim intellectuals whose works swept Christian Europe after their translation into Hebrew and Latin. Born three generations after Ibn Hazm, he was also a product of the Córdoban ruling class. He applied himself to science, mathematics, medicine, philosophy, and theology. He held positions of high responsibility, but also suffered sanctions over political rivalries, as had Ibn Hazm. Muslim Spain was not tranquil as far as ambitions and factions were concerned. Averroes argued against the mysticism of Al-Ghazali, and considered philosophy an elite pursuit. He is famous for his commentaries on Aristotle, a pretext for him to develop his own philosophy, which achieved dominance in Christendom, surpassing the doctrines of St. Thomas Aquinas and Duns Scotus in prestige. Aquinas adopted his style, and although he argued against Averroes's interpretations, he greatly admired him, as did Dante.

If the martyred Suhrawardi *saw* the dawn, the adherents of Ibn Arabi believe he is the dawn or, at least, that his spirit abides within the first, sublime gleams of light at the beginning of every day, throughout creation. His insights are so exceptional that he is one of the most admired figures in Islamic spirituality, with thousands of Westerners interested in his message today. He also was widely read by Jewish mystics. The Islamic Spain in which Ibn Arabi was born was under intense pressure from Christian forces driving southward out of territories reconquered from the Muslims. During his life, the Spanish Muslims lost the climactic Battle of Navas de Tolosa in 1212 to combined armies of Castilians, Aragonese, and Catalans.

The Islamic state collapsed in an array of quarreling entities incapable of uniting against the invader, although Muslim rule would continue in the peninsula for nearly three centuries more. Ibn Arabi died in Damascus a quarter century before the taking of his native city, Murcia, by Christian soldiers.

Ibn Arabi had, as a youth, met Averroes. But his character was entirely different from that of an Aristotelian philosopher. Ibn Arabi had begun experiencing spiritual visions relatively young, and the pursuit of esoteric truth became his life purpose. His most important treatises are his *Meccan Openings* and *Bezels of Wisdom*. The title of the former volume, sometimes translated as *Meccan Revelations*, refers to the "opening" of Mecca by mercy, without violence or revenge, after the town surrendered to Muhammad. The latter work is a summation of each unique truth delivered by the Prophets recognized in Islam. William Chittick, an honored scholar of Ibn Arabi, has noted that the Spanish Arab master believed "no one after him would inherit fully from the Prophet Muhammad." That is, the mystic saw himself as the final spiritual heir of the final Prophet.

The most important of Ibn Arabi's contributions of Islamic thought dealt with the principle of the unity of all being, a concept attacked by fundamentalists as "pantheism." Ibn Arabi followed Hallaj in proclaiming the unity of the monotheistic faiths, since Jews, Christians, and Muslims all pray to the same God. His most appealing, if challenging, work is his collection of poems, *Stars and Sparks of Mystical Love Revealed*, also known as *Treasures for Lovers* and as *The Interpreter of Desires*.[2] This incredible sequence of passionate odes is the real Muslim equivalent of the Jewish *Song of Songs*. Its classic edition includes his poems as well as the poet's commentaries on them. The author identified the images in the verses with specific spiritual lessons, and his own prefaces explained the circumstances under which the poems were composed.

The Interpreter of Desires reflects the experience of Ibn Arabi after his first trip to Mecca, where he encountered mystics from Persia. His host in the city had an adolescent daughter who was "exceedingly beautiful," in the poet's words, and "renowned for her asceticism and eloquent preaching." Ibn Arabi added in one version that he would say more about her physical and moral perfection but was deterred by the temptation of sin. Nevertheless, he poured into his verses a desire of such intensity that it seems a force of nature, and of such inspiration it could transform the universe. He wrote:

> When she walks on the glass pavement[3] you see a sun on a
>   celestial sphere . . .
> When she kills with her glances, her speech restores to life, as if
>   she, as a giver of life, were Jesus.
> The smoothness of her legs is like the brightness of the Torah,
>   and I follow it and walk in its steps as if I were Moses.
> She is a female bishop, a daughter of Rome, unadorned, with a
>   radiant goodness.
> Wild is she, none can make her his friend; in her solitary cham-
>   ber she has a tomb for remembrance;
> She has baffled every learned scholar in our religion, every
>   student of the Psalms of David, every Jewish doctor, and every
>   Christian priest.

The poet's commentary explains each startling turn in his text as a reference to mystical study. She, who is wisdom, walks arrogantly, proud of her power over the heart. Death by the glance of the beautiful woman symbolizes complete loss of the self in contemplation of God. The text also shows the extent and force of Ibn Arabi's belief in the unity of monotheism. *Torah* has four faces, our Muslim believer writes with devotion: these are *Qur'an*, the *Pentateuch*, the *Psalms*, and the *Gospels*. Later in the work appears his most famous utterance:

> My heart is a pasture for gazelles and a convent of
>   Christian monks,
> A temple for idols and the Ka'bah of pilgrims,
> The Tablets of the Law in Torah and the Book of Qur'an.
> I follow the religion of Love, wherever Love takes me,
> There is my religion and my faith.

Protest as the author might, to later readers as well as his censorious contemporaries—who saw in these verses naught but shameless lust—their essence remains admiration of the young woman's beauty. No love affair is known to have taken place. Yet it is no wonder that Ibn Arabi remains a deeply controversial figure in the *ummah* today, loathed and forbidden by fundamentalists and their governments, under whose rule his works are banned, while on the other hand he is beloved as "the Greatest Shaykh" by many traditionalists.

The influence of Islamic Spain, especially in its spirituality, transformed the religious culture of the Spanish Jews and Christians. The greatest 20th-century Jewish cultural historian, Gershom Scholem, who pioneered the analytical study of *Kabbalah* or Jewish spirituality, wrote that the mystical impulse toward "a more intimate communion with God and for a religious life connected with this" appeared in medieval Judaism "from fusion of internal (Jewish) drives with the external influence of the religious movements present in the non-Jewish environment. Since their proponents did not find the answer to all their needs in the Talmudic (and other Jewish sources) which purported to bind man closer to God . . . they also drew extensively on the literature of the Sufis." The first important expression of this attraction was an 11th-century Jewish work, *The Duties of the Heart* by Bahya ibn Paquda, composed in Arabic. This book was translated into Hebrew by Jews living in France.

The sources of medieval *Kabbalah*, beginning a series of stupendous spiritual revolutions in Judaism, were found on both sides of the geographical border dividing Muslims and Christians in Western Europe. The classic *Kabbalah* appeared in the Christian realms of Provence, Catalonia, and Castile. But a Jewish strain linked to Sufism had long been visible in Spain. Scholem notes that the mystical aspect of works by Abraham ben Moses ben Maimon, son of the great Judeo-Arabic jurist, Maimonides, "is entirely based on Sufi sources and bears no evidence of any similar Jewish tradition known to the author."

These Jewish mystics were, and some remain today, at home in both the House of Israel and the House of Ismail, the synagogue and the mosque. The Islamic impact on Jewish spirituality was not limited to the Spanish borderlands; it also came to the Jews of Christian Spain from the Muslim East. Moshe Idel, the leading present-day historian of *Kabbalah*, describes "an unbroken chain of (Jewish) authors . . . who developed a mystical trend under Sufic inspiration." This tendency was "transmitted" from East to West, in "a fascinating 'migration' of Kabbalistic theory." Idel concludes, "Palestine made a great contribution to (*Kabbalah*). This contribution, ironically, was nurtured by Muslim mysticism."

A yet wider Islamic influence is visible in religious Judaism, beginning at the time of the Muslim conquests of the Middle East. Greek-speaking Jews had produced the *Septuagint*, the first translation of *Torah* out of Hebrew, as well as founding Christianity and writing the *Gospels*. But with Arabic as a new and more advantageous medium, the use of Greek by Jews rapidly diminished except among small communities in the Byzantine Empire. Bernard Lewis describes a Judeo-Arabic civilization in the early caliphate, in which Judaism was, quite simply, Islamized: "What is intended here is not the adoption of the Islamic religion but assimilation to Islamic modes of thought and patterns of behavior—in a word, a Judaeo-Islamic tradition parallel to the Judaeo-Christian tradition." Remarkable similarities exist between the training of a Muslim scholar and that of a rabbi that can only be explained by this historical relationship, and Lewis indicates more points where Judaism and Islam coincide. "The Jewish notion of *Halakha* and the Islamic notion of *Shariah*—both words mean 'path' or 'way'—are surely closely related . . . [I]t would seem that in this case the initial influence was from Judaism to Islam, and not vice versa."

Rabbinical precedents are found in Islamic legal thought. The compliment was then returned: The intellectual framework and even the terminology of Islamic jurisprudence were borrowed by later codifiers of Jewish law. The *fatwa*, or religious-legal opinion, is identical to the *responsa* issued by rabbis. Indeed, Lewis declares that the very concept of a Jewish theology, meaning the organization of beliefs in a set of principles, "was alien to the Jews of biblical and talmudic times," and was created by Jews utilizing an Islamic form of religious dialogue or disputation. The Masoretes, the group of Palestinian Jewish scholars who settled on the authoritative text of the Hebrew *Torah* during the 10th century, did so in emulation of the Islamic scholars similarly working to establish a firm text of *Qur'an*. There is also significant Muslim influence on ritual and worship in synagogues. Finally, medieval and Renaissance *Torah* commentators described Islam as the fulfilment of God's promise to Ishmael.

Although there was no similar Islamic suffusion in Christian theology and practice, the impact of Spanish Muslim mysticism on Christian spirituality was extremely strong, especially in the literature of love, both spiritual and profane. The greatest Spanish Catholic mystical work is *The Book of the Lover and the Beloved*, by the 13th-century Catalan classic Raimon Llull. It includes an explicit reference explaining its composition, by Llull's imaginary philosophical hero, Blanquerna: "a Saracen [i.e., Muslim] once told him that the Muslims have various holy men. The most esteemed among these or any others are some people called Sufis. They offer words of love and brief examples that inspire a person to great devotion. Their words require exposition, and thanks to the exposition the Intellect rises higher, which develops it and spurs the Will to devotion. After considering this, Blanquerna proposed to make a book in this manner."

Seven hundred years later, an inspired analyst of courtly love, the Swiss philosopher Denis de Rougemont, wrote, "a highly refined rhetoric, with its set forms, themes, and characters . . . and indeed its symbolism, pushes out from Iraq and the Sufis . . . and reaches Arabic Spain, then, leaping over the Pyrenees, it comes in the south of France upon a society that seems to have but awaited its arrival in order to state what it had not dared and had not been able to avow either in the clerical tongue or in the common vernacular. Courtly lyrical poetry was the offspring of that encounter . . . From the one East along either shore of the Civilizing Sea, there was born the great western model of the language of passion-love." Thus did Islam liberate the hearts and minds of seekers among the Jews and Christians. These contributions to world culture would have been inconceivable had Islam remained paralyzed in its fundamentalist form.

The Crusades brought about further cultural links between the *ummah* and Christendom. Christian armies invaded the Holy Land numerous times, battling Muslims and ultimately conquering Jerusalem. But in history's greatest irony, the confrontation of Christian and Muslim arms soon took second place to intellectual and spiritual encounters. War between the faiths may even have done more than peace to foster these connections. One thing is certain: The Crusades meant more to Christians than to Muslims, notwithstanding latter-day agitation by Islamic extremists. The wars over the Holy Land had little real impact on the Islamic world.

Christian historians follow chronology in assigning weight and impact among the Christian-Islamic conflicts. Westerners treat the Crusades as first in importance, the fall of Muslim Spain second, and the Muslim invasions of and from Central Asia third. Islamic historiography reverses this order. This seems justified when the effects of the Crusades on the Muslim world are compared with those of either the Christian reconquest of Spain or the colossal changes wrought by the coming of the Turks to center stage in world history. Even more disturbing, but ultimately more benevolent for the Muslim world, were the Mongol conquests of Persian and Arab dominions.

In 1258, the Mongols fell upon and obliterated Baghdad. The siege of the city was perceived by its inhabitants as a sign of the "end time." It ended Baghdad's power in the Islamic world for centuries. These events had wide consequences for the Mongols themselves and for the whole *ummah*, creating controversies that, more than any other, have complicated the later history of Islam.

The Mongol rulers of Baghdad became Muslims. This produced a reaction by a Hanbali legal scholar named Ibn Taymiyyah (1263–1328). Born in the generation after Baghdad's fall to a family from the devastated city, Ibn Taymiyyah rebelled against the Islamized Mongol rulers. He insisted on a purist attitude toward Islam that directly anticipated and is honored above all others by the Islamic fundamentalists of the 21st century. This extremism was most fully expressed in his theories of governance.

Muslim legal authorities traditionally held that local Muslim rulers should be obeyed by their subjects if they were recognized by the caliphate. Ibn Taymiyyah denied that a caliphate existed after the first four caliphs succeeding Muhammad. He argued that the rulers of differing

Islamic states should command the loyalty of the Muslims whether a caliphate was recognized or not. But he offered the Islamic rulers a means of religious legitimation: They were to be obeyed if they instituted a rigid interpretation of *Shariah*. For Ibn Taymiyyah, the political state and the religious scholars were to function as a single entity. This view was later echoed in the rise of Wahhabism in Saudi Arabia, which sought the same result, and in the governance of Ayatollah Khomeini. But in reality, political and religious authority, though formally combined, could not avoid a division of responsibilities in which religion would inevitably become a tool of political necessity.

Ibn Taymiyyah argued that Muslims who did not live under *Shariah* represented the worst of all evils. He alleged, incorrectly, that the Mongols had not accepted *Shariah*; he claimed that although they had made the profession of Islamic faith in One God and the Prophecy of Muhammad, they were unbelievers. Shocking the *ummah* of his time, he went on to argue that the Mongols who had accepted Islam were suitable targets for attack and despoliation.

The Mongol ruler of Baghdad, Ghazan Khan, was denounced by Ibn Taymiyyah and later extremists. But Ghazan Khan was a fervent Muslim even though he was presented as a disbeliever with the intention of justifying Ibn Taymiyyah's pretensions as a reformer and a great soldier in *jihad*. Ghazan Khan was the grandson of Hulagu Khan, the invader who had devastated Baghdad. Brought into Islam by a Sufi Shaykh al-Juwayni, he built a distinguished mosque in Tabriz among many other Islamic religious works.

Ibn Taymiyyah also declared total war on Sufism, Shi'ism, and the study of Greek philosophy. He even attacked those who visited the grave of Muhammad, or commemorated his birth, insinuating that such celebration of the Prophet was an imitation of the Christian worship of Jesus as God. He denounced Ibn Arabi as an unbeliever. Finally, he introduced an anthropomorphic view of God into Islam, declaring that the Creator had a physical body. As in Judaism, this position is firmly rejected by Muslims, who hold that the divine form is limitless and unknowable—a view more consonant with modern physics than with religious obscurantism. Ibn Taymiyyah was also markedly ignorant, anticipating the flat-earth fun-

damentalists and terrorists who, centuries later, idolized him. He seems to
have believed, for example, that Greek and Armenian Christians kept the
same dietary laws as Jews and Muslims, an astonishing gap in his knowledge. Above all, he renewed the threat of extremism, which was repudiated, but which was revived and reinforced by the Wahhabis.

Ibn Taymiyyah's encouragement of *jihad* as a means of dividing Muslims meant a return to the destructive mentality of the Khawarij. It led
him to press the ruler of Syria, al-Nasir, to wage war on Ghazan Khan. It is
unsurprising that Ibn Taymiyyah's extremism brought about his imprisonment; he became ill and died in confinement, having been condemned
by the highest religious authorities of his era.

Sufism, in contrast, served as the bridge to new Muslims and became
widely favored by the Ottomans as a tool of imperial statecraft. The Sufis,
with their exemplary behavior and teachings, as well as their assimilation
of local spiritual customs, aided the consolidation of the Ottoman state.
Later Western commentators have completely misunderstood this phenomenon, especially in their apologies for the Saudi cult of Wahhabism.
Wahhabism, following Ibn Taymiyyah, warred on the spirituality and traditions preserved and nurtured by the Sufis. Contemptuous attacks on
Sufis as superstitious tricksters, combined with phobic hostility to the
Ottomans and erroneous identification of the Wahhabis with the Protestant Reformation, skewed the entire Western view of Wahhabism. Colo-
nialist orientalism obscured the fact that Sufism was a cornerstone of
tradition and the bulwark of tolerance and pluralism, as well as the source
of great fighters in the cause of Islam.

In the years of the Mongol ascendancy Sufism also flourished as a
means for ordinary believers to contend with the convulsions of war and
conquest. Central Asia was then the most fertile ground for Sufism, which
had organized itself in orders or *tariqa*, meeting in regular assemblies and
keeping houses of study, prayer, *dhikr* or remembrance of God (whether
in collective observance or individually), charity, and hospitality. But
Sufism spread everywhere in the Muslim world. There have always been
claims that Sufism was the model for Christian bodies such as the Knights
Templars, as well as the Franciscan orders, and similarities between the
Sufis and Chasidic Jewish communities are notable.

The most important of the many Sufi orders have included the following:

The *Qadiris* were established by a Persian, Abdul Qadri Jilani (1077–1166). His influence was immense; in the words of Baba Rexheb Beqiri, his beliefs "permeated Muslim society as far as India." The Qadiris, highly disciplined and devoted to the outward practices of Islam as codified in the *Sunna*, went beyond the subcontinent, penetrating West Africa in one direction and Indonesia in the farthest East. The Qadiri dervishes are known for their combat in defense of Islam and the freedom of Muslim peoples in places as diverse as Algeria, Kosovo, and Chechnya. But the peaceable penetration of India by them and other Sufis, who introduced Islam to the subcontinent by their articulate preaching and examples of saintly living, is typically contrasted by traditional Muslims with the conquest of non-Muslim territories through *jihad*.

The *Rifa'is*, formed by an Iraqi named Sayid Ahmed Rifai (d. 1182), are famous for their practice of body piercing, cutting their flesh with blades, swallowing burning coals, and handling poisonous snakes as ecstatic affirmations of faith. These customs were borrowed from Mongolian shamans who practiced their rituals during the invasion of Iraq, i.e., before the Mongol rulers of Baghdad became Muslim.

The *Yasawis* are named for the 12th-century saint or *Pir* of Turkestan, Ahmad Yasawi. Yasawi was the first major Sufi to appear in the Central Asian heartland. His teaching and methods, as well as the regulations he developed for his order, had a lasting influence and his organizing principles were adopted by many other Sufi orders. These rules include obedience, conviction, loyalty of the seeker to his teacher, and secrecy about Sufi teachings. As described by the historian H. T. Norris, the pre-Islamic, shamanic spiritual traditions of the Turks "lasted long in their memory, subconsciously or consciously influencing the later Sufism of the Yasaviyya, the first Sufi order to be fully 'acclimatised' among the Turks." In addition, the heritage of Buddhism is visible in local dervish meditation practices.

With the death of Yasawi, his order fragmented. Two other orders gained importance in the Islamic world beyond their original mystical horizons. They became as distinguished as the Yasawis were in the active transformation of newly acquired territories into Islamic lands through spirituality. One was the *Naqshbandis*, established by Muhammad Bahauddin Naqshband, born near Bukhara in 1317. The Naqshbandis are famous for their popular preaching, their devotion to the *Sunna* and *Shariah*, and their valiant self-sacrifice, defending Islam, often alongside the Qadiris. The Qadiris and Naqshbandis are the two most widespread Sufi orders today. But the Naqshbandis are also known for their powerful meditative and chanted remembrance of God (*dhikr*), based on repetition of the divine names and the oral formulas of Islamic faith. Strict Sunnis, they developed a close relationship with outstanding scholars as well as the rulers of Muslim states in Central Asia and, later, the Ottoman sultans.

The other major variant following on the collapse of the Yasawis is the *Bektashi* order, which emerged before the Naqshbandis and also gained great influence under the Ottomans. The Bektashis are Shi'a-oriented and are known for their heterodox practices, such as drinking alcohol, which is anathema to the overwhelming majority of Muslims. Their mentor is the Turkish poet Hajji Bektash Wali, born in 1248 in the Khorasan area of Iran. From the Yasawis they inherited the use of Turkish as a devotional language, in contrast with Arabic and Persian, which gave them great authority in Turkic culture. Their second great master, Ballem Sultan, restructured the order at the end of the 15th century and is credited with initiating Sultan Bayazid II, who welcomed the expelled Spanish Jews to his dominions, into Bektashism. The Bektashis were powerful in Hungary when it was Turkish-ruled. They carried on a Yasawi practice in promoting the role of women in their order, and therefore the equality of women in the broader society. The Naqshbandis have been called the "most contemporary" of the dervish orders, and the Bektashis the "most progressive."

Other important orders include the Halvetis, followers of *Pir* Omer Halvet, who gave rise in turn to many later orders. These included the Cerrahis, Bayramis, and the followers of Gulsheniy, whose shaykh was born in Azerbaijan, and of Niyazi Misri, an important poet who had significant contacts with Jewish mystics of his time. The Halveti and post-Halveti orders remain a powerful component of Islamic culture. Their distinguishing characteristic is the seclusion of adherents, with intense repetition of God's names. A process of outer purification, in which one asks for God's forgiveness for sin, precedes an inner purification involving the suppression of temptation and lust by prayer.

The Saadi-Jibawis originated in Palestine and are also a major force, as are the Shazalis, based in North Africa, to which they are related. Ahmed Badawi was born in Fez, Morocco, and later moved to Egypt, where the Badawi order remains extremely influential, with Badawi a popular saint. Like the Rifa'is, this order is associated with extremes of ecstatic behavior. The Chishtis, founded in Syria, played an important role in bringing Islam to India. Aside from these orders, perhaps the most famous Sufis among non-Muslims are those of the Mawlawi order. The Mawlawis were founded by the poet Rumi (1207–73), whose authorial name means "The European" though he was born in Afghanistan. As previously noted, his verses proclaiming divine love, translated into the Western languages, have made him a best-selling modern author. The Mawlawis are known as the "whirling dervishes" for their *dhikr* while turning on one foot.

The Ottoman Turks were crucial in the development of the most heterodox forms of Sufism, and their open mentality paralleled the unique role of their empire in strengthening and maintaining Islamic power in the world, especially after the conquest of Constantinople in 1453. The capture of the imperial city by Sultan Mehmed the Conqueror, or Mehmed al-Fatih, came at the apex of a series of victories in the Balkans. But it had a special religious significance as the fulfilment of a prediction by Muhammad. The fall of the Byzantine Empire was an unparalleled stroke for Islam, and made possible a spectacular renewal of Islamic creativity. Trade between the Ottomans and Italy made both dominions rich—also making possible the Christian Renaissance.

In the final reckoning, neither Jerusalem, held by the Crusaders from 1099 to 1244, nor any city in Spain retaken by the Christians, nor even Baghdad, was as significant to the medieval world as Byzantium, the fabled capital of Eastern Christianity. To the Muslims it, not its Italian counterpart, was *Rum*, i.e., Rome. Western writers impressed by Arab rhetoric about the misdeeds of the Crusaders seem never to have realized that the conquest of Constantinople avenged the crimes of the Crusaders a thousandfold, not in blood, but in shifting the direction of history. Unfortunately for the Muslims, the later effects of the fall of Constantinople undermined their power. Turkish control of the Bosphorus closed off major eastern trade routes to Christian exploitation; without that impressive material fact Christian merchants and navigators might have been long delayed looking westward to the Atlantic, and encountering a new world. This was, of course, an unintended outcome of Mehmed the Conqueror's victory in 1453.

The Ottoman Empire differed significantly from the Arab and Persian dominions that preceded it in Islamic governance. In the first phase of its expansion, Islam, whose Prophet and Book were both Arabic, had gained ascendancy over the Arab heartland and adjoining areas of the Middle East, many of which had previously been ruled by Christians. The Turkish period of Islamic expansion was very different. Their heartland was Central Asia, where the majority of the Mongols, the Turks' distant kin, rejected monotheism, cleaving first to shamanism and then to Buddhism. Because their subjects were generally not of their own ethnicity, while their fervor for spreading Islam increased, so, paradoxically, did their need for pluralism. The Islamized Turks carried out great military efforts across thousands of miles of land and sea. But the Turks themselves were relatively few in number, and in their empire they were a minority; as they advanced they recruited and allied with non-Muslim rulers more frequently than had the Arabs. At the center of Ottoman society Christians and, later, Jews played more important roles than they had under any Arab ruler; the Turkish elite was simply too small to govern effectively without them.

The result was a multiethnic, pluralistic, and tolerant Ottoman Empire that established a new, all-powerful caliphate and fostered an Islamic "style" that set the intellectual pace for the faith for the next 450 years. Ottoman Islam, parallel with the character of its state, but impregnated by Central Asian Sufism, was also multiethnic, pluralistic, and tolerant. The Turks were anything but primitive; the Greek Orthodox Patriarch has remained their guest as a resident of Constantinople since 1453. Muslim cities and states of Central Asia such as Bukhara, whose culture was Persian but in whose sphere the Turks had long lived and whose legacy they inherited, had produced some of the finest theologians, scientists, mathematicians, poets, and mystics, from the beginning of Islam. These included Al-Khwarezmi, inventor of algebra, whose own name comes to us as the word "algorithm."

Similar Islamic achievements included contributions to astronomy, seen in the names many Westerners find unpronounceable, such as that of the star Betelgeuse, which may be translated as "House of the Twins," *bayt al-jawzah*, or as "hand of Orion," *yad al-jauza*. Similarly, Aldebaran comes from "the follower" (of the Pleiades), *al-Dabarah*. Several other stars bear names based on the Arabic word for "tail" (*deneb*); we may also note Fomalhaut, from "mouth of the fish," or *fam al-hut*. The Muslims named the brightest stars in the sky, for use in traveling through the desert and in navigation. Their contribution to astronomy parallels the similar influx of Arabic terminology into chemistry, geology, metallurgy, botany, and other physical sciences in the West. Borrowings from Islamic culture include such common words as abacus, albacore, albatross, alcohol, alkali, amber, arsenal, average, azimuth, balsam, cane, cider, cipher, coffee, cotton, gypsum, nadir, sequin, sesame, silver, soda, zenith, and zero.

In its next phases, moving farther outward from Central Asia, Islam consolidated its rule in India, where the Muslim faith had been introduced by Sufis; then, carried by seaborne traders, it penetrated the Malaysian and Indonesian islands. The Ottoman sultan, as caliph, stood as the religious authority for all these Muslims. Meanwhile, for much of the period from 1300 to 1924, the Ottoman Empire tested its borders with its European Christian foes. These wars had a very different character than either the Crusades or the Christian reconquest of Spain. The Spanish reconquest saw a series of conflicts in which, slowly but inexorably, the Iberian Peninsula was retaken from the Arabs. By contrast, the Ottoman wars in Europe showed unpredictable turns of fate until the end of the 17th century. Repeatedly, the Turks reached the environs of Vienna; Hungary remained an Ottoman province for more than 150 years.

While the Spanish reconquest was limited in its geographical theater, the Ottoman combat in Europe involved well-organized, extensive operations both by the Muslim forces and their Christian opponents, including the Poles and Hungarians on land and the Venetians, Genoese, and Catalans at sea. These wars involved all of southeastern Europe. The small Spanish Muslim states disappeared one after another, but Muslim culture in the Balkans persists into the 21st century in Bosnia-Hercegovina, Albania, Kosovo, Macedonia, Montenegro, Bulgaria, Serbia, and Greece. It is news to nobody, however, that the survival of this indigenous European Islam in the Balkans has been threatened by the Islamophobia of Christian (and especially Orthodox) Europe. This is disturbing because the Balkan Muslims are a unique, precious, and rich resource for a world in which the survival of humanity depends on reconciliation between the three Abrahamic faiths.

Western Europeans of a half-millennium ago did not view a local Islamic culture on the north coasts of the Mediterranean as a possible cultural asset. The last Spanish Muslim kingdom, in Granada, was defeated by the Christians in 1492. The end of Spanish Islam profoundly affected Christianity and Judaism throughout the Mediterranean. Although Muslims had been promised religious freedom if they surrendered to the Christian monarchs Ferdinand and Isabella, this pledge was soon abrogated. Spanish Muslims who remained loyal to their faith were driven out along with the Spanish and Portuguese Jews. In succeeding generations, the descendants of many Muslims and Jews who had become Christians under compulsion were also expelled or fled from Spain, pursued by the Catholic Inquisition.

Islamic fundamentalists argued that the Spanish Muslims were better off leaving the Christian-ruled lands. Many refugees settled in Morocco, whence "Andalusian" or Spanish Muslim culture, remaining vigorous in music and related arts, spread throughout North Africa. Jews who converted to Christianity in Spain but regretted their decision or suffered or feared persecution left for Italy. Many Jews who defended their faith heeded the invitations of Ottoman rulers to go to Turkey, the Balkans, and the Middle East. Sultan Bayazid II, son of Mehmed al-Fatih, threw the gates of his empire open wide to the Spanish and Portuguese Jews. These Jews, who became known as the Sephardim or Spaniards, settled in every major city in the Ottoman dominions. Bayazid II is said to have questioned how King Ferdinand of Spain could be considered a wise ruler, since he had expelled his most intelligent and productive subjects, to the profit of the Muslim foe.

The Turks did not see the Jews in the same light as the Christians. The standard Ottoman terminology in referring to People of the Book was "unbelievers [i.e., Christians] and Jews," which Bernard Lewis traces back to recognition of "the unflawed monotheism of the Jews." But Christians, including Greeks, Armenians, Romanians, Bulgarians, Serbs, and Croats, as well as the Sephardim, were permitted by the Ottomans to develop their religious life and literature, mainly without serious handicap. Among the Jews, the entry into the Ottoman Empire heralded a new wave of *Kabbalah*, as well as the writing of many works of Jewish law, collections of *responsa*, and other contributions. Numerous books were printed in the Jewish languages, Hebrew, Aramaic, and Spanish, as well as, much later, in Turkish and Arabic, under the Ottoman authorities. Shi'ism was largely tolerated, and the Bektashi Sufi order became one of the most powerful institutions in the empire through an association with the Janissaries, a body of youth from Christian families trained to administer the military and other affairs of the sultans. Central Asian Sufism, with its Turkic legacy, endured as the greatest single cultural influence in the empire. Only rarely, when mystics became infected with rebellion, were they repressed.

The Ottomans were also the greatest *jihad* power in the history of Islam. Lewis has described the Turks as "of all the major dynasties, the most fervently and consistently committed to the Muslim faith and to the upholding and enforcement of the Holy Law." Yet, as we have seen, Ottoman Islam was tolerant, pluralist, and spiritual, and its treatment of Jews was admirable, although its relations with its Christian subjects were strained by the role of Christian powers as enemies in *jihad*. The Ottoman *jihad* was brilliantly and successfully pursued as a rational system of war.

The Ottoman sultan ruled from the eastern frontier of Morocco to the Indian Ocean. As caliph, the same personage exercised religious authority over every Sunni Muslim from West Africa to the Philippines. Until the 17th century, the Ottoman Empire was equal to Christendom in prosperity and enlightenment—the latter point especially illustrated by its

friendly attitude toward the Jews. How can we understand the reality of
Ottoman life at the empire's height? Some of Ottoman religious and popular culture survives today in Bosnia-Hercegovina, a province notably traditionalist in its Islam, precisely because it was on the border with the
enemy, remote from Constantinople. Bosnians had entered Islam in the
middle of the 15th century en masse (excepting, of course, those who considered themselves Catholic Croats or Orthodox Serbs). Theirs was the
only example of a near-total acceptance of the Muslim religion in the
Balkans.

The sons and daughters of the Bosnian villages, set between breathtaking mountains and revivifying rivers, became known as lions of God for
their valiant combat in the Ottoman wars that repeatedly tore their land
asunder. The mentality of Muslim Bosnia is deeply spiritual, and the
country was famous for its Sufis before the arrival of Communism after
the second world war. But these qualities of the heart nurtured an environment in which the Franciscans of Central Bosnia flourished alongside
some of the most brilliant and nonconforming rabbis in Jewish history.
Balkan Muslims attended Christmas observances while Christians participated in the end of Ramadan. In Bosnia, tender and eloquent love ballads, merging physical passion with Sufi discourse, were sung by Muslim,
Jew, Serb, and Croat, while all celebrated the coming of spring on May 6,
St. George's Day, an archaic and very likely a pre-Christian festival. In
Sarajevo, *Sing, little nightingale,* a melody expressing the sadness of an
Ottoman soldier knowing he must die, became *Noches, noches, buenas
noches,* a Spanish Jewish ballad evoking the desperation of a lover left
alone. These folk were neither Turks nor Arabs. They were and are native
Europeans who have inhabited their exquisite and breathtaking land for
many centuries, and who can never be torn from it completely, no matter
the horrors of war, exile, famine, or ideology. Theirs is a Slavic language
that is no less European than the Czech spoken in Prague, and their Islam
is no less a European religion than Christianity or Judaism. Today they are
the indispensable bridge between the worlds, battered, bloodstained, and
weakened, but intact and perhaps indestructible.

After deeply penetrating Europe, the Ottoman Empire ceased to
progress. Its long decline was aggravated by the economic and technologi-

cal advances made by Christendom, which benefited enormously from
the wealth of the New World. But the Ottoman stalemate also reflected
the bureaucratic character of the empire, as well as the isolated situation
of the Turkish elite, much of whose imperial business was done by others.
In the Ottoman realm, the princes were Turkish; but the grand counsel-
lors or *vizirs* and numerous governors and military commanders were
Bosnians, Albanians, and Kurds; the scribes, accountants, and builders
often Greeks and Armenians; and the merchants and metallurgists Jews.
Many of the empire's Muslim religious and cultural elites favored Persian
as their medium of written expression. The Arabs, who saw themselves
(rather than God) as progenitors of Islam, were left the furthest behind in
an empire that itself soon began falling behind Christendom in wealth
and technical capacity.

Unfortunately, the disintegration of the Ottoman order has been confused in the Western mind with the perceived failure of the Islamic world
to participate in modernity. In a fascinating paradox, modernity had
begun with Spain's rejection of Hebrew and Islamic traditions in 1492,
just as exploitation of the New World commenced, while the Ottoman
realm that rescued the Jews could be seen as the ultimate victim of
modernity. But the long fall of the Ottoman Empire was not a unique
process. In yet another paradox, the Spanish empire, the world's greatest
in geographical breadth, failed to fully embrace modernity, in virtually
the same way as Turkey. Indeed, the decline of both Catholic dominions
ruled by Spain and the *ummah* led by the Ottomans began at the same
time—early in the 17th century—and may have a common origin in the
devastating global inflation created by the vast inflow of gold and silver
from the New World. The historian David Hackett Fischer has noted,
"the crisis of the 17th century was a time of troubles throughout the
world." In its aftermath, the later, longer crisis of the Arab nations may
best be compared with the struggle of Latin America to attain stability.

Spain did not attain a prosperous state of capitalist democracy until the
last quarter of the 20th century. The Ottomans' neighbor and rival, the
immense domain of the Russian tsar, was no more hospitable to modernity than the court of the Ottoman sultan. Few today would argue that the
degeneration of the Spanish empire or the backwardness of tsarism were

symptomatic of fundamental weaknesses in Christian civilization. Even the mighty British empire has passed from the scene. By contrast, Japan, a society no less traditional and delayed in its entry into modernity, became a successful capitalist power—though not a democracy—in 20 years, at the end of the 19th century. Turkish Islamists today look to Japan as their favored model.

Ibn Khaldun, a 14th-century Islamic thinker and historicist, sometimes called the father of the historical sciences, would doubtless have said that the downfall of the Ottoman Empire, like that of any other political structure, was inevitable. In his *Muqaddima* or *Introduction*, he argues convincingly that every dominion has its time of ascent followed, usually over a longer period, by its time of descent. New blood, he declares, is always needed to revitalize a civilization once the downward process has begun.

The Ottoman Empire had fatal weaknesses. Yet the deadliest challenge to its rule would come not from the artillery of Christian princes but from a fundamentalist movement among the Arabs. The apocalyptic, militaristic, and totalitarian cult called Wahhabism would shed the blood of many fellow Muslims before eventually hurling a murderous challenge to the Judeo-Christian world.

CHAPTER 3

Haters of Song

THE EARLY WAHHABI MOVEMENTS

Muhammad Ibn Abd al-Wahhab, founder of Wahhabism, was born in 1703, the son of a judge, in Uyaynah, a village in the central Arabian region of Najd. The word *najd* means "plateau." It is a large and extremely dry area, with great extremes of heat and cold in summer and winter, and little water. Until about 500 years ago, it was mainly uninhabited, its only human activity limited to Bedouins grazing their animals. It is isolated from the more important areas of the Peninsula; Mecca and Medina are far to the west, and its only commerce at the time of Ibn Abd al-Wahhab's birth was with Kuwait and the island of Bahrein to the east. But barren and inhospitable Najd would end up exercising an immense influence on world history after the establishment there of Riyadh, the future capital of Saudi Arabia, by followers of Wahhabism.

Little can be confirmed about the early life of Ibn Abd al-Wahhab; he emerged from an emptiness that was not only physical and economic but social, intellectual, and spiritual. But he is said to have shown extremist religious tendencies in his youth. Both his father and his brother Suley-

man, who were Islamic scholars, warned others against him, and Suleyman even wrote a book in opposition to him, with the piquant title *Divine
Thunderbolts*. It is also said that in early adulthood Ibn Abd al-Wahhab
traveled widely, to Basra and Baghdad, to Damascus, and through Kurdis-
tan, Iran, and India, intending to become a merchant. But how would an
unsophisticated, narrow-minded wanderer from Najd have seen himself
and his surroundings, while passing through these distinguished and opu-
lent places?

In the disconnected, footloose son of the remote oases, doubtless baf-
fled, hypnotized, and dismayed by the life of fabled cities and great
empires, we see the archetype for all the famous and infamous Islamic
extremists of modern times. Some say that during this vagabondage Ibn
Abd al-Wahhab came into contact with certain Englishmen who encouraged him to personal ambition as well as to a critical attitude about Islam.
Soon, the itinerant Arab and the imperial British shared a goal: the liquidation of the Ottoman Empire.

Ibn Abd al-Wahhab returned to Najd with a group of African slaves as a
bodyguard. In 1737–40, he publicly announced his call to his version of
religion and was joined by some of his younger relatives. From the lava
beds and wastelands of Najd, where walls and gardens were nearly
unknown, he demanded that Muslims everywhere—in the rich provinces
of the Balkans and Turkey, the ancient towns of Syria, and the legendary
capitals of Iran and Central Asia; in the mountains of Morocco, in tropi-
cal Africa, and in the islands of the south seas; in a Muhammadan India
that was a wonder of the world—must all surrender to his vision of an original, authentic Islam such as he imagined had existed in the time of the
Prophet. He therefore advocated rebellion against the Ottoman caliphate.
His chief written work was titled *The Book of Monotheism (Kitab al
Tawhid)*. His main inspiration was Ibn Taymiyyah.

These events occurred at a critical moment in Islamic history. The
Turks had ruled Arabia a little more than 200 years at the time of Ibn Abd
al-Wahhab's birth. But as he correctly perceived, the Muslim caliphate
had entered a deep crisis. Fifty years before, in 1683, the Ottoman campaign against Christian Europe had been decisively defeated at the Battle
of Vienna. Throughout the *ummah*, Muslims asked themselves what was

happening, why the cause of Islam had encountered defeat, and where the global community was headed. But the Muslim world was also affected by other social and theological turbulence from outside.

Christendom had been disrupted for at least five centuries by a series of uprisings and outbreaks of religious excitement, and Jewry had lately undergone the appearance of a false messiah. These movements are usually referred to as millennial or apocalyptic. Most of them originated in social dislocations—wars, migrations, economic adjustments, and similar incidents. The effect of these religious upheavals was to foster teachings and explanations that assisted confused folk in "understanding" history. Vast numbers responded to rapid change and sudden uncertainty with beliefs that the "end time" had arrived; that humanity was about to be redeemed supernaturally. Charismatic preachers rose to lead revival movements, which mobilized armies and fought wars against noble and ecclesiastical elites. Rebellious peasants and disaffected city-dwellers sometimes convinced themselves that church leaders had become satanic servants, and that the world itself was a literal hell, ruled by the devil.

Many of these dissenters revived an aspect of the ancient Zoroastrian religion, known as dualism—a vision of the universe as a struggle between two beings of equal power, a God and a Demon. Judaism underwent a successful struggle to remain free of such doctrines, and they had never significantly infected Islam. In early Christianity dualistic tendencies were ruthlessly stamped out. But in the later history of Christendom, the evident corruption of religious authority revived this suppressed tendency, leading an agitated populace to reverse the principles they were taught and to believe that the churches and monasteries were in the hands of God's enemy. Other seemingly unavoidable outcomes were demands for purification, separation, fundamentalism, and a mystical-anarchist abandonment of God's law. Some religious rebels proclaimed that since the morality of the church reflected satanic influence, sin would lead to redemption. In the Christian world, these phenomena culminated in the Protestant Reformation, unleashing a series of religious wars lasting 200 years.

In the late 17th century, the large Jewish community in Turkey produced a massive movement, led by the self-proclaimed messiah, Shabbetai Zvi. This individual's claim that the "end times" had arrived attracted enormous attention among Christians and Muslims, but it completely conquered world Jewry, bringing about immense changes in the Jewish sensibility. Similar phenomena were limited in the Islamic world, with some Shi'a communities susceptible to such conflicts with authority.

Ibn Abd al-Wahhab's movement represented a distillation of "end time" fears in Islamic dress. Other Muslims in the Ottoman Empire had argued that the defeats of the imperial armies in Europe were caused by insufficient devotion to religious fundamentals, as well as mysticism fostered by the Sufis. Some critics claimed that the heterodoxy of the Bektashi order had undermined the fighting capacity of the troops. Such blame was irrational, since the dervishes continued producing great warriors and contributing to the internal consolidation of Islamic societies. But with the crisis of the empire and the caliphate, the stage was set for a new explosion of purism and fundamentalism among Muslims. In addition, Ibn Abd al-Wahhab and others living in Najd seem to have been stirred by Arab resentment of Ottoman domination. His doctrines broke completely with traditional Islam as embodied in the Ottoman caliphate.

In his main written work, *The Book of Monotheism*, he argued that a Muslim's identity, and the protection of his life and possessions because he is Muslim (a principle of Islam), could not be considered secure unless it was based not merely on belief in a sole God, alone worthy of worship, but on actively denying any other object of worship. If the believer's adherence to the uniqueness of the creator should be doubted, or not be actively declared, the security of life and property was forfeited. These were innovations in the requirements for being a believer. Further, Ibn Abd al-Wahhab wrote that his own writing had made this "grave problem, singular in its seriousness and importance . . . absolutely clear, and its solution established without question." *The Book of Monotheism* is, therefore, an inquisitorial handbook, rather than a juristic work.

The essence of Ibn Abd al-Wahhab's preaching came down to three points. First, ritual is superior to intentions. Second, no reverence of the dead is permitted. Third, there can be no intercessory prayer, addressed to God by means of the Prophet or saints. This latter precept was borrowed directly from Ibn Taymiyyah. Prayers to God by means of a pious person

or even honors to any individual other than God were condemn
atry, despite their acceptance by all previous generations of Mu
the Prophet himself. At the same time, defying centuries of Islam
ogy, Ibn Abd al-Wahhab's followers ascribed a human form to God, as Ibn
Taymiyyah had also done. An anthropomorphic view of God had hitherto
been considered scandalously heretical in Islam.

Ibn Abd al-Wahhab further condemned as unbelievers those who did
not observe all the prescribed times of prayer, a position absent from traditional Islam. As to prayer itself, he called for a revision in how it was
to be carried out. Specific bodily postures were imposed and supplemen-
tary prayers after the standard practices of worship were restricted. He
demanded that the Muslim profession of faith be made a second time, as
an adherent to his Wahhabi sect—a practice not dissimilar to English
Puritanism or contemporary "born again" Protestantism but deeply
shocking to traditional Muslims, for whom the profession of faith is
unquestionable. Ibn Abd al-Wahhab further followed Ibn Taymiyyah in
assailing local religious and spiritual customs. The earlier fundamentalist
had condemned river festivals and other traditional celebrations that are
extremely popular in many Muslim lands, as well as visits to hot springs,
forests, mountains, or caves for spiritual or physical health.

Many more long-established Muslim practices were assailed by Ibn
Abd al-Wahhab, including praying in favor of Muhammad and the recitation of blessings on the Prophet at the beginning of Friday congregational
prayers. Ibn Abd al-Wahhab is said to have killed a blind caller to prayer,
or *muyezin*, who insisted on praying for the Prophet at the conclusion of
his summons to worship, as required by the four established legal schools.
Ibn Abd al-Wahhab also condemned the habit of those making *hajj* in
Mecca to visit the Prophet's tomb in Medina. He particularly hated celebrations of the Prophet's birthday, or *mawlid an-nabi*, which had given
rise to a noble and beautiful corpus of religious compositions in every language spoken by Muslims. He would not even permit the name of the
Prophet Muhammad to be inscribed in mosques, which he ordered
should be free of all decoration. At the same time, however, he and his followers demanded that Muslims not shave or trim their beards, supposedly
in emulation of the Prophet.

Wahhabis explain their hatred of traditional praise for the Prophet by comparing it to the Christian worship of Jesus, which, because it treats Jesus as God, is rejected by Muslims. In Islamic parlance, Christian belief in the divinity of Jesus means adding "partners" to God, which is to say, denying monotheism and returning to the pagan belief in many gods. But anti-Wahhabi polemics point out that the Muslim profession of faith, as well as the call to prayer, include two parts: "I affirm there is no God but Allah; and I affirm Muhammad is the Prophet of God." Thus, one cannot be a Muslim without recognizing and honoring the Prophet. In support of this argument, Muslim scholars point to the ultimate precedent, derived from Judaism: When the House of Israel was oppressed by Pharaoh, liberation came through Moses, not directly by God's hand.

Ibn Abd al-Wahhab's doctrines explicitly downgraded the status of Muhammad. Yet he claimed to live a life so close to the exemplary *Sirah* of Muhammad that he could stand as a peer to the Prophet himself. It seems clear that Ibn Abd al-Wahhab saw himself as an equal of the Prophet, a view that is also thoroughly heretical in Islam. Some critics assert that he even saw himself as surpassing the Prophet. But, above all, for Ibn Abd al-Wahhab's radical interpretation of Islam to gain followers, the Prophet's personality, and especially his dedication to compassion and mercy, had to be amputated from the body of Muslim doctrine. Similarly, although Turkish rule in the Arabian Peninsula had been loose, disorganized, and benevolent, the openness and imagination of Ottoman Islam could not but clash with the puritan demands of Ibn Abd al-Wahhab. Unsurprisingly, he was immediately repudiated by scholars who found his theses in conflict both with *Qur'an* and with the four schools. His brother Suleyman accused him of trying to add a "sixth pillar" to Islam: the infallibility of Ibn Abd al-Wahhab.

He, in turn, preached abandonment of the four traditions, although his followers would claim to be followers of the Hanbali school. He denounced his opponents, and all Muslims unwilling to accept his views, as idolaters and apostates, and abused the prophets, scholars, saints, and other pious figures of the past. Al-Zahawi states that Ibn Abd al-Wahhab "made no secret" of his opinion that all Muslims had fallen into unbelief and that if they did not follow him, they should all be killed, their wives and daughters violated, and their possessions confiscated. Shi'as, Sufis, and other Muslims he judged unorthodox were to be exterminated, and all other faiths were to be humiliated or destroyed. With this terrible doctrine, the basis had been laid for two and a half centuries of Islamic fundamentalism, and ultimately terrorism, in response to global change.

The Wahhabi call for Islamic "reform" had no support in the *Sunna*. In his predictions of the future, which were many, Muhammad never once forecast that the Muslims would fall back into polytheism, as Wahhabis have strenuously accused them of doing since the 18th century. The Prophet believed that "at the head of every century Allah would send someone who would *revive* the faith," as opposed to reforming it. Soon Ibn Abd al-Wahhab ordered that graves of Muslim saints be dug up and scattered, or turned into latrines. He also burned many books, arguing that *Qur'an* alone would suffice for humanity's needs. Above all, Ibn Abd al-Wahhab and his followers despised music, which they viewed as an incitement to forgetfulness of God and to sin. Many Sufis, by contrast, used music as a means to heighten consciousness of God.

The innovations proposed by Ibn Abd al-Wahhab seem bizarre and repulsive to traditional Muslims, who have often sought the intermediation of the Prophet, of saints, living and dead, have visited tombs, and have celebrated the Prophet's birthday for generation upon generation. But the Wahhabi loathing of music must identify them to normal people throughout the modern world (excluding, that is, fundamentalist Christians who share such an outlook) as extremist to the point of derangement.

Music is perhaps the greatest glory of Islamic civilization, as well as having been a major form of social communication and means for preservation of culture throughout the history of the *ummah*. Of the magnificence of Islamic Spain, one of the greatest living memories consists of the schools of "Andalusian music" that flourish today in North Africa. In the same region, Moroccan Sufis play music, chant, and sing with a unique freedom of inspiration and mystical fulfillment. The stringed instruments of the Atlas Mountains convey the purest ecstasy of union with God. Turkish bands with percussion, brass, and wind instruments transformed Western classical and military music. The essence of the Bosnian Muslim national tradition is romantic song, or *sevdahlinke*; every Bosnian Muslim, tormented by the horrors of the 1992–95 war in that country, knows in the deepest part of his or her soul that without the stirring and intimate art of *sevdah* performers, their cultural identity would have long since disappeared. Indeed, the patriotic ballads from the recent war explicitly said that Bosnian Muslims fought for their music as well as their mosques; for gorgeous songs of love and nature along with the Islamic call to prayer. At the other end of the northern Muslim world, the crown of Uzbek culture is its people's devotion to the lute, on which Uzbek women, their faces uncovered, perform works that are breathtaking, exquisite, with an extraordinary austerity and depth. Few personalities in the modern Arab world have the unique and profoundly moving appeal of musical performers like Fairuz and the Egyptian nightingale, Umm Kultsum. Islam without music would be like God without his creation, Earth. Yet that is the Islam, and the vision of God, on which the cult called Wahhabism was founded.

Ibn Abd al-Wahhab's puritanism and heresy-hunting had precedents in Islam, chiefly in the form of the Khawarij. Nor were they completely novel in the broader stream of world history. At the time he began recruiting followers, the burning of witches was well remembered in Britain and Massachusetts and was a continuing practice of the Catholic Inquisition in Peru and Mexico as well as in Spain. The burning of books was so widespread as to almost escape notice.

This bleak creed was fit for the nothingness of Ibn Abd al-Wahhab's birthplace in Najd, a part of Arabia the Prophet himself did not favor. Anti-Wahhabi Muslims cite a *Hadith* recording of the Prophet praying aloud and asking "O Allah, give us blessings in our Syria, O Allah, give us blessings in our Yemen." Someone called out, "And in our Najd?" But the Prophet ignored him. The Prophet repeated his request for blessings upon Syria and Yemen, and again the onlooker shouted, "And in our Najd?" Finally, the Prophet replied, "From that place will come only earthquakes, conflicts, and the horns of Satan."

Enemies of Wahhabism point out that Najd had never before produced a major Islamic theologian. However, the district supported various false prophets, such as one Musaylima the Liar, an obscurity who posed as a rival to Muhammad during the early years of Islam. Muhammad is said to have called the people of Najd "naked and destitute shepherds and camelherds," and Muslims hold that the applicability of such comments by the Prophet to the Khawarij, Wahhabis, and other sowers of discord in the *ummah* who came after him is proof of his prophethood. It is, at least, evidence of his insight into human character.

Najd was a hotbed for early factionalists in Islam, particularly the Khawarij, known for their extreme outward pietism while preparing rebellion and mass murder. Many leaders of the Khawarij came from the Banu Tamim, a powerful Najd tribe, of which Ibn Abd al-Wahhab, more than 1000 years later, was a member. As noted by recent commentator Kerim Fenari, the Banu Tamim came late to Islam. They first demanded a public debate with Muhammad, and there is a *Hadith* indicating they asked to be paid to become Muslims. Fenari writes, "An attribute ascribed to the Tamimites . . . is that of misplaced zeal. When they finally enter Islam, they are associated with a fanatical form of piety that demands simple and rigid adherence, rather than understanding." The Tamimites called for prayer in a way that undermined the dignity and worth of prayer. Such was the heritage to which Ibn Abd al-Wahhab succeeded.

He began his campaign of "reform" in Islam by cutting down a tree beloved of local mystics. Soon he organized a demonstration for the education of the populace: the stoning of a woman in Uyaynah accused of "fornication." Ibn Abd al-Wahhab had mounted a challenge to the Ottoman order, and a *fatwa* was issued calling for his arrest. Like his own family, the people of Najd began to split between his supporters and his opponents. In 1744 he took refuge in the village of Dariyah, in a district that was ruled by a local rebel, Muhammad ibn Sa'ud, and his family, known as Al Sa'ud.

The early history of Al Sa'ud, like that of Ibn Abd al-Wahhab, is almost nonexistent. Prior to the 18th century, this Arab clan was largely unknown to the broader societies of the Peninsula. As rulers of Dariyah, the Al Sa'ud engaged in the only organized economic endeavor found in the backward environment of Najd: banditry. This brought them into constant conflict with the Ottomans. It also created a propensity for them to ally with the

British, who were then taking control of the richer and more valuable parts of the Arabian Peninsula: the coastal emirates from Kuwait to Aden. The Al Sa'ud were not known as firm Muslims; indeed, they belonged to the tribe of Bani Hanifah, who were tainted by having supported Musaylima the Liar. From the beginning, then, the family's religious bona fides were somewhat doubtful.

Dariyah was a lawless place ruled by the whims of Al Sa'ud until 1747, when Ibn Abd al-Wahhab and Al Sa'ud established a crude government based on a unique power-sharing agreement, with the former as religious authority and the latter as political ruler. They contracted marriage between their families—a typical means of cementing alliances in tribal and clan-based societies—and agreed that power should be inherited exclusively by their descendants, as if their lineage carried greater author-ity than that of Muhammad, who neither imposed his successor nor made any attempt to establish a dynasty.

This alliance between two families of outsiders, fanatics, and bandits, in a place God seemed to have forgotten, represented a historical novelty. Marriage pacts are usually contracted to preserve the wealth and power of each family or to bring an end to feuds or other conflicts. But the two men who came together at Dariyah had no significant wealth or power to share and no grievances to settle. Their true aim was conquest and world domi-nation. For his part, Ibn Abd al-Wahhab imagined himself a new Prophet who would replace the Ottoman caliph as the sole theological authority within the global Islamic *ummah*. For Al Sa'ud, meanwhile, the extrem-ism of the Wahhabis provided a means for the legitimation of political power. Many commentators, Muslim and non-Muslim, have character-ized the Wahhabis' labeling of other Muslims unbelievers as nothing more than a pretext for robbery, murder, and rape, which would naturally appeal to the desert brigands who rallied to Al Sa'ud.

Ibn Abd al-Wahhab may not have been the Antichrist, or *Dajjal*, as this figure is known in Islam, but he was something equally fearsome: the first known exemplar of totalitarianism, which may be defined as the merging of an extremist ideology with an absolute state. Unknown to the world at the time, the diabolical personality manifested in Stalin, Hitler, and the other monsters of 20th-century history first appeared in a central Arabian black hole almost 200 years earlier. The outstanding biographer of Hitler, Konrad Heiden, called this human type "the armed intellectual." By marriage and inheritance, the bloody swords of Al Sa'ud came to aid the perverse vision of Ibn Abd al-Wahhab in a unique fusion of religious and political control, a system in which faith and statecraft would be run as a family business. This political formula has its fullest expression in modern Saudi Arabia. It also represents a complete break with the traditions of the scholars of Islam, who were typically thoughtful, unworldly men, not political schemers after global power.

The Wahhab-Sa'ud alliance first conquered a few local settlements and imposed Ibn Abd al-Wahhab's doctrines on them. The first of his political partners, Muhammad ibn Sa'ud, died in 1765 and was succeeded by his son Abd al-Aziz ibn Sa'ud. By 1788, the Wahhab-Sa'ud alliance controlled most of the Arabian Peninsula. In 1792, Ibn Abd al-Wahhab died, and Abd al-Aziz took over leadership of the Wahhabi-Saudi alliance, extending their raiding over the next three years to Medina, Syria, and Iraq. These campaigns saw mass murder and rape of Shi'a Muslims as well as adherents of the Hanafi and other legal schools rejected by Ibn Abd al-Wahhab.

The Wahhabis had an extraordinary hatred of Shi'ism, which became an early target of their violence. Some of this rage may have originated during Ibn Abd al-Wahhab's travels in Shi'a Iraq and Iran, but it is also known that the Shi'as of Hasa, the region directly east of Najd, contemptuously rejected his pretensions. However, the Shi'a may simply have become objects of Wahhabi assault because they were richer than the Bedouins of Najd and offered tempting opportunities for plunder. Whatever its source, however, bile against the Shi'as has remained a constant throughout Wahhabi-Saudi history. Today the Saudi school systems, following Wahhabi tenets, teach their children and other Muslims throughout the *ummah* that Shi'a Islam was invented by an imaginary Jewish convert, that Shi'a theologians are liars, that their legal traditions are false, and that they are not Muslims at all.

In 1801, the Wahhabis attacked the Shi'a holy city of Karbala, in Iraq between Baghdad and the Arabian frontier, and in a horrifying magnification of the atrocities enacted there more than 10 centuries before they slaughtered thousands of its citizens. They also wrecked and looted the tomb of Husayn, grandson of the Prophet. As a result, the second battle of Karbala retains immense symbolism for the Shi'a and other enemies of Wahhabism.

The Saudi chief Abd al-Aziz was murdered in 1803, possibly by a Shi'a avenger. His son Sa'ud bin Abd al-Aziz succeeded him. The year before Mecca fell to the Wahhabis, who forbade the entry of a caravan of Ottoman pilgrims. These events were of such moment that they were reported in Christian Europe, where they stirred a not inconsiderable interest. But for more than two centuries, real understanding of Wahhabism eluded Westerners, even though it ultimately grew to become a world power under Saudi patronage.

Unfortunately, most Western writers on Islam have taken Wahhabi claims to represent reform against the alleged decadence of traditional Islam at face value. Because the Wahhabis rejected ostentatious spirituality, much as Protestants detest the veneration of saints in the Roman Church, Western observers have seen the movement as analogous with the Christian Reformation. Thus American journalist Thomas W. Lippman, in a widely read book, declares that Wahhabism "had a therapeutic and invigorating impact upon all of Islam, similar to that of the Reformation on Christianity." We all know the cliché that one man's terrorist is another's freedom fighter, but we forget the universal lesson of religious fundamentalism: One man's reformer may be another man's murderous bigot.

Jihad, or struggle to promote the faith, had been the guiding principle throughout a millennium of uninterrupted Islamic expansion. Ibn Abd al-Wahhab and his followers called for "*jihad*" against Muslims. In this they imitated the grim example of the "reformer" Ibn Taymiyyah, who had incited "*jihad*" against the Islamized Mongols. Turkish scholar Hilmi Ishik has assembled an authoritative chronicle of religiously motivated Wahhabi cruelty. After the sacking of Karbala, this was most dramatically illustrated by their conduct following the surrender of Ta'if, a western Arabian city assaulted in 1802 during the Wahhabi campaign against Mecca. The Ottoman governor of Mecca, Sharif Ghalib Effendi, failed in attempts to negotiate peace with the Wahhabis and retreated into the fortress of Ta'if, where he prepared the citizens to defend themselves. The city was threatened by some 10,000 Wahhabi bandits, as they were described by the Islamic sources of the time, led by 20 desert brigands under the Wahhabi commander Salim ibn Shakban. The citizens of Ta'if administered a serious defeat to the extremists. Yet the confused situation and the decision of Sharif Ghalib to go to Jeddah for help left the people of Ta'if weak in the face of persistent Wahhabi harassment. Many fled with their families. Finally, the citizens of Ta'if petitioned for an honorable surrender, based on guarantees for the security of their lives and the chastity of their women. But a parley with a brutal and avaricious Wahhabi envoy, under a flag of truce, was interrupted by the Wahhabis' direct attack on the town.

In the taking of Ta'if, it is said that the Wahhabis "killed every woman, man, and child they saw, slashing with their swords even babies in cradles. The streets were flooded with blood." Citizens who surrendered in their houses were executed, their bodies trampled by horses and left unburied. Their homes were looted and their possessions scattered, later to be washed away by rain. The Wahhabis then set about destroying all the holy tombs and burial grounds in the city, followed by the mosques and Islamic schools, or *medresas*. When a scholar of the city pleaded that a certain mosque be spared, a radical among the Wahhabis, named Matu, commented, "anything doubtful should be annihilated." This would prove the quintessence of the Wahhabi outlook. As Al-Zahawi wrote,

> They killed everyone in sight, slaughtering both child and adult, the ruler and the ruled, the lowly and well-born. They began with a suckling child nursing at his mother's breast and moved on to a group studying Qur'an, slaying them, down to the last man. And when they wiped out the people they found in the houses, they went out into the streets, the shops, and the mosques, killing whoever happened to be there. They killed even men bowed in prayer until they had exterminated every Muslim who dwelt in Ta'if and only a remnant, some 20 or more, remained.
>
> These were holed up in Beit al-Fitni with ammunition, inaccessible to the Wahhabis' approach. There was another group at Beit al-Far numbering 270, who fought them that day, then a second and third day, until the

Wahhabis sent them a guarantee of clemency; only they tendered this proposal as a trick. For when the Wahhabis entered, they seized their weapons and slew them to a man. They induced others to surrender with a guarantee of mercy and took them to the valley of Waj where they abandoned them in the cold and snow, barefoot, naked and exposed in shame with their women, accustomed to the privacy afforded them by common decency and religious morality. They then plundered their possessions: wealth of any kind, household furnishings, and cash.

They cast books into the streets, alleys, and byways to be blown to and fro by the wind, among which could be found copies of *Qur'an*, volumes of Bukhari, Muslim,[1] other canonical collections of *Hadith* and books of Islamic jurisprudence, all mounting to the thousands. These books remained there for several days, trampled upon by the Wahhabis. None among them made the slightest attempt to remove even one page of *Qur'an* from underfoot to preserve it from the ignominy of this display of disrespect. Then, they razed the houses, and made what was once a town a barren waste.

It is said that the leather and gilt bindings of the Islamic holy books they had destroyed were used to make sandals for the Wahhabi warriors.

Next the Wahhabis entered Mecca. Sharif Ghalib drove them away, but Wahhabi raids continued until Ghalib surrendered the city. The Wahhabis then turned to Medina. Sa'ud bin Abd al-Aziz addressed the people thusly: "There is no other way for you than to submit. I will make you cry out and vanish as I did the people of Ta'if." On taking Medina, they stole the Prophet's treasure. This included holy books, works of art, and other priceless gifts sent to the city during the previous 1,000 years. While they controlled the Two Holy Places, they imposed Wahhabism as an official creed, barred pilgrims from performing the *hajj*, covered up the Ka'bah with a rough black fabric, and began the demolition of shrines and cemeteries. The disruption of the *hajj* provoked an uproar throughout the Muslim world. Murders of leading citizens of both holy cities continued. The Wahhabis, under the third Saudi ruler, Sa'ud bin Abd al-Aziz, had established a prototype for a modern "Islamic" terrorist regime.

Within a few years of Ibn Abd al-Wahhab's initial agreement with Al Sa'ud, a hitherto-remote element entered the picture: British interest in the penetration of Arabia. Motivated by concern for its Indian enterprise, in 1755 Britain made a first, unsuccessful attempt to wrest Kuwait from Ottoman control. Ten years later, Muhammad ibn Sa'ud died and his son Abd al-Aziz became the ruler of Dariyah. During the following two decades, the Wahhab-Sa'ud alliance further extended its area of influence, paralleling British infiltration in the Peninsula. Britain again showed interest in Kuwait in 1775, seeking protection for their mail service through the territory, and attempted unsuccessfully to take Kuwait in 1786, when they were defeated by the Ottomans.

The next year, Ibn Abd al-Wahhab declared himself leader of the worldwide *ummah*. This insanity was backed with a *fatwa* in which Ibn Abd al-Wahhab ordered *"jihad"* against the Ottomans. The full import of Ibn Abd al-Wahhab's pretensions to universal religious authority became clear in 1788, when Abd al-Aziz ibn Sa'ud was joined by British forces in occupying Kuwait. The Wahhabis turned to the Christians for direct military help in their *"jihad"* against the Turks.

During this period, Britain acquired a client in southeast Arabia: Oman, a state with sovereignty over Zanzibar in Africa and parts of the Iranian and neighboring coasts. Britain also expanded its influence northward into the area now known as the United Arab Emirates. In the other direction, the British subjugated Aden, on the southern Yemen coast, in 1839. Yet remarkably enough, Wahhabi violence was almost never turned against the encroachments of this aggressive Christian power; the fanatics seemed concerned only with destroying the Ottomans. For this reason, anti-Wahhabi Muslim writers have repeatedly denounced them as a tool of the British who sought the destruction of Islam. Clearly, however, the British were more concerned with the coasts of the Arabian Peninsula, which were of immediate value as imperial possessions. Central Arabia was of no apparent use, and the British were glad to leave control of it to usurpers like Ibn Abd al-Wahhab and Al Sa'ud.

Bernard Lewis has noted that the incipient crisis of the Ottomans also generated a more spiritual response, toward Islamic revitalization. After the Battle of Vienna in 1683, two powerful movements had appeared in the empire. Counterposed to Ibn Abd al-Wahhab and his followers, the Naqshbandi Sufis underwent a new burst of inspiration. Lewis writes that these contrasting developments "expressed, in different ways, the Islamic reaction against the growing power of the West." Both were attempts to restore the "pristine purity" of the faith. But the Wahhabis sought to purge Islam, while the Naqshbandis worked to renew its spiritual wealth.

One of the great Naqshbandi shaykhs of that era was Nur Muhammad al-Badawani, whose burial shrine is in Lahore, Pakistan. Of him, Muhammad Hisham Kabbani writes, "He spent all his time in meditation and contemplation . . . from his excessive contemplation, his back became bowed." Al-Badawani was only 59 when he died in 1722/3. Naqshbandis from India promoted Arabic learning anew in Egypt, along with a return to the original piety and simplicity of the *Salaf*, the "Forerunners," or early successors to Muhammad. Naqshbandi writings defending the Islam of the *Salaf* may have contributed to the emergence of Wahhabism, and Lewis observes the irony that while the Wahhabis would claim the mantle of the *Salaf*, they were murderous in their hatred of dervishes, as an element of their attack on the entire legacy of the *Sunna* upheld by the Ottomans.

The Wahhabis continued their career of bloodshed in Arabia until 1811, when one of the most remarkable personalities of the 19th century, and an outstanding figure in Islamic history, was dispatched by the Ottoman Sultan Mahmud II to subdue them. Ottoman tolerance did not extend to open subversion.

The hammer of empire and caliphate against the Wahhabis was Muhammad Ali Pasha, the governor of Egypt, and an Albanian born in the heart of the Balkans. As the historian H. T. Norris writes, "He looked fondly towards his home town of Kavalla in Macedonia, and always seemed to breathe some distant, fresher mountain air beyond it." Muhammad Ali Pasha's pride in his Albanian heritage led him to promote Albanians, their language, and their culture everywhere he could. He was also widely claimed as a sympathizer, if not a member, of the Bektashi dervishes.

Muhammad Ali Pasha was the ideal man to fight Sa'ud bin Abd al-Aziz, the defiler of the Holy Places, and he acquitted himself gloriously in liberating Mecca and Medina from Wahhabi dictatorship. He appointed his son Tosun Pasha commander of the troops, but Tosun Pasha's forces were badly defeated and Muhammad Ali Pasha reassumed command. In 1812, augmenting his artillery and coordinating with Sharif Ghalib, he swept through western Arabia, lifting the darkness of Wahhabi domination. Al Sa'ud's men fled before the punitive advance of the Ottoman army. Two of the worst Wahhabi terrorists, Uthman ul-Mudayiqi (the tormentor of Ta'if) and Mubarak ibn Maghyan, were sent to Istanbul where they were paraded through the streets before being executed, their severed heads posted in the imperial precincts.

Next Muhammad Ali Pasha sent troops under his second son, Ibrahim Pasha, to cleanse Syria, Iraq, and Kuwait of the Wahhabis. The Arabs who had suffered under the Wahhabi-Saudi gang rose and joined Muhammad Ali Pasha's forces. In 1818, the Wahhabi capital, Dariyah, was subjugated and destroyed by the Ottomans, but some of the Al Sa'ud received British protection in Jeddah. Sa'ud bin Abd al-Aziz had died of fever in 1814. However, his heir, Abdullah ibn Sa'ud, fourth in the lineage of upstart rulers, was sent to Istanbul, where he was executed with more captured Wahhabis. The first Saudi state and the terror it inflicted existed no more.

The parallel struggle of Ottoman religious scholars against Wahhabism generated an immense literature of *fatwas* and other writings against them. These included many titles eloquently expressing the anger the Wahhabis provoked among traditional scholars. Ata' Allah al-Makki turned his pen to *The Indian Scimitar on the Najdi's Neck*, referring to the origin of the movement in Najd. Al-Sayyid Ahmad ibn Zayni Dahlan, *Mufti* of Mecca and Shaykh al-Islam (the highest Ottoman religious authority) for the Hejaz region of western Arabia, died in 1886, after writing many works against them, including one with the mild heading, *Pure Pearls in Answering the Wahhabis*. His contemporary Dawud ibn Sulayman al-Baghdadi al-Hanafi returned to the more combative mode, with a work generally known as *The Most Strenuous Jihad* or *Ashadd al-Jihad*, calling for sustained resistance to Wahhabi blandishments. Al-Sayyid al-`Alawi ibn Ahmad ibn Hasan ibn al-Qutb al-Haddad also favored the cutting edge in polemics: He composed *The Sharp Sword for the Neck of the Assailant of Great Scholars* as well as *The Lamp of Mankind and the Illumination of Darkness Concerning the Refutation of the Errors of the Innovator from Najd by Which He Had Misled the Common People*. These volumes represent but a few of some 80 anti-Wahhabi classics.

Nevertheless, like many rebellious movements, including the Khawarij, the Wahhabis proved resistant to repression. From the 1820s through the 1860s, they husbanded their resources and prepared new assaults on the empire's political and religious authority. Britain for its part encouraged the Wahhabis, with an eye to the eventual Turkish collapse and division of Ottoman possessions. This became a major aim of the Western powers once it was clear the empire had been seriously weakened. In addition, an entirely novel phenomenon had begun to intrude into Ottoman affairs: the rise of European nationalism among the Christians of the western border. Ibn Abd al-Wahhab and his supporters and descendants did not conceive of an Arab national identity. But the emergence of revolutionary France, the conquests of Napoleon, and steps toward the unification of the Germans and Italians had led to an uprising against the Ottomans in Serbia in 1804. The theater of anti-imperial revolt soon shifted to Greece. These nations and the Romanians attained varying degrees of autonomy and independence from the Ottomans in the first half of the 19th century.

Meanwhile, after his successful campaign against the Wahhabis, Muhammad Ali Pasha pursued a project for imperial reform that failed but had wide impact. His vision reflected the influence of the triumphant idea of global progress represented by Napoleon, who had conquered Egypt in 1798. The devotion of Muhammad Ali Pasha to Egypt and his conception of a modernized Ottoman Empire were so influential that he has been called the founder of modern Egypt.

In 1700 Turkey had still been a great and vital power. But with the passage of a century, its decadence was unmistakable. Muhammad Ali Pasha's suppression of the Wahhabis, though stunningly effective, had been delayed for years by lassitude and congestion in the bureaucracy at

Istanbul. Napoleon's Egyptian campaign dramatized the apparent need of the Ottoman Empire to adapt to new technologies, as well as new military and political doctrines. Successive sultans of the 19th century attempted to adjust the imperial order to European models by introducing new institutions, forms of education, and theories of citizenship, with varying success.

A major institution in the administration of the empire, the Janissary corps, was mainly composed of children of Christian families, drafted for military service. Widely viewed as an obstacle to change, the Janissaries were brutally suppressed in 1826, following a rebellion against imperial reforms. The great Istanbul lodges of the Bektashi dervishes, the chaplains of the Janissaries, were also destroyed and their properties handed over to the Naqshbandis. But sympathy for the Bektashis remained deeply rooted in the Turkish elite, and their rights were restored. Ironically, the Wahhabis had pledged to carry out a similar campaign to drive the Bektashis, Qadiris, and other dervishes out of the vicinity of Mecca and Medina. The Two Holy Places had, for 1,000 years, been Islamically inclusive, with shrines for the Shi'a and other Islamic sects. But the extirpation of pluralism was the essential Wahhabi goal in theology. Ottoman weakness, blamed by the Wahhabis on a lack of strict observance, was entirely dictated by geopolitical factors.

Underlying the aspects of the 17th-century Ottoman stalemate discussed in the previous chapter, Christian civilization had continuously pushed outward, across new horizons, while Islamic civilization mainly proceeded in an eastern direction that inevitably, it seemed, turned inward, even as it gained new power as far from Arabia as the Philippines. Christians and Muslims had met at many points in their colonizing competition, but while the Christians had the luck to explore and exploit virgin territories in the Western Hemisphere, their populations unacquainted with modern arms and their resources never before extracted on a large scale, the Muslims infiltrated regions possessed of long-stabilized cultures and economies that were already ancient at the time of their first encounters with dervishes and Arab merchants. Indeed, the Muslims explicitly viewed themselves as heirs of the ancient Greek and Persian empires. Thus the Christians and their Jewish allies invented an entirely new

nment, while the Muslims and their Jewish advisors adminis-
and then a shrinking, reality.

how the weakness of the Ottomans is analyzed, in the 18th
century they who had fought and often defeated the Greeks, Albanians,
and Serbs, the Hungarians, Poles, Germans, and Croats, the Venetians,
Genoese, and Catalans, clearly faced a new and most formidable foe in
the alliance of British interests and the House of Sa'ud. In addition, the
Russian empire also pressed the Muslim dominions from the north. It is
in this context that we must return to the pairing of Naqshbandi Sufis and
Wahhabis as two exemplars of Islamic regeneration.

On the frontier between the Muscovite empire and the Islamic lands,
an entirely different kind of *jihad* occurred, offering an instructive contrast with the nihilistic power ideology of Ibn Abd al-Wahhab and Al
Sa'ud. This was the struggle of the Chechens and other Caucasian Muslim peoples, commencing around the same time as the campaign against
the Wahhabis by Muhammad Ali Pasha. The small nations on the peaks
of the Caucasus had only lately become Muslims when *jihad* began
against the Russians in the region. American Muslim commentator
Mateen Siddiqui has written, "Islam did not take root in the Caucasus
until well into the 18th and mid-19th centuries, with the mountain
regions last. However, when Islam finally did enter the hearts of the Caucasian mountaineers, it was impregnated with iron firmness, like the tow-
ering Caucasian ramparts themselves."

Prior to their Islamization, these peoples shared a very ancient religion,
worshipping features of the landscape and natural spirits. They had a
complicated system of clan relationships and a customary law, really a
code of honor, for the settlement of disputes. They were chiefly distinguished by the extraordinary diversity of their languages, which belong to
several completely different families. To the extent they were ruled by others, which was not very much, they were subjects of the Christian Geor-
gians, the Ottomans, and the Shah of Persia. But the 1813 Treaty of
Gulistan transferred sovereignty over the Caucasian districts to the Russian tsar.

The call to *jihad* in those parts possesses a picturesque legendry, which
might be true, but probably is not. The tale is told that a certain Shaykh

Mansur, who some say was a dervish and others claim was an Italian Jesuit who embraced Islam, had traveled through the Caucasus at the end of the 18th century. He preached resistance to the Slavs, and his forces defeated the Muscovite army in battle in 1785, gaining support from Chechens and Daghestanis. Captured by the Russians in 1791, near the end of the Second Russo-Turkish War, he was exiled to the Solovietsky Islands in north Russia, where he died. Imperial Russia, in the meantime, had turned her face back toward the Black Sea and Europe. A generation passed before Tsar Aleksandr I, fresh from overcoming the levies of Bonaparte, decided on a new advance into the Caucasus.

Whether thanks to a Catholic cleric turned Sufi or not, the seeds of resistance had been planted in the mountains. The Naqshbandi dervishes, who contributed seven illustrious shaykhs to the Caucasian *jihad*, reject the fables about Shaykh Mansur. He was, they say, a Chechen, originally named Ushurma, born in 1732. Although he summoned the Caucasian Muslims to *jihad* against the Russians, the Naqshbandis credit the real spiritual preparation of the struggle to the outstanding personality of their order in the later Ottoman period, Shaykh Khalid al-Baghdadi (1779–1827), who reorganized the dervishes and restored their enthusiasm. A historian of the Caucasian rebellion, Moshe Gammer, notes that with the full annexation of the Caucasian territories the tsarist regime began to persecute the local dervishes. One of al-Baghdadi's disciples, Shaykh Ismail al-Kurdumuri (also known as Ismail ash-Shirwani), stepped forward to prepare the Muslims of the mountains for combat. He became an unforgettable figure in Islamic history: In the words of Muhammad Hisham Kabbani, "In his century he was the Sufi to whom all eyes turned."

Organizing the Caucasian Muslims for a wide-scale defense against the Russians, the Naqshbandi shaykh strengthened the resolve of the *jihad* fighters or *mujahidin* as a mystical collective, just as the Bektashis and other Sufis of the past had educated the Central Asian warriors and Janissaries for Islam. Ash-Shirwani was joined by four other *mujahidin* of his generation. Khas Muhammad, a follower of Shaykh ash-Shirwani born in 1786, initiated Muhammad Effendi al-Yaraghi (b. 1777); al-Yaraghi brought Jamaluddin al-Ghumuqi al-Husayni (b. 1788), known as the *Gazi* or holy hero, into the Naqshbandi order. The fourth was Abu Ahmad as-Sughuri (b. 1793). These five Daghestani shaykhs, men from obscure villages and towns alight with the fire of faith, dramatically changed the history of their dervish order, the Caucasian Muslims, and the Russian empire. All of them remain beloved Muslim saints among Sufis and the Caucasian peoples.

Khas Muhammad said, "God did not send anything to this earth except as a lesson for His servants to learn from." Another Sufi reported that Khas Muhammad appeared to him in a vision and uttered a phrase of extraordinary power, expressive of the dervish *esprit*: "When you are with us, you must not feel fear." Kabbani notes that when Khas Muhammad walked in the towns of Daghestan, the streets were lined by pious folk seeking a glimpse of him. Of al-Yaraghi, Kabbani comments, "He trained his disciples who numbered in the thousands. During the day he taught them military strategy for fighting the Russians. During the nights he taught them spiritually." Al-Yaraghi defined his faith as follows: "Islam is to surrender your heart to your Lord and not to harm anyone." Of al-Ghumuqi, Kabbani writes, "He comprehended the speech of the birds." This was considered the ultimate weapon of the dervish in *jihad*, his unity with God's creation.

Al-Yaraghi had two young followers, dear friends and Naqshbandi dervishes who together would lead the Caucasian Muslims to world renown. These were Ghazi Muhammad ibn Ismail ad-Daghestani, known as Kazi Mullah, and *Imam* Shamyl, both members of the small mountain nation of Avars.

Shaykh al-Yaraghi declared *jihad* against the Russians in 1830. Kazi Mullah, commanding the dervishes, won his first battle without violence: Assembling at the mountain community of Andi, which cooperated with the Russians, the silent ranks of the Sufis were so impressive that the inhabitants capitulated. But in confrontation with the Slav armies, these men fought fiercely for the right to be left in peace in their homes, their religion, and their spiritual communities, and they used the advantages of the landscape, the steep ranges, wild valleys, and woods to outwit and devastate the tsar's forces. The Russians launched a terror campaign, burning villages and slaying their residents; in many clashes, no quarter was given on either side, and the Caucasian *mujahidin* killed many Russian soldiers. Kazi Mullah died in the siege of a mountain redoubt called Ghimri, the birthplace of his comrade Shamyl, who carried on the struggle.

Born at the end of the 18th century, Shamyl would become a hero to the whole Muslim world, as well as to many non-Muslim observers of the struggle against Muscovite imperialism; he even excited the respect and admiration of his Russian foes. As a child he kept his family's sheep in the high peaks, and Kerim Fenari has written, "Often he would look over the edges, down into the 5,000-foot abyss beneath the village, and watch the lightning flash in the thunderclouds below." He evaded encirclement at Ghimri and spent months recovering from 18 wounds, before returning to arms. A description of his successful escape from Ghimri, written by a tsarist soldier, has become a classic vignette of Russian history:

> It was dark: by the light of the burning thatch [roof] we saw a man standing in the doorway of the [house], which stood on raised ground . . . This man, who was very tall and powerfully built, stood quite still, as if giving us time to take aim. Then, suddenly, with the spring of a wild beast, he leapt clean over the heads of the very line of soldiers about to fire on him, and landing behind them, whirling his sword in his left hand he cut down three of them, but was bayoneted by the fourth, the steel plunging deep into his chest. His face still extraordinary in its immobility, he seized the bayonet, pulled it out of his own flesh, cut down the man and, with another super-human leap, cleared the wall and vanished into the darkness. We were left absolutely dumbfounded. The whole business had taken, perhaps, a minute and a half.

Brutal warfare ravaged the Caucasus for almost 30 years thereafter. To the considerable frustration of the tsarist court, Shamyl established a new Islamic dominion in much of Chechnya and Daghestan and was severe in the application of *Shariah*. As a child he had threatened suicide if his father would not abstain from alcohol, and as a man he was especially dedicated to the extirpation of banditry. The Russians had unlimited resources, but the conflict turned in their favor only after 1851, when they began leveling the forests in which the *mujahidin* sought shelter. After eight years more, Shamyl was exhausted. He retreated to a village in the farthest mountain reaches, but after resisting many Russian attacks, he agreed to end his *jihad*. He was interned near Moscow until 1869, when he was permitted to leave for Mecca and Medina. He died in 1871 and was buried in Jannat al-Baqi, the cemetery of the Prophet's Companions in Medina.

The Caucasian *jihad* deeply undermined the tsarist empire. The respect the Russian intelligentsia felt for the dervishes and their struggle is best expressed in Leo Tolstoy's famous work *Hajji Murad*. Karl Marx, who loathed Russian expansionism, wrote memorably of the Caucasian Muslims, "People, learn from them, see what people who want to remain free can do."

The Wahhabi and Caucasian Islamic movements delineate in the sharpest terms the two faces of *jihad*, and of Islam in general. In Arabia, the Wahhabis chiefly fought other Muslims in a war against saints, shrines, graveyards, and mosques, while in the Caucasus Sufis pledged their lives to defend their native lands from a real and consequential opponent: Russian imperialism. Writ larger, this contrast illumines an everlasting struggle for the soul of the *ummah*. Would Muslims respond to the crisis of the Ottoman caliphate by withdrawing into violent self-purging and criminality in the Wahhabi style, or by spiritual purification and self-defense, as practiced by the dervishes? And how would the Wahhabis fight their "*jihad*" in societies where Muslims lived alongside non-Muslims?

Wahhabism was first seen outside the Arabian Peninsula among the pirates of the Persian Gulf. But the true face of Wahhabism in dealing with non-Muslims was revealed in India, by a man named Sayid Ahmad Barelvi. This personage had gone on pilgrimage to Mecca in 1820. When he returned two years later he established a Wahhabi center in Patna on the upper Ganges in northeast India. He and his agents began preaching in Afghanistan, and in 1826 launched "*jihad*" against the Sikhs in Punjab. In 1830 his forces seized Peshawar, and he was soon killed in battle, fighting Pashtuns who had sided with the Sikhs. But the Wahhabi group in Patna continued to organize uprisings until the late 1860s. The "*jihad*" of Sayid

Ahmad called for combat against Sikhs, Hindus, and the British alike, according to the principle of flight or withdrawal from unbelievers. In India, this quintessential Wahhabi concept flourished: Muslims were called upon to separate violently from the company of non-Muslims. No mixed societies would be tolerated, much less rulership over Muslims by non-Muslims. The Indian subcontinent—including Afghanistan as well as what would become Pakistan and Bangladesh—would serve as the laboratory of global Wahhabism, a role it has continued to play until the present.

In Bengal in 1831, a peasant named Titu Mir led a Wahhabi uprising. Born in 1782, Mir had earned a living as a wrestler and as a guard for local men of wealth. In the mid-1820s, he made pilgrimage to Mecca and came under the influence of Sayid Ahmad. Titu Mir returned to Bengal and began fomenting separation by Bengali Muslims from the Hindus with whom, and under whom, they lived; many of the bigger landowners were Hindu. In his view, Bengal was part of the "house of war," a concept the Indian Wahhabis had adopted with great avidity. Contact between Muslims and Hindus, the Indian Wahhabis argued, had imbued the former with objectionable spiritual practices. This attitude combined the demand for separation from non-Muslims with the Arabian Wahhabis' condemnation of traditional Islamic spirituality as expressed in Sufism. It is true that in Bengal the Muslim poor had grown so close to their Hindu counterparts that they observed Hindu rituals and holidays and occasionally adopted Hindu names. But traditional Islam had come to define Hindus as People of the Book, finding a monotheistic essence in the religion of Brahma.

In addition to their anti-Hindu separatism, the Bengali adherents observed the typical Wahhabi rejection of the company of Muslims who did not share their views. Their ultimate goal was political power, as in Arabia. But in India, Wahhabism acquired new features: In addition to violence against other religions as well as uncompliant Muslims, it also made a claim of social justice. After all, the Arabian followers of Ibn Abd al-Wahhab were desert wanderers and bandits. They had not even reached the stage of economic development, or produced social grievances, such as existed among the Muslim peasants and poor craft-workers of India. Thus an Indian Marxist historian, Narahari Kaviraj, has argued that Indian Wahhabism was little more than a vessel for class protest by the poor against the "exactions" of Hindu exploiters.

The Bengali Wahhabi revolt began when several hundred of them burst into the marketplace of a village called Poorwa and slaughtered a cow, the holy animal of the Hindus. As Kaviraj narrates, "With the blood of the animal they defiled a Hindu temple." They beat up a Hindu, threatening to force him into Islam, and then "attacked and ill-treated an Indian-born Christian of the name of Smith, an overseer of a native indigo plantation, and wounded his servant, who happened to be passing on an elephant." They spread through the countryside committing similar provocations against the Hindus and imposing a real terror in the district. Frightened locals referred to the fanatics as having "eaten the dinner of death." The extremists laid waste to colonial as well as local enterprises, appropriating vast assets and defeating troops sent against them by the British authorities. In the areas that fell under their control, they robbed non-Wahhabi Muslims and ordered them to grow beards in the Wahhabi fashion. Muslims joined Hindus and Europeans in hastily leaving the region.

The uprising was finally suppressed by British troops, though not without a battle in which the Wahhabis displayed the corpse of a murdered European in their front line, as if it were a banner. Golam Masum, who had become the military commander of the group, was executed. Of the rest, 189 were tried, of whom 49 were acquitted and one released as insane; the remainder were sentenced to varying terms of prison and hard labor. Notwithstanding their profession of faith and claim to religious reformation, they were viewed by most observers as outrageous criminals. The Marxist Kaviraj cheerfully points out, "Considering the standard of the times, the rebels . . . showed a wonderful sense of discipline and organization." Nevertheless, they never gained the support of the majority of local Muslims. Kaviraj notes "the inveterate hostility of the rebels to Muhammadans[2] of the old faith. They made forced conversion their chief weapon. They plundered and maltreated rich Muhammadans. They did not hesitate to cruelly butcher the Muhammadan judges and . . . public servants who failed to agree with them. The old Muhammadans became as terror-stricken as the Hindus and they joined hands to destroy the Wahhabi menace."

During later Wahhabi trials in India the defendants' posture would range from refusal to recognize the authority of the court to employment of British lawyers—another fascinating parallel with more recent incidents. In the late 19th century, Wahhabism assumed a dual pattern it would repeat at the end of the 20th: Accommodation by its Arabian branch with Britain, the leading Christian imperial power, while its Indian branch conducted a violent *jihad* against the same British in the subcontinent. Similarly, the Saudi kingdom would hold, in their own territory, to an extraordinarily beneficial relationship with the Americans while encouraging terrorism against American interests everywhere else.

Between 1865 and 1891, the Wahhabis launched further attempts to gain control of the whole Arabian Peninsula. Although defeated by the Ottoman-Egyptian forces of Muhammad Ali Pasha, they had not given up their dreams of conquest, moving their headquarters to Riyadh, a new settlement near the former Dariyah. Sa'ud ibn Faysal was their new chief, and he launched a fresh campaign of pillage, and rebellion against the Ottomans, from 1870. This renewed attempt at Wahhabi-Saudi hegemony in the Peninsula was undermined by internal quarrels among the Al Sa'ud. But it became the basis of an unstable "second Wahhabi state," following that suppressed by Muhammad Ali Pasha in 1818. Ishik cites an opponent of the Wahhabis who noted that while the inhabitants of Arabia were highly intelligent, they were also "extremely ignorant, cruel and murderous." The critic continued, "Their allegiance to Sa'ud increased the intensity of their barbarism."

Perhaps more important for the tragic details of history was a bit of business unfortunately left unfinished by Muhammad Ali Pasha when he defeated the Wahhabis. In the region of Asir, between Ta'if and Yemen, lived about a million "savages," as they have been described by Ishik, who were converted to Wahhabism. Muhammad Ali Pasha had put off the repression of the Wahhabis in Asir, where the local folk refused to recognize the Ottoman governor, obeying only their own chief or *emir*. Finally, imperial troops were sent to flush the Wahhabis of Asir out of their mountainside nests. In the 20th century, the area would be re-Wahhabized, with special torments visited on Shi'a Muslims who lived in the region, and Wahhabism in Asir became known for its cruel and fanatical character. But Ta'if and Asir would remain obscure to the rest of the world until the beginning of the 21st century when certain of its sons would attain a dolorous notoriety: Of the 19 terrorists who hijacked four jet aircraft on September 11, 2001, 12 of the 15 Saudis among them originated in those areas. As reported by Charles M. Sennott of the *Boston Globe*, investigators of the events believed Osama bin Laden's terror recruiters specifically targeted inhabitants of Ta'if and Asir for this and other operations. Hani Hanjour, a leading member of the terror team, hailed from Ta'if. Three hijackers came from the nearby area of Al Baha. More originated in the Asir localities of Abha and Khamis Mushayt. Sennott wrote of hearing boasts there that "sons of Asir" were key participants in the September 11 atrocities. Such horrific acts and utterances were pure expressions of the Wahhabi traditions from which they sprang, geographically as well as religiously.

As the 19th century came to a close, Wahhabism waxed and waned. In 1891, Sa'ud and his Wahhabi followers were expelled by the Rashid dynasty, their main rivals in central Arabia, from Riyadh to the Empty Quarter of the Peninsula, before settling in Kuwait where British influence was paramount. Eight years later the ruler of Kuwait was granted an annual subsidy by Britain, which assumed responsibility for its foreign relations and security. Sa'ud and the Wahhabis bided their time until 1901 when the latest representative of the dual lineage, Abdul-Aziz Ibn Abdur-Rahman Ibn Muhammad Al Sa'ud, then aged 21, departed Kuwait for a new try at subduing the Two Holy Places. He went first to Riyadh, murdering the city's ruler, and took control of it, thereby laying the foundation of what would become Saudi Arabia, a global power of the 20th century. This scion of the Al Sa'ud would be known as Ibn Sa'ud, and we shall refer to him as such hereafter. Another century would pass before Wahhabism exploded into the consciousness of the world, devastating lives in other cities far away.

CHAPTER 4

Global Gamblers

THE WAHHABI–SAUDI CONQUEST OF ARABIA

In 1924, the Wahhabis reconquered Mecca, thereby acquiring the right to the collection of taxes and fees from pilgrims in *hajj*. The Hashimite family, which had previously held the position of governor, or *sharif*, of Mecca, were expelled, and an "Islamic" order was established reflecting the Wahhabi vision. Primitive Wahhabi frenzy led the conquerors to smash mirrors and burn windowframes and doorways (typically finely decorated in the Turkish style) for fuel. The seizure of the city of the Ka'bah came at the end of a 23-year campaign by Ibn Sa'ud, accompanied by the usual mass murder: Nearly half a million people had been killed or injured by Wahhabi zealots. A million people had fled the areas they seized.

The triumphant reassertion of Wahhabi-Saudi power produced the third, and most lasting, of the Wahhabi states. The new regime emerged from the confusion of the first world war, the collapse of the Turkish empire, and the end of the Ottoman caliphate as the religious authority for the world's Muslims.

The following year saw the extension of Wahhabi authority to the port of Jeddah and to Medina. Soon Ibn Sa'ud ordered the destruction of the most sacred tombs, graveyards, and mosques. Wahhabi militia, the *Ikhwan* or Brotherhood, first leveled the "heavenly orchard" cemetery, or Jannat al-Baqi, in Medina, which was viewed by the local folk and by visiting pilgrims as an honored burial site. There one of the early Companions of the Prophet, Uthman bin Madhun, was buried under Muhammad's own supervision. Muhammad's son Ibrahim, who died in childhood, was also interred there, accompanied by the Prophet's tears. Hassan, son of the caliph Ali, grandson of Muhammad and brother of Husayn, honored by Sunni and Shi'a Muslims alike, was buried at the site. The graveyard also sheltered the remains of thousands more of the Companions, two other leading *imams*, and various relatives of Muhammad. All these tombs and gravestones were wrecked by Ibn Sa'ud's minions, who then, like their Wahhabi predecessors in the 19th century, looted the treasure at the Prophet's Shrine.

The *Ikhwan* went on to completely demolish the cemetery in Mecca that included the graves of the mother and grandfather of Muhammad and of his wife Khadijah. Within a short time they had reduced to nothing many more distinguished mausoleums, mosques, and honored sites, devastating the architectural achievements of Arabia, including Muhammad's own house. Of the graves, only that of the Prophet remained intact, although the Wahhabis wanted to get rid of it as well, having begun but abandoned such an attempt during their first seizure of the city.

Indignant protests against Wahhabi vandalism rang throughout the *ummah*. At first, Ibn Sa'ud claimed the occupation was temporary, and many Muslims demanded that Mecca and Medina be placed under a separate religious authority. But in 1926, Ibn Sa'ud called a global Islamic conference to ratify his control over the Two Holy Places. Anti-Wahhabi delegates from India walked out and were then expelled from the country.

These victories represented the culmination of decades of intrigue and combat. Beginning in 1902, from his base in Riyadh, Ibn Sa'ud had pursued the original goals of the Wahhabis with relentless ambition: to undermine the Ottomans, subdue the Two Holy Places, and impose the Wahhabi dispensation on the entire *ummah*. These theological ambitions allowed the desert raider Ibn Sa'ud, little more than a bandit chief, to be called *imam*, or religious leader, by his followers, along with the title of king. While they eventually succeeded in their first two goals, the Wahhabis and Ibn Sa'ud would never attain domination over the world's Muslim faithful. Nevertheless, fortuitous combinations of crude diplomacy, corruption, and the resource needs of global industry and warfare would provide the Saudi ruling class with almost unimaginable wealth, power, and influence.

Ibn Sa'ud had first concentrated on destroying the remaining power of Al Rashid, a rival dynasty from Najd. Al Rashid had allied with the Ottomans to drive Al Sa'ud into exile toward the end of the 19th century and ruled Riyadh until Ibn Sa'ud's recapture of the city in 1902. Consolidating his authority before launching the Wahhabi *"jihad"* anew, Ibn Sa'ud maneuvered to remove the competing family from the scene.

This effort has been painted by admirers of Saudi power, both Arab and Western, as the commencement of a great enterprise of Arabian unification. In truth, a far greater contribution to the welfare of the Peninsula was then being made by the Ottomans, who built the Hejaz Railway from Damascus to Medina. The railway was intended to make travel by pilgrims to the Two Holy Places more efficient and safer—particularly against the depredations of Al Sa'ud and other bandits, as well as Wahhabis who sought to bar anybody but their own acolytes from making *hajj*.

This investment by the Ottoman authorities followed the religious and reconstructive works undertaken after Muhammad Ali Pasha's suppression of the Wahhabis. Many structures in the Two Holy Places had been destroyed by the fanatics during their first occupation, including the tombs of Muhammad's later wives, many of the Companions, and important Muslim martyrs. But the empire could not continue in the progressive direction represented by the opening of the Hejaz Railway in 1908, even though the same year also brought a revolution to Turkey. A conspiratorial military group, the Committee of Union and Progress, known as the Young Turks in the West and as Unionists among the Ottoman masses, forced Sultan Abdul Hamid II to adopt a constitution.

The Ottoman constitution was not new—it had originally been promulgated in 1876. But the European powers had viewed that reform as a sign of weakness and incited Serbia in an attempt to annex Bosnia-

Hercegovina, which set off a series of massacres. An uprising in Bulgaria led to Turkish atrocities there. In 1878, Turkey was attacked by Russia, and the constitution was abrogated. Seeking to defend the empire, Sultan Abdul Hamid II embarked on an absolutist course that accelerated its breakdown. In the aftermath of 1878, Austria-Hungary occupied Bosnia-Hercegovina as a protectorate. Thirty years later, the Ottoman territories were under increasing pressure from all sides. By then the European powers clearly sought the definitive dismemberment of "the sick man of Europe," as Turkey had come to be known. Partition of the Ottoman possessions was seen as a logical step after the successful European conquests of Muslim lands in Africa and the rest of Asia during the 19th century.

In 1907 Russia and Britain had split Persia into spheres of interest, following a constitutional revolution in that country, while France and Spain even more boldly divided Morocco. Stirrings among the Arabs were also favored by Britain. Much of this turmoil reflected the eastern impact of the first Russian revolution, in 1905. The year 1908 also saw Austria-Hungary's direct annexation of Bosnia-Hercegovina. Russia, notwithstanding its internal crisis, encouraged the Armenians to revolt against the Turks, and backed Serbian schemes for a continuing anti-Ottoman crusade. Bulgaria declared its formal independence from Ottoman sovereignty in the same year, and yearned to expand its boundaries at the expense of Turkey's remaining Balkan provinces. Greece, electrified by an anti-Turkish rebellion in Crete in 1908, as well as tiny Montenegro, harbored similar designs. Even Italy, a brash newcomer to imperialism, rushed to begin its hour in the sun by detaching sections of the Ottoman dominions in Africa and the Mediterranean. Meanwhile, an independence movement erupted among the Ottoman-ruled Albanians.

The Unionist regime was radical in some of its conceptions, such as their proposal for a modernized, single Turkish citizenship regardless of religious differences. This had unforeseen effects: Christians and Jews, formerly exempt as People of the Book, would now be subject to compulsory military service, which the non-Muslims resented. Thus, a measure intended to diminish distinctions aggravated them. The Committee for Union and Progress was split between a liberal, federalist trend and a nationalist, centralist faction, with the latter soon dominant. The old imperial equilibrium, in which power was maintained mainly by compromise among numerous differing ethnic and religious groupings, and only occasionally by direct repression, had been completely undermined, and in 1909 Sultan Abdul Hamid II was deposed. Power devolved to three pashas, Enver, Djemal, and Tala'at, who ruled jointly, but with uncertain authority.

Chaos at the center of the Ottoman realm naturally contributed to unrest in Arabia. Unionist rule was viewed as usurping and criminal by many Muslims who believed that if the new ruling clique was not against religion altogether, it certainly favored unacceptable alterations to Islamic authority.

During this period the Wahhabis and Ibn Sa'ud were somewhat eclipsed as the Arabian symbols of the anti-Ottoman posture. Opposition to the Turks among the Arabs of the Peninsula crystallized instead around the scion of the Hashimite clans that traced their ancestry directly to Muhammad: the ruler of Mecca, *Sharif* Husayn ibn Ali Pasha. *Sharif* Husayn was a traditionalist, who sought to return the empire to Islamic, but non-Wahhabi principles. He did not support the destruction of the Ottoman caliphate, but its renovation.

The collapse of the Ottomans entered its acute phase in 1912 as the Balkan Christian partners—Serbia, Montenegro, Bulgaria, and Greece— shot and slashed their way to the conquest of Kosovo, Macedonia, and Thrace, among the last Turkish possessions in the region. Widespread massacres of Slavic Muslims and Albanians excited world condemnation of Serbia and Bulgaria. Agitation for a further revision of borders in southwestern Europe, through Serbian absorption of Bosnia-Hercegovina, also threatened the Habsburg rulers of Austria-Hungary, which like Turkey was a multiethnic empire filled with fractious nationalist movements. Pan-Slavism, the ideology of "national liberation" championed by the tsar of Russia, contributed to the insecurity of both Austria-Hungary and Turkey, since vast numbers of Slav subjects were divided between the two realms.

While the Muslim Balkans were drenched in blood, the Wahhabi-Saudi alliance struck out in a new and noteworthy direction. In 1912, the fascinating Wahhabi-Saudi combination of theology and theft metastasized into an explicitly ideological form, aimed at completely reorganizing society in Arabia. This was the formation of the Brotherhood, universally known by its Arabic name of *Ikhwan*, a paramilitary body of young Bedouins, mainly belonging to tribes from Najd, established in agricultural colonies called *hijar* at oases across the Peninsula. These communities were created with the aim of stabilizing the Bedouin and assuring their loyalty to the Wahhabi-Saudi alliance. But their spirit clashed profoundly with the individualistic and free traditions of the Arabs. Wahhabism introduced into the Arab world the essence of totalitarianism: a quasicompulsory social experiment aimed not at social modernization, as in the Marxist case, but at the perpetuation of reactionary fanaticism. The *Ikhwan* represented the ideal of Wahhabi separatism—from other Muslims, from non-Muslims, from the world. Between 1916 and 1928, 26 insurrections by the Bedouin against Wahhabi-Saudi authority were suppressed by the *Ikhwan* with great bloodshed, including the murder of women and children.

The choice of the word *hijar* with its echo of the *hijra*, or "flight" of the Prophet Muhammad, was intentional. The Wahhabis falsely identified their separation from normal existence with Muhammad's departure from Mecca to Yathrib, which became Medina. But as we have noted, the Prophet engaged with life in all its variety; he did not seek to evade it or cancel it out. Wahhabi separatism, the most extreme version of the face of Islam that had been seen intermittently since the time of the Khawarij, represented a concept repudiated by centuries of Islamic civilization as exemplified by the Ottomans.

According to economic historian J. B. Kelly, as early as 1910 Ibn Sa'ud had begun sending out Wahhabi preachers (*mutawiyah* or "volunteers") to the desert tribes "to kindle in them a zeal for holy war." The *Ikhwan* were unquestioningly devoted to Wahhabism and very quickly became the backbone of Al Sa'ud's rule. Its militants were trained and maintained as a raiding shock force against non-Wahhabi Muslims. This ended up being their main activity, since the Bedouin who were pressed to join the colonies naturally preferred "*jihad*" to farm labor. However, the creation of a theocratic militia in the hinterlands of Najd did not attract much attention outside the *ummah*, which had not forgotten the outrages committed during the earlier Wahhabi attacks on the Two Holy Places.

The 20th century's first set of Balkan wars ended in 1913, after many atrocities and with the amputation of most of European Turkey. In 1914, the arena of Slavic provocation—now centered on the lovely city of Sarajevo in Bosnia—was the scene of a terrorist assassination, that of the Austrian Archduke Franz Ferdinand and his wife, by a Serb extremist. The shooting touched off the first world war, which would destroy the entire imperial system in the East. Neither the Austro-Hungarian nor the Ottoman dominions nor Russian tsardom would survive it. Meanwhile, even as Muslims around the world cried out in pain at the Balkan nightmare, Ibn Sa'ud saw the defeat of the Turks in Europe as the opportunity to revive the Wahhabi *"jihad"* against the Ottomans. He gathered his forces for the conquest of Hasa in Eastern Arabia, a Turkish-governed region with a population about half Shi'a.

Turkey, in alliance with Germany and Austria, went to war with Britain. London became more interested than ever in developing connections among the Arabs, especially in the Peninsula. The British would first offer a cordial and financially generous arrangement to Al Sa'ud, but in the end they settled on the Hashimite *Sharif* Husayn of Mecca as their favorite. Husayn received a subsidy and the direct help of T. E. Lawrence (1888–1935), who became famous as "the organizer of the Arab revolt." Lawrence, an archaeologist and mapmaker, saw the *sharif* of Mecca as the most legitimate contender among the Arabs. But he did not grasp the direction history was taking. Power throughout the world, in the wake of the great war and the general moral collapse attendant on it, would go not to the defenders of tradition as exemplified by Husayn and the Hashimites, but to the most ruthless and nihilistic power seekers. In retrospect, however, the sincerity of Lawrence and his appreciation of the *sharif*'s character speak well for him.

Sharif Husayn had been alarmed by the entrance of Turkey on Germany's side in the world conflict. He recognized that it would end in disaster for the empire, even though the Unionists titled the declaration of war a proclamation of "The Greatest *Jihad*" and transmitted copies of it to all Islamic countries. The *sharif* of Mecca saw the Unionists sacrificing thousands of Muslim youth to the horror, and in 1916 he issued two calls to Arab revolt.

The first appeal emphasized the early adherence to the Ottoman Empire and the strict loyalty to it of the Meccan rulers of the past. It proclaimed the independence of Hejaz from Unionist rule and promised "We shall learn every branch of science which is conformable to and fit for Islam. We shall found advanced industry. We shall try with all our hearts and souls to advance on the way of civilization."

The second declaration outlined the disaster of Ottoman involvement in the first world war, based on two main arguments. First, the empire had been devastated by the attacks of the Balkan Slavs as well as the Italians, who had seized Libya and other territories. Ottoman society and the army were exhausted by these struggles: The Muslim masses were indignant at the imposition of heavy taxes to support the increased technological demands inflicted by participation in the first world war, which, the *sharif* observed, "is extremely terrible and destructive compared to previous wars." Second, the Ottoman armies had suffered repeated defeats at the hands of the English and Russians. He wrote, "Is there anyone who does not see that the Unionists have broken the huge empire into pieces and led the people into deep trouble? The huge empire is being sacrificed for the pleasure of Enver, Djemal, Tala'at, and their friends." The empire had long prospered, Husayn insisted, by its friendship with Britain and France, but was now aligned with their enemies.

Husayn called on the Arabs to cease support for the Ottoman war against the Allies, in order to rescue the empire. But his own willingness to ally with Britain against the Unionists alienated most Arabs from the *sharif* and his confidant, Lawrence. Aside from Wahhabis, who had profited from their relations with Britain, few Muslim believers would countenance alignment with a Christian and imperialist power to the detriment of the Ottoman rulers, who still embodied the caliphate that had guided the Muslims for centuries.

With war and intrigue in full cry, Ibn Sa'ud soon had an Englishman of his own, a sinister double to the idealistic Lawrence. Ibn Sa'ud's main interlocutor to the West for the next four decades was one of the most remarkable and most appalling figures of the 20th century: a former colonial official in India named Harry St. John Bridger Philby (1885–1960). Philby was a talented linguist and an accomplished explorer and geographer. He was also pathologically vain, filled with hatred of his own country, and a born dissembler and schemer. And he was the father of the British traitor and Russian spy H. A. R. (Kim) Philby. The younger Philby betrayed his country, its American ally, and the West in general by providing information that allowed the Russians and other Communist police states to protect their foreign espionage assets while murdering those who resisted them. But when we weigh the activities of the elder Philby in the balance we find, in the longer run, much worse consequences for the world at large.

St. John Philby had been a minor British military figure in India. Sent to Iraq early in the first world war, he used the opportunity to refine his command of Arabic. He also caught the attention of Miss Gertrude Bell, a legendary figure in British Middle Eastern affairs. Miss Bell was a formidable Arab expert and influential adviser at the highest levels of imperial policymaking. *Sharif* Husayn and Lawrence were the main players in Miss Bell's project of the moment, which was to unite the Arabs for a campaign to conquer Palestine and Syria. But she found uses for Philby in her plans: In 1917 he was sent to Riyadh to secure the cooperation of Ibn Sa'ud in protecting the *sharif*'s forces from an attack by the rival Al Rashid, who remained loyal to the Ottomans.

Ibn Sa'ud had agreed to a treaty with Britain in 1915, making his domain a protectorate. He promised, in return for cash and arms, to fight Al Rashid. But Al Sa'ud hung back from the anti-Ottoman struggle once it became acute and instead adopted a policy of playing the British and Turks off against each other. Having taken Hasa, Ibn Sa'ud was confirmed by the Turkish authorities as *emir* of Riyadh. The Saudis would pursue similar strategies with the British and Americans during the 1930s and, later, between the United States and the forces of anti-Western Islamic extremism.

By 1918, the conflict in Arabia was no longer of strategic importance to the Allies. But St. John Philby, appropriating the British government's funds for his own adventurous uses, backed Ibn Sa'ud in a new campaign of Wahhabi expansion in northern Najd. Philby's British superiors ordered the effort stopped. It was clear that Britain saw itself as the postwar guardian of order in the Arabian Peninsula. But the Allies had pledged repeatedly that the defeat of the Ottomans would produce an independent Arab state, and as the first world war came to an end it seemed inevitable that in redeeming this pledge, Britain would have to choose between its two main clients in Arabia: *Sharif* Husayn of Mecca, who was now styled King of Hejaz, and Ibn Sa'ud.

Both the Hashimites following Husayn and the Wahhabis backing Ibn Sa'ud saw their leaders as candidates to succeed the Ottoman sultan as caliph of Islam worldwide. British recognition of either as the ruler of Arabia would greatly substantiate the chosen one's claims to legitimacy. For their part, a stable continuation of Islamic religious authority was viewed by the British and French as necessary for the tranquil governance of their colonies in India and North Africa, as well as the territories they coveted in the Middle East. But Ibn Sa'ud's theological ambitions were greater and drove the stakes even higher. British patronage, combined with his control of Mecca and Medina, and his hoped-for establishment of a new caliphate, would make possible the first serious effort at rapid Wahhabization of the world's Muslims.

Ibn Sa'ud has been described by both his admirers and detractors as a conniving desert chieftain. The Wahhabi-Saudi alliance had always decided its course on the basis of power politics, and it never rejected British aid if it could be obtained on Wahhabi terms. The British granted Ibn Sa'ud significant honors and favors—he and the emir of Kuwait, who had provided Al Sa'ud shelter, would be the first Arabs to be granted British knighthoods. The British then represented the mightiest Christian empire in history, a power aggressively committed, from the Islamic perspective, to the spread of unbelief. They had reduced Muslim India to impotence; throughout the 19th century English-speaking Protestant missionaries had flooded the Middle East, and in 1917 the British promised a national homeland to the Jews in the soon-to-be-divided Ottoman dominions. To arrive at an understanding with the British, with the goal of transforming

the *ummah* into a community of Wahhabi fundamentalists, was a concept
so daring in its perversity it would seem to have sprung from the brain of a
demon, not a man. This was precisely the gambit Ibn Sa'ud made his
own, with advice from St. John Philby.

In the political and financial realms, the Sa'ud-Philby strategy succeeded for generations. At first the Wahhabis interpreted this success as a
sign of God's favor; but it was much more a consequence of British—and,
later, American—intellectual, religious, and political obtuseness. When
we examine the two pairs of actors in the Arabian drama—*Sharif* Husayn
and Lawrence on one side, and Ibn Sa'ud and Philby on the other—it is
easy to assume that they represented differing British interests. Certainly,
their forces were at odds in Islamic terms. *Sharif* Husayn sought nothing
other than the security of the Two Holy Places and the consolidation of an
Arab state, while Ibn Sa'ud envisioned control of the Two Holy Places as
the basis for Wahhabization of global Islam. But rather than adherents
and tools of disparate British policy options, they seem more symbolic of
contrasts in British imperial psychology: *Sharif* Husayn, the sincere religious figure, and Lawrence, the high-minded intellectual, versus Ibn
Sa'ud and Philby, a couple of adventurers whose mental horizons, regardless of their political gifts, could not have been lower.

Lawrence himself seemed to partly understand the differences among
the Englishmen who went to Arabia at that time. In the introduction to
his memoir of the Arab Revolt, *Seven Pillars of Wisdom*, he wrote memorably, "All men dream, but not equally. Those who dream by night in the
dusty recesses of their minds wake in the day to find that it was vanity; but
the dreamers of the day are dangerous men, for they may act their dream
with open eyes, to make it possible." Lawrence saw himself as such a
dreamer. He dreamt of "a new nation," to provide the Arabs with "an
inspired dream-palace of their national thoughts," built on "the inherent
nobility of their minds." But in his idealism, Lawrence did not see, or did
not choose to notice, that dreams, whether in sleep or in real life, also dif-
fer in content. It is difficult to imagine Ibn Sa'ud or St. John Philby
dreaming of anything but personal aggrandizement. They were schemers
rather than dreamers. Lawrence stipulated, "for my work on the Arab front
I had determined to accept nothing" as material payment. Philby, by con-

trast, had his eye on the main chance from the beginning. Lawrence made his contribution and returned to Britain; Philby established himself at the court of Ibn Sa'ud and spent the rest of his life buying and selling for his patron. He even became a Wahhabi Muslim.

The Arabist's son, Kim Philby, would describe Lawrence in contemptuous terms, as having "misjudged both the balance of power in the Arabian Peninsula and world interest in the Middle East." The dominant figure in contemporary Arabia, Philby wrote, would be neither Lawrence nor a Hashimite prince, but Ibn Sa'ud.

Either way, the aims of British policy in the Arabian Peninsula were the same: to add new and strong links to the chain of imperial authority in the Indian Ocean. An arc of power, with India the prize at its zenith, extended from south and east Africa, past Aden and Oman, to the coasts of today's Pakistan, through India to the Malay Peninsula and south to Australia. In this vast area, Britain ruled without challenge. Territories were held in Africa by Italy and Portugal, and today's Indonesia was a possession of Holland—but all these minor partners did Britain's bidding. Iran was virtually a British puppet; only Thailand was fully independent, and even it came under British pressure. Although seldom viewed in such terms today, the Indian Ocean represented a single sphere of British domination. Furthermore, Islam had followed Indian Ocean maritime routes to establish itself in the same region. The imposition of a pro-British regime over the Two Holy Places would therefore serve two overlapping ends: It would strengthen imperial strategic security while reinforcing the loyalties of the millions and millions of Muslims who were British subjects.

It is useless, at this point, to imagine how their broader interests might have been affected had Britain more consistently favored *Sharif* Husayn over Ibn Sa'ud. Since the *sharif* of Mecca had never had authority in the eastern Arabian regions where oil was found, the wealth of hydrocarbon resources would probably have remained in Ibn Sa'ud's hands and might well have been exploited by U.S. rather than British enterprises. But two things are certain: Had Britain defended the Hashimites in the Two Holy Places, Wahhabism would have remained an obscure, deviant cult, and the Peninsula would very likely have developed modern political institutions.

The British seem never to have thought that a "reformed" Islam, stripped of its customary culture and impregnated with separatism, supremacism, and violence in the name of virtue—the values that had stirred Britain's own Puritan past—might someday launch a suicidal, destructive challenge to the Christian world. Or perhaps they did not care; like Ibn Sa'ud, they were gambling with the future. Eventually, the Wahhabis interpreted the failure of the Western powers to perceive their intent as a sign of the unbelievers' stupidity and as a license to continue swindling and otherwise taking advantage of them. The success of this deception would be repeated by the Saudis in their dealings with the United States, through the rise of the Arabian oil industry, the war in Afghanistan in the 1980s, and the events and even the aftermath of September 11, 2001.

However, the paradox of Ibn Sa'ud's situation cut in both directions. While the British could be fooled about the real nature of Wahhabism, numerous Wahhabis could not be fooled about the intentions of the British. They knew the British, in their Arabian intrigues, had their own interests at heart, which did not ultimately coincide with those of the Wahhabis. The City of London might have been perfectly happy, in the interest of short-term profits, to bankroll Muslim extremists bent on the imposition of a worldwide theocratic terror regime, but some of the fanatics, back in the wastelands of Najd, seem to have had reservations about the arrangement from the beginning. The problem would not go away, and it did not only involve the British and Al Sa'ud. Over the long run the greatest grief for both the Wahhabis and their Christian accomplices would come from neither Arabia itself nor the West, but from the rest of the Muslims, who never reconciled themselves either to Wahhabi dictation or its patronage by non-Muslim diplomacy. The painful and convoluted history of the Middle East throughout the 20th century would owe a great deal to decisions made in the 1920s about Mecca and Medina by global gamblers in London and Riyadh.

Sharif Husayn of Mecca lent himself to the decision by which Mecca and Medina came under Wahhabi control. The Hashimites had become deeply involved in the Allied disposition of the Middle East after the war's end, but Husayn grew disaffected with the British-French arrangement under which Syria and other successor states would be governed—and which would also lead to the establishment of a Jewish state. In 1924 Husayn recognized the Soviet Union, thus aggravating the deterioration of his relations with Britain. Ibn Sa'ud then summoned the *Ikhwan* anew to the conquest of Mecca and Medina. He seemed confident that the British would not interfere. His subsidy from them had ended, but that also represented his release from foreign restraint.

Dissatisfaction appeared in the Wahhabis' own ranks even as Al Sa'ud consummated Wahhabi-Saudi ambitions toward rulership in Arabia. Indeed, Ibn Sa'ud would soon be plagued by the conflict between the extremism of the *Ikhwan* and the requirements of statecraft in a world where his power owed more to the benevolence of the British, and later the Americans, than Wahhabi beseechings to God. The dichotomy between the Wahhabis' absolute rejection of saintly intermediaries and their preaching of absolute dependence on God, on the one hand, and the political necessity of support from unbelievers on the other, has been the source of the dangerous dissonance within the Wahhabi mentality. In every generation a Wahhabi trend has appeared that was dissatisfied with this obvious hypocrisy.

More important, at first, than its theological contradiction, was the political nature of the Wahhabi-Saudi regime. Wahhabism had created a totalitarian system—a dictatorship resting on an ideological militia, the *Ikhwan*. When the *Ikhwan* was founded in 1912, the phenomenon of totalitarianism barely existed. In European society, it was chiefly represented by Lenin's Russian socialist faction and the modernist/imperialist rhetoric of Italian Futurism—products, let it be noted, of second-rate powers active in the destruction of the Ottoman Empire. Extremist nationalist movements in the Balkans, as well as in India, also assumed conspiratorial and militaristic forms. However, it does not seem that any political developments outside Arabia directly influenced the formation of the *Ikhwan*. The *Ikhwan* were young sons of the desert who had emerged from a hopeless nothingness of petty rivalries and banditry, and who viewed human life in terms devoid of sophistication or cosmopolitan understanding. They could not imagine learning from the rest of the Islamic *ummah*, much less the rest of global society. Rather, they would teach the world about the emptiness in their hearts, which reproduced the void of their social existence.

Muhammad had taken the Arabs out of the desert and, through Islam, brought them to a great destiny in the world. Now the *Ikhwan*, whose psychology was rooted in the suspicion of all isolated rural folk toward the outer world, would seek to drag the peninsular Arabs, and then the world's Muslims, into the abyss from which the *Ikhwan* had come and from which there was, finally, only one escape: death in *"jihad"* and attainment of Paradise.

Remarkably, the Wahhabis came up with a premonitory form of fascism on their own, independent of other models or examples. Building on a paramilitary political structure comparable to the Bolsheviks and Nazis, the Wahhabis established a system of governance based on a monopoly of wealth by the elite, backed by extreme repression and a taste for bloodshed. Their subsidiary methods included a brutal secret police, censorship, rigid control of education, and incitement to genocide against minorities (mainly, the Shi'as, but by extension, all non-Wahhabi Muslims, as well as Christians and Jews).

Wahhabi ideology had previously revived, in a more vigorous form than any ever seen in Islam, the tendencies toward separatism which had existed since the time of the Khawarij. In its 20th-century form, its theology was fundamentalist, but its political tools were surprisingly modern. In one of the greatest of all historical paradoxes, this reactionary utopia gained ascendancy through the newest totalitarian methods. Far behind the rest of the globe in economy and technology, Wahhabis had leaped far ahead of it in political sociology. This experience would be repeated, as the 20th century gave way to the 21st. The *Ikhwan*, who reproduced the mentality of the Khawarij, also anticipated the terrorism of the Saudi-backed Hamas in Israel, which became infamous for their suicide bombing attacks on civilians. But the *Ikhwan* and the later phenomenon of Hamas both evinced another feature of Islamic totalitarianism: Created for limited, political ends, they tended to escape or challenge their mentors' manipulation. In 2002, Hamas, Palestinian Islamic Jihad, and the Wahhabi-style Al-Aqsa Martyrs Brigade, a wing of the secular Fatah movement of Yasir Arafat, appeared to defy Saudi offers of peace with Israel. It was tempting to see the gap between Saudi peace rhetoric and Hamas bombings as typical, two-faced deception from the Arab side. But a real breakdown in control could not be excluded.

Certainly, the Wahhabi-Saudi regime of the 1920s was plagued by its internal inconsistencies. After taking power, Ibn Sa'ud had swept aside the forward-looking political structures, including a written constitution and civil courts, that had developed in Hejaz prior to the Wahhabi reconquest of Mecca. The new state was based on three powers: the whims of Ibn Sa'ud, the Wahhabi interpretation of *Qur'an* (which became the country's constitution), and the sword—specifically, the ruler's personal implement for executions, the saber known as "The Neck-Cutter" or *raqban*. In the following years, the rigid Wahhabi form of *Shariah* would be imposed as an exclusively religious-based law. Wahhabi doctrine called on the people to read only *Qur'an* and Wahhabi texts and to refrain from composing literary works, including poetry. However, even as he consolidated his rule, Ibn Sa'ud began to experience open tensions with the *Ikhwan*. The conflict was expressed first on the issue of modern technology. The Wahhabis had never rejected the use of rifles and other military inventions, but the *Ikhwan* were deeply suspicious of the introduction of the telegraph and telephone, radio and automobile transportation, which were viewed as inventions of Satan. (Reconstruction of the Hejaz Railway, built by the Ottomans and wrecked in the first world war, did not begin until the end of the 20th century.)

Another major conflict involved music, the bane of the Wahhabis. During the 1926 international Muslim conference in Mecca, a party of Egyptian pilgrims approached the city with musical accompaniment, a long-established custom. A group of *Ikhwan* who had reputedly never heard music before were so inflamed that an exchange of gunfire occurred, in which numerous people were killed. Cautious about offending the already irritable participants in the Muslim conference, Ibn Sa'ud refrained from punishing the Egyptians involved in the incident, as the *Ikhwan* wished. The *Ikhwan* were further aggravated by this weakness in the face of "unbelievers" who happened to be pious Muslims. But it was clear that the *hajj* would, hereafter, be administered by Wahhabi rules.

This was even more shocking to the Shi'as, who also accompanied the *hajj* with their own customs.

As a check on the extremism of the *Ikhwan*, Ibn Sa'ud founded the body that would become the country's secret police. Headed by two Wahhabis, the League for the Encouragement of Virtue and Prevention of Vice would establish Public Morals Committees to act as its eyes and ears among the masses. (They are known in Arabic as the *mutawiyin*, or "volunteers," a title borrowed from the earlier Wahhabi agitators.) Apparently unknowing, the Wahhabis paralleled the Bolshevik regime in Russia and the Fascist state in Italy, both of which used local vigilance committees to control public life. That one state was based on a narrow interpretation of Islam, while another cleaved to revolutionary socialism and the third to futurist nationalism, meant very little; the state form was virtually identical.

The dictatorial Wahhabi state also had much in common with the secularist military regime of Mustafa Kemal in Turkey. A Soviet diplomat reporting from the country, cited by a Wahhabophile Russian historian of Saudi Arabia, Alexei Vassiliev, explained the fanaticism of the regime in terms of its dependence on the *hajj* income; obviously, a country whose budget was derived from religious works could not embrace secularism. But the Soviet Union was the first government to recognize Ibn Sa'ud as King of Hejaz, in 1927.

That Wahhabi obscurantism and its totalitarian state had to do with more than the collection of religious fees escaped the Bolshevik observer. Theft was a much greater incentive to Wahhabi extremism and even to *Ikhwan* dissatisfaction with Ibn Sa'ud. Vassiliev writes, "The 'brethren' felt that they had not had their fair share of the spoils in Hejaz and Ibn Saud's prohibition on raids across the borders of Kuwait, Iraq, and Transjordan deprived them of the opportunity to improve their material conditions by plundering 'infidels,'" i.e., non-Wahhabi Muslims. But the Bolsheviks in Moscow seem clearly to have recognized in the monarchy of Ibn Sa'ud, and in Wahhabism generally, a phenomenon not unlike their own movement. Neither they nor the Saudis seem ever to have mentioned to the other that the Russian Communists had established their power in the

Central Asian Soviet republics through a ruthless struggle against Islamic resistance, and especially against the Sufi orders.

The early regime of Ibn Sa'ud reproduced the structure of Bolshevism and Nazism at the commencement of their rule and, also like Bolshevism and Nazism, quickly reduced their unwieldy third element—the mass of ordinary people drawn into the political struggle—to a more manageable and concentrated dual partnership of power. All such systems began with a division of influence between ideological cadres (in the Saudi case, the Wahhabi scholars), the "popular" militia (the *Ikhwan*), and the state structure (occupied by the royal family). In all of them, the elites—party cadres and state—combined to suppress the "popular" or "mass" groupings. Hitler, once attaining power, drew his party closer to the state by purging the Brown Shirts, an unruly force of street fighters, in the 1934 "night of the long knives."

With the death of Lenin, Stalin greatly enlarged what had been a select Bolshevik membership into a mass organization, which he used to conquer the heights of the Soviet bureaucracy. But he, like Hitler, devastated the human machinery he inherited, as well as the Red Army, leaving in their place flaccid, deactivized bodies characterized by supine loyalty to his will, although the Russian ruling party retained its immense social and political privileges. In addition, in all these instances, the purging of the mass movements widened the role of the secret police, although it remained clearly subordinate to the party and state in a way the militias were not. The Soviet KGB, the Nazi Gestapo, and the Saudi *mutawiyin* were identical in this regard. The sole major distinction between the two European examples and the last was the dynastic relationship between the Wahhabi ideological element and the Saudi ruling family, based on their 18th-century marriage alliance. The course of Ibn Sa'ud after he gained power was therefore inevitable; he could not help but follow the pattern of all totalitarian states.

A group of dissident *Ikhwan* presented a bill of particulars to Ibn Sa'ud at the beginning of 1927. They complained against the maintenance of a favorable relationship with Britain, introduction of new communications and transport technology, and toleration of the Shi'as in Hasa and elsewhere, who should be compelled to accept Wahhabism or else be liqui-

dated. Ibn Sa'ud came away from this confrontation victorious; the assembled leaders named him King of Najd and Hejaz. Yet his position was still
somewhat insecure in the face of Wahhabi agitation. Britain chose this
moment to renegotiate its treaty with Al Sa'ud, strengthening their recognition of his sovereignty. But an *Ikhwan* faction commenced provocative
raids into Iraq, ruled by King Faisal, the Hashimite son of *Sharif* Husayn
of Mecca. The *Ikhwan* incursions were met by British air raids.

Ibn Sa'ud responded by refining the two-faced policy that has been a
constant in Saudi history. He demagogically denounced the British to the
Ikhwan, while at the same time acting to prevent a serious clash with the
British, the real masters in Iraq. Philby wrote, "He was at one with his subjects in condemning the attitude of the British government; and his subjects, whose fanaticism had been fanned into flame by infidel insults and
injuries, were ready to fight to the death for his cause. . . . He also knew
that the desert was in ferment to the point of challenging his policy of
accommodation with the infidel." Unlike postwar Turkey, which imitated
Italy in the stabilization of its authoritarian regime, Arabia under Al Sa'ud
began to resemble revolutionary China and Mexico, which had dissolved
into warlord zones. But in Najd such had always been the way power was
exercised, so that it appeared the Peninsula would simply relapse into disorder after a brief period of artificial unification under the Wahhabis.

A real civil war broke out in 1929, marked, among other incidents, by
the murder of an American missionary. But the conflict ended quickly in
another victory by Ibn Sa'ud over the recalcitrant *Ikhwan*, and the radical
wing of Wahhabism was firmly subjugated. The totalitarian state had triumphed over its restive storm troopers, while the Wahhabi religious
bureaucracy was left untouched and retained its control over the Two
Holy Places. Thus by 1932, all power had been concentrated in Ibn
Sa'ud's hands and the kingdom of Saudi Arabia was proclaimed—the
only country in the world named for a living person.

The Saudi society of the 1930s had been subordinated to Wahhabi religious command, but the country's population did not submit uniformly,
notwithstanding the reports of Western apologists who reproduced Wahhabi claims that they held the enthusiastic and loving allegiance of an
overwhelming majority. Non-Wahhabi Sunnis have proven impossible to

remove completely from the country. Heroic groups of Sufis have also persisted, carefully hiding their activities, while in parts of the oil-bearing Eastern Province, Shi'as have never numbered fewer than 90 percent; only the ruling commercial and landholding classes were Wahhabi in the years before the second world war. Shi'a communities have held on, under extremely difficult conditions, in the vicinity of Medina and in the southern area of Najran. In addition, although both Wahhabis and, recently, Westerners have dwelt on the banishment of non-Muslims from Arabia, local Christians maintained a church in Jeddah until the Wahhabi reconquest of the 1920s, and some have doubtless survived clandestinely through the following decades. With a large Jewish community remaining in Yemen, moreover, some Jews were also present within the borders of the Saudi kingdom until fairly recently.

Against much opposition, the Wahhabis worked to spread their rigid variant of Hanbali jurisprudence to the whole country from their stronghold in Najd. Shi'as, who followed their own legal canons, were not the only group to resist. The Wahhabi-Saudi state also sought to eradicate customary law, which had much tribal support, and non-Hanbali legal schools, although repressed, long remained present in Hejaz, the region of the Two Holy Places, and in the towns that had been governed by the Ottomans. As was typical of them, the Ottomans had supported a pluralistic jurisprudence headed by four representatives of the standard Sunni schools, although the Hanafi school tended to dominate as elsewhere in the empire. Such pluralism was anathema to the Wahhabis, who dedicated themselves to a relentless unitarism and centralization of legal practice.

Wahhabism also was and remains the backbone of the Saudi educational system, founded soon after the reestablishment of the dual family power in the 1920s. From the beginning, Wahhabi pedagogy emphasized religion to such a degree that even after the second world war, almost 80 percent of elementary schooling consisted of instruction in Wahhabi doctrine—that is to say, in the violent hatred of all non-Wahhabi Muslims as well as adherents of other faiths.

Undeveloped in commerce and industry, purged of its traditional spiritual and intellectual life, dependent on other countries for its food supply,

Saudi Arabia, at the beginning, did not undergo the social and political conflicts and rivalries seen in most other Muslim countries. Without a laboring class, it generated no unions or strikes; locked into the prison of Wahhabi doctrine, its educated folk remained unaffected by new ideas from abroad; nor did it possess the significant peasant strata that played a leading role in other Islamic lands from Morocco to Malaysia. In the isolated Wahhabi experiment, only religious differences were a source of ferment. Such was Saudi Arabia on the eve of its entry into the world's petroleum markets.

With the discovery of oil in Arabia, the Wahhabi-Saudi state would soon pass irrevocably from the British to the U.S. sphere of influence. Hydrocarbons turned the Wahhabis and Al Sa'ud, already the most extreme totalitarians on the planet, into the world's richest and most powerful ruling elite. Yet at the same time, the sudden windfall of wealth would greatly aggravate the contradiction between Wahhabi extremism and Saudi political opportunism.

Oil, more than control of Mecca and Medina, made Saudi Arabia a global power and its theopolitical ideology an issue for the world. In the process, Al Sa'ud expended very little more of its own blood. In 1931, the year before Saudi Arabia's formal establishment, two Americans, Charles R. Crane and Karl S. Twitchell, visited Ibn Sa'ud and were commissioned to carry out the country's first geological survey. Twitchell reported the strong probability of oil deposits in Hasa. He was temporarily hired by the Standard Oil Company of California, or Socal (predecessor of today's ChevronTexaco), which sought an Arabian petroleum concession.

The stage was set for the transformation of politics, religion, and economy not only in Arabia but throughout the world. The active players aside from Ibn Sa'ud—Crane and Twitchell, who had originally come to Arabia as hydrologists, and the representatives of Socal—were being manipulated from behind the scenes by St. John Philby, who perceived that petroleum would make Al Sa'ud incalculably rich. In 1932, Socal struck oil in Bahrein and serious negotiations began between Ibn Sa'ud and the company, which hired Philby. The Socal salary paid to Philby was spent on his son's education at Cambridge, where the younger Philby was recruited as an active Soviet spy. (We have convincing evidence that the elder Philby previously benefited from a clandestine financial relationship with Moscow.) By the middle of 1933, a deal had been concluded: Socal gained a 60-year concession for oil development in Saudi Arabia. Thanks to Philby, Britain, which had previously dominated the oil business in the Middle East, was left out of the arrangement, at least temporarily.

Much may be said about the enterprise that had obtained the concession—Standard Oil of California. A contract involving Ibn Sa'ud, St. John Philby, and Socal has the air of a witches' Sabbath bringing together the most extreme reactionary state in the world, a flamboyant example of the degeneracy of the British ruling class, and the most hated capitalists in American history. Through the second half of the 19th century, Standard Oil and the Rockefeller family that created it garnered a reputation as overwhelmingly abusive corporate neighbors and employers, the very incarnation of commercial greed. The Standard Oil combine had driven rivals large and small out of the marketplace; indeed its anticompetitive policies led to the creation of antitrust law in the United States.

Rockefeller's labor policies were symbolized by the "Ludlow massacre" of 1914, in which a dozen wives and children of coal miners striking against the Rockefeller-owned Colorado Fuel & Iron Company were shot and burned to death by company-hired detectives, along with eight men participating in the work stoppage. None of the company guards was ever arrested or punished. The day after this incident, when news of the atrocity was printed in gigantic, blood-red headlines from coast to coast, the workers of America felt a deep, murderous anger at John D. Rockefeller. Thousands, if not millions, of Americans would have slain him if given the chance.

Standard Oil of California had not learned very much from its history; or perhaps it had learned too much. The original Standard trust had been broken up into a group of allegedly independent companies, of which Socal was one. But political sanctions against monopoly did not encourage Socal to adopt more enlightened public policies. On the U.S. West Coast in the 1930s, the company was infamous for its persecution of union members through surveillance and blacklisting; it was enemy number one of the resurgent Pacific Coast labor movement. In 1935 it attempted to frame a group of striking sailors in California on terrorism charges. The abysmal conditions in which its tankship crews and refinery workers toiled were notorious. So were the misery and squalor of its company-controlled towns, such as Richmond and El Segundo. In many respects California was simply an economic possession of Standard Oil. It might seem, then, that the alliance of these dark forces was a natural one.

It is well to recall the state of Europe, the Americas, Africa, and Asia in the late 1930s, when Socal was poised to locate the richest oilfields on the planet. The industrial world struggled with the Great Depression. Everywhere the existing order was in profound crisis. The European control of world markets was the subject of a vicious rivalry between the Anglo-French alignment and the aggressive fascist and militarist powers, Germany, Italy, and Japan. In Europe, much of the working class, even in leading countries like Britain and France, was impoverished and aggrieved. Revolutionary movements promised the overthrow of capitalism. In Spain, a social-revolutionary war had broken out, and in Russia Stalin had embarked on the physical liquidation of the generation whose revolution had put him in power. The United States was busy erecting a social welfare system to rescue its society from the collapse of the international economy.

By 1950 every one of these deep conflicts had passed from the scene. They had not been drowned in blood by the combat of the second world war, but in Arabian oil, which allowed the swift recapitalization and restructuring of the world economy and the foundation of permanently affluent societies in Europe, the Americas, and east Asia. The old class divisions that had wracked Europe and fed the radical appeal of Soviet Communism simply vanished. The capitalist and democratic world was reborn. But there was a trade-off. In the West, all would benefit from the illumination and prosperity made possible by the flow of Saudi petroleum. But the Muslim *ummah*, and the subjects of the Saudi monarchy, would suffer under an unrelenting and ever-greater corruption and hypocrisy.

Socal did not find oil in Saudi territory until 1938. In 1936, Socal and the Texas Oil Company had created a partnership, which would come to be named Aramco—the Arabian-American Oil Company—to drain, refine, and sell the Saudi kingdom's subsoil resources. The first oil strike, at Dammam Dome Number 7, produced 100,000 barrels before the end of two months. Ten years later, in 1948, Aramco located Ghawar, which remains the largest oil field on the planet.

Saudi oil production was interrupted by the second world war, and royal income fell. In addition, *hajj* revenues were again threatened by the outbreak of global combat. Although the regime was aligned with Britain, Saudi Arabia remained neutral. History has concentrated on the fighting in Europe, but the real war aims of the Axis—Germany, Italy, and Japan, as well as their "silent partner" in 1939–41, Stalinist Russia—involved a new division of world markets and colonial territories. Saudi Arabia was surrounded by war fronts. The Germans, who lacked energy resources, were aggressively interested in Arab oil, and repeatedly attempted to replace the British as the Saudis' protectors. Nazi propaganda emphasized the injustices of British imperialism while also fostering anxieties about Zionist interests in Palestine. After the fall of France, the pro-Nazi Vichy regime controlled Syria.

In 1941, a pro-Nazi coup took place in Iraq, but was defeated within weeks by the British. However, Nazi agents on the Iraqi-Saudi border attacked the oil fields in the Eastern Province. Soon afterward, the Vichy regime was overthrown in Syria by British and Free French troops. The Axis challenge in the Middle East had clearly been rebuffed, even though German and Italian forces continued fighting in North Africa. Ibn Sa'ud again revealed his family's penchant for duplicity by giving asylum to Rashid Ali, leader of the Iraqi coup. In addition, St. John Philby, who was quite a loudmouth, had spent much of the beginning of the war in Saudi Arabia, giving vent to defeatist opinions in his discussions with Ibn Sa'ud, including expressions of admiration for Hitler as a "mystic." He was arrested by the British and interned for seven months in 1940–41.

American authorities attempted to turn Socal into a firm asset in the war effort, but by all indications the company turned the tables and used Washington to secure its interests, rather than serving the immediate military needs of the United States. Thus Saudi Arabia suddenly became a major American ally even though it maintained its neutral stance until the end of the European war. Socal convinced the administration of Franklin Roosevelt that support for Ibn Sa'ud on its, and his, terms would result in the United States permanently excluding Britain from the exploitation of Arabian oil. American officials concluded that the shift of oil development from Latin America and the United States to the Arabian Peninsula would make the supply more plentiful, cheaper, and easier to process. Accordingly, the Saudi monarchy was granted millions of dollars in lend-lease aid.

The Saudi monarchy entered another new phase in 1945 when Roosevelt met with Ibn Sa'ud aboard the USS *Quincy* in Egypt's Great Bitter Lake. The American president tried unsuccessfully to gain Saudi approval for increased Jewish settlement in Palestine. However, the monarch agreed to a U.S.-Saudi economic alliance, which would prove far more useful to Al Sa'ud than their former links with Britain. Under the new conditions obtaining between the two countries, American military and technical personnel would be admitted to the kingdom; a U. S. Air Force base was built at Dhahran in 1946. But Saudi Arabia had become a business partner of the United States, more than a military asset, and Britain retained major responsibility for Western security interests in Arabia for another decade. The new arrangement was predicated on Saudi Arabia declaring war on the Axis, which it did within a month of the Roosevelt-Ibn Sa'ud encounter—and which allowed it to be included in the founding conference of the United Nations.

At the time of the meeting with Roosevelt, curiously, the Saudis seem to have made their first contacts with American Jew-baiters and fascist agitators. But the United States had clearly adopted a "hands off" policy toward Saudi internal and ideological matters. It was also then that Aramco and its friends in American public life began a long and shameless effort to prettify the extremist and terrorist origins of the monarchy. Hypocrisy about the backward and corrupt nature of the Wahhabi-Saudi regime was not limited to Arabia itself. J. B. Kelly wrote that Aramco "constituted itself the interpreter of Saudi Arabia—its people, its history, its culture, and above all its ruling house—to the United States at large, and because there were no other sources of information about that country open to the American public, ARAMCO could put across its version of recent Arabian history and politics with almost insolent ease. . . . Naturally, little prominence was accorded in ARAMCO's publicity to the fanatical nature of Wahhabism, or to its dark and bloody past."

The flight of European Jews to Palestine in the years after the second world war, and the foundation of Israel in 1948, aggravated the duplicitous nature of Saudi relations with the West. Britain had never been a consistent friend of the Zionist movement, and Ibn Sa'ud had managed to keep British support by an elaborate series of hints, ambivalent statements, and plots. A Hashimite dynasty, which he viewed with extreme dislike, had been placed in power in today's Jordan under King Abdullah and asserted sovereignty over Palestine, in contradiction to the 1917 Balfour Declaration and its pledge that a Jewish homeland would be established in the Middle East. Since he would not support Hashimites, Ibn Sa'ud aided the more radical *Mufti* of Jerusalem, Haj Amin al-Husayni, who became a German agent, while also encouraging clans opposed to the *Mufti*. After 1945, the British sought al-Husayni for trial, but Ibn Sa'ud provided secret shelter to the *Mufti*, as he had previously welcomed Rashid Ali, the Nazi agent from Iraq.

When the Jewish state was proclaimed, its Arab neighbors invaded it and were badly defeated. Ibn Sa'ud publicly supported the war on Israel but did not send troops to the front and arrested those among his own subjects who went there to fight. It has long been believed by Arabs that Ibn Sa'ud and his successors feared their unification against Israel, which could turn against him, more than he resented the foundation of the Jewish state. After the war was over, displaced Palestinians were barred from entering the Saudi kingdom, out of anxiety that they, having never lived under a Wahhabi-style regime, would stimulate discontent. This hypocritical stance proved extremely durable. Throughout the half-century that followed, the House of Sa'ud attempted to balance its dependence on an American power that was also pro-Israel with anti-Jewish rhetoric, given extra spice by Wahhabi hatemongering. Classical Islam lacked a major body of writings attacking the Jews and their religion, but the Wahhabi clerics rushed to fill the gap with new interpretations.

The greatly expanded postwar oil revenues were monopolized by the Houses of Ibn Abd al-Wahhab and Al Sa'ud to maintain their unique variant of family governance. Even though their influence was eclipsed by the political authority of the offspring of Al Sa'ud, the descendants of Ibn Abd al-Wahhab were provided with generous subsidies and the two lines continued intermarrying. For example, King Faisal, a son of Ibn Sa'ud and a female member of the family of Ibn Abd al-Wahhab, reigned from 1964 until he was murdered by a nephew in 1975. Meanwhile the voracious demand of Ibn Sa'ud and his cohort for women produced armies of wives and concubines, as well as an enormous dynasty of princes. By the end of the 20th century the ranks of the main princely lines were estimated at 4,000. History had seen many hereditary monarchies, but the Wahhabi-Saudi regime remained unique in also maintaining a hereditary religious hierarchy. The descendants of the Wahhabi founders, the second most powerful family in the land, continued directing its theological affairs, while still casting jealous eyes on the rest of the global Islamic community.

The vast mafia of princely parasites, over some 70 years, further exacerbated the clash between Wahhabi claims of fundamentalist puritanism and the real character of their rule. Previously known for mixing religious piety and political opportunism, the Saudis introduced the new and even more outrageous problem of their private immorality. The Saudi aristocracy would become known as "airport Wahhabis"—once their private jets left the runways, bottles of whisky appeared, women's veils disappeared, and a high time was had by all. The "Saudi oil prince" became an unparalleled symbol of debauchery, ostentation, and waste, as well as ignorance, prejudice, and brutality. Expenditures to clothe and bejewel their women, indulge their children, build and decorate their palaces, and otherwise satisfy their appetites became legendary. Their tastes led them to taverns, casinos, brothels, and similar establishments. They bought fleets of automobiles, private jets, and yachts the size of warships. They invested in valuable Western art they did not understand or like and which often offended the sensitivities of Wahhabi clerics. They spent as they wished, becoming patrons of international sexual enslavement and the exploitation of children. Yet at the same time, they dedicated a large proportion of their wealth to the promotion of international Wahhabi radicalism, in a desperate attempt to bridge the gulf between pretense and reality.

One of the beneficiaries of both Wahhabi fanaticism and Saudi royal squandering was an illiterate Yemeni, formerly a laborer for Aramco, named Muhammad bin Laden, who became known as the personal construction boss of the monarchs. Bin Laden supervised such large, garish, and very expensive projects as the oversized "mosques" built around the Ka'bah in Mecca and in Medina, in the style best known as Islamic kitsch. He shared the extremism of the Wahhabis, and his 17th son, born in 1957, would become an outstanding figure in the history of the Wahhabi death cult: He was named Osama.

How was it that the grotesque duplicity of the Saudi regime—fostering official puritanism and unofficial degeneracy, proclaiming loyalty to Islam while rooting out its traditions, and agitating for the wholesale destruction of Israel while proclaiming its loyalty to the United States—was ignored for so long by Western leaders and public opinion? A closed society and the political demands of the oil economy are insufficient explanations, although the Aramco partners played the greatest role by their consistent favorable publicity. The fruits of this decades-long campaign may be found in virtually any Western volume on Islam, where Wahhabism is either ignored or treated with great courtesy, if not admiration. Often this latter outlook is overlaid with "political correctness." Here, for example, is the best-selling Thomas W. Lippman: "In the West, we may think of Saudi Arabia as a country where reactionary attitudes and obscurantism still prevail while other Muslim societies are modernizing, but the Saudis would hardly agree. They see Wahhabism as the movement that freed Islam . . . Literalists in interpretation of the Koran, the Wahhabis paradoxically liberated the individual believer." This would be paradoxical indeed, if it were true. Lippman further observes that Wahhabism "enhanced the world's image of Islam as a serious and dignified religion . . . it demonstrated that Koranic literalism, the *Shariah*, and Islam itself were not incompatible with technology and science." This opinion is hard to reconcile with the Wahhabi opposition to telephones and automobiles, acceptance of which Ibn Sa'ud forced on them. But it should be even more difficult to sustain given such examples as that of the blind Wahhabi *imam* Abdul-Aziz bin Baz, who died at 85 in 1999.

Six months after September 11, 2001, in a private gathering in Washington, a former U.S. ambassador to Saudi Arabia, Wyche Fowler, Jr., an appointee of Bill Clinton, after losing his seat as U.S. Senator from Georgia (Democratic), fondly recalled his many chats with bin Baz in which they pondered the differences between American and Saudi life. These colloquies were presumably conducted through translators, since Fowler and bin Baz were equally lacking in their knowledge of the other's language. Glorified by the Saudi regime as a pillar of Islamic wisdom, bin Baz issued a *fatwa* in 1969 stating that the earth is a flat disk around which the sun revolves and that any belief otherwise was heresy, to be severely punished. He corrected himself after Prince Sultan, a grandson of Ibu Sa'ud, took a ride in an American space shuttle in 1985 and told bin Baz that he had personally witnessed the roundness of the earth.

Forty years after Ibn Sa'ud imposed modern communications and transportation on the Wahhabis, little in their worldview had changed. Television transmissions during the early 1960s were restricted to images of nonanimate life, such as palm trees, and advanced little beyond this for decades. Bin Baz also authored a notorious *fatwa* against women driving. He opined, "Depravity leads to the innocent and pure women being accused of indecencies. Allah has laid down one of the harshest punishments for such an act in order to protect society from the spreading of the causes of depravity. Women driving cars, however, is one of the causes that lead to that." As late as 1994, his colleagues in the Saudi religious structure issued a *fatwa* against the preservation of historical buildings on the grounds that it encouraged "polytheism."

Lippman mistakenly writes, "Wahhabis are no longer thought of as being outside the mainstream of [Islam]. In many ways they are the mainstream." Fortunately, this naive and erroneous view was and remains more common among Western Wahhabophiles than among traditional Muslims worldwide. But between the first flows of oil and money from and to the Peninsula in the 1930s and the crisis of Islam and its relations with the non-Muslim world at the end of the century, Wahhabism went a long way toward achieving this nefarious end. The flattering platitudes of Lippman are echoed redundantly, here, there, and everywhere. Daniel Yergin, in his canonical volume on the oil industry, *The Prize*, passes over Wahhabism on two of his 900-plus pages. The Wahhabis, he observes, "espoused a stern, puritanical version of Islam." Yergin dresses up the exactions visited by the Wahhabis on the Shi'a Muslims of Hasa, declaring that Ibn Sa'ud, in 1913–14, "regulariz[ed] their status and prevent[ed] their harassment." This comment contrasts sharply with the view of the more clear-eyed J. B. Kelly: "When Ibn Sa'ud regained Hasa in 1913 the Hasawis were again subjected to persecution—though not enough, to be sure, to slake the *Ikhwan's* thirst for vengeance—a persecution which was not eased until many years later." The Shi'as of Hasa finally experienced some relief only because the Socal wells were in their district and it became the treasure house of the kingdom.

Diminishing the extremism of the Wahhabis is, however, especially pronounced among historians of comparative religion. For example, Karen Armstrong, widely cited in the aftermath of September 11, in her brief survey of Islamic history, refers to it in mild terms. For her, its founder was a "reformer" who "tried to create an enclave of pure faith." She describes the cult as it functions in Saudi Arabia today as "a puritan religion based on a strictly literal interpretation of scripture and early Islamic tradition," adding little to these benign phrases.

Likewise, the Russian writer Vassiliev, whose *History of Saudi Arabia* has become a standard text in English, praises the Wahhabis as an "egalitarian popular movement" in the mold beloved of second-rate Marxians. It is clear that Vassiliev equated the Wahhabi-Saudi dictatorship with the Communist regime in Russia, with some accuracy as well as considerable sentimentality. A Soviet journalist in Riyadh for a decade and a pure exemplar of Stalinist sociology, Vassiliev gives the impression of mastery of Arabic sources on Wahhabi-Saudi history, yet he asserts, quite falsely, that it is "difficult nowadays to find anti-Wahhabi writings."

St. John Philby himself launched the 20th-century school of Western sycophancy toward the Wahhabis. While it may be difficult to imagine certain of his successors and imitators having been directly paid, as he was, to purvey these myths, if they were not, they should have been. And many of them were and remain recipients of Saudi funds.

But Western gullibility about Wahhabism and the Saudi state involved more than obliviousness about religious history. For 35 years after the first well began gushing at Dammam, the Wahhabis, Al Sa'ud, and Aramco pursued their activities in an untroubled manner. The line between the business of Aramco and the affairs of the United States disappeared. Aramco was enlarged. To Socal and Texaco were added two more successors of the Standard Oil Trust, namely Standard of New Jersey and Socony-Vacuum, the progenitors of ExxonMobil. The Aramco partners, along with British Petroleum (which merged with Amoco, another of the Standard heirs), Royal Dutch Shell, and Gulf Oil became known as The Seven Sisters. These enterprises, together with Al Sa'ud, controlled the world's largest single source of petroleum. But they also bound successive American presidencies, the Congress of the United States, and the U.S. military establishment to an unquestioning defense of the Saudi status quo. The instrument of this entanglement was and remains a Saudi lobby of extraordinary power and effect.

The Saudi lobby has always depended first and foremost on the services of former diplomats like Fowler and journalists like Lippman. It seems to be a virtual law that American ambassadors to the court of Al Sa'ud come back to the United States as honorary Saudi ambassadors to Washington. Often directly paid by the Saudis through various think tanks and academic programs, they have become assiduous defenders of the Wahhabi-Saudi status quo, ready for action whenever they are called upon, backed up by retired managerial and technical personnel from the various Aramco partners. Since few normal scholars and almost no independent journalists from other countries are admitted to the kingdom, those who are granted permission to pursue their professions there seem inevitably to return under Saudi influence, like the historical "specialists" described above.

The most important cog in the machinery of the Saudi lobby is doubtless the Middle East Institute (MEI), based in Washington, with a million-dollar Saudi endowment. It should come as no surprise that six weeks after the hideous events of September 11, MEI appointed Wyche Fowler, Jr., chairman of the board, and that in March 2002 it named Lippman an adjunct scholar, noting that he was preparing a new book on the kingdom. With more U.S. attention than ever before focused on Saudi deception, the regime had hurried to assemble an effective damage-control team.

After the second world war, the course of Wahhabi-Saudi history, as well as the broader fate of the *ummah*, was influenced by other global developments. Among these were the abdication of British power in the Middle and Far East and the founding of Pakistan. The liquidation of other imperialist enterprises included the end of Dutch sovereignty over Indonesia and, eventually, the reduction of France's role in the Arab world. Imperial patronage was taken over in some cases by the United States, in others by the Soviets. But many new Arab and Muslim states were artificial constructs left over from the colonial age, and their political legitimacy was often fragile. Of equal importance, in political terms, was the foundation of the state of Israel in 1948. With the establishment of the Jewish state, much of Arab political thought took flight into Nazi-style conspiratorialism.

In one example of such fantasies, the Wahhabis had long fostered the claim that the Jews aimed at sovereignty over Mecca, to redeem its Abrahamic origin. This lunatic notion remains prevalent in Arab media today. Along with it we find the more predictable belief that the weakness of the Arab states is a consequence of behind-the-scenes control over the United States by Zionism. St. John Philby unsuccessfully tried to arrange a cash payoff for Ibn Sa'ud for a supposed solution in Palestine. But the Saudi king's real understanding of such matters was unsophisticated. He complained in the 1950s that 5,000 Jews in New York City controlled American policies abroad. Meanwhile, the United States built and operated the massive air force base at Dhahran, beginning in 1946, to protect Saudi interests. Dhahran, not coincidentally, was the site of Aramco headquarters.

Ibn Sa'ud died in 1953, and the only country in the world run as a private business came under a new ruler, Sa'ud bin Abdul-Aziz. Just before Ibn Sa'ud died the first strike by Aramco workers took place. But that event had remarkably little impact on the life of the kingdom. The 1956 British-French raid on the Suez Canal and ensuing Egyptian-Israeli fighting, both opposed by the United States, stirred anger in Arabia; in a premonitory incident, King Sa'ud cut off oil export to Britain and France. In 1961 Saudi troops were sent to protect Kuwait from an invasion by

Iraq, which had long asserted a claim on the emirate. In 1962 the U.S. Dhahran air base came under the authority of the Royal Saudi Air Force. Beginning the same year, revolutionary chaos struck the kingdom's southern neighbor, Yemen.

The year 1967 was far more traumatic. Israeli forces delivered a serious defeat to a coalition of Arab states, including the Saudi kingdom, in the Six Day War. The Jewish state took control of Jerusalem, the West Bank of the Jordan River, the Gaza Strip, the Sinai Peninsula, and the Golan Heights. A summit of Arab leaders resolved to use their oil wealth to finance a continuing confrontation with Israel. The more notable outcome of this decision came in 1973, when Egyptian forces crossed the Suez Canal into Sinai and were again badly beaten by the Israelis. The Arab oil exporters, with the Saudi kingdom in the lead, cut output and embargoed sales to the United States and Holland. Aramco was "nationalized" as Saudi Aramco, that is, as a Saudi corporation controlling production.

The conversion of Aramco into a Saudi firm was perhaps the murkiest operation in global business history. Saudi Aramco continued its exclusive export contracts with the U.S. corporations that had created it, and American personnel remained in its leading management strata. Saudi-citizen employment by Saudi Aramco was slow and was expected to reach 87 percent in the year 2005. The replacement of Aramco by Saudi Aramco was a remarkable example of international financial sleight-of-hand.

But more important, during the 1973 oil boycott, American citizens woke up to discover that the cheap gasoline on which their post-1945 dream of mobility and leisure had been built was suddenly so expensive it made any but necessary travel almost impossible. Drivers lined up at the pump, cursing the Arabs. Auto manufacturers began retooling for adoption of energy-efficient designs. Environmental concern about the depletion of fossil fuels, which many had considered hysterical, suddenly became U.S. government policy. And with the restructured business relationship between the kingdom and Saudi Aramco, payments to Al Sa'ud increased manyfold.

Americans were reluctant to seriously moderate their demands for cheap gasoline, which made them both good customers for Aramco and hostages of the Wahhabi religious bureaucracy and the Saudi monarchy. Indeed, it is amazing to ponder, in retrospect, how quickly American concerns about dependence on foreign energy resources, and the nexus between the oil giants and the Saudi elite, receded from popular discourse. That was, of course, the best possible outcome for the corporations and their Arab accomplices. But ultimate responsibility for the continuation of dishonesty and injustice in Arabia, as well as, eventually, the rise of Islamic terrorism, belongs with the Aramco partners and the American political and media elites that have served them.

At the end of the 20th century, global society was convulsed with controversy over issues of cultural relations and noninterference. Leftist academics and intellectuals throughout the world excoriated the United States for its "insensitivity" to Arab and Muslim feelings, opinions, and sentiments. Globalization was attacked for imposing American values on the planet. Yet no American entity could have outdone the Standard Oil successors, Chevron-Texaco and ExxonMobil, in sensitivity toward the Saudi oil elite. Certainly, globalization as represented by the oil giants was not meant to crack the thick layer of Wahhabism that stifled Arabian society. Nonetheless, globalization (especially through information technology) inevitably undermined Wahhabi domination in Arabia. The problem was worse in the West. The failure of American public opinion to engage with the issues of Saudi governance may be blamed mainly on lassitude and even isolationism. But the oil giants must stand accused for assuring that the topic of Wahhabism would be almost completely ignored in the Western academy until September 11. Even after the atrocities of that dark day, questions about Wahhabism were met with blank looks and embarrassment, followed by shocked protestations, attempts to silence discussion, and frequent accusations in New York and Washington that any such investigation must be intended to serve foreign, i.e., Israeli, interests.

In reality, the most powerful Jewish and Israeli leaders had little or no knowledge of what went on in the *ummah* outside the narrow cockpit on which their attention was focused. They did not believe the internal contradictions in Saudi Arabia were of much consequence to them. Israelis and other Jews were much more concerned about Iran. Even among committed Zionists, comments about the responsibility of the Wahhabi-Saudi kleptocrats for the actions of Osama bin Laden and his new *Ikhwan*, al-Qaida, were met with amazement and disbelief. Jews wished to convince themselves that Saudi wealth and the Saudi alliance with Washington would somehow, in the end, make them real moderates. The successful camouflage of Saudi reality depended on the failure of Jewish advocates to expose them, as well as on the immense bribes paid by the kingdom to diplomats and other former visitors, and the extraordinary abdication by Western scholars. Put simply, nobody influential in the West wanted to hear bad news about the Saudis.

Yet the fact remains that the Wahhabi core of the Saudi state had survived unchanged since its creation. The kingdom cleaved to a fundamentalist doctrine under which women were generally confined to the home, and when in public had to cover themselves completely, in excess of the recommendations of traditional Islamic jurisprudence. Television, movies, and other modern inventions were delayed in their introduction, and the ludicrous beliefs of religious functionaries like bin Baz, along with separatism, supremacism, and the inevitable Wahhabization of the whole globe, still dominated the school curriculum. Western friends of Wahhabism happy to denounce traditional Muslims for honoring saints and observing Sufi rituals saw nothing at all to criticize in the unrestrained adulation granted the Saudi rulers and their Wahhabi acolytes. According to many Westerners, it was more sensible for Muslims in Arabia to believe that the earth was flat than to imagine, like the Sufis, that trees might have a spiritual significance. And Westerners either did not notice, did not comprehend, or did not care that after 1973 the Wahhabi-Saudi institutions began a new and immensely ambitious global campaign for the Wahhabization of the *ummah*. Increased petroleum income paid for free trips by foreign Muslims to make *hajj*, construction of new mosques, founding of *medresas* around the world that exclusively promoted the sect's ideology, distribution of free copies of *Qur'an* with Wahhabi commentaries, training of *imams*, dissemination of hate literature, and similar works.

American politicians, military leaders, and intellectuals, it seemed, were obligated by Chevron-Texaco and ExxonMobil to act as low-rent security guards for the local gangsters protecting their assets in the Arabian

Peninsula, even if it meant that thousands would die in New York and Washington when the wild element in the ranks of Big Oil's Saudi protection racket finally cut loose.

At the same time, Wahhabi-Saudi dependence on Western technology and finance, and ultimately, on the sword of the unbelievers—the military forces of Christian America—for their security, inevitably sowed profound instability in Saudi Arabia. This deceit would foreshadow a new series of challenges to the Saudis' credibility, from their own citizens, from the world's Muslims, and from the non-Muslim states that supported Riyadh. The crisis began in 1978, in the countries of Iran, Russia, and Afghanistan, and has yet to end. A new personality appeared on the Islamic horizon: Ayatollah Ruhollah Khomeini. Thanks to Saudi influence, the U.S. government and public were set up to view this previously obscure Iranian cleric as a demonic figure. We shall examine how much justice this portrayal embodied. But it is unarguable that Khomeini would both divert attention from and contribute to the crisis of Saudi society.

CHAPTER 5

The Coming of the *Imam*

KHOMEINI'S ISLAMIC REVOLUTION

The revolutionary era in Arab and Muslim history began in July 1952 with the Egyptian Revolution, led by an army colonel named Gamal-Abdal Nasser. For six months, Egypt had experienced brutal riots against foreign control of the Suez Canal and the long-term presence of British troops on Egyptian soil. On July 23, the Free Officers Committee, a conspiracy organized by Nasser, seized military and government installations and communications. The coup succeeded, with almost no fighting. The victory of the Free Officers was announced over Egyptian radio by one of Nasser's closest comrades, Lieutenant Anwar Sadat. Three days later, King Farouk abdicated and fled the country.

Nasser and his group did not immediately assume power; rather, they governed from behind a figurehead, General Muhammad Naguib. But Naguib was eventually removed, and Nasser came forward as the country's ruler. He thereby joined the ranks of other new national leaders produced by the post-colonial world after the second world war, such as Jawaharlal Nehru in India and Sukarno in Indonesia, both of whom oversaw the departure of imperial power from their populous lands. But

Nasser was also young, virile, and possessed immense charisma. Martial and handsome, seeming more an athlete than a politician, Nasser contrasted dramatically with the old men who then ruled the world, including U.S. President Dwight Eisenhower, the statesmen of Britain and France, and the successors to Stalin in Russia and Ibn Sa'ud in Arabia.

He was also more radical than Nehru or Sukarno. Nasser's ideas and ambitions centered on unification of the Arab nation and modernization of Arab society, under Egyptian leadership, as the means of reviving their past greatness. In this regard, the formative event in Nasser's consciousness, like that of the whole Arab world of his time, was the creation of Israel. When Israel became independent in 1948, it was invaded by the armies of five Arab states: Syria, Lebanon, Jordan, Iraq, and Egypt. All of them, including the Egyptians, were beaten. Nasser was on the front lines and personally witnessed the weakness and incapacity of the Egyptian army in fighting the Israelis; the resulting humiliation was the most significant lesson of the young officer's life. To Nasser the debacle of the Egyptian army symbolized the general crisis of the Arab world.

The crushing of Arab military power was not the only aspect of the Egyptian revolutionary process to which the rise of Israel contributed. Although the parallel is generally overlooked, the successful Zionist struggle against the British occupation of Palestine could not but instill in the Egyptian Arabs the conviction that the long-established imperial proprietor of the Suez Canal could be successfully challenged.

The establishment of Israel was the second in a series of five modern shocks in the relations between the Muslim world and the dominant West. The first was the emergence of a stream of Islamic fundamentalism similar to Wahhabism, but originating outside the Arabian Peninsula, in great part as a protest against Western colonialism. Its adherents were known as "Salafis," appropriating the title of the first two generations of Muslims, the *Salaf* or "Forerunners." After the emergence of the "Salafis" and the victory of Israel, the next succeeding shocks were Nasser's triumph over the West at Suez in 1956 and the Arab energy embargo of 1973.

Between Nasser's revolution and the oil boycott, Arab radicalism mainly followed a path reflecting the difference between the two faces of

Islamic civilization. Nasser himself would not seek to alter the essential pluralism of Egyptian Islamic culture. Indeed, he and other Arab nationalists long cleaved to a secular outlook.

In the context of the Cold War, both the United States and Russia wooed Nasser. Moscow, which had briefly flirted with the state of Israel as a means to oppose British interests in the Middle East, saw Nasser's Pan-Arabism as a potential ally of the worldwide Communist movement in its struggle against Western "imperialism." Nasser, however, was by no means won over by Russian flattery. By 1955, he had joined with Tito, the maverick Communist dictator of Yugoslavia, and with Nehru and Sukarno to form a "neutralist" coalition of nations that would hew to an independent line in the Cold War.

Influential as it was, however, Nasser's Pan-Arab nationalism was but one of several responses to the manifest difficulties in which the Arab states found themselves after the second world war. Some Arab intellectuals had turned to earlier forms of Pan-Arab nationalism and radicalism, while others had immersed themselves in Wahhabi-influenced fundamentalism and separatism. One variation of Pan-Arab radicalism that gained power in Syria and Iraq was the Arab Renaissance Movement or Ba'ath. While the Soviets failed to completely co-opt Nasser's Egypt, they had better luck with the Ba'ath regimes, which was unsurprising in that Moscow had considered Syria and Iraq to be within its geopolitical sphere of influence since the end of the 1930s. In May 1941, Russia had recognized the pro-Nazi regime of Rashid Ali in Baghdad.

The Ba'ath, originally a conspiratorial anticolonialist party, possesses a tortuous history. Founded in 1941, thanks mainly to the efforts of an Orthodox Christian named Michel Aflaq (1910–1989), one of the growing Arab class of radical schoolteachers, the Ba'ath party's ideology combined Pan-Arab unitarism with a nebulous socialism closer to fascism than to the historic left. Notwithstanding his Christian origins, however, Aflaq had many Muslim comrades and eventually sought to merge Arab nationalism with Islam—a fusion with no legitimacy among traditional Muslims. However, the Syrian Ba'ath did develop a strong constituency among Alawis, a powerful Shi'a trend in that country, and extensive political involvement with its military.

In other countries, the reactionary religious movements that called themselves "Salafis" had greater appeal. In claiming the Salafi title, they asserted, like the Wahhabis, that every development in Islam after its early period should be expunged. Also like the Wahhabis, they rejected the four established schools of Islamic jurisprudence and hated Sufism. In addition, they would attack established Islam as unbelief. They only differed from Wahhabism in paying more attention to Western injustices against the Islamic world, about which the Saudis were then unconcerned. Much later, international Wahhabism, exported thanks to Saudi oil revenues, appropriated the "Salafi" name as a cover, much as European Communists taking direction from Moscow called themselves "socialists."

At the beginning, the most powerful of these movements (outside Saudi Arabia) stood behind Nasser's Free Officers. This was the *Ikhwan al-Muslimun* or Muslim Brotherhood, a radical neo-Wahhabi organization founded by an Egyptian schoolteacher named Hassan al-Banna (1906–1949). This modern *Ikhwan* had no direct connection with the Arabian original, although it had similar characteristics—mainly, the condemnation of contemporary Islam as corrupt and in need of violent redemption. Hassan al-Banna was also among the first to introduce into modern Islamic discourse a corrosive hatred of the Jews, which he seemed to have adopted from Nazism.

But Nasser was uninterested in a flight into fundamentalism, seeing the desired Arab revival as a consequence of ethnic solidarity and social reform rather than promises of religious purification. This outlook again revealed the two faces of Islam: Nasser sought to rally Muslims to his cause, but on a basis of Islamic tolerance, not by consigning all who differed with him to hell as unbelievers. By contrast, the Muslim Brotherhood preached that a purge in Muslim ranks must precede a cataclysmic global battle with the Christian powers and the Jews.

As noted, Nasser and his followers throughout the Arab world, who soon numbered in the millions, were courted by the Soviets as prospective anti-Western allies and foot soldiers. These efforts could not but trouble the Americans. But notwithstanding Moscow's propaganda, its offers of massive aid, and the financial backing enjoyed by Soviet-controlled Communist parties throughout the Islamic world, Marxism proved to have little popular appeal in the *ummah*. Muslims disliked Communists as atheists and mercenaries, and Nasser, who was too clever to abandon his neutralism, soon sidelined the Egyptian Communists (many of whom had in any case been Jewish).

Nevertheless, Nasser's Arab nationalism set loose a series of international clashes that would make the Muslim countries of North Africa and the Middle East the cockpit of global rivalries for the next half-century. The first and, in some ways, the most traumatic for the West was the controversy over the Suez Canal.

On July 26, 1956, the fourth anniversary of King Farouk's abdication, Nasser proclaimed the canal's expropriation. (Historians claim that the decision reflected rage over the U.S. government's decision to grant substantial foreign aid to only one neutralist leader—Tito, not Nasser.) Britain and France determined to regain control of the canal by military means. For Britain, the issue was the waterway's importance for the transportation of oil to Europe. The French, who had originally paid for and built the canal, were angry at Nasser for financing, training, and otherwise supporting a nationalist-Islamic revolutionary movement in Algeria. In addition, Egyptian-based raiders frequently struck Israel, and the Europeans cultivated the Jewish state as an ally against Nasser. The British in particular convinced themselves that allowing Egyptian control of the canal would lead to Arab disruption of world oil markets. This in turn might cause the collapse of the European economy and of the Western military bulwark against the Soviets.

The Russians, who were at that moment occupied with drowning the Hungarian Revolution in blood, loudly supported Nasser, threatening nuclear war against the European powers, which Eisenhower warned would be answered in kind. But Washington also announced that it would not support the British, French, and Israelis in a military seizure of the canal and would demand they stop once it began. Eisenhower was reluctant to support an aggressive stance by Israel. But his administration was also focused on the struggle against Russian Communism and did not wish to see Western energies diverted to a hopeless attempt to preserve Anglo-French imperialism that might further reinforce the Soviet appeal to the colonial peoples. Eisenhower even threatened to block oil supplies to the Europeans if they persisted in attacking the Egyptians. The Western military alliance embodied in the North Atlantic Treaty Organization (NATO) was split. Finally, the Europeans and Israelis withdrew from Egyptian territory.

To his immense prestige, Nasser had triumphed over the European powers with the unenthusiastic but very real help of the United States. Nasser thus became the champion of the Arabs—a status to which many, including Saddam Husayn, later aspired. The Saudi reaction to the emergence of a secular nationalist as the leader of the Arab nation was one of intense concern and even fear. But the Suez crisis had also exposed a new factor in Arab relations with the West: Few outside the highest levels of the European political elite were prepared to go to war over the canal. Indeed, the protests in Europe against the Suez campaign marked the beginning of a new left movement that steadily grew until it came to dominate the younger generation during the 1960s. This homegrown anti-imperialist radicalism was further enhanced by the Algerian Revolution, the revolt against the French which Nasser subsidized.

Suez opened the door to a broader radical upsurge in Arab sensibilities, symbolized above all by Algeria's anti-French struggle, but also by the creation, in 1958, of a short-lived United Arab Republic combining Egypt, Syria, and Yemen. Nasser's Egypt thus became a modernist and anticolonialist pole in Arab politics, increasingly opposed by reactionary (and pro-American) Saudi Arabia. Egypt and the Saudis fought a proxy war in Yemen, and in 1962, the Saudis founded the Muslim World League—a kind of Islamic "International"—as a buffer against Nasserism. The resulting split between the two faces of Arab Islamic culture, represented by Egyptian pluralism and Saudi Wahhabism, persisted and widened. The Muslim Brotherhood and other neo-Wahhabi "Salafis" were already suspicious of Nasserism, which they rightly considered more nationalist than Islamic. In addition to these, however, other militant groups had emerged in the *ummah*, beginning in the 1930s. Some involved a mélange of anti-Western protest and borrowings from socialism. But others assumed a cover of theological purification, and over time the Wahhabi-Saudi power drew many of these groups into its orbit. By 1978, Islamic radicalism had been in great part Wahhabized.

A central figure in this process was Sayyid Abul-Ala Mawdudi (1903–1979), an Indian Muslim radical who greatly influenced the course of Arab nationalism, becoming one of the most controversial figures in recent Islamic history. Mawdudi was not a scholar or theologian but a journalist who had completed only the most basic religious and spiritual studies. His ideology was almost anarchist, but with a strong Wahhabi component. Like the Wahhabis, he idolized Ibn Taymiyyah and declared that the entire *ummah* was characterized by unbelief. For him, traditional Muslims were living in a second period of superstition and ignorance comparable to that of the pre-Islamic Arabs of Mecca. He also condemned the mixing of diverse religious populations, blaming Muslims who lived among Hindus, or who permitted the latter to live among them, for the weakness of Indian Islam in modern times.

Mawdudi's first book, *Jihad in Islam*, appeared in 1927. In it Mawdudi argued for curtailment of the rights of non-Muslims residing under Islamic rule and the destruction of existing governments, Muslim as well as secular. With more forthrightness than his Wahhabi counterparts, he declared, "Islam is a revolutionary doctrine and system that overturns governments. It seeks to overturn the whole universal social order . . . and establish its structure anew. . . . Islam seeks the world. It is not satisfied by a piece of land but demands the whole universe. . . . *Jihad* is at the same time offensive and defensive. . . . The Islamic party does not hesitate to utilize the means of war to implement its goal." Based on these ideas, in 1941 Mawdudi founded a militant movement in India, the Community for Islam or *Jamaat-i-Islami*, and his anti-Hindu doctrines and incitement to violence have been blamed for continuing conflict in Kashmir. When the Muslim World League was established by the Saudis, he was among its leading figures. (Strangely, Mawdudi died in Buffalo, New York.)

Mawdudi was richly honored by the Saudi regime and enjoys immense prestige among Muslim fundamentalists today; but the judgment of established scholars upon him is as harsh as that voiced by the traditionalists against the Wahhabis. He was denounced as a reviver of the Khawarij and condemned for his rejection of the scholars of the past. His obsession with political revolution was deemed un-Islamic, since traditional Islam based its guidance on knowledge and ethics rather than violence and subversion. His Muslim critics have grouped him with later figures like Hassan al-Banna and Sayyid Qutb (1906–1966) as seditionists whose seductive effect on young Muslims has been wholly evil. These men and their acolytes reinforced the extremist tendencies promoted in Islam by the Wahhabis. Rather than seeking to fortify the *ummah* against atheist Marxism and the political corruption common to many postcolonial societies, they demanded a murderous purge of alleged unbelievers, who also happened to make up the vast majority of Muslims.

Sayyid Qutb, like Hassan al-Banna, was an Egyptian schoolteacher, and like Mawdudi, an aspiring man of letters. He was born in the remote village of Musha, or Qaha, in Upper Egypt. As a young man he was a Western-oriented progressive, but he shared with Mawdudi a fixation on revolution that puts both men in the class of political rather than theological thinkers. Also like Mawdudi he was drawn to the United States, where between 1948 and 1951 he made a study of school curricula, sponsored by the Egyptian Ministry of Education, and was horrified by America's lack of prudery and its manifest materialism.

The great Bektashi teacher Baba Rexheb Beqiri fled to America to escape the Albanian Communists during the same period and found it a haven of religious liberty. Similarily, Turkish Islamists have drawn inspiration from the force of religion in American life. But Qutb came to America and encountered nothing that stirred his heart positively. An Egyptian bumpkin from an obscure village in a distant district nobody had ever heard of, much like Ibn Abd al-Wahhab, he viewed the Islamic world as a vast rural hinterland and America as an immense and unholy city. Despite his travels, he never grew beyond the mental horizon of an isolated and impoverished peasant. For example, at the end of his life he wrote that the great age of modern science in the West had been limited to the 18th and 19th centuries, and had already ended. But while he decried the materialism of the West, he admitted its technological superiority, and saw no contradiction in these postures.

Returning to Egypt filled with revulsion and disgust for America, Qutb joined the Muslim Brotherhood. Urban Muslims of the lower middle

class had flocked to the Egyptian *Ikhwan*, giving it the character of a genuine fascist movement that was absent in Saudi Arabia where no middle
class had yet emerged. So too did the professions pursued by Qutb distinguish him from the bandits and Bedouin who made up the Saudi *Ikhwan*.
Petty schoolteachers who yearned for recognition as literary figures were
plentiful in the ranks of the European totalitarian movements. But the
doctrines of the Egyptian *Ikhwan* were replete with the fundamentalist
separatism and supremacism characteristic of Wahhabism. It called for
the imposition of a rigid interpretation of *Shariah*, and in the Wahhabi
manner also emulated by Mawdudi, described existing Islam as a profound darkness, like the void of unbelief in which the Arabs had dwelt
before Muhammad. Also like the Wahhabis and Mawdudi, Sayyid Qutb
admired Ibn Taymiyyah and aspired to lead his followers to world domination—though less to the global triumph of existing Islam, with its pluralism and love of tradition, than to the absolute reign of his own narrow
dispensation.

The Muslim Brotherhood and even Sayyid Qutb himself have been
described as the ideological inspirers of the officers who brought down the
Egyptian monarchy. Nasser had been drawn, briefly, into their orbit, but
once in power he and his comrades turned their backs on Islamic fundamentalism. As the years went by, Nasser's regime embarked on the brutal
repression of the Muslim Brotherhood. Given the threat to public order
the fanatical Brothers represented, as well as their profound challenge to
pluralistic Egyptian Islam, this suppression was both necessary and justified. Nor was Nasser the only modernizing Arab leader who found that
the welfare of his people required the destruction of neo-Wahhabi extremism. King Husayn of Jordan was also compelled to deal mercilessly with
fanatics. Qutb himself was repeatedly jailed before his execution by the
Egyptian authorities in 1966. He is said to have smiled at his death,
embracing "martyrdom" in the Wahhabi manner, before he was hanged.

Sayyid Qutb is widely read in the Islamic world today, overshadowing
Mawdudi as probably the single most important influence in the formation of young Muslim extremists. His hostility to the West expressed itself
in an exaltation of his concept of *"jihad."* This *"jihad"* embodied a guerrilla ethos of radical assault, from below, on Western societies, as well as

attacking contemporary Muslims for their alleged lack of purity. As we have seen in discussing the doctrines of Ibn Taymiyyah and Ibn Abd al-Wahhab, traditional Muslims have often warned against the call to "*jihad*" between Muslims. Some opponents of Qutbism argue that the correct Islamic meaning of "sacred struggle" denotes a set of invariable regulations, based first of all in the legal essence of Islam as a bringer of order to the world. Indeed, political legitimacy has always resided for Muslims in the principle of acceptance of authority, often leading to civic passivity, and almost never approving of insurrectionary actions. Traditional Islam thus abhors the idea of subverting or otherwise disrupting any governments, including those of unbelievers, as sedition, the ultimate Muslim sin. Qutb declared, "Muslims are revolutionists. They revolt against cruelty and injustice." But some Muslims consider it sinful to rebel even against cruel authority, citing clear *Ahadith* as proof. Tradition holds that Muslims cannot oppose a ruler who does not forbid prayer.

In the aftermath of September 11, heightened concern has been expressed around the world about the meaning of Islamic *jihad*. Enthusiasts of Mawdudi, Sayyid Qutb, and, more recently, bin Laden and the partisans of terrorist bombings in Israel have reportedly drawn inspiration from a verse of *Qur'an* that says, "Permission to take up arms is hereby given to those who are attacked, because they have been wronged."[1] Such citations are used to justify crimes against Americans and Israelis on the grounds that they are aggressors against Islam itself, not merely opponents of some Muslim leaders or competitors over territory. Other Muslims point out that when the unbelievers in Mecca oppressed and slew Muhammad's followers, permission to rise against them was repeatedly asked and refused. The above verse from *Qur'an* came to Muhammad after the formation of the Islamic state in Medina. According to the commentaries assembled by Hilmi Ishik, this verse does not authorize Muslims to rebel against those who rule over them, no matter how abusive they may be. Rather, it allows a Muslim state to fight against non-Muslim governments, if they prevent their subjects from learning about the message of Muhammad. By this standard, Soviet Russia, which imposed atheism on Muslims, and Serbia, which razed mosques and murdered Islamic divines in large numbers, were proper enemies. However, *Sharif* Husayn of Mecca had called for *jihad* against the Unionist rulers of Turkey, viewing their actions as tantamount to abandonment of Islam.

The traditional Islamic definition of *jihad* is war against unbelieving countries in which few or no Muslims live, or in which Muslims are denied religious rights, not internal subversion in pluralistic, mixed societies, much less Muslim lands. The Ottomans were the greatest *jihad* power in their campaigns against foreign, Christian rulers. But these wars were fought by organized armies from without, not by terrorist irregulars from within.

The unity of Arab rhetoric—though not action—against Israel has obscured the persistence of essential, permanent differences among the Arab states. To a considerable degree, pluralist and modernizing Egypt and the reactionary Wahhabi kingdom of Saudi Arabia continue to represent rival ideological trends in the development of Arab societies. Just as the acolytes of Mawdudi and the Muslim Brotherhood rejected Nasser's nationalism, so did Saudi Arabia view the Egyptian leader as a dangerous challenger to its claims to hegemony over the Arab world. In opposing him, the Saudis were pleased to consider the United States as their ally. But Zionism and Israel, which Ibn Sa'ud had assailed even before 1948, would not go away, and remained a major beneficiary of American support at the same time as Washington backed the Saudis. The accommodation of the Saudis to U.S. demands is seen by many fundamentalists as a betrayal of Islamic integrity by the regime that, as the vessel of Wahhabism, advances the loudest claims to Muslim purity.

Meanwhile, as the Ba'ath movement gained power in Syria and Iraq, its revolutionary pretensions drove it inexorably toward Moscow. Its importance in two leading Middle Eastern countries aggravated tendencies toward radicalism in Arab politics. Nasserites and Ba'athists equally favored guerrilla warfare against Israel, while the Saudis believed they could use their relations with the United States to undermine the Jewish state. But with typical duplicity, the Saudis also subsidized terror.

The 1948 war, Arab attacks, and Jewish retaliation had caused the flight of hundreds of thousands of Arabs from Israeli territory. In the years that followed, some trickled back across the border, which was then largely deserted; these were considered infiltrators by the Israelis. Some were armed and exchanged fire with Israelis. Soon, Arab refugees who had gone to Syria and were paid by Saudi agents crossed into Israel, aiming to kill Jewish civilians. Then, in October 1953, an incident occurred that set a long-lasting pattern for future relations between the Jewish state and its Arab neighbors.

A grenade was thrown at a house in the Israeli community of Yehud, and a woman and two infants were killed. The British officer John Bagot Glubb, or Glubb Pasha, commander of Jordan's police (and of a larger military force, the Arab Legion), which patrolled in what is now known as the West Bank, offered to hunt down the perpetrators. But the Israelis chose to deal with the problem by sending Ariel Sharon, an army reservist then 27 years old, into Jordanian territory at the head of a special commando group called Unit 101. Dressed in civilian garb, the Israeli troops attacked the Arab village of Qibya on October 14. At least 66 people, mainly women and children, were killed. The incident provoked worldwide condemnation and led to a deep crisis in the Israeli leadership, pitting David Ben-Gurion, the father of the Israeli state, against his foreign minister and long-time comrade, Moshe Sharett. Ben-Gurion had authorized Sharon's action, and Sharett, who had been left uninformed of its ramifications, was horrified. Ben-Gurion prevailed and was encouraged to later launch the Israeli action at Suez in response to Egyptian military raids. Sharon himself would forever after symbolize, in Arab and Israeli minds alike, the policy of harsh retaliation against any attack on Israel.

As Islam has two faces, so has Israel. With their substantial history of Orthodox religious rejection of Zionist claims for the authority of the Jewish state, as well as their traditions of socialist internationalism in Europe and liberalism in the United States, global Jewry, as well as Israel, have always produced critics of hard-line Israeli policies. These dissidents have often proclaimed the justice of Arab protests against the Jewish state. Whatever the truth of these grievances, it must be acknowledged that the vigor of Jewish anti-Zionism and Israeli self-criticism contrasts strongly with the weakness of liberal self-criticism in Arab states.

It has long been debated whether the Arab states that attacked Israel in

1948 adopted a deliberate policy of refusing to assimilate the Palestinian refugees. The United Nations decision to administer permanent relief for the expelled relieved the Arab states of the burden, but left the refugees clustered in camps on Israel's borders. In 1964, these Arab states cooperated in the creation of the Palestine Liberation Organization (PLO) as an umbrella for various groups of nationalist radicals, headed by a certain Ahmed Shukairy. It was quickly endorsed by Moscow.

Armed beyond the wildest fantasies of any revolutionaries of the past, a mass of factions soon festered in the Palestinian body politic. As each new group appeared, they were courted and flattered, justified and financially rewarded not only by the Arab regimes but by the Russians, their Chinese rivals, and Western leftists. Despite the proliferation of these groups the differences among them came down to matters not of ideology but of personal ambition among mediocre pseudo-intellectuals. Nor, despite Wahhabi-Saudi incitement against Israel, were any of them, at first, explicitly religious in nature. Instead, each tried to justify its existence by recourse to obscure points of Leninist, Stalinist, Trotskyist, Maoist, and nationalist theory.

From the outset, the largest and most powerful of these groups were the Palestine National Liberation Movement, or Fatah, headed by Yasir Arafat, and the Popular Front for the Liberation of Palestine (PFLP) directed by a Christian, Georges Habash. Their original members were drawn from among Palestinian students at the American University in Beirut as well as the educated urban classes of Egypt, Jordan, and other countries. Inspired by Nasser, they dreamed of Arab unification and modernization through "revolution until victory" against Israel. The PFLP's title was reminiscent of that of the Union of Soviet Socialist Republics—of which the Russian dissident Vladimir Bukovsky said "five words, five lies." It was not popular or a front, but a personalist conspiracy run by Habash. It stood not for the liberation of Palestine but its destruction through terror and totalitarianism, and the absolute rejection of peace appeals by the Israelis. The PFLP are mainly remembered for introducing airplane hijackings into Middle East politics. They also brought forth such variant groupings as the PFLP–General Command and the Popular Democratic Front for the Liberation of Palestine.

The Arabs—above all, the Palestinians—had proven incapable of extricating themselves from their long political crisis. They made no progress against Israel; they could not form prosperous, democratic regimes, and they most certainly did not unite the Arab nation. The deep frustrations engendered by this situation gained the serious attention of the world in 1972, when a group of Palestinian militants murdered several Israeli athletes at the Munich Olympics. This dramatic assault alarmed the population of the globe. Many Arabs, as well as the majority of the *ummah*, were not yet so inured to political violence that they were not in some way disturbed at the terrorist crime. But while the Palestinians had so far failed to gain the real (as opposed to rhetorical) backing of the Arab states, they found ample support outside the Arab world. Though Westerners assumed that the Palestinian terrorists were backed by the Arab regimes, more significant support came not from other Arabs but from the worldwide anticapitalist left. By the early 1970s, with the help of the Russians, Czechs, Cubans, Yugoslavs, North Koreans, and other Communist powers, the Palestinians had formed a "terrorist international" that also included bombers and assassins in Northern Ireland, the Basque country, Colombia, Argentina, Uruguay, Peru, Nicaragua, the former Portuguese colonies in Africa and Asia, Germany, Italy, Spain, Japan, Turkey, and even the United States.

Wave upon wave of atrocities have crossed the front pages and screens of world media in subsequent decades. Initially, these horrors had little or nothing to do with Islam. Indeed, some of the most violent and irreconcilable terrorist chiefs and their apologists were Christians like Georges Habash or the Palestinian-American academic and activist Edward W. Said. One Arab demagogue, the Libyan Muammar al-Qadhdhafi, in his time a prolific supporter of terrorism, gave his regime some Islamic trappings, but they counted for little.

But notwithstanding its success at grabbing headlines, the failure of Palestinian nationalism to fully unify its constituency, to gain consistent support from the rest of the Arab world, or to make serious gains against Israel reflected the more general weaknesses of the Pan-Arab movement, which could never attain maturity so long as regimes like Egypt and Saudi

Arabia, the two main leaders in the Arab world, differed so greatly in their vision of the Arab future.

In 1973 the fresh defeat of Arab armies in a war against Israel stirred the Wahhabi-Saudi state to assist the Arab leftists with a boycott on oil sales to the West. The realization that oil could be used as a weapon brought about a fourth shock in Islamic relations with the West. The first, the metastasis of Wahhabi-style separatist and nihilist extremism, provided doctrines and recruits for a new challenge to the global powers. The rise of Israel, the second, exacerbated Arab and Islamic frustrations. The third, the confrontation at Suez, was proof that the former colonial rulers were unprepared to reimpose their past control. The boycott illustrated that the West's dependence on oil was an even greater weakness than its leaders' unwillingness to carry through foreign intervention. Each of these lessons for the *ummah* seemed inexorably to point to a Judeo-Christian civilization in decline, unable, in the long run, to resist a reassertion of Islamic aggressivity. Americans fuming in gas lines were, it seemed, helpless; the great powers had finally been rendered powerless.

Enormous changes, largely unperceived by outsiders, gestated in the Muslim world in the years following the 1973 oil convulsion, as increased oil royalties fueled a new Saudi effort, more ambitious than ever, to Wahhabize the worldwide Islamic community. Vast numbers of "Salafi" enthusiasts of the Egyptian Muslim Brotherhood, Sayyid Qutb, and Mawdudi were employed in this enterprise. The boycott had also shifted the international political advantage, at least temporarily, to the Arabs. But the new relationship of forces led to a weakening, rather than a reinforcement, of the Arab position. It was as if, suddenly handed an opportunity to dictate to the world, Arabs had become intoxicated with their new power and chose to waste their moment in a suicidal display of self-inflicted cruelty. This self-mutilation of the Arab nation came to a head in 1975 in the form of an atrocious civil and religious war in Lebanon.

Lebanon had long been dominated by France. It was a cosmopolitan and prosperous society, with a richly pluralist Islamic and Christian culture. But in the postcolonial era the country's multireligious character, with large numbers of Sunni and Shi'a Muslims as well as Orthodox and Maronite Christians, made it perhaps the weakest link in the Middle Eastern order. After 1943 its political system had been based on an unsatisfactory power-sharing arrangement between Christians and Sunnis brokered by the French on their withdrawal. The Christians had been granted political dominance although they constituted only a slender majority of the population: 54 percent according to a 1932 census. Indeed, despite lingering Arab resentment of Great Britain, in the longer run of history the French were by far the most irresponsible colonialists to appear in the Arab world.

In Algeria, France had implanted a large settler population and promoted the ludicrous fiction that an ancient Arab and Berber Muslim society could be merged into France as a political unit indistinguishable from any other *département* of the "mother country." Such a policy led inevitably to terrible bloodshed in the independence war, followed by European flight. But in Lebanon the French had outdone themselves: By favoring the Arab Christians they had fostered a sense of immutable privilege among the country's rulers and festering resentment among the disenfranchised. Generational and demographic pressures may also have contributed to the breakdown of political authority. When fighting broke out in Lebanon in 1958 (blamed by Beirut's Maronite Christian leader, Camille Chamoun, on Syria) it led to a brief United States military intervention. But it was really the arming, funding, and proliferation of Palestinian guerrilla groups during the late '60s and early '70s that played the decisive role in the devastation of Lebanon.

Armed Palestinian groups and their refugee supporters had earlier fostered gangsterism and other serious problems in Jordan. The PFLP's airline hijackings were particularly awkward for the royal authorities in Amman. Following the group's seizure and destruction of three Swiss, British, and American jetliners on Jordanian territory, King Husayn moved against the Palestinians in September 1970 with violent repression. PLO leader Yasir Arafat responded with calls to overthrow the Jordanian monarchy. The ensuing chaos, memorialized as "Black September" by Palestinian militants, was described by Arafat as a "genocide" of the

Palestinians. Blood ran in the streets of Amman as well as in the refugee camps. A long series of attempted negotiations under the patronage of Egypt and the other Arab states failed to resolve the conflict. Finally, in July 1971, the Jordanians drove Arafat and his fighters into Lebanon. The Black September organization, which carried out the Munich atrocities, was born as a weapon of Palestinian vengeance.

At the end of 1975, just as the battles began in Beirut between Christian extremists and Palestinians, Arab-backed terrorism exploded anew in Europe. A gang headed by a Venezuelan named Ilich Ramirez, who called himself Carlos, burst into a meeting of the Organization of Petroleum Exporting Countries in Vienna, killing three people before escaping. In addition, the "Arab street" was encouraged that year when the United Nations adopted a resolution equating Zionism and racism, and the Suez Canal, closed since the 1967 war with Israel, was reopened by Egypt.

When the Lebanese war began, many leftists around the world were exalted by the fantasy of a new revolutionary wave. But they were profoundly mistaken. Lebanon marked the end of the era of terror as a form of alleged protest by youthful revolutionaries. In its place came a new world disorder in which terror brought about the complete breakdown of societies, wholesale violence between neighbors, and urban populations held hostage for years by implacable gunmen. Later wars and uprisings would have much to do with anticapitalism, but offered little in justification of the doctrinal shibboleths of radical socialism.

The revolutionary dawn that seemed to have appeared in the late 1960s was sputtering to an end. The Lebanese agony coincided with the farce of an attempted Stalinist takeover in Portugal and suicidal massacres caused by guerrilla adventures in the Southern Cone of South America. The Communist triumph in Indochina, also in 1975, led to the migration of millions of Vietnamese and the mass murder of millions of Cambodians. Meanwhile, Moscow and its Cuban mercenaries took over the last Portugese possessions in Africa, which also resulted in cruel civil wars. The Castro regime, which had seized the reins in Cuba under the banner of anti-imperialism, was now a minor surrogate within the Soviet imperial system. Ethiopia established a brutal Marxist nightmare in the form of a revolutionary state. Moscow also backed the expansion of violent extremism by domestic European radicals and revolutionary cadres in Nicaragua and other Central American countries.

Beirut, however, became a unique symbol of the collapse of a sophisticated urban culture in a world that had lost its bearings in the last quarter of the century. The catastrophe began in a clash between Palestinian gunmen and followers of a Christian Arab politician of fascist sympathies, Pierre Gemayel, who headed the Kataeb or Phalange, founded in 1936. Although the Kataeb declares its belief in Christian-Muslim coexistence, it is strongly anti-Palestinian, having viewed the Palestinians as Muslim interlopers on Lebanese soil. With the coming of the Lebanese war, the religiously mixed population of the country divided between Christian and Muslim camps. The new repertory of urban terror included very large and well-organized militias, rigidly segregated communal zones, expulsion of opposing populations, street barricades and identity checks, uncontrolled sniping, and massacres. (Some of these practices had become standardized near the heartland of Western political culture, in Northern Ireland.)

The Lebanese Christian forces included armed groups supporting the Chamoun and Franjieh families. The Muslim side comprised the Palestinian guerrillas and assorted leftist groups such as the Progressive Socialist Party headed by the Nasserite Kamal Jumblatt, a member of the Druze sect. Jumblatt's party had undergone curious wanderings in the direction of the anti-Communist left. In 1952 Jumblatt represented Lebanon before the Congress for Cultural Freedom, meeting in Switzerland. The Congress was, as is now well known, controlled by the United States Central Intelligence Agency. But Jumblatt, who led the 1958 Lebanese uprising that led to the landing of U.S. Marines, later went to China and became a fixture in Communist-affiliated "Afro-Asian solidarity" activities. He closely aligned his Lebanese adherents with the Palestinian extremists in their struggle against Israel.

Lebanon also saw the emergence of two Shi'a militias, the Lebanese Resistance Squads, or Amal, and the Party of God, or Hezbollah. Amal had been formed under Iranian influence and was a major element in the Lebanese war. But in the early 1980s, the Khomeini regime encouraged the rise of Hezbollah, and Amal became a Syrian client. Hezbollah, which murdered 241 U.S. Marines in Beirut in 1983, would never have existed without the challenge to the *ummah*, the Wahhabi-Saudi alliance, and the Western powers represented by *Imam* Khomeini. Accordingly we turn to the next great seismic event in Muslim affairs, the Iranian Revolution.

In 1951, an eccentric Iranian politician named Muhammad Musadeq, acting as prime minister under a constitutional monarchy, nationalized British oil holdings in the country. Two years later, with the complicity of Britain and the United States, Shah Muhammad Riza Pahlavi attempted to remove Musadeq, but the prime minister briefly drove the shah from his throne. Musadeq was then overthrown with help from the CIA, and the shah was restored to power. Iran thus became one of America's main political supporters, with Turkey and Saudi Arabia, among the Muslim countries.

The American victory in Iran nurtured a sense of false confidence among Western leaders, who convinced themselves they could easily suppress further outbursts of radicalism in the Muslim world. But the course of history during this period was kind neither to the shah nor to his American patrons. The upstart Pahlavi dynasty had ruled Iran since the 1920s; they were established at the same time as, and were otherwise comparable to, Al Sa'ud. Shah Muhammad Riza, the last of the line to exercise power, had also benefited from Western oil royalties, and like his Saudi counterpart, he spent without care. Pahlavi had attempted to impose political changes aimed at undermining the country's Islamic opposition. The most provocative of these actions involved the monarch's penchant for the extravagant celebration of pre-Islamic Iranian traditions. The worst indulgence came in 1971 when the shah spent millions on a national festival celebrating two and a half millennia of Iranian royalty. With his love of pageantry focused on imitation of the most ancient rulers, the shah was perceived as seeking to revive paganism and idolatry. Almost as destructive was his decision to replace the Iranian Islamic calendar with an imperial one. This was viewed by Muslims as a direct attack on the faith.

In addition, the shah's regime had gained a horrific reputation for human rights abuses. His secret police, SAVAK, was widely believed to be almost an extension of the CIA, which had overthrown Musadeq—a fact recalled daily by all opponents of the monarchy. Further, the shah had aligned Iran strategically with Israel.

Everything changed in 1978 with the arrival of Ayatollah Ruhollah Khomeini and the Shi'a clerics of Iran at center stage of world history. Khomeini embodied all the most dramatic and sentimental aspects of Shi'a tradition. He was charismatic, learned, articulate, idealistic, philosophical, mystical, had suffered for his principles, and above all, was deeply angered at the West—mainly at America, but also at Israel.

For centuries, Shi'as had believed that a "hidden *Imam*"—a religious redeemer—would emerge from concealment to lead his fellow Muslims to glory. Khomeini seemed to many to have fulfilled that promise, and thus became known as "the *Imam*." His was a revolution for Islam, not, as in the preachings of the "Salafi" radicals, Islam as a factor in an Arab revolution. The revolution in Iran led to that country being universally viewed, and greatly feared in the West, as the fountainhead of fanatical Islamism. But these anxieties were skewed by Western ignorance of Muslim history. The worst excesses of Islamic intolerance and aggression had always derived from the Wahhabi-Saudi ideology, and nowhere else. Khomeini and his fellow clerics, being Shi'as, repudiated the claims of the Saudis and "Salafis" such as Mawdudi and Qutb that the overwhelming majority of the world's Muslims, neither Wahhabis nor "Salafis," lived in a state of unbelief. But viewing themselves as champions of the oppressed, they also rejected the traditional Islamic condemnation of revolutionary movements. In this regard they betrayed, to an extent, the influence upon them of the "Salafi" radicals.

Almost no other Muslim country had produced a body of scholars comparable to the Iranians. Their Shi'ism had long reconciled them to a minority position in the Islamic world, but they were also used to acting collectively in a way seldom seen among Sunni scholars; even among the Wahhabis, discord and fractiousness was the norm. The Iranian clerics had never accepted the shah's regime. Rather, they steadfastly opposed it.

They were personally free of corruption, and it was simply impossible to imagine the Iranian Muslim leaders wallowing in the decadent lifestyle of the Saudi oil princes. When they confronted the West, they did so with extraordinary firmness, tenacity, and conviction, even as they made minor concessions here and there.

The rise of Khomeini and his colleagues electrified the *ummah*. His movement represented a diametrical opposite to the Wahhabi-Saudi axis ruling Arabia, combining all the things about Islamic civilization, Sunni as well as Shi'a, that the Wahhabis hated most. They enjoyed music. They did not destroy classic works of art and literature of the kind that the Wahhabis grimly burned and shredded. They belonged to Sufi orders and practiced *dhikr*, achieving ecstatic trance states in their quest for unity with God. They loved, honored, and praised Muhammad and his family, especially Ali and Husayn, with exceptional passion. They frankly admitted and sought to understand the esoteric, Gnostic essence in Islamic tradition, the very mention of which stimulated Wahhabis to murderous frenzy. They rejected the paganism of the pre-Islamic Persian past but nonetheless studied and preserved its cultural remains. They looked to the pluralist face of Islam, even though their anger and pietism made them appear profoundly reactionary and narrow-minded to the West.

The rage of the Iranians toward the world order reflected something other than the primitive suspicion and nihilism of the Wahhabis, lurking in the lava beds of Najd. The Iranian Muslims were heirs of a national identity as old as that of the Jews, Greeks, Hindus, and Chinese. Unlike the Egyptians, they still spoke their original language. They had sheltered the Hebrews, faced the Athenians in battle, and had a long and fruitful cultural dialogue with the peoples of India, the obscure provinces of Inner Asia, the Siberian steppes, and the Yellow River Basin. Their name rang throughout the chronicles of the ancient world; their rulers' works were noted in Jewish scripture, and a Persian had been among the original Companions of the Prophet. They had been the artistic and literary powerhouse of the *ummah* for centuries and had penetrated European culture in subtle ways. As words borrowed from their language were common in the Slavic dialect of Bosnia-Hercegovina, so their spiritual classics had been read by the Spanish Catholics. What the Arabs had been to the original Muhammadan revelation, and the Turks to the concept of an Islamic state, the Persians represented for the most sensitive Muslim intellectuals.

The Iranian Muslims wanted respect from the West on their own terms and were determined to get it. They were certain that a new era had come, represented by *Imam* Khomeini, in which they would once again be recognized as one of the greatest and most powerful countries. They were well educated and ready to stand on an equal footing with the Western elite, if not in values then in knowledge. They had studied the revolutions of the past, organized the overthrow of the Pahlavi dynasty carefully and intelligently, and were fully prepared to rule once he fled. But above all, they were Shi'a. Nothing could more shock the holders of Wahhabi-Saudi power in Arabia than the spectre of an Islamic revolution led by Shi'as, whom they had sought to wipe off the face of the planet. And the Iranians were no hypocrites. Their political order would be severe. The Iranians would grant no exceptions to Islamic morals to princes, prostitutes, pornographers, peddlers of influence, or any of the other hangers-on that pullulated in the House of Sa'ud.

Imam Khomeini's revolution provided the fifth, and most significant shock to Muslims and the world at large in the second half of the 20th century. Mawdudi and Qutb had laid the basis for an assault on the West's power; Israeli success had seemed to justify it; Suez showed that the West might be effectively resisted; the oil boycott revealed that Western vulnerability went much deeper than the foreign ministries responsible for global policy. *Imam* Khomeini showed that the West could be beaten, at least psychologically. He issued his revolutionary appeal, stood by it, and survived.

Ruhollah Al-Musavi Al-Khomeini was born in 1902, the year Ibn Sa'ud and his Wahhabis, having recaptured Riyadh, launched their adventure in politics and plunder. His birthplace was Khomein, a small town south of the Iranian capital, Tehran. His father, a Shi'a cleric, was murdered when the boy was only five months old. He began his religious studies at 19. He was mainly drawn to philosophy and ethics, and he would teach these subjects at Qom, the intellectual center of Iranian Shi'ism. Foreigners ignorant of Islamic culture would doubtless have scoffed at the notion that a man so wedded to religion and mysticism could lead a revolution. His admirers point out that in Khomeini, neither Islam as a faith nor Muslim spirituality stimulated a desire to separate himself from the world. Rather, both gave depth to his demands for political change. In 1962, when he was already old, he began his career of direct, public opposition to the shah.

Khomeini took aim at the series of modernizing reforms that the shah had proclaimed as a way to make the country prosperous and powerful, but which the clerics viewed as pretexts for the consolidation of the monarchy. Violent clashes came the next year, coinciding with Shi'a observances of the martyrdom of Husayn. Khomeini warned his people against needlessly sacrificing themselves, in the classic vocabulary of Shi'a Islam: "Keep calm. You are the followers of those leaders in your religion who suffered greater atrocities. It is up to you to preserve this sacred heritage." He was arrested, confined, and then exiled, first to Turkey, then to Iraq where he remained until the onset of the revolutionary crisis in 1978, when he briefly took up residence in France. Throughout his exile he preached and published denunciations of the shah, remaining popular inside Iran. The death of his elder son Mustafa, in Iraq in 1977, was widely blamed on the shah's secret police and helped spark the protests that began the Iranian overturn.

That year had also seen the worldwide broadcast of a television image that, like many another news picture, seemed pregnant with symbolism: The Iranian monarch and U.S. President Jimmy Carter wiped tears from their eyes at a meeting in Washington, as local police battled anti-shah demonstrators. The meaning was obvious: The Iranian regime depended on tear gas and other tools of violent repression, and the American president was forced into complicity with its brutalities. Throughout 1978, Iran was shaken by mass demonstrations. Awestruck Western leftists, as they had at the beginning of the horrors of Lebanon, again imagined they were seeing a new upsurge of world socialism. Exiled Iranian radicals had plowed the academic fields in Europe and the United States for years. Top Western decision makers expressed increasing anxiety about Iranian oil. Iran had become the central element of American strategy in the Gulf. Would the shah fall? Would the country's oil production be affected?

Experts, journalists, religious intellectuals, and politicians throughout the world were stunned when the shah fled and Khomeini declared an Islamic Republic. Many traditional Sunni Muslims as well as Westerners objected to the strict interpretation of *Shariah* imposed on Iran, but it was imposed uniformly, with no double standards. *Imam* Khomeini and his fellow scholars displayed the kind of impassioned commitment one would expect from those who drew their own blood in recollection of the sufferings of Ali and Husayn and who saw themselves as divinely chosen redeemers of injustice. They would bring the same dedication to their rulership, even though many Shi'a as well as Sunni scholars reject Khomeini's merger of faith and governance.

On October 22, 1979, the United States admitted the shah to asylum. Iran was swept by rumors of a new imperial restoration such as that in which Musadeq had been overturned a quarter of a century earlier. On November 4, 1979, radical Islamic students seized the U.S. embassy, taking 52 Americans hostage. They would remain captive for 444 days, until the election of President Ronald Reagan and their release on January 20, 1981.

Iran also adopted an aggressive posture toward Israel and supported the terrorist Hezbollah in Lebanon. But Khomeini's rise represented an even greater challenge to Wahhabism and Al Sa'ud. A revolution in Iran would naturally draw on Shi'a traditions of identification with the suffering and oppressed. But more, it embodied a repudiation of Wahhabi pretensions about world *jihad*. For the first time since the 1920s, Wahhabi claims to leadership of an Islamic revival had been exceeded. If Muslims were to organize and fight on a global level, it seemed clear that the despised Shi'as now had more credibility than the jaded and cynical Wahhabi-Saudi ruling class. To note a single symbolic detail, Khomeini's first published book, *Secrets Revealed*, issued in 1941, was a reply to a Wahhabi-inspired polemic as well as a guarded critique of the Pahlavi monarchy.

By any measure, *Imam* Khomeini was an extraordinary figure. He and his colleagues in the leadership of the Islamic Republic of Iran had overnight shown themselves to be more effective in challenging Western interests than any Arab Muslim since the time of the Spanish caliphate. In addition, unlike so-called Islamic revolutionaries such as Mawdudi and

Sayyid Qutb, Khomeini was a genuinely distinguished religious scholar. His concept of revolution, although illegitimate from a traditional Islamic perspective, contrasted with their turbulent fantasies no less than the Ottoman idea of *jihad* differed from the bloodthirsty depredations of Wahhabism.

Khomeini's authoritative biographer, Hamid Algar, has written, "The aspiration 'to pierce the veils of light and attain the source of magnificence' may . . . be regarded as a constant element in the devotional life of [Khomeini], and only by bearing it in mind can the totality of his struggles and achievements, including the political, be correctly understood." Khomeini had studied and written on the *Bezels of Wisdom* by Ibn Arabi, anathematized by Wahhabis. Here was a manner of thinking totally at odds with the latter's narrow doctrines. Although a fierce defender of tradition, Khomeini was a deeply unorthodox personality. His poetry praised the martyred Sufi Hallaj, judged a heretic for merging his personality with God. Khomeini had also written in one of his most famous and characteristic verses in praise of "divine drunkenness,"

> At the door of the tavern, temple [of idols], mosque, and
> monastery,
> I have fallen in prostration, as though you glanced upon me.

No Wahhabi would ever contemplate such a vision, much less write it down or publish it. Yet while Khomeini could express a religiosity symbolized by drunken abandon, he was nothing if not sober in his personal life, and indeed it was in their personal morals that Khomeini and the Iranian clerics contrasted most dramatically with the Wahhabi-Saudi elite. One could more easily imagine Khomeini or one of his colleagues joining the Israeli Defense Forces than disporting himself like a Saudi prince in a Thai brothel, dropping thousands of dollars in the most expensive boutiques of New York and Beverly Hills, or partying down in Marbella. Nor could the Iranians forget or forgive the Wahhabi-Saudi demolition of Shi'a mosques and other sacred sites in the Two Holy Places, their restriction of Shi'a pilgrims to Mecca, and other insults.

Khomeini's revolution caused immense global anxiety, especially as it was assumed that he would seek to export it aggressively. Western media codified the claim that Iran had designs on the whole Muslim world. But the Western powers failed to understand that the Iranian revolution could not be effectively internationalized, based as it was on Shi'ism, a minority tradition in Islam, and in the Iranian nation, which is not Arab. Thus while Hezbollah, a Shi'a militia in Lebanon, had been financially assisted by the Tehran regime, its concerns were local. The real exporters of international Islamic extremism were the Saudis. Nevertheless, the Saudis did not miss the opportunity to stoke the Western fear of Iran in order to bolster their false image as Arab "moderates."

Equally alarmed by the Iranian Revolution, Saudi Arabia soon found a weapon against it in the person of Iraqi dictator Saddam Husayn. Shi'a but non-Arab Iran had always disliked Arab Iraq, which happened to possess the holy sites of Shi'a Islam at Karbala and Najaf. In 1980, the Saudis backed Saddam in a war of aggression against Iran that would last nine years. Although Saddam's Ba'athist regime had a leftist and pro-Soviet past, the Saudi King Fahd, taking power in 1982, paraded around the Muslim world seeking support for Saddam and memorably described him as "the sword of Islam." Even when the war turned into a disastrous bloodletting for Iraq, the Saudi kingdom moderated its rhetoric but continued supporting Saddam against the Iranians.

The Iraq-Iran war ended in a costly standoff. Meanwhile, as we will see in subsequent chapters, the Saudis dramatically increased their own program for the worldwide expansion of Wahhabi extremism.

Khomeini's advent, coming close on the heels of the oil boycott and Beirut, changed more than the Islamic status quo that had existed since the end of the second world war. The Iranian revolutionary regime worried the Russians almost as much as it did the Saudis and the Americans, and they suddenly looked with anxiety at their Islamic possessions in Central Asia—Kazakhstan, Uzbekistan, Tajikistan, Turkmenistan, and Kyrgyzstan. The Slavic empire at its height included millions of Muslims. Russian Communism had forcibly lifted them into the contemporary world by compulsory education, industrialization, and modern communications and transportation, but it had cut them off from the historical legacy they shared with Arab divines, Turkish conquerors, and Persian poets and mathematicians. The vast majority of Muslims under Soviet rule were Sunnis. But how would they respond to the call of the *Imam*?

Late in the day as it was for the Leninist system, Communism *seemed* solidly established as a permanent element of the global political landscape. If anything, the Russians appeared to have tipped the worldwide balance of forces decisively to their advantage when their Vietnamese clients harried the United States and its allies out of Southeast Asia. Yet at the same time the internal crisis of the Soviet system—almost uncanny in its resemblance to that of the Saudi kingdom—advanced, largely misunderstood in the West, through the 1970s.

No sooner had they gained an impressive apparent victory over the West in Indochina than the Communist ship ran aground on the shoals of history. The election of a Pole, Karol Wojtyla, to the papacy, also in 1978, represented the first challenge to Muscovite imperialism that could not be answered by force alone. The authority of political dictatorships could vanish, to be brusquely replaced by that of sincere men of God—whether the benign John Paul II or the harsh Khomeini. Suddenly aware of how quickly the breath of chaos might descend upon their necks, the Russian Communist rulers began casting about for a new internal enemy that could be manipulated to unify their people as well as an external target against which to mobilize their Slav subjects. In the past, the Jews would have filled the bill admirably. But Western condemnation of Soviet anti-Jewish measures had stung painfully, and a return to total, frenzied Judeophobia in internal Russian politics seemed an uncertain path.

Muslims, however, presented an ideal target for the suppressed resentments of the Russians. There were millions of them inside the Soviet Union. They represented a hereditary enemy of the tsarist empire. They had never liked Communism. They differed from the Slavs in appearance and language. They had a high birth rate and could be presented as a demographic threat to the Russian nation. Muslims were overrepresented in the criminal classes thanks to brutal Russian discrimination. This was especially cruel against the Chechens, who along with other small nations had been deported from the Caucasus in their entirety by Stalin during the second world war. In addition, they had kept their Sufism alive in secret, and who could say what those mystics were up to when they met to praise their God? Doubtless, the Chechens and other Muslim subjects of the Communist dominion dreamed of *Imam* Shamyl and the humiliation he once inflicted on Russia. The moment might soon come when an assertion of Russian national power against a Muslim foe would save the Communist system.

CHAPTER 6

Permanent *Jihad*

THE SHADOW OF AFGHANISTAN

Russian troops marched into Afghanistan following a Communist coup in Kabul in 1979. Alarmed by events in Iran, the Soviet leadership had found itself compelled to demonstrate its power to the Muslims of the world, especially in the countries within and bordering the Soviet Union. And so the Russian Army crossed the frontier into Afghanistan, no more than a thin line on a map. They carried bright banners that would soon lie trampled, along with the Communist order itself. But in Russia the Afghan war destroyed an ideology, while in Afghanistan the country and its people were physically devastated.

Soviet forces quickly completed the seizure of Kabul on the evening of December 27, 1979. Until then, Afghanistan had been considered one of the most remote, undeveloped, and traditional countries in the world, a Muslim Tibet or Nepal. Indeed, it was known in the West similarly, as an exotic tourist destination for the footloose lotus-eaters of the 1960s. But the Russians made a terrible mistake in crudely attempting the direct conquest of Afghanistan. Afghanistan was not Czechoslovakia; it could not be overpowered. Nor was it a Cuba or Angola that could be drawn into Moscow's orbit on the pretext of anticolonialism.

With the Russian occupation, Afghanistan ceased to resemble Tibet and Nepal and rapidly emerged as a Muslim counterpart to Poland and Nicaragua, both in its religious culture and its essential rejection of the Communist mentality. Each of these countries defeated Communist colonialism in a different way: Poland through labor organization and Catholic activism; Nicaragua through a combination of civic opposition, armed resistance, and the same Catholic inspiration. Afghans had lived on the border of the Communist empire long enough to know that the new regime would seek to regiment them, beginning with the replacement of Islam by official atheism. But the difficult environment, in which geography fit the temper of the people, seemed to determine that the Afghan struggle would be more military than political or even religious.

Yet as it happens, the real story of Afghanistan was enacted neither in that country nor in Russia, but in Saudi Arabia and the United States. In Central Asia, the Wahhabi mind, never at rest, had stumbled on an opportunity to repeat the bold trick by which, a half century before, Ibn Sa'ud had gained British acquiescence to Wahhabi-Saudi claims on Mecca and Medina. Now the gambit would be repeated, with the help of the United States, in an unrestrained effort to subdue the whole worldwide Muslim community, with Afghanistan as its training ground.

Some in the West were thrilled by the Soviet invasion. The radical gadfly Alexander Cockburn opined with startling crudity: "If ever a country deserved rape it's Afghanistan. Nothing but mountains filled with barbarous ethnics with views as medieval as their muskets, and unspeakably cruel too." As time passed and the rigid character of the Khomeini regime further alarmed the Judeo-Christian world, the attempt at Communist transformation of Afghanistan came to be viewed by other Westerners with approval. But not by all, most notably Ronald Reagan, who was elected president in 1980. Jimmy Carter had protested against the illegality of the Soviet invasion, but Reagan noticed that the de facto annexation of Afghanistan was the first such action by Moscow in 40 years. The Communists had adopted a strategy of heightened pressure against the West, and it was necessary to rebuff it.

From the beginning, Afghan refugees had poured over the border into Pakistan, providing recruits for an anti-Russian *jihad*, as the Afghans began mass resistance to the invaders and their puppets in Kabul. The Russians responded by filling the country with ever more conscripts, many from the Soviet Central Asian republics, particularly Uzbekistan and Tajikistan. They were ill-trained, maltreated by their officers, low in morale, and promiscuous about committing atrocities. The Reagan administration decided correctly to grant substantial aid to an Islamic counter-revolution in Afghanistan.

But the Americans failed to understand the Afghan resistance, which was composed of both traditional Afghan Muslims, including some distinguished Sufis, and fundamentalists controlled by the Pakistanis, under the influence in turn of Wahhabis bankrolled by the Saudis. The penetration of the Afghan resistance by Wahhabi manipulators reflected the induction of Pakistani acolytes of Mawdudi into the activities of the Muslim World League. The Pakistan regime and its InterServices Intelligence (ISI) were permeated with Wahhabi-style fundamentalism. The journalist Ahmed Rashid comments, "Saudi arms and money flowed to Saudi-trained Wahhabi leaders among the Pashtuns . . . thanks to the CIA-ISI arms pipeline, the engine of the *jihad* was the radical Islamic parties."

Less than six months after the Russian invasion the Afghan resistance split into two rival bodies. The National and Islamic Revolutionary Council was made up of traditionalists and tribal chiefs. The Revolutionary Council of the Islamic Union for the Liberation of Afghanistan favored Wahhabism, a doctrine foreign to Afghanistan and similar in its radical spirit to the Communism it sought to supplant. Simply put, the Islamic Republic of the traditionalists would be theologically pluralist, while that of the Wahhabis would be fundamentalist. The former would fight for their culture, while the latter would seek the destruction of established Muslim customs and the chance of personal martyrdom.

A pioneering group of Afghan fundamentalists was promoted by Pakistani dictator Zia ul-Haq; they were upper-middle-class adherents of Mawdudi's neo-Wahhabism. The leading figure among them was a Pashtun, Gulbuddin Hekmatyar, who founded a movement called the Party of Islam or *Hezb-i-Islami*. Hekmatyar and his followers dominated the Afghan scene for years before being driven out by the Taliban, long after the triumph over the Russians.

The Saudis viewed Afghanistan more or less exactly as the Russians had: as prey for political experimentation and as a buffer against the baleful Khomeini. The Wahhabi-Saudi power had found in Afghanistan not only a chance to "prove" that they were more militant than the Iranians, but to impose their own form of Islam under the pretext of defending Muslims. Using Pakistan and the anti-Russian struggle as a cover, they launched their most ambitious attempt to date at direct religious colonization of a Muslim country that was neither Arab nor a neighbor of Arabs.

Even more significant, perhaps, the *jihad* in Afghanistan provided a unique opportunity for the Saudis to dispose of restless Wahhabi youths in their own country, who could be sent to martyrdom abroad. The Soviet invasion, and the ensuing international movement of *mujahidin* to fight it, coincided with a sociological phenomenon that nobody in the West seems to have anticipated. This was the emergence of the first mature generation of the Saudi middle class—the Arabian equivalent of the Western baby boomers. Products of educational and economic changes in the Peninsula beginning after the second world war, these young people constituted a middle class without capitalism. Brought up under a bureaucratic theocracy and drilled in fanaticism, they encountered few of the opportunities available to the middle class in the industrialized nations or even in transitional states like Malaysia. Trained to be semi-idle state functionaries in a system destined to shrink, not to expand, they were cut off from global reality.

The young Saudi middle class of the 1970s greatly resembled the German middle class of the 1920s. Both had enjoyed enormous social advantages, and both had been promised the world; yet both found themselves in a historical impasse with no apparent exit. Just as the German middle class had been raised to believe in the superiority of their imperial power, so had the Saudis been indoctrinated in the separatist, supremacist, intolerant, and brutalizing curriculum of Wahhabism. Faced with marginalization, in both cases a deranging anxiety drove them to seek a "conspiratorial" understanding of their misfortunes. In their irrational search for explanations and scapegoats the German middle class of the

Weimar period and their Saudi counterparts in the 1970s also anticipated the confusion of the Communist cadre in Moscow during the ultimate crisis of their system in the 1980s. All three found their ideal enemies in capitalism and supported totalitarian terrorism.

The arrival of this unstable Saudi middle class made Wahhabism and "Salafism" more virulent than ever. It now had millions of young, vigorous, semieducated, indoctrinated, and frustrated followers. These youthful misfits from the urban centers of the Arabian Peninsula, as well as from Egypt and other Arab countries, took up the *jihad* in Afghanistan, a country of which they typically knew nothing. They became "sacred soldiers" as *mujahidin*, and were known as "Afghan Arabs." Their main Afghan enabler was a Wahhabi of Pashtun origin, Abdul Rasul Sayyaf, who received vast sums from the Saudis but fell out with them when he backed Saddam Husayn in the 1991 invasion of Kuwait. During much of the anti-Russian war, Hekmatyar and Sayyaf served as two legs of a Wahhabi colossus that rose on the Afghan-Pakistan border.

These "Afghan Arabs," once they had stood in the front ranks of battle, found it unattractive to return to their mediocre existence back home. Some of them seem to have become attached to the rough mountain beauty of Central Asia, which differed so much from their places of birth. But in addition, death as a martyr or *shehid* in *jihad* guaranteed that one would never have to submit to the demands of ordinary existence. The lure of death in combat was increased by the belief that religion in all its forms had always taught: that the rewards of the hereafter are superior to those of the material world. References to these concepts, in addition to the appeal of the Black-Eyed Virgins awaiting the *shehid* in Paradise, are replete in narratives left by Arab volunteers who died in Afghanistan.

Marriage to the Black-Eyed Virgins in Paradise could also be a preferable alternative to arranged weddings and suffocating family situations in one's original environment. Thus, for example, Yasin Al-Jazairi (Abdur-Rab-un-Noor Hamid), an Algerian killed in Afghanistan in 1989, was described by his associates as "one who fled from marriage in this Life, to marriage in the Next." A memorial written for him by Abdullah Yusuf Azzam (mentor of Osama bin Laden as well as "Afghan Arabs" in general) speaks volumes on this question: "He graduated from high school, and then worked in administration. His parents got him engaged to a girl, because they desired to gratify their eyes with the sight of a grandchild. The engagement took place and the preparations for the wedding began. A short while before the wedding Yasin was flicking through a magazine on *jihad* in the Land of Courage and Sacrifice [Afghanistan]—what could there be after this?" The memorial continued, "Does marriage count as an excuse to abstain from the *jihad?*" In the end, "He finally decided absolutely that he must buy a ticket to take him to the *jihad* with the money he had saved for his wedding. As for marriage, perhaps it might be in Paradise with the Wide-Eyed Paradise Maidens."

Similar evidence of abandoned commitments and personal adventurism, of a kind that is strictly condemned by traditional Islam, is found in other "Afghan Arab" narratives. Diraar ash-Sheeshani, a Jordanian veteran of Afghanistan and devoted follower of Abdul Rasul Sayyaf, was killed in 1989 in a terrorist incident in Israel. He habitually recited a verse to Azzam, "cowards see cowardice as courage," which could apply as much to himself and other terrorists as to those who supposedly failed to accept the *jihad* challenge. Azzam wrote of him, "Diraar tried to bring his wife with him to the *jihad*, but she refused, so he left her to her worldly life." Indeed, once the real *jihad* in Afghanistan had ended and the Azzam–bin Laden terror command had established itself under the Taliban regime, it seems to have become common for the wives and children of combatants to be dragged off to live in "*jihad*" communities. Some operatives in the West also seem to have used their families as a cover for their activities.

In a similar example of irresponsibility masquerading as religious heroism, a citizen of the United Arab Emirates known as Abu Muslim al-Imaraati was killed in Bosnia in 1995 while serving as commander of the foreign *mujahidin* there. He had left his pregnant wife to fight and never saw his son. Azzam's acolytes offered his family scant comfort: "He did not see his son in this world, but God willing, he will be reunited with his family in paradise." The pathos of these atomized individuals is also reflected in a memorial to Jamal-ad-din Yamani, an "Afghan Arab" veteran from Yemen, killed in Bosnia in 1993, at 19. He had, it was said, "dreamed of his wife in Paradise and Paradise itself, while in the *jihad* in Afghanistan."

A delirious commentary on these themes appeared in 2000, written by an individual calling himself Amir Sulaiman, who from internal textual evidence appears to have been an American. Titled *The Battlefield: the Safest Place on Earth*, it declared, "I have found no safer place for me in the heavens or earth than the battlefield fighting (physically) for the sake of Allah." It listed the rewards promised the martyr in paradise:

- "All his sins are forgiven from the first drop of blood.

- "He is saved from the punishment of the grave.

- "He will cross the *sirat* with the speed of light (the *sirat* is the bridge that crosses over the Hell fire that every Muslim has to cross on Judgment Day; some will make it and some will fall).

- "He will receive 72 women of Paradise.

- "He [will be] given a special crown and garment in Paradise so all will recognize him as a martyr.

- "He will be given the honor of interceding (with the permission of Allah) for 70 members of his family.

- "His soul will be kept in the bodies of green birds to fly around in Paradise."

The text continues, "The *mujahid* on the battlefield is in the safest position possible because the one who fights physically for the sake of Allah does not die. This is the closest thing that Allah has given the Children of Adam to immortality." But the writer also admitted that his search for existential commitment was motivated by fear, not by courage: "I am just scared that my life will not be acceptable to Allah on the Day of Judgment . . . The reason I want to fight *jihad* is not because my *iman* [faith] is strong. Rather, I want to fight *jihad* because my *iman* is weak."

For traditional Muslims as well as non-Muslims knowledgable about Islamic history, nothing could be more wretched and perverse. The heroes who fought their way under Ottoman command almost to Vienna over half a millennium between the 14th and 18th centuries were overwhelmingly ordinary, normal men, even when they were called by their faith, and exalted by Sufi spirituality, to combat for God. To compare them with confused middle-class youths who deserted their families and sought death out of boredom and a weak spirit would seem disrespectful, to say the least.

Abdullah Azzam, who enticed so many of these alienated youths to their deaths, was Palestinian, not Saudi; but his mentality was thoroughly Wahhabi, and he formulated the diabolical conception that led "Afghan Arabs" to launch a *"jihad"* against America. A text produced by his followers declares,

> The Americans, to this day, arrogantly claim that the victory of the *Mujahidin* in Afghanistan was due to their support. They further claim that the training of the *Mujahidin* was by American CIA agents. Thus, they falsely claim the credit for a victory that Allah had bestowed upon the *Mujahidin* through his Grace and due to their perseverance.
>
> America did send some support to the Afghan *Mujahidin*, but that came after a minimum of two years into the war, when the *Mujahidin* were already gaining victory after victory. This support also was very limited. Many a *mujahid* is heard saying: "Where was that support when we needed it? We never saw a single American-made weapon that came to us . . . our weapons were old broken rifles that our donkeys would carry over the mountains for us . . ."

Forced to address certain obvious facts, the same extremists write,

> It has to be said that America did provide Stinger missiles and more support in terms of advanced weaponry towards the end of the war—when it was apparent to everyone that the *Mujahidin* would emerge victorious. And, furthermore, that support was coupled with a malicious design to coerce signing of the "Geneva Accord" and to create in-fighting between the dif-

ferent groups. This was with the aim of preventing formation of a *Mujahidin* government based on *Shariah*. It was to this end that a large quantity of the so-called American "support" was used! So much for their false claims and propaganda!

Although Azzam clothed his complaints in such rhetoric, in reality he had developed a fantasy, based on the hatreds of Mawdudi and Sayyid Qutb, that the United States could be swindled and then attacked, just as the British had been fooled by Ibn Sa'ud into helping install the Wahhabi state as sovereign over the Two Holy Places. Also like Mawdudi and Qutb, he traveled in America; indeed, during the 1980s he conducted an extensive tour of U.S. cities, raising money and recruiting for the Afghan *jihad*.

Azzam was born in 1941. Like many other Islamic extremists, he had worked as a schoolteacher, although he gained an education in Islamic jurisprudence. He was described in his official biography as "the cleverest and smartest" among the students at an agricultural college that awarded him a diploma. With the Israeli occupation of the West Bank in 1967, he crossed the river and remained in Jordan. Curiously, he was slow to join in direct confrontation with the Jewish state. According to his biography, he was "determined to migrate . . . to learn the skills necessary to fight." In 1970 the Palestinian guerrillas were driven out of Jordan, but Azzam remained as a teacher at the University of Jordan in Amman. He studied at Al-Azhar, the famous Islamic university in Egypt, where he became acquainted with the family of his idol, Sayyid Qutb. He was irritated to realize that the Palestinian war on Israel was led by people uninterested in religion and who, indeed, violated every one of the Wahhabi strictures, including those against music and other pleasures. His biography states, "One day he rhetorically asked one of the *mujahidin* what the religion behind the Palestinian revolution was, to which the man replied, quite clearly and bluntly, 'This revolution has no religion behind it.' This was the last straw. Shaykh Abdullah Azzam left [Jordan], and went to Saudi Arabia to teach in the universities there."

The truth is more revealing. A University of Jordan professor of religious law, Azzam was among the leaders of the local branch of the Muslim Brotherhood. He was dismissed from the faculty for his attacks on

Jordanian state policy, especially with regard to Israel. He then fled to the Saudi kingdom where he worked as a professor. Impressed by the purity of faith of the Afghan Sufis fighting the Russians, he decided to use them and their battleground as a field to generate a new zeal among Arabs for the "lost art and science of *jihad.*"

Azzam therefore went to Pakistan and founded an organization, known in English as the *Mujahidin* Service Bureau and in Arabic as Bayt ul-Ansar or House of the Helpers (the Helpers were the residents of Yathrib who had invited Muhammad to found Medina). The Service Bureau, funded extravagantly by the Saudis, administered travel and training for volunteers coming to fight in Afghanistan. But Azzam was isolated as a Palestinian in the Afghan war. The volunteers who came to him were mainly citizens of the Saudi kingdom, Yemen, the United Arab Emirates, and other parts of the Peninsula, followed by Egyptians and Algerians. Even the rage of Palestinians against Israel was little inducement for them to go fight in a country they did not know, inhabited by people who spoke a different language. The Russians had supported the Palestinians in the past and would probably do so again. More important, few Palestinians then saw their struggle as an Islamic one. They felt little in common with the Afghans, whom they viewed as backward and uncivilized. The active soldiers in Azzam's war were therefore drawn from communities most infected with the disease of Wahhabism.

For native Afghans, *jihad* was the only possible means of liberating their country from Communist colonialism, while Wahhabis were motivated by yearning for death and exaltation of martyrdom. However, not all of them, regardless of the misfortunes of their birth and upbringing, suffered the malady in equal measure. Some celebrated when their comrades were killed, and some who were preparing to die, or who knew they were mortally wounded, rejoiced. But many they left behind wept at the loss of their brethren.

The adroit propagandist Abdullah Azzam apparently saw no contradictions in this situation. Exploiting and, no doubt, exaggerating reports of inspiring and extraordinary experiences undergone by the fighting Afghans, he wrote a book describing such "combat miracles." In it, and in his lecture tours, including several across the United States, he described countless incidents in which, against incomparable odds, *mujahidin* units or individuals were able to destroy whole Soviet battalions or tank columns or avoid inevitable death in close confrontation with the enemy. He never mentioned the Soviet Army's poor record in fighting nondefensively, or the role of American arms assistance. Describing these occurrences as similar to the great battles Muhammad fought against the unbelievers and idolaters, he declared that the success of the *mujahidin* was made possible by the invisible swords of avenging angels. This propaganda was powerfully persuasive to many young men, who, having been raised in the fundamentalist subculture, had no context for judging such claims.

Among ordinary Afghans, Wahhabis and "Salafis" were almost as rare as Palestinians, except among young people impressed by Mawdudi and Sayyid Qutb after 1973. Islam had come to Afghanistan during the period of Muhammad's immediate successors, and mature Afghan Islam was traditional, Sufi, and pluralist; the Naqshbandi, Qadiri, and Chishti dervish orders were especially strong. A European writer, Bo Utas, who visited Afghanistan in 1978, observed that "almost every grown-up man in the country seemed to have some kind of relationship with a Sufi" teacher. Shi'as had lived in the country since the beginning of their movement, and Mazar-i-Sharif, or "the noble tomb," derived its name from the belief that the fourth rightly guided caliph, Ali, was buried there. The anti-Soviet resistance included respected Sufis, including Sibghatullah Mujaddidi (who served after the Russian defeat as interim head of state in 1989 and as acting president of the country in 1992) and the Qadiri *Pir* Sayyid Ahmad Gailani. Both remain active political leaders in Afghanistan in the aftermath of the 2001–2002 antiterror war.

Mujaddidi traced his unbroken ancestry to an outstanding Islamic theologian and Sufi, Shaykh Ahmad al-Faruqi as-Sirhindi, also known as *Imam* Rabbani, and recognized in Muslim tradition as the "Reviver of Islam." Mujaddidi had been imprisoned by the Afghan government during the 1960s, in a period of pro-Soviet alignment, on the amazing charge of plotting to assassinate Soviet Premier Nikita Khrushchev. The Mujaddidi family lived in a large walled compound outside Kabul. The Russians announced their visit to the site in December 1979, when a tank round destroyed the gate and Communist soldiers arrested all within, except for a 10-month-old boy who was left in his crib. The child was rescued and smuggled to a relative who remained free. Sibghatullah had also escaped and became an early leader of the anti-Russian combatants. But 79 other family members had already been slaughtered by the Communists at the beginning of 1979, and 40 more, including the elderly Shaykh Ibrahim Mujaddidi, head of the Naqshbandi-Mujaddidi order, were deported to Russia where they disappeared, their fate unknown to this day.

Notwithstanding their domination of the anti-Russian military struggle, the Wahhabis had relatively little luck implanting their religious dispensation in Afghanistan. However, a group of Pashtuns studying in the *medresas* on the other side of the Pakistan border—known as the Students or Taliban—came within their gravitational field. After the Saudis broke with their former client, Sayyaf, they adopted the Taliban as protégés, and the latter were quickly Wahhabized.

Why did U.S. policymakers fail to understand the conflict within the Afghan resistance? The error was colossal. Yet it was merely one example of a set of mental habits in a State Department and a Washington policy community characterized by bureaucratic conservatism. In 1980, foreign observers simply and stupidly condemned the Afghan fighters as psychologically and culturally prone to divisiveness, ignoring the significance of the conflict between traditional Islam and Wahhabism. And what other factors brought about this failure? The refusal of Western academic and media experts on the Saudi kingdom to understand and warn the world about Wahhabism was clearly a major issue. Intellectual incapacity and automatic affirmation of the alliance with Riyadh were both rooted in the reality of U.S. energy economics. Certainly, Western media that had never reported on Wahhabism or its imitators could not be expected to understand the inner life of the "Afghan Arabs," much less real Afghans. But the situation was aggravated by the Pakistani government, which through its ISI controlled the Afghan *mujahidin*.

The two faces of Islam were revealed in the confrontation between traditionalists and Wahhabis in the Afghan resistance. The inability of U.S. policymakers to grasp this division and its possible consequences was, and remains, both disturbing and dangerous. It was as if the Reagan and Bush administrations had refused to back Polish Solidarity or the Nicaraguan presidential candidacy of Violeta Chamorro. But it was much easier for Washington policy experts to comprehend the Solidarity trade union or the opposition struggle of the Nicaraguan anti-Communists than the Sufis of Afghanistan. In the Western cases the Catholic church played a major role in guiding events; there was no comparable religious institution to help the traditional Afghan Muslims make Washington understand that their disagreement with the Wahhabis represented a historic combat for the soul of the world's Muslims. As far as Westerners were concerned, Sufism was a highly esoteric phenomenon that had nothing discernible to do with anything political or newsworthy.

Twenty years later, while working in the Balkans, I was told by a Foreign Service veteran, when seeking to bring up the issue of Wahhabi infiltration into Kosovo, that the United States was not in the business of starting religious wars (my reply: how about stopping one?). The same individual informed me that as far as he was concerned dervishes were people who spent all their time whirling (this in Kosovo, where a third of all Muslims are Sufis).[1] Few Americans knew enough to comprehend the fractious Afghan resistance. On one side, there was the bright aspect of Sufi traditionalism, ever renewed, happy, filled with love of God and humanity, seeking to embrace believers in the other monotheistic faiths, always committed to the defense of human dignity. On the other was the ugly visage of Wahhabi fundamentalism, narrow, rigid, tyrannical, separatist, supremacist, and violent. Had they been able to distinguish between them, Western rulers might have made the correct choice—to support the real struggle of the Afghan people against Soviet domination as they had helped the Poles and Nicaraguans. But they did not, and at the time they probably could not: Islam, especially in the days of Khomeini, remained too alien and frightening. The State Department was simply unprepared for so great a challenge, as it would again prove unprepared in the aftermath of September 11.

Besides, in the previous decades the Western academy's "Middle East Studies" branches had come under the baleful influence of leftism. Innumerable professors had imposed a paradigm under which conflicts and issues throughout the Islamic world were viewed exclusively as consequences of Western imperialism, "Orientalism," economic dependency and poverty, and the alleged need for a Muslim "Reformation." In such an intellectual environment, it was unsurprising that many academics viewed the Soviet invasion as a benign development.

One of the worst blunders by American policymakers was to ignore the importance and potential contribution of the former Afghan king, Zahir Shah. The United States failed to realize that the restored monarchy could create a stable and traditional government prepared to deal with the modern world in a mature but balanced manner. The American incapacity to help the Afghans create a civil alternative to Soviet colonialism also meant that the existing traditional social institutions would be undefended against both Communism and Wahhabism. In some sense, then, the United States shares the blame for the devastation of Afghan society.

The sequence of events reminds one of the biblical story of Jacob, the son of Isaac and nephew of Ishmael, and the two daughters of Laban. Jacob was promised the beautiful Rachel, but found himself the morning after his wedding in bed with the ugly Leah. Arthur Koestler cited this scripture as a metaphor for the disillusionment of Communist intellectuals with Stalin. But it could also be applied to the disastrous mistake of American policymakers in Afghanistan, who went into the tent thinking they would be embraced by angels of religious freedom and discovered much, much later that they had consummated a marriage with a Wahhabi succubus. Moreover, it took the Americans much longer than Jacob to find out they had been swindled. Widespread recognition of the ugliness of the Wahhabi face of Islam would be delayed until the horror of September 11.

A significant turning point on the road from Afghanistan to the Twin Towers was the encounter in 1985 between Abdullah Azzam and two other men, Ayman al-Zawahiri and Osama bin Laden. The latter, a typical rich Saudi and Wahhabi fanatic whose father had overseen the Wahhabi "rehabilitation"—actually an uglification—of the Ka'bah, was moved to go to Afghanistan by Azzam's speechifying. By 1989, and doubtless thanks to infusions of cash from his family fortune, bin Laden had risen high in the ranks of Azzam's organization. That year Azzam was blown apart by a car bomb. No suspect in the murder has ever been named. The year 1989 saw the withdrawal of Russian troops and the commencement of the open crisis of Soviet Communism. Triumphalism became visible among the "Afghan Arabs." As Abdullah Azzam exulted in a speech delivered in the United States in December 1988, even before the Russian retreat: "O brothers! After our experience in Afghanistan, nothing in the world is impossible for us anymore! Small power or big power, what is decisive is the willpower that springs from religious belief." Thus the "Afghan" Wahhabis, having helped knock Communist Russia off its foundations, fantasized that they could do the same to Israel, India, and, above all, the United States.

Also in 1989, the Islamic world was moved by the death of Ayatollah Khomeini. Khomeini had responded in a curiously different manner to the Russian agony, which he saw as an inevitable consequence of Godless materialism. As recounted by his biographer, Hamid Algar, in 1988 he sent a letter to the last of the old-style Soviet rulers, Mikhail Gorbachev, in which he analyzed the weakness of Russian society as a product of atheism and recommended that Soviet scholars come to Iran to study the works of the philosophers Al-Farabi and Ibn Sina (Avicenna) and the Sufis Suhrawardi and Ibn Arabi. Khomeini believed that such an intellectual reorientation would set Russian society on the new and morally healthy basis necessary for its rebirth.

Khomeini's will, made public in 1989, contained words that struck the Wahhabis like arrows: "Satanic powers have, through their puppet regimes who sham Islam, undertaken to reprint and publish the Holy *Qur'an*, distorting sacred verses to serve their devilish ends. Such *Qur'ans* are published with attractive calligraphy and binding and are distributed everywhere with the aim of eventually removing the Holy Book from all scenes . . . We note that each year King Fahd of Saudi Arabia spends a good deal of the wealth of the people in printing the Holy *Qur'an* and considerable publicity and propaganda material in support of anti-Quranic ideas propagating the baseless and superstitious cult of Wahhabism . . . Fahd abuses the *Qur'an* . . . He uses the noble Islam and the Holy Book to destroy both."

Khomeini was now out of the way. Even at this supreme moment, however, Wahhabism was confronted with its own contradictions: Everybody in the world knew that the provision of U.S. Stinger missiles had contributed far more to the victory over the Russians than Saudi religious blandishments. Here was yet another imperative for Wahhabism to surpass its previous limits and launch the worldwide *"jihad"* it had always promised.

The next phase of the global Wahhabi campaign involved the penetration of Muslim societies within the former Communist empires of Russia and Yugoslavia, suddenly opened up by the disintegration of the Marxist-Leninist order. "Revival of Islam," which Wahhabism had transformed into a massive commercial enterprise, would provide cover for aggression in countries like Tajikistan and Uzbekistan. Most important, the entire range of programs that had been devised for Wahhabi-Saudi infiltration, from free *hajj* tickets to free education for *imams*, would lay the basis for the attempted Wahhabization of these countries and the destruction of their indigenous Islamic cultures, which were and remain mainstream Sunni, Sufi, and pluralist. Where Wahhabism appeared, its companion and scout would always be war, including terror against local Muslims carried out by mercenary forces funded and trained by the Saudis. Western observers missed this because they did not see the hidden connections between the various struggles going on in the Muslim world. This was a result of a successful strategy to intervene in or initiate not one but a number of small-scale *"jihads,"* in Central Asia, the Caucasus, Kashmir, and elsewhere—seemingly separate conflicts that were all elements of a larger design.

Throughout the 1980s, the Wahhabi-Saudi power and the West had shared an apparent common interest in containing Iran's perceived threat of exporting Shi'a radicalism throughout the Gulf. The eastern regions of the Saudi kingdom, Bahrein, and other Gulf states with sizeable Shi'a populations appeared to be ripe for such an appeal. The Saudis repeatedly stressed this menace to U.S. officials. To the extent that this was true, which was not much, it was not due to the attractions of Khomeini's radicalism but to the long chronicle of dreadful abuse suffered by the Shi'as in Iraq and the Arabian Peninsula at the hands of the Wahhabis. But the Saudis had sold the West a false depiction of Shi'as everywhere as wild-eyed fanatics and of Wahhabis as trustworthy defenders of the traditional Islamic order. The truth was exactly the opposite: In Albania, Turkey, Iraq, and other countries, Shi'as were a force for progress and social reform, while Wahhabis pursued their usual program of indoctrination in hatred and intolerance.

But the West had been so frightened by Khomeini that its leaders enthusiastically supported the Saudi line. Western academics who should have understood this problem and warned Western leaders were too hypnotized by the spectres of imperialism, "Orientalism," and dependency even to begin to understand it. For this reason, the Western academy was complicit in the disaster. In the first attempt to confront the Shi'a challenge, the West had backed the demoniacal Saddam Husayn against Iran. Providing Saddam with billions of dollars and vast quantities of military aid, the Saudis fueled the war against the Shi'a state, from which the Iranian regime emerged stronger than ever. Saddam became a regional threat thanks to American ignorance of the real Wahhabi agenda in confronting Iran, as well as of Saudi ambitions as a competitor, not a subordinate, to the United States in global politics.

Internationally projected Wahhabism could not recruit new soldiers without finding Muslims undergoing extraordinary suffering of the kind that had wracked Lebanon and Afghanistan. Much discourse had presented the Palestinians as victims, but if anything the war against Israel enjoyed a surfeit of ready volunteers, and the Wahhabis could not exclude Palestinian Christians from that struggle, as they would have wished. Further, because of the continuing involvement of the United States, Europe, and various Arab states at the highest levels of Middle East diplomacy, the Palestinian conflict could not easily be reduced to an exclusively military effort such as would have favored the "Afghan Arab" strategy. Guerrilla tactics had failed in Israel, although the Palestinians were unwilling to give them up. With the rise of the Wahhabi group Hamas, the Palestinian guerrilla struggle degenerated into pure terrorism.

Hamas had emerged as a religious alternative to the secular emphasis of Arafat's classic form of Palestinian nationalism. At the beginning, it was allegedly supported by the Israelis to counter Arafat's influence. But its ideology was always "Salafi"/Wahhabi, i.e., deeply extremist, and Saudi influence, thanks to petrodollars, soon came to predominate within it. Nevertheless, the controversy over land rights and political sovereignty in Israel and the Palestinian territories, though bloody at times, was never as dramatic as that between the Afghans and the Russians.

The failure of the Palestinian guerrillas to gain victory was easy to understand. Notwithstanding Palestinian rhetoric about Israel as an alleged "settler state," Israelis were never colonizers in the usual sense, however European their sensibilities and regardless of how many "colonies" in the form of cooperatives or settlements they created. They were simply not alien to the land, historically or psychologically; they were and felt themselves to be redeemers of it. The Jewish link to the country was attenuated but undeniable. Perhaps most important, the Jews saw their return to Israel as a fulfilment of God's promise, a divine destiny they would not be denied. The majority of Palestinians, on the other hand, had varied in their allegiances, many having welcomed the British in their "liberation" of the Holy Land from the Ottomans.

Patrons and survivors of the Afghan Wahhabi campaign, thirsty for the opportunity to kill and die for God, and compel others to do the same, looked for new fields of fire into which they could plunge themselves. They had to make their "*jihad*" permanent. Unfortunately, the breakup of Sovietism and a revival of Christian Orthodox nationalism would create such theatres of war in the Balkans and the Caucasus. If the Russians and their imitators learned a lesson in Afghanistan, it was that a strategy of political aggression, terrorism, and the use of irregular forces would be more useful in stirring Slavs to fight an Islamic scapegoat than one resting on conscript armies and the manning of permanent garrisons. Afghanistan, though a catastrophe for the Soviet Union, was only the first of a series of new assaults on Muslims by disaffected Slavs.

The Russian confrontation with Muslims, first in Afghanistan, then in Chechnya and elsewhere in the former Soviet Union, had its parallel, which came to fruition, in the Balkans. The Bulgarian, Serbian, and Macedonian Communist parties artificially fostered Christian Orthodox nationalism as a means to maintain their power. There was no Wahhabi instigation or involvement until after bloodshed had begun, and it remained manipulative rather than provocative.

But where the Russian assault on the Islamic "other" had failed in Afghanistan, a strategy of Slavic Orthodox confrontation with domestic Muslims would, at the beginning, succeed in the Balkans, which housed large Islamic minorities. Bulgaria and Yugoslavia proved far more apt as battlefields for the transformation of Slavic Communist dictatorships into Slavic nationalist states. This leads one to wonder if extremism among Slav Orthodox Communists might not have originated in a plan developed by the ramshackle and tottering Soviet hierarchy. Such a scheme may well have involved a "dry run" in Bulgaria, followed by "wet operations" in Yugoslavia, with further applications in Azerbaijan, Chechnya, and other Muslim nations within the convulsed Soviet empire.

After the occupation of Afghanistan in 1979 came a generally successful campaign by Communist Bulgaria, during the 1980s, to expel or forcibly "Bulgarize" its Muslim populations. As much as 15 percent, or about 2.5 million, of Bulgaria's population was Muslim at the beginning of the decade. Suddenly, without pretext or warning, nearly a half million were expelled to Turkey. Thousands who considered themselves culturally Turkish fled east across the border, and thousands more, purely Slavic Muslims and historically Bulgarian in culture, but who bore Islamic names, were compelled to adopt new, "national" identities. This demographic experiment coincided with the rise in Yugoslavia of anti-Muslim propaganda, as a background for the emergence of Slobodan Milošević, who would kill more Muslims in Europe than any other Christian ruler in recent times. Both of these Balkan assaults on the security of local Muslims occurred while a weakened Moscow contended with the Afghan quagmire.

Soon the borderlands were aflame: Everywhere Slavic conquests had impinged on the Muslim world. As the Soviet "Union" fell apart, Armenian nationalists attacked Azerbaijan, resulting in horrific carnage. The Chechens, who had become handy targets for police aggression in the country's major cities, reemerged as a central element in the Soviet breakdown. Chechens in the Soviet Army supported Baltic and other small nations in their struggles for independence, and Russian troops in the Caucasus resumed their legendary habits of pillage, torture, and massacre.

The worst such clash came in Bosnia-Hercegovina in 1992. This beautiful, tranquil Alpine country, only an hour by air from Vienna and Rome, was an unknown laboratory for the development of an indigenous European Islam, of a kind unseen since the fall of Granada in 1492. Its traditions were pluralist, and Bosnian Communism had combined economic development with neutrality toward Islam, which shielded the populace from any threat of Wahhabi or other extremist appeals. Bosnia, in other words, was poised to create a truly modern Euro-Islam. As H.E. Mustafa efendija Cerić, head of the Bosnian Muslim clerics, has written, "These Muslims, born in Europe, wish to preserve their identity in a challenging European political, economic, and cultural environment, and are waiting for those who will help them be proud of their Islam as well as their European identity."

The educational level of Bosnians was high, although Yugoslavia showed surprising gaps in this area. In addition, a distinguished Sephardic Jewish remnant played a leading role in urban Bosnia, unique in contemporary Europe. The University of Sarajevo drew students from throughout the *ummah*. In 1984, Sarajevo hosted the Winter Olympics. In winter sports alone Bosnia had immense potential for prosperity based on tourism. Indeed, it had the option of becoming a Balkan Singapore, an entrepôt between East and West drawing investment and finance from all the leading countries. But this was not to be; instead, Bosnia would become a Balkan Lebanon. The Serbian Communist regime, which had monopolized tax and other functions in a Yugoslavia now crumbling, was to be preserved at any price, by launching the Yugoslav Army, assisted by unemployed and alienated Serbian youth, into genocidal wars against their neighbors. Milošević and his clique embarked on this campaign in a desperate bid to preserve their rule, surrounded as they were by Communist regimes giving way to democracy. In so doing, they attempted to destroy a European outpost of cosmopolitan Islamic culture that was prepared for a harmonious, multireligious existence.

The horrors inflicted by the Serbs and Croats in Bosnia were unlike anything seen in Europe since the second world war. They included mass executions, the assassination of women, children, and the elderly and infirm, mass rapes, sexual enslavement, wholesale torture, deportations of the residents of whole districts, the erection of concentration camps, and the attempt at complete destruction of a cultural legacy, including historic religious structures as well as libraries and other resources.

The Bosnian war had an impact on the *ummah* unlike anything else in recent times. Whatever could be said about the Arab-Israeli wars, the Israeli Defense Forces had never engaged in the mass rape of Muslim women and girls; such a thing was inconceivable. Nor had the West turned away from the conflict in Israel, to say nothing of Afghanistan, as policymakers and diplomats did in the Bosnian case. Christian Europe was, it seemed, unwilling to accept an independent and viable Muslim-majority society in its heartland (Albania had a Muslim majority but was considered a Mediterranean basket case and therefore negligible). The entire series of Arab-Israeli wars, from 1948 to the end of the millennium, had taken no more than 30,000 lives, while at least 200,000 people were wiped out in Bosnia in three years. The horrors of Bosnia were profoundly distressing, and they seemed interminable. Each atrocity was exceeded by some new, ghastly event; observers of the situation had no chance to recover from one before another would occur. This was effective terror.

The siege of Sarajevo, in which 12,000 ordinary citizens, including more than 1,100 children, were coldly shot down by snipers or killed by heavy-gauge shellfire while attempting to go about their normal affairs, offered an unsurpassable benchmark for modern brutality. In addition to the blood in the streets of Sarajevo, the city, one of the loveliest in the world, was lashed by hunger as the Serbs closed all entryways for relief supplies. During the siege, people starved in Sarajevo while others looked on; people stole in Sarajevo, from their oldest neighbors and friends; people who never, previously, told even a minor lie to a compatriot, swindled each other in Sarajevo, and women who would otherwise have become good and caring wives and mothers sold themselves in Sarajevo. All while from the peaks where Olympic athletes, only eight years before, had begun their graceful descents through the deep, clean snow, a storm of hellfire poured down, from the artillery, sniper weapons, and rocket launchers of the Yugoslav and Serbian forces.

Yet in the dark night of Sarajevo, the Muslim call was still heard: God is great! God is great! *Allahu-akbar! Allahu-akbar!* The *tekbir* became the battle cry of the Army of the Republic of Bosnia-Hercegovina (ARBH), even though that military body, routinely described as "Muslim forces" by world media, included Serbs, Jews, and others as well as Muslims. Several Jews played leading roles in the defense of Sarajevo and Bosnia, and the state of Israel, operating through the Joint Distribution Committee, air-lifted medicines into the city, establishing three free pharmacies and saving Sarajevo from epidemics. In addition, the Sarajevo Jews operated a soup kitchen with food free to all comers, and a pre-Communist Sephardic community relief organization, La Benevolencia, was revived as a nonsectarian institution serving all Sarajevans.[2] The ARBH, which employed the rhetoric of Tito's multinational Partisan tradition, had more in common with the Soviet Army at Stalingrad than with the *mujahidin* in Afghanistan. It was a regular army drawn from former Yugoslav ranks, commanded by experienced officers and structured according to established military principles. Hundreds of thousands served in it or functioned under its command; the citizens of Sarajevo all submitted to its discipline. Yet its supply train was always tenuous, and nobody knew from one day to the next if it would not disappear from the earth, taking its obscure nation, of which many people had never before heard, with it.

News of Muslim women and girls raped in Bosnia stabbed to the heart of every Muslim in the world. The repetition of these reports in global media generated feelings of fear, helplessness, and outrage. The complicity of Christian Europe in the nightmare aggravated these feelings. The whole *ummah* idolized Bosnian President Alija Izetbegović. Millions around the world learned that the British General Michael Rose openly expressed his contempt for the Bosnian Muslims and friendship for the Serbs; that a Japanese humanitarian functionary, Yasushi Akashi, as much as accused the Muslims in Sarajevo of shelling themselves; that French troops permitted the murder of Bosnian leader Hakija Turajlić, who trusted them to protect him from the Serbs, and that Dutch troops helped the monstrous Serb criminal Ratko Mladić carry out the murder of some 8,000 Muslim men and boys at Srebrenica. Blood had run in streams through the country's waters, torrents of tears were shed, chastity was violated, holy sites were profaned, graves were uprooted. To Muslims, Bosnia had the impact of a Holocaust, in the heart of a Europe that had claimed no such genocide would ever happen again within its borders. Despite the common European and leftist tendency to blame Islamic extremist rage on American and Israeli policy in the Middle East, their own contribution to this anger—represented by European passivity in the face of the Bosnian horror—is rarely, if ever, acknowledged.

Stories about the murders and rapes in Bosnia were employed by the acolytes of Abdullah Azzam and Osama bin Laden as recruiting propaganda. Yet strangely, few of the "Afghan Arabs" joined the Bosnian *jihad*. Bosnian Muslims needed friends, and they were grateful for the participation of "Afghan Arabs," numbering no more than a few thousand, in their defense. The ARBH, as noted, included hundreds of thousands of fighters, and the *mujahidin* did not influence the course of a single battle in the Bosnian conflict. They did, however, become known for committing atrocities against Bosnian Croats and Serbs. While the level of war crimes on the Bosnian Muslim side was markedly lower than that among their adversaries, several incidents are known where *mujahidin* engaged in torture and murder of prisoners.[3]

The *mujahidin* were largely Saudi or Gulf state adventurers who loved war; the Bosnians were typical Europeans who had come to hate war after their experience of Fascist occupation and Partisan struggle in 1941–45, a torment revived a generation later. The Bosnian Muslims, like the traditional Muslims in Afghanistan, fought for their country and for things Wahhabis despised: their distinctive Balkan music, their decorated Ottoman mosques, their Sufi and other long-established Islamic customs, not for the "purification" of Islam or death as escape from a banal existence. While the frustrated middle-class youth of the Saudi kingdom sought martyrdom as an alternative to uselessness and boredom, the Bosnian Muslims, whose forebears were lions of the faith, refused to die. Here were the two faces of Islam in their most compelling images: the true *jihad* of the Bosnians versus the false *"jihad"* of Saudi vagabonds.

The conduct of the Bosnian Muslims also contrasted dramatically with that of Palestinian extremists in their war against Israel. In Bosnia-Hercegovina thousands of Muslim women were raped, half a million people were driven from their homes, many thousands were brutally murdered en masse, and thousands of mosques were leveled. Yet Bosnian

Muslims never engaged in suicide terrorism, even though it would have been much easier for them, since they spoke the same language and had the same appearance as their enemies. And when the United States intervened to end the Bosnian war, nobody on the Muslim side thought of prolonging the *jihad* either by further violence or by advancing excessive demands. The Bosnian Muslims wanted peace, while the Palestinian terrorists and their Wahhabi-Saudi mentors only wanted to destroy Israel. When the Bosnian war ended in 1995, no Bosnians followed the *mujahidin* off to Chechnya or Central Asia. Most of the "Afghan Arabs" departed the Balkans, although a few who had acquired Bosnian citizenship by their war service or by marrying Bosnian women settled in central Bosnia, occasioning much rumor but little local trouble, aside from conspiratorial and espionage activities carried out under Saudi protection by the al-Qaida network. (Iran had sent military technicians to Bosnia but they maintained an extremely low profile during the war and were immediately withdrawn afterward.)

It would be difficult to imagine anybody less attuned to the nuances of the Balkans than the Wahhabis. Fanatics for complete separation from unbelievers, they abhorred the very concept of mixed Islamic and non-Islamic societies such as exist throughout the region. However they might exploit the image of Muslims murdered and raped to elicit recruits, the expulsion of Muslims by Serbs and Croats caused them little concern. Some Bosnians have told me they believed the Arabs favored reduction of Muslim Bosnia-Hercegovina to its most narrow ethnic territory (a strip from Mostar to Tuzla, including Sarajevo) if this would advance a fundamentalist, separatist, and supremacist agenda. For these Wahhabi foreigners, a "green," i.e., Muslim island in Europe meant nothing unless it became a Wahhabi enclave. Needless to say, this condescending view of Balkan Islam as an object of colonization disregarded the vast contribution of Bosnians and Albanians to the development of Islamic civilization in general and the Ottoman Empire in particular. Similarly, the Saudi view of Afghanistan ignored that country's historic contributions to Islamic tradition.

In the case of the Bosnian Muslims, it also contradicted a truly ancient tradition of interfaith coexistence and intrareligious pluralism. The Bosnians had supported an independent Christian church before the Turkish conquest of the country. During Ottoman times, Bosnian Catholics enjoyed religious autonomy, while the Serb Orthodox Church functioned as the main representative of the Christian religious community. The Sephardic Jews, considered the "fourth Bosnian nation" after the Muslims, Serbs, and Croats, had been welcomed in Bosnia after their expulsion from Spain and Portugal. There were never any ghettoes or other residential restrictions on Jews in Bosnia; four synagogues remain intact in Sarajevo alone, a city that in 1941 was almost 20 percent Sephardic. Notwithstanding the horrors of the 1992–95 war and the predictable resurgence of Islamic aspects in Bosnian Muslim ethnic identity, almost no native Bosnians could conceive of their country undergoing a Taliban-style experiment in Islamic "reform."

The irrelevance of the "Afghan Arabs" and their rootless, itinerant habits, after the Russian retreat from Afghanistan, to the struggles of Balkan Muslims are epitomized by the experiences of Sabri Ibrahim al-Attar, a member of the Egyptian terrorist Islamic Group or *Gamaa al-Islamiyya*. Al-Attar was a leading witness in the 1999 investigation of the "Albanian Returnees," a Wahhabi network deported to Egypt from that Balkan nation at the instance of the U.S. Central Intelligence Agency. Born to a poor family with five children, he graduated from a technical school and began frequenting an extremist mosque in 1986 before joining the *Gamaa*. Because of his hard-line views, he rose in its ranks. In 1991 al-Attar traveled to the Saudi kingdom, following "the very traditional scenario" typical of the time, according to an Arabic media account. He was unable to find work there, but met some *mujahidin* and was passed from one to another until he encountered a bin Laden associate known as Abu Ahmad, who recruited him to go to Afghanistan, furnishing him a false passport to travel via Yemen and Pakistan. In Peshawar he landed in a house controlled by bin Laden. He received some military training from a delegation of the Muslim Brotherhood and ideologically fell between them and the *Gamaa*. Military instruction was continuous, with courses on the use of grenades, both Russian and Chinese, and bombs, as well as marksmanship.

The courses were extremely rigorous, and al-Attar was wounded in an explosion. He sojourned in Yemen and Sudan before returning to Afghanistan. In 1996 he went to Bosnia. However, these *mujahidin*-come-lately found Bosnia inhospitable—for the Wahhabi "internationals," the *jihad* of the sword in the Balkans had ended with the U.S. imposition of the Dayton agreement a year before. Al-Attar recalled, "After signing of the Dayton agreement, we Arabs felt that our stay in Bosnia was no longer desirable." Arabs in the Balkans ran afoul of U.S., European, and local law enforcement, as best illustrated by al-Attar's own arrest in Albania and repatriation to Egypt.

With the collapse of the Soviet state, Wahhabism effectively replaced the Communist movement as the main sponsor of international ideological aggression against the democratic West. One variety of extremism was replaced by another, suggesting that such madness, whatever its form, had become endemic to modern life.

Did Communist hatred of the West metastasize into a renewed Wahhabi totalitarianism? Were they simply too alike to remain distant from one another, or did some unknown, functional link exist? Certainly, Soviet Communism and Wahhabism shared many characteristics. Both were totalitarian and terroristic, and both had acquired such negative reputations that their leaders chose to disguise the identity of the movement; as the Communists called themselves "socialists" or, in the United States, "progressives," the Wahhabis appropriated the term *Salafis*, referring to the original, pious successors of Muhammad.

Wahhabism, Stalinism, and Nazism had another hidden aspect in common. All indoctrinated their followers in the mentality of "two worlds," that is, of two utterly separate realities within human society. These were, for the Communists, "the camp of imperialism" and "the camp of peace and socialism." This division of the world laid the basis for the Cold War. Wahhabis viewed the world in similar terms. They sought an *ummah* sufficient unto itself, with no "external" relations except those between Wahhabi rulers and the minority of their subjects who remained protected as People of the Book. All others were to be liquidated, beginning with the Shi'a and Sufis. Thus they split the planet between the "house of war" and the "house of peace" or "house of Islam," as the Communists divided the globe into two spheres, capitalist and socialist. This division of the world had been codified in Islam when Muslims were uniformly barred or expelled from non-Muslim communities, where "the call to prayer could not be heard," i.e., Muslims could not pray openly and Islam could not be taught. It was reinforced by periods in which Christendom was effectively closed to Muslims. But the Wahhabis made it a permanent item of faith, in line with their ferocious separatism; indeed, echoing the Khawarij, they said all areas in which non-Wahhabi Islam obtained were part of the "house of war."

The Bosnian Mustafa efendija Cerić has argued that the West should be seen as neither part of the "house of war" nor of the "house of Islam," but as belonging to a middle alternative recognized in Islamic jurisprudence as the "house of the social contract." Drawing on the French sociologist Emile Durkheim, Cerić wrote, "Europe is 'the house of social contract' because it is possible to live there in accordance with Islam," even though Muslims do not dominate and *Shariah* cannot be implemented. The United States would fall into the same category. The "house of war" represented by Soviet Communism had collapsed. Yet the Wahhabis insisted on seeing the world in rigid, binary terms. They knew no other way to think. For this reason, Cerić's conception represents one of the most powerful weapons against Wahhabi-inspired terrorism.

The ideological division of humanity into "two worlds" has been promulgated on different bases: Wahhabism applied a religious distinction, Communism a class standard, and Nazism a racial criterion. But in all cases, fanatics, repeating the fundamental error of the radicals in the French Revolution, sought to split their own societies between the virtuous, entitled to hold power and property, and the virtueless, condemned to disappear. For this reason, all three forms of totalitarianism required a constant inquisition against alleged internal enemies—traditional Muslims for the Wahhabis, Trotskyists or other dissident socialists for the Stalinists, Jews and other "antisocial elements" for the Nazis. In all three cases, the necessary internal enemy was presented as an agency of "the opposing world": Wahhabis, including the later fanatics encouraged by Mawdudi and Sayyid Qutb, attacked traditional Muslims as unbelievers,

Stalinists accused Trotskyists of being fascist agents, and the Nazis labeled the Jews as representatives of Anglo-American plutocratic finance. Finally, all three of the totalitarian collective illnesses, Wahhabism, Communism, and fascism, represented the stunted, underdeveloped, and deformed modernism of backward societies attempting, by a forced march, to catch up and surpass the more advanced and prosperous cultures.

Yet another element visible in both Stalinism and Wahhabism is the presumption that as "reforming the world" continues, crises do not diminish, but increase; the desire of all totalitarian rulers being to maintain their subjects in a condition of permanent turmoil and anxiety. In this social-Darwinist view, war is a test of purity, and those who cannot survive it do not deserve to. Wahhabism had always had this attitude, holding that the problems of the Ottoman Empire were produced by its lack of puritan rigor, and that it therefore deserved to fall, regardless of the human cost. Similarly, however they might dwell in their propaganda on the suffering of Bosnian Muslim women raped by Serbs, in their hearts the Wahhabis believed these women deserved such a fate for going out in the street without covering up from head to toe. In private, many Saudis, and in public, other Wahhabis, admitted to the view that if the Balkan Muslims were slain in the Slav Orthodox onslaught it was because God had deemed them unworthy. This was not merely a matter of passivity in the face of events that seemed ordained by the Creator, but of hatred for traditional Islam.

On these bases, Wahhabism, like the other totalitarian ideologies, inevitably assumed a posture of hostile confrontation with the Western democracies. It compelled members of the new middle classes in the Saudi kingdom and the Gulf states to eagerly kill and die, rather than to procreate and live. As bin Laden repeatedly said, his followers loved death as much as Westerners love life. Similarly, representatives of Hamas jeered at life-loving Jews in Israel. But this was something different from a yearning for the rewards of Paradise. Wahhabism is not merely a variety of religious revitalization or a hitherto-overlooked radical protest against Western imperialism; it is Islamofascism. It is thus that we must discriminate between "Islamism," "political Islam," and other categories of simple Islamic extremism and the particular influence of Wahhabi intolerance, metastasized through Mawdudi and Sayyid Qutb, in the rise of Islamic terrorism.

Even before September 11, much ink had been expended on the topic of Arab and Muslim anger at their humiliation by the West. Arabs and other Muslims, it was said, had suffered deep and repeated traumas: the decline of their civilization, their subjection to Western colonialism, and the disenfranchisement of the Palestinians. But while many Muslims had been mistreated by British, Dutch, Russian, and French imperialism, and Arabs were demoralized by the repeated victories of Israel, the humiliation of Saudi society was entirely the product of the Saudi rulers themselves. No Western army had defeated the Saudis; rather, they protected them. No Western corporations stole Arabian oil; rather, they assured payment for petroleum beyond the imaginings of any other energy exporter. No Western government imposed the corruption of the Saudi monarchy; rather, the sons of Ibn Sa'ud gratified their degenerate tastes by their own wish. But the dependence of Wahhabi authority on American arms, of Saudi profligacy on non-Islamic business practices, and of an irreligious global materialism on Arab energy resources could no longer be explained away, much less hidden. For the Arabian youth, these contradictions are unbearable, and they provide the only reasonable explanation for the presence of 15 Saudis out of 19 participants in the horror of September 11.

Western leaders have previously made the mistake of believing that corrupt and opportunistic extremists, exemplified by the Saudis, were less of a threat than convinced radicals like Khomeini and his colleagues. They did not learn the lesson of Soviet history: that the Bolsheviks of the 1920s, although they presented an open challenge to international capitalism, were less disruptive of world order than Stalin. Nor did they really understand why Mao Zedong and his Chinese Communists, although they had fought in the Korean War and were given to extraordinary outbursts of Marxist purism like the violent Cultural Revolution of the late 1960s, proved easier for the United States to deal with than the Russians.

As with Trotsky and Mao, there was never a doubt where Khomeini and the Iranian clerics stood, and their behavior could therefore be reliably predicted. And like Trotsky and Mao, Khomeini was personally disinterested. The Ayatollah said openly that he hated the West, and acted consistently with his statements. Further, aside from Hezbollah in Lebanon, few foreign groups were armed and financed by Iran—notwithstanding the widespread identification of its government as the main sponsor of state terrorism. Iran made no effort to mobilize the wider community of Shi'a Muslims on their behalf—if only because other Shi'as were Albanian, Turkish, Arab, Pakistani, Indian, and otherwise non-Iranian, and some hewed to forms of piety the Iranians found questionable. By contrast, the conduct of the Saudis was devious. They assured the West of profound affection, while fomenting worldwide adventurism and seeking to bring every Sunni Muslim on the face of the earth under their control.

Wahhabism, including its successive incarnations represented by Mawdudi and Sayyid Qutb, is as different from ordinary Islamism or Khomeinism as Stalinism was from the militant socialism that preceded it, and as Nazism differed from established conservative nationalism in Germany. To see the present global crisis as a simple conflict between Islamism and the West would therefore be as incorrect as viewing the battle for the fate of Weimar Germany as a mere confrontation between the capitalist right and the radical left. The Wahhabi-Saudi regime was never moderate, although it was presented that way to the West, nor does it reflect resentment of alleged Western injustices, as in Iran, nor is it truly conservative. It embodies a program for the ruthless conquest of power and a war of extermination against "the other," Islamic as well as Judeo-Christian. The face of Wahhabi Islam is a great deal uglier than that of a general Islamism, or Iranian anger at the West, or radical Arab nationalism, or even of Soviet Communism, and its threat to the peace and security of the whole world is immensely greater.

Wahhabism exalts and promotes death in every element of its existence: the suicide of its adherents, mass murder as a weapon against civilization, and above all the suffocation of the mercy embodied in Islam. The war against terrorist Wahhabism is therefore a war to the death, as the second world war was a war to the death against fascism. But triumph over death is the victory of life: With the Western defeat of the Taliban-Wahhabi regime in Afghanistan in 2002, the other, beautiful face of Islam was again revealed. Anthony Shadid wrote in the *Boston Globe,* "The Sufi movement, a branch of Islam in which adherents disavow dogmatic interpretations of the faith for a more personal relationship with God, is witnessing a revival, providing a new face for the religion after the Taliban's fall." The Sufi masters Mujaddidi and Gailani, who had become the most consistent opponents of both Soviet and Saudi imperialism, could now resume their spiritual mission while returning to public life in the struggle to find the right direction for the country.

Nevertheless, the Wahhabis had other places ready in which to continue their illegitimate *"jihad."* The shadow of Afghanistan continues to darken the world.

CHAPTER 7

Sword of Dishonor

THE WAHHABI INTERNATIONAL

Between the Afghan and Bosnian wars, the contradictions facing the Wahhabi-Saudi power were greatly aggravated in 1991 when Saddam Husayn invaded Kuwait. For one thing, the invasion exposed Saudi weakness and its reliance on Western support. Although billions of riyals had been spent on its military forces, the state of Al Sa'ud was incapable of defending its own territory, to say nothing of its petroleum partner, Kuwait. Americans fought and died in the Gulf War to repel Saddam's invasion: The U.S. rescued Kuwait even more directly and actively than it had assisted the Afghan resistance. Wahhabism, supposedly victorious against Soviet Communism, was thus humiliated by the upstart Ba'athist ruler of Iraq, the longtime Saudi proxy against Iran.

But the peculiar Western decision to allow Saddam to stay in place further complicated matters. Because of the inefficacy of the Saudi military, U.S. forces, including Christians, women, and, it was widely believed, Jews, remained in eastern Arabia to monitor any new Iraqi threat. In addition, renewed dependence on American forces reflected the Saudi royals' distrust of their own military's loyalty. To the reinvigorated Wahhabis, richer than ever with oil royalties after the changes of the 1970s, a scandalous defilement of the sacred territory of the Prophet Muhammad had occurred.

Never mind that the Wahhabis had always depended on military assistance from the unbelievers. They were first protected by the British, then by the United States, which maintained the air base at Dhahran from 1946 to 1962, then by French elite troops who were called on to eject a band of ultra-Wahhabis from the Ka'bah in 1979. The reappearance of the U.S. military in Arabia was the pretext for a new flight into Wahhabi fanaticism, with ultrafundamentalist scholars, as in the late 1920s, again wary of the canny statecraft of Al Sa'ud.

Osama bin Laden, burning with hatred for the unbelievers after his Afghan adventures, was among the lesser-known protestors against the return of the U.S. military presence. Flushed with the relatively easy victory over the Russians, bin Laden called on the Saudi monarchy to rely on his "Afghan Arab" *mujahidin* to repel Saddam, instead of inviting in the U.S. forces. The Saudis' rejection of this offer, doubtless motivated by fear of later subversion by the fundamentalists, caused great anger in bin Laden, leading him to a parting of ways with some of his homeland's rulers and a search for other venues for his *"jihad."*

Ibn Taymiyyah, Mawdudi, Sayyid Qutb, and Abdullah Azzam—the four horsemen of Islamic fundamentalism—would likely have been proud of bin Laden. Ibn 'Abd al-Wahhab and Ibn Sa'ud, however, would probably have chided him for his impatience, reminding him that the Wahhabis had always fooled the unbelievers into helping them—Afghanistan providing an outstanding example—and would continue doing so. But the new generation would not listen. Certain Wahhabis presented the Afghan and Gulf War victories as examples of their cunning in tricking the United States into protecting their interests. But the younger fanatics saw Muslim wars contaminated by the involvement of the unbelievers, whose motivations could only be evil.

The spoiled victories of Afghanistan and Kuwait, combined with the challenge of Iran to Wahhabi pretensions, made a difficult situation intolerable. Wahhabism owed the West far more than it was owed in return, but its perverse worldview allowed for no balancing of accounts. Wahhabism was in trouble. Unlike the Arab oil producers, the Wahhabi clerics would not allow their blackmail to be paid in cash; nothing less than blood would do. It thus became necessary for the Saudi rulers to again divert the energies of the younger fanatics by assisting bin Laden in further extending the Wahhabi "*jihad*" abroad. Since then, every country where Muslims are found has witnessed a sharpened struggle between Wahhabis and traditionalists. Some places, like Uzbekistan and Chechnya, have produced an anti-Wahhabi *jihad*.

By the year 2000, two streams of rhetoric dominated public discourse in the Saudi kingdom. For example, on February 13 of that year, Princess Noaf presided over a seminar on women's issues. Dr. Raja Bint Muhammad Audah of King Saud University in Riyadh commented on the role of women in Islam, but quickly turned to the paranoid thesis of "cultural invasion" by the West. She warned of the role of Christian missionaries in such penetration. Dr. Suheila Bint Zeinal Abdeen Hammad of the International League of Islamic Literature condemned globalization, then swung into classic Wahhabi territory by arguing that "the illiteracy and cultural stagnancy prevalent in the Arab and Muslim world resulted from the isolation imposed by Ottoman rule." Dr. Hammad also blamed the Ottomans for the spectral menace of "cultural invasion." Finally, Dr. Sara Bint Abdulmuhsin Bin Jalawi Al-Saud, from the Girls' College of Arts in Dammam, summed up the problem of "cultural invasion" by identifying it with "centers of orientalism"—the academic ideology invented by the Palestinian-American Edward Said and alleged to rule the Western mind. It would be difficult to imagine a more ridiculous display of the intellectual backwardness of the Saudi elite.

Less than two months later, the other voice of the Saudi aristocracy was heard when defense minister Prince Sultan met with his then-U.S. counterpart, William Cohen, on April 10, 2000. In a flight of language that was exaggerated even by the standards of a Saudi prince, Sultan told Cohen, "We regard the policy of the United States of America as one that follows the recommendation of the *Torah* and the *Bible* in serving humanity and justice." Prince Sultan's comments might have been motivated by a mistaken impression that Cohen is Jewish. Nevertheless, at just that time, the Wahhabis were increasing the rhetoric of world "*jihad*." The *Imam* of

Mecca, Shaykh Salih Bin Abdullah Bin Humeid, in a Friday sermon on April 22, 2000, offered a panorama of continuing massacres in the Balkans and the Caucasus, along with suffering by the Palestinians and Muslims in Kashmir, Burma, and the Philippines. His aim was to dramatize the appeal to *"jihad"* by portraying Muslims everywhere as under attack.

However, the *"jihad"* inevitably brought catastrophe, much sooner than anybody among the Wahhabis had imagined. The events of September 11, 2001, with compelling evidence of the true nature of Wahhabi extremism, exposed the "religious dilemma" facing the Saudi monarchy. In February 2002, the on-line periodical *Saudi Times* quoted Saudi journalist Dawood al-Shirian: "Shirian said the ruling Al Saud family . . . had a problem with a new breed of Muslim extremism that combines Wahhabi doctrine with activist models that took hold in the Middle East after the 1979 Islamic revolution in Iran." Shirian indicated the consequence of these developments: "Men like [Osama] bin Laden and [Taliban chief] Mullah Omar, based in a poor country, managed to raise an army of followers."

But this Wahhabi army would never have existed without oil revenues. The Saudi state sustained the global *"jihad"* by its funds for religious works. Additional efforts were developed through Kuwait and the United Arab Emirates, both of which had come under Wahhabi influence since the consolidation of the Saudi kingdom. Many more billions of dollars were expended to pay for new Wahhabi mosques and *medresas*, free *hajj* trips, training of foreign clerics in the kingdom, and printing of sectarian literature. In March 2002, the official Saudi newspaper, *Ain Al-Yaqeen*, described royal expenditures for these purposes as "astronomical." Subsidies established 1,500 mosques, 202 colleges, and some 2,000 schools for Muslim children "in non-Islamic countries in Europe, North and South America, Australia, and Asia."

In societies with many Muslims, the *medresas* were the basis for the proliferation of Wahhabi influence. The Pakistan newspaper *Jang* reported in January 2002 that the number of *medresas* in that country had risen from 2,861 in 1988 to 6,761 in 2000. At the end of the period, 1,947 belonged to the Wahhabized Deobandi sect—source of the Taliban—and 310 were directly linked to the Wahhabi-Saudi network. Sources in India, where Muslims were a minority, reported that the construction in that country of new *medresas* from 1980 to 2000, paid for by the Saudis and Kuwaitis, far exceeded the number built over eight centuries of Islamic rule. On the Indian frontier with Nepal, 384 had opened on the Indian side and 195 in Nepal. On Indian territory at the Bangladesh border, 208 had been built. In the Indian state of West Bengal, 238 *medresas* were founded between 1780 and 1977, and 269 between 1977 and 2002. The Communist government of West Bengal spent $30 million for *medresas* in 2001, and nothing on Hindu religious education.

The Saudis and other Gulf authorities maintain religious charities to which rich and poor donate, as prescribed for Muslim believers. Major beneficiaries included the previously mentioned Muslim World League (MWL), the World Assembly of Muslim Youth (WAMY), and the International Islamic Relief Organization (IIRO). Many of the charities were exposed after September 11 as backers and supporters of bin Laden. "Aid" officials, religious missionaries, and assorted hangers-on, in furtherance of extremist ends, appeared from San Francisco to Sarajevo to Singapore, coordinated by such hitherto-respectable entities as the MWL. They had powerful associations in the Saudi kingdom as well as in Pakistan, and with the organizations making up a "Wahhabi lobby" in the United States. As the *medresas* trained suicide warriors, the charities provided them with organizational assistance and cover, including travel expenses and jobs.

In the aftermath of September 11, enormous pressure came to bear on the Saudis to cooperate with U.S. and allied efforts to unravel the terrorist network behind the attacks. The Saudis were slow to respond and were notably uncooperative—understandably, considering how much they had to hide. On February 5, 2002, the Saudi Embassy in Washington finally replied to U.S. media inquiries about the role of its Islamic charities in terrorism. An embassy press release noted "reports that individuals associated with some foreign branches or offices affiliated with the International Islamic Relief Organization, the Al-Haramain Foundation, and the al-Birr Committee of the World Assembly of Muslim Youth have relationships with [terrorist] organizations." The Saudi government declared it would "take every measure possible to prevent use of these charitable efforts for any unlawful activities."

However, the very next day, the embassy issued another statement, which could not but stir doubts about Saudi commitments. In it, the Saudi Arabian Monetary Agency (SAMA) denied it was monitoring the private bank accounts of any individuals and stated that although the United Nations Security Council had advised it of 150 names of suspected terrorists, only 53 had dealings with Saudi banks, and only four accounts had been frozen. On May 14, 2002, SAMA went further when its vice-governor, Muhammad al-Jasser, declared that "not even a single bank account has been frozen in Saudi Arabia" in connection with terror funding. SAMA added to this admission the impudent charge that Israel, rather than "most Arab states," had refused to comply with international recommendations to prevent money laundering.

The International Islamic Relief Organization had already produced a rebuttal of charges that it had collaborated with terrorists, pointing out its numerous links with humanitarian nongovernmental organizations such as the United Nations High Commissioner for Refugees and the World Food Program. The IIRO claimed to assist refugees and other deserving people in Kenya and Tanzania, where bin Laden supporters had blown up two U.S. embassies in 1998, in Sierra Leone, where al-Qaida terrorists were believed to be involved in diamond trading, and in Azerbaijan and Pakistan. The Al-Haramain Foundation was accused by Russian security agencies, in May 2000, of using Chechen relief operations as a cover for recruitment, training, and support of extremists. In 2001, the Saudi Red Crescent Society, another charitable agency involved in the global expansion of terror, had paid for refugee facilities in Ingushetia, a small Muslim neighbor of Chechnya, which served as a center for Wahhabism.

Evidence of Saudi charitable institutions being used to advance terrorism was found early in 2002, in the offices of the Saudi High Commission for Relief to Bosnia-Hercegovina. Documents seized by the Sarajevo authorities revealed the scope of the Saudi-backed Wahhabi *"jihad"* in the Balkans during the previous decade.

After the Dayton agreement was negotiated in 1995, agents of the Saudi kingdom and other Gulf states had flooded the Bosnian Muslim zone. While the scruffy *mujahidin* enlisted by Abdullah Azzam and bin Laden found the streets of Sarajevo inhospitable—filled with loud music, women dressed in the latest European fashion (all black, as it happened), and Western troops and police—the Saudi High Commission had come, with considerable assurance, to take over local Islam. Rape victims and other refugees from Serb massacres, the handicapped, the widows and orphans of soldiers as well as of ordinary citizens, demolished mosques and schools—all provided pretexts for the Wahhabi infiltration of the "Pearl of the Balkans." The needy and destitute would be fed and housed—and pushed to adopt Wahhabism. Mosques and schools would be "rebuilt"—according to the strictures of Wahhabism, with Wahhabi *imams*, prayers, and other baggage imposed on local believers.

On July 13, 2001, the Saudi High Commission disclosed its income and expenditures over the previous nine years. Since the Bosnian war had begun in 1992, the Commission had collected $600 million—that is, only three times as much as the 2001 Saudi annual donation for the protection and maintenance of Islamic structures in Jerusalem. Although the Saudis preened over this effort, claiming it as uniquely grand and successful in the *ummah*, the suffering of Bosnian Muslims was clearly low on the Saudi list of priorities. In the same nine-year period, about 110,000 tons of relief supplies, or less than two shiploads in a modern container vessel, were sent to the war-torn Balkan nation. Two million food baskets were provided—about one basket per person throughout the length of the relief operation. However, $33.79 million was spent on the "restoration" of 160 mosques, along with "cultural centers, Islamic institutes, orphanages, and housing."

But Wahhabism attracted few Bosnian recruits. Instead, Balkan Muslims rebelled against Wahhabi attempts to impose puritanical strictures on their pluralist religious culture. The main conflict between Wahhabi acolytes and Bosnian Muslims took the form of a "mosque war" over the architectural styles to be adopted in the reconstruction of religious monuments destroyed by the Serbs and Croats. (Forty percent of Bosnian mosques, including the oldest and most important, were leveled during the war, most of them in territory that remains under Serbian control.) Bosnians wanted their mosques rebuilt in their original and refined

Ottoman style. The Saudis would only pay for the erection of Wahhabi-style mosques. The building the Saudis were proudest of, the King Fahd Cultural Center in Sarajevo, is a monstrous exercise in kitsch that looks as if it belongs in Las Vegas.

The Saudi High Commission occupied one of the most prominent official buildings in the Bosnian capital. But Saudi aid was not always appreciated by ordinary Muslims. Thus, at the Alipasha mosque in Sarajevo, a lovely Ottoman structure with a slender, graceful minaret only yards away from the Commission's headquarters, the word "Saudi" was scratched off the commemorative plaque announcing a donation for its restoration. The issue was resentment over the Wahhabi-Saudi disapproval of Ottoman mosques.

In October 1999, the sensationalist Bosnian weekly *Dani* (Days) published a revealing interview with Kemal Zukić, director of the Center for Islamic Architecture in Sarajevo. Asked about the destruction of wall decorations in the Governor's Mosque—the largest in the former Yugoslavia and the most famous Islamic monument in Sarajevo—Zukić answered, "There were several layers of paintings, so that in the end we were in a quandary about which layer merited preservation. . . . The biggest contribution came from a Saudi donor. . . . Parts remain but most of the walls are now blank." Pressed as to whether the panels would be preserved, Zukić answered testily, "I find it really hard to get excited over decorations inside the mosque. We are not in a situation like the more fortunate European nations, such that we could preserve our cultural heritage. . . . That was only an internal decoration and it was not intended to last forever."

Zukić was a graduate in architecture from the University of Sarajevo who had never practiced that profession, but who was now engaged in producing elaborate plans for new Bosnian mosques. According to one foreign expert, "His ideas for mosque design involve knockoffs of Saudi-modern shopping mall architecture with odd touches inspired by the décor of *The Love Boat*, including portholes!"

At least the outer walls of the Governor's Mosque remained standing. Elsewhere in Bosnia-Hercegovina, the fundamentalists pursued a more aggressive course. *Dani* reported that Muslims in the rural town of

Vrbovik were angry because they understood funds were available for the reconstruction of their traditional Ottoman mosque, which was destroyed in the 1992–95 war. But the money was diverted elsewhere, while two new mosques and six smaller prayer structures were erected in the Saudi style. The local cleric, Hadji Salih Avduković, commented angrily, "These people are hypocrites. They want to do everything from scratch."[1]

Walking the streets of Sarajevo today, one might think that the Wahhabis have gained considerable influence. Many young men wear "Islamic" beards, and numerous young women have adopted head and shoulder coverings or *hijab*. The campus of the University of Sarajevo is especially notable for this habit, and a women's store with the amusing name "*Hijab* Boutique" opened near the old Ottoman market. But as the defaced plaque at the Alipasha mosque demonstrated, the fundamentalists are definitely unpopular with Bosnian Muslims. In Sarajevo, *hijab* may be more a fad than anything else. In 2002, when a group of six Algerians was arrested by U.S. forces in Bosnia and removed to Camp X-Ray in Cuba, local Wahhabis mobilized to impede the deportation. But in Sarajevo no more than 300 deluded young people turned out to defend the extremists—in a city of 400,000 that today is 92 percent Muslim. Although various local and foreign gadflies loudly protested American unilateralism in the Sarajevo arrests, most Bosnian Muslims supported close cooperation with U.S. authorities and were thrilled to see the Algerians leave.[2]

On March 19, 2002, Bosnian officials executed raids in Sarajevo and the central Bosnian town of Zenica. They seized evidence that formed the basis for perjury charges filed on April 30 in Chicago, Illinois, against Enaam Arnaout, a Syrian confederate of bin Laden and the head of the Benevolence International Foundation, an Islamic charity used as a front for terrorist funding. In the same investigation, the Bosnian authorities exposed the activities in their country of al-Qaida leader Mamduh Mahmud Salim, a Sudanese involved in bin Laden's efforts to obtain nuclear and chemical weapons. Salim, imprisoned in the United States as a conspirator in the 1998 bombings of U.S. embassies in Kenya and Tanzania, stabbed a New York prison guard in the eye with a sharpened comb. Benevolence International provided extensive cover for his activities.

Bosnian police raided seven offices of the Al-Haramain Foundation, including two in Sarajevo and one in the old Turkish town of Travnik on June 3, 2002. Based in Saudi Arabia, Al-Haramain was deeply implicated in the transfer of funds to al-Qaida. On March 11, Treasury Secretary Paul O'Neill—acting jointly with the Saudi government—had frozen transactions with Al-Haramain in Bosnia and Somalia. The foundation's offices in Sarajevo had fallen under the control of the Egyptian Islamic Group or *Gamaa al-Islamiyya*, the terrorist outfit that spawned Osama bin Laden's lieutenant Ayman al-Zawahiri and carried out the Luxor massacre of 62 people, 58 of them foreign tourists, in 1997.

Bosnian foreign minister Zlatko Lagumdžija emphasized his country's bold stand on these issues. "The world has split into a modern civilization and one of barbarism and terrorism," he said. "Bosnia-Hercegovina has chosen to ally itself with the civilized world. It has decided to be part of the solution, not part of the problem." He added, "For our own sake, we have done the best we could in the past seven months" to locate and arrest terror suspects. On September 11, he declared, "we chose sides." At the end of May 2002, reputable sources in Sarajevo reported that Bosnian secret service chief Munir Alibabić had proof that $800 million had recently been moved to al-Qaida from Saudi Arabia.

The year 1999 saw the commemoration, following the Islamic lunar calendar, of the centennial of Ibn Sa'ud's seizure of Riyadh, the event leading to foundation of the third Saudi state. On January 22, King Fahd inaugurated the centennial celebrations with the opening of a massive historical center. As the year wore on, vast resources were expended for such observances.

But the festival atmosphere was complicated by the human rights disaster in Kosovo, where, for a year, two million Albanians, the majority of them Muslims, had suffered continuing attacks by Serb authorities. The kingdom therefore embarked on an ambitious and very public campaign for Kosovo relief. In April 1999, after the commencement of the NATO bombing of Serbia and the attempted Serb expulsion of the Albanian majority, King Fahd ordered two aircraft sent to Albania with 120 tons of tents, blankets, rice, flour, sugar, cooking oil, and milk. Cash donations and in-kind gifts were solicited both inside and outside the kingdom.

Later such allocations included medical assistance, 2,000 tons of Saudi dates, shelter for refugees, and grants to Albanian families that took in refugees. Saudi relief activities were extended to Macedonia, where most of those driven out by the Serbs were grouped after the NATO military intervention began. A hospital was erected in Tirana and two helicopters were assigned for the use of Saudi relief functionaries in the Balkans. But Wahhabi soul-catching operations were not to be neglected; a religious school for Kosovar Muslim boys was established, also in Tirana, by the World Assembly of Muslim Youth.

Thanks to the inexhaustible resources of Saudi Arabia and the Gulf states, Wahhabis also appeared all over Kosovo once fighting ended there. On August 9, 1999, the Saudi Joint Relief Committee for Kosovo (SJRCK) announced a 20-day training course for 50 *imams* and *muftis* in Arabic language and *Shariah*. A few days later the SJRCK moved its headquarters from Albania to Prishtina, the Kosovo capital. On August 22, SJRCK stated that in addition to extensive health facilities and repatriation of 50,000 refugees from Albania to Kosovo, it was also busy distributing copies of *Qur'an* and "books on Islam." The prospective Wahhabization of Kosovar Islam had begun in earnest.

According to a September 9 SJRCK news release, out of four million Saudi riyals spent in Kosovo, nearly half went to sponsor 388 religious "propagators" (i.e., missionaries) with the intent of converting Kosovars to Wahhabism. Another 600,000 riyals went for the reconstruction of 37 mosques, and 200,000 riyals was spent on two religious schools. The amount of money involved was fairly modest (four million riyals is a little more than a million U.S. dollars), except when one considers that the Saudis had only been on the scene for a little over two months. It was characteristic that a greater proportion of Saudi aid was spent on fundamentalist "propagators" and on mosque building than on broader humanitarian needs.

Many aspects of Balkan Islam excite Wahhabi disapproval. One of these is veneration of the dead and graves or funerary monuments. In

Kosovo, Wahhabis from the United Arab Emirates offered to rebuild several mosques in Vushtrri that were destroyed during the 1998–99 fighting. Emirates troops patrolled the town as part of the NATO-coordinated occupation, and an Emirates-based agency was the main relief institution in the region. The Wahhabis promised that the new mosques would be "better and more Islamic." But first, they said, the Albanian Muslims would have to uproot the Ottoman graveyards nearby. Andras Riedlmayer, a Harvard University librarian and expert in this field, recalls numerous such events: "Kosovar Muslim laymen in Prizren, Vushtrri, and Peja told me that while they disagreed with the Wahhabi agenda, they were afraid to talk openly about it. 'It's easy for you to speak,' they said, 'but we have to live here. You don't know these people. They and the local people they've recruited are really dangerous.'"

In the town of Peja in 1998, according to Riedlmayer, as the villages in the surrounding countryside were in flames, a group of Wahhabi missionaries—Arabs and their Kosovar acolytes—arrived and sought to impose their own way of praying (the locals described the physical position of the Wahhabis during religious observances as "odd"). The Wahhabis, sledgehammers in hand, tried to smash the 17th-century gravestones in the garden of Peja's ancient Defterdar mosque. But angry local residents beat them up and chased them out of town. Riedlmayer was shown the vandalized monuments, carved with exquisite floral motifs and verses from *Qur'an*. Six months afterward, in the spring of 1999, Serb paramilitaries came and burned down the mosque. Riedlmayer commented, "Unlike the fundamentalist missionaries, the Serbs were not interested in the gravestones."[3]

This sort of outlook could scarcely appeal to the nationalistic Albanians, who, like their Serb adversaries, considered their graves to be evidence for the justice of their claims on Kosovo. But fundamentalist proscriptions went on and on. Wahhabi hatred of music and of Sufism both ran counter to Balkan Muslim traditions. Balkan Muslims are especially devoted to a practice that drives Wahhabis to fury: *mawlid an-nabi*, or, as it is locally called, *mevlud*, the commemoration of Muhammad's birth. In Bosnia-Hercegovina, many Islamic officials disliked fundamentalist activities but, until September 11, were reluctant to denounce them.

The Bosnians were avid for the money. Only a few local Sufis openly criticized Wahhabi missionizing in Bosnia, arguing that the long presence of Sufi spiritualism in the Balkans was incompatible with fundamentalist fanaticism. But Balkan Muslims are desperate to be viewed as European, and submission to the will of the Wahhabis will certainly do nothing to advance that agenda.

In Kosovo, Wahhabism encountered far greater public opposition than in Bosnia-Hercegovina. The main reason is that Shi'a-oriented Sufism—a double abomination in Wahhabi eyes—is the dominant form of religious expression among Albanian Muslims in Dukagjini (western Kosovo), the territory most distinguished by its history of anti-Serb resistance. It has been estimated that there are more Sufis or dervishes in the cities of Dukagjini, such as Gjakova and Prizren, than there are regular Sunni Muslims. Indeed, among Albanians, patriotism and Sufism are closely identified. In addition, *mujahidin* were not welcome in Kosovo during the 1998–99 war, although some Arabs went there to fight. Ramush Haradinaj, a leading figure in the Kosovo Liberation Army (KLA), stated in a book of interviews that "about 20" non-Albanians fought in the organization's ranks in Dukagjini. Haradinaj identified their places of origin as "Sweden, Netherlands, France, Germany, Algeria, Italy, and some other countries. There were martyrs from [among] these volunteers," he added.

Kosovo Albanian Muslims were more forthright in airing their irritabilities about Saudi and other Gulf-backed religious colonialism. After all, they do not need the money. The Kosovars have a large emigration that supports their various reconstructive activities, and, in addition, the Kosovo Albanians are far more enterprising than the Bosnians.

In one of the more remarkable developments in Kosovo, Islamic fundamentalists came under fire from the KLA's Kosovapress news agency. Kosovapress declared: "For more than a century civilized countries have separated religion from the state. [However], we now see attempts not only in Kosovo but everywhere Albanians live to introduce religion into public schools. . . . Supplemental courses for children have been set up by foreign Islamic organizations who hide behind assistance programs. Some radio stations . . . now offer nightly broadcasts in Arabic, which nobody understands and which lead many to ask, Are we in an Arab country? It is time for Albanian mosques to be separated from Arab connections and for Islam to be developed on the basis of Albanian culture and customs." The Grand *Mufti* of Kosovo, H.E. Rexhep Boja, expressed himself similarly, stating boldly that Albanian Muslims had followed their faith for more than 500 years and did not need anybody to teach them how to be Muslims or how to decorate their mosques.

Paradoxically, however, the Wahhabis, until September 11, made more visible inroads in Kosovo than in Bosnia-Hercegovina—notwithstanding Albanian tetchiness and the fashion addiction of Kosovar Albanian women, which makes *hijab* a rare sight indeed in Kosovo. Here, too, it had to do with elemental requirements. The Bosnians lacked financial resources, but they did not want for books or trained *imams*, because the Yugoslav authorities had been more tolerant of them under Tito. The Kosovar Albanians did not need money, but they had a thirst for books and a shortage of clerics thanks to decades of ferocious Serbian imperialism. Once Kosovar religious students began going to the Saudis for training, they ran the risk of returning home imbued with Wahhabi extremism. Worse, their recruitment was supervised by the World Assembly of Muslim Youth, which the Saudi authorities themselves have admitted was tainted by terrorist activities.

Local residents were not the only people concerned about Wahhabi infiltration in the Balkans. In Albania as well as Bosnia-Hercegovina, anxiety over the activities of bin Laden supporters led American diplomats to entrench themselves behind high, thick walls, observing exceptional security measures at their embassies and other diplomatic facilities. At the end of March 2000, a group of Saudi "aid workers" was rousted by U.N. police from a building in Prishtina, the Kosovo capital, and accused of surveilling foreign vehicles, presumably in preparation for a terrorist attack. A representative of the Saudis, one Al-Hadi, complained that the telephone in the building where they resided had been tapped. The real story behind this was never reported: A KLA commander had discovered the "aid workers" spying on American diplomats and was preparing to kill the Saudis.

The upshot of this situation was evident in the first week of April 2000, when Prishtina saw a spectacle unheard of in Sarajevo. A massive funda-

mentalist "cultural program" was held in the local sports stadium. Thousands of Albanian Muslims, young and old, walked away from the event
happily clutching works in Albanian that professed Wahhabi fanaticism.
In May, the familiar Saudi Joint Relief Committee laid the foundation of
a multimillion-dollar cultural, sports, and religious center in the Kosovo
capital.

In 2000, the "mosque war" that had upset Bosnian Muslims expanded
to Kosovo, where the Serbs had destroyed almost half the mosques—
about 240 structures wrecked out of 550. Many Kosovo mosques were
completely blown up, including several Ottoman architectural treasures.
At the end of July 2000, Saudis who had taken over the refurbishment of
the Hadum mosque complex in Gjakova, dating from 1595 and devastated by the Serbs during the 1999 war, suddenly turned up in the old
Ottoman cemetery inside the walls and began removing its centuries-old
gravestones. They also demolished the remains of the library, which could
have been restored. The Albanians again reacted with predictable rage.
Gazmend Naka, an expert with the Institution for Protection of Kosova
Monuments, commented: "The Saudis say NATO and the United
Nations will let them do whatever they want, and that we Albanians have
nothing to say about it. The Serbs killed us physically, but these fanatics
want to kill our cultural heritage." Naka wanted NATO's Kosovo Forces
command, which mounted guards at Serbian churches threatened by
Albanians, to place similar protective units at Islamic structures. But
NATO was trying to get out of the monument protection business: Sitting in armored cars and tanks watching Serbian Orthodox churches was
not an efficient use of military resources, and there was no interest in
extending the program to mosques. Fortunately, on August 5, 2000, the
U.N.-backed authorities barred the Saudis from the Hadum mosque rehabilitation project.

Kosovar Albanian resentment of Arab meddling was even more sharply
expressed when an Emirates diplomat promised that 50 beautiful new
mosques would be built around Kosovo, to be paid for out of the diplomat's own pocket. Naim Maloku, a former KLA commander, brusquely
rejected this proposal, stating that Kosovo needed employment opportunities more than mosques.

Kosovar resistance to Wahhabi mosque demolitions and cemetery vandalism was not an insignificant matter. Wahhabi missionaries in Kosovo sought to do what the "Arab Afghans" and the Taliban did in Afghanistan, when they demolished the great Buddhas at Bamiyan. After the NATO bombing ended, Kosovar Albanians also attacked Serbian religious structures, with about 90 churches and monasteries damaged out of a claimed total of more than 1,000 Serbian Orthodox monuments in the province. But Albanian vandalism, while despicable, was motivated by revenge rather than religion. The Wahhabis who went to Kosovo played no role in the destruction of Serbian churches but were preoccupied with eliminating the Ottoman architectural legacy.

The physical eradication of a rich cultural heritage is itself an act of barbarism, whether by Serb militias, vengeful Albanians, or Wahhabi zealots. In Afghanistan, no one was able to stay the hands of the iconoclasts. In Kosovo, the story has been different, as the Kosovars have made it clear they will not suffer the imposition of a foreign and totalitarian form of Islam. This is a victory for moderation and a great asset for the United States in its future approaches to the Muslim world. The Saudis were hopeful of penetrating Kosovo's fertile plain. In 2000, 300 Kosovar Albanians were provided free tickets for *hajj* as guests of the regime—through the Saudi Embassy in Tirana, not through the Saudi Joint Relief Committee for Kosovo—and the year after featured visits to the province by leading Saudi state and charitable functionaries. In mid-2002, however, the Saudis seemed to have had enough of dealing with the Kosovar Muslims. "The Muslims here behave like Christians," Al-Hadi, still running the Saudi Joint Relief Committee, told the *Los Angeles Times* irritably. "They have accepted living like in Europe. I think in 10 years it will be worse. . . . We will not stay." This constituted an admission that in Kosovo, the Wahhabi-Saudi "*jihad*" had failed.

In the wake of the atrocities of September 11, American and other Western commentators asked a perplexing question. The aim of three previous wars fought by the United States and its allies had been to rescue Muslim or Muslim-majority peoples from aggression. The Gulf War saved Kuwait from Iraqi invasion, the 1995 intervention in Bosnia-Hercegovina halted Serbian attacks on Muslims, and the NATO campaign against Serbia four years later prevented the expulsion from Kosovo of two million Kosovar Albanians, of whom at least 80 percent were Muslims. Western intervention also saved the Iraqi Kurds. Why then should so many Arab Muslims hate America? Had they forgotten these acts?

A disregard among Arabs for U.S. protection of the Kuwaiti rulers, as well as the Saudi monarchy, is understandable. Even pious Muslims among the Arabs have been known to admire Saddam Husayn, or to think that his invasion of Kuwait paled in comparison with Saudi corruption. But did Arab Muslims not care that the United States saved the Balkan Muslims and Albanians from extermination or exile? Were the new Balkan wars not a clear-cut case of massive U.S. military and humanitarian intervention on behalf of Muslims in distress?

Yet no credit was given where it was due. Fouad Ajami confirmed the point in an interview with the *Washington Post*. Why had no Arab or Muslim leader given the United States thanks or credit for taking military risks on behalf of two Muslim populations in Europe: the Bosnians and Kosovars? "I have heard no one acknowledge any gratitude for that," Ajami said. "It's a mystery." The mystery deepens when one hears or reads what many Arabs do say about the U.S. interventions in the Balkans. These Arab assessments tend to be overwhelmingly negative—so much so that Osama bin Laden himself made denigration of the U.S. role there an item of his standard repertoire. In a 1996 interview, the terrorist chief denounced America for "withholding of arms from the Muslims of Bosnia-Hercegovina." Many of his Arab listeners would have known the truth: That it was Europe and the United Nations, not the United States, which had erected and maintained the embargo on arms to the Bosnian Muslims. The U.S. intelligence community cooperated with other countries, including Iran, to arm the Bosnian Muslims in secret.

Bin Laden, under U.S. attack in Afghanistan in November 2001, thought it useful to return to this theme in a manifesto broadcast on Qatar's Al-Jazira television. There he referred to "a war of genocide in Bosnia in sight and hearing of the entire world in the heart of Europe. For several years our brothers have been killed, our women have been raped, and our children have been massacred in the safe havens of the United Nations." It was a claim whose efficacy relied on Arab ignorance. Considering the passionate concern for Bosnia felt throughout the *ummah*, however, it was bound to fail, since many Muslims were well aware that there had been no mass rapes or massacres in the country since U.S. intervention and the imposition of the Dayton agreement; that the United Nations Tribunal had indicted the Yugoslav leadership for genocide; and that even as bin Laden spoke, Slobodan Milošević sat in prison in The Hague awaiting trial. After all, Turkey, Malaysia, Morocco, Jordan, the United Arab Emirates, and Bangladesh contributed troops or police to the pacification of the Balkans, giving the media public in those countries particular reason to be informed about the real situation there.

But the willful self-deception about U.S. actions in the Balkans expressed by bin Laden had a surprisingly wide echo among Arab Muslims, and especially among bin Laden's fellow Saudis. Even Saudi interior minister Prince Nayef, in August 2000, referred to Bosnians as if they were still fighting with arms in hand. An "Open Letter to President Bush" penned by the Saudi cleric Safar ibn 'Abd ar-Rahman al-Hawali, a leader of the country's extremist opposition, taunted the Americans: "One of your smart missiles infuriated the Yellow Giant [China] by destroying its embassy in Belgrade." Al-Hawali failed to mention that the accidental bombing of the Chinese Embassy to Yugoslavia had taken place during the Kosovo intervention, and that China had sided with Milošević in the United Nations in order to block action to save the Albanians.

Nevertheless, this myopia has been peculiar to the Arabs. Turks, for example, know better. The Turkish journalist (and former diplomat) Gündüz Aktan provided a typical Turkish assessment of the U.S. role in the Balkan wars, in the midst of the Afghan bombing of 2001: "The United States, [after] it could not convince our European friends, stopped the Serbian aggressions with a military intervention in Bosnia-Hercegovina . . . the forces of the United States constituted 90 percent of the NATO forces which brought Yugoslavia to heel, after it [repressed] the Kosovar Albanians and [sought to expel them]; and it is observed that the United States also played an important role in the recognition of extensive rights for the Albanians in Macedonia."

Even more telling was the pro-American position taken by many Balkan Muslims as the antiterror offensive unfolded in Afghanistan. Bosnia's leading Islamic cleric, Mustafa efendija Cerić, had set the tone for this attitude at the end of 1999, when he declared, "Saddam Husayn is a Muslim the way that Hitler was a Christian, and [Radovan] Karadžić is an Orthodox Christian the way that Osama bin Laden is a Muslim." The Albanian government, which helped the CIA break up the terror cell deported to Egypt and known as the Albanian Returnees, put bin Laden in the same category as Milošević: "Enemies of civilization like Milošević or bin Laden should end up in the defendant's dock . . . bin Laden will soon be held accountable alongside the 'Butcher of the Balkans.'"

Islamic leaders in Albanian-speaking territories, including Kosovo and western Macedonia, were even more outspoken in support of the United States. The day after the September 11 attacks, Haxhi Dede Reshat Bardhim, world leader of two million Albanian Bektashis, headquartered in Tirana, sent a message to President George W. Bush referring to America as "the pride of this world" and declaring, "May Allah be, as always, on the side of the American people and the American state!" On October 12, 2001, in the Kosovo capital of Prishtina, Grand *Mufti* Boja prayed for the American dead at a commemorative meeting organized by the U.S. diplomatic office (Washington has no official ambassadorial or consular representation in Kosovo). The prayer service was led jointly with the Albanian Catholic bishop of Kosovo, Monsignor Mark Sopi. Chief *Imam* of the Kosovo Islamic community, Burhan Hashani, commented: "The people of Kosovo will never forget America and its assistance."

The day after the beginning of the Afghan bombardment, the Tirana daily *Koha Jone* offered a stirring headline, showing that some Muslims eagerly wished for the punishment of Islamic extremists: "Nobody Veils the Statue of Liberty's Face." The Kosovapress news agency printed statements from the two political formations that emerged from the KLA, the Kosovo Democratic Party (PDK) headed by Hashim Thaci, and the Alliance for Kosovo's Future (AAK) led by Ramush Haradinaj. They criticized the refusal of the Taliban regime to hand over the leaders of al-Qaida as demanded by the United States, and affirmed that "the people of

Kosovo bear a natural and special responsibility to the United States and its allies."

December 2001 saw raids in Kosovo similar to those that would take place in Bosnia-Hercegovina. Representatives of the Global Relief Foundation were arrested in Prishtina and Gjakova in an operation coordinated with raids on its offices in the United States and, on the same day, the American operation of the Benevolence International Foundation. Meanwhile, a Kosovar Albanian group called the Students Movement for an Open and Democratic Society had begun mobilizing, and accused the Islamic humanitarian agencies of terrorist training. The ethnic Albanians of Kosovo were, if anything, even more avid than the Bosnians to be counted in the anti-terror coalition. "Every Albanian in Kosovo knows that without the help of the United States we would have been devastated by Serbian imperialism," Kosovar journalist Daut Dauti emphasized. "Muslim Albanians are no less pro-American than others. Our Islamic traditions are pluralist and antiextremist. We will never turn against the United States."

In February 2002, the authorities in Tirana continued their "zero tolerance" policy toward Islamic extremists by seizing the local assets of a rich Saudi agent of bin Laden, Yasin al-Qadi, who co-owned two tall buildings in Tirana known as the "Albanian twin towers." Al-Qadi, interviewed in an Arab daily, admitted to having met with bin Laden "a few times long ago during some religious lectures," but also claimed to be a friend of U.S. Vice President Dick Cheney. "I spoke to [Cheney] at length and we even became friends. I also got to know former U.S. president Jimmy Carter," al-Qadi said. The interview bore the headline, "Yes, I know bin Laden and U.S. Vice President is My Friend." Identified as a terror financier by the U.S. State Department, al-Qadi had abused the Bosnian cause to advance the bin Laden agenda.

There was therefore nothing surprising about the enthusiasm for U.S. global leadership expressed by Albanian Muslims. They knew the lengths to which the United States had gone to protect them and other Balkan Muslims. The resentments they harbored over betrayal by false friends were directed not against America but against Arab leaders, who either sided with Milošević or treated Balkan Muslims with supreme condescension. Many local Muslim politicians and intellectuals are bitter that the Saudis and other Arab states watched passively as thousands of indigenous European Muslims were slain in the Balkans, offering almost no assistance aside from press releases, aid donations, and religious propaganda, while exploiting the suffering of Bosnian Muslims as a pretext to raise funds and recruit for Wahhabi wars elsewhere.

In addition, conspiracy theories about Arab behavior abounded among Balkan Muslims. Some pointed to Arab resentment of the cultural association between Balkan and Ottoman Islamic traditions, despised by the Wahhabis. Others believed there had long existed an alliance between Milošević's Yugoslavia and the Arab states, resting on the role of the Arab Orthodox Christian churches in Palestinian nationalism, historic links between Arabs and the former Soviet Union and other Communist states (including former Yugoslavia), and a common anti-Americanism. One of the most fascinating and disturbing phenomena in recent global interfaith relations has been the two-faced position of the Orthodox churches, which incite genocidal violence against Balkan and Caucasian Muslims at the same time as they accommodate Palestinian terrorism. During the 2002 conflict in the West Bank, Arab Orthodox Christian writers defended suicide bombings by Wahhabized Palestinians—most notably, during the standoff at the Church of the Nativity in Bethlehem—while the Russian and Serbian Orthodox sought to turn the U.S.-led war on terror into a pretext to continue killing Chechens and to rehabilitate Milošević. Meanwhile, many Orthodox Greeks criticized the United States as an imperialist power.

There can be no doubt that Milošević found many bedfellows among radical Arab states and movements, which rallied to his defense during the NATO operations against him. Iraq and Libya both described the NATO action in Kosovo as an anti-Yugoslav aggression, while Syria and Lebanon registered no reaction to events there. Earlier, Libyan foreign minister 'Umar al-Muntasir had announced, after a meeting with the Yugoslav ambassador to Libya, that Libyan leader Muammar al-Qadhdhafi supported "dialogue" between Belgrade and the Kosovars without foreign intervention. This amiable exchange came one month after the first pitched battle between Serb forces and the KLA in the Kosovo town of Rahovec.

Rahovec enjoys an especially beautiful setting, with the city on two levels, in a green plain where vineyards are tended and on a hill. On July 19, 1998, open fighting in the streets culminated in a Serb assault on the Halveti-Karabashi Sufi lodge in the upper town, known as the Sheh Myhedini *teqe*, in which hundreds of terrified residents had sought refuge. The elderly and extremely distinguished leader of the Sufis, Shaykh Myhedin Shehu, was killed. At Rahovec, up to 150 Albanians died; within two days the Serbs had buried the victims in two mass graves in Prizren. The incident was among the most traumatic of the Kosovo conflict, but it came during a season of horrors. In August and September 1998—while the Libyans and Serbs were chatting familiarly—Serb mass executions were recorded in Ranca (11 people killed, eight of them children), Galica near Vushtrri (14 dead, mainly young men), and Golluboc (eight child victims), while in Abria e Epërme, a whole family of 22 persons was wiped out. By the end of 1998, half a million Albanians had fled their homes. Yet on May 3, 1999, with the NATO bombing of Serbia underway for weeks, Qadhdhafi called for a halt to all military operations in Kosovo and the withdrawal of Serbian and NATO troops.

Libyan involvement with the Milošević regime and its defense was not merely rhetorical. Throughout the NATO bombing, Libya maintained firm trade and economic relations with Serbia. Serbian management cadres have participated in running Libyan industry, and Serb officers assisted in training Qadhdhafi's personal guards. In May 2002, U.S. undersecretary of state John Bolton pointed out that Serbian assistance remained critical to Libya's ballistic missile program. Leading Palestinians, incredibly enough, nurtured a similar sympathy for Milošević. What may be considered the most surrealistic gesture during the entire decade of recent Balkan wars occurred eight months after NATO's Kosovo campaign began. On December 1, 1999, the Palestinian Authority (PA) invited Milošević to Bethlehem to celebrate the Orthodox Christmas. News of this invitation, though more or less ignored in the West, was reported with banner headlines in the Balkans. An Israeli foreign ministry spokesman said that if Milošević accepted the invitation he would be arrested on arrival, since Israel, as a U.N. member, is obliged to fulfill arrest orders issued by The Hague Tribunal, which had indicted him. The PA, not being a U.N. member, was under no such obligation. Nor was the PA the only Palestinian element to vacillate over Kosovo. Earlier in 1999, the Palestinian Wahhabis of the Hamas movement denounced the U.S. intervention to settle the Kosovo crisis as "hiding under the slogans of human rights to impose its power in the Balkans." Hamas thus echoed the allegations of Milošević's own media, as well as the Russians and various leftists worldwide.

All this contrasted sharply with Israel's conduct in the early phase of the Kosovo intervention. The Jewish state sent a mobile hospital to the main Kosovar Albanian refugee camp in Macedonia; the Israeli labor federation, Histadrut, donated 10 metric tons of food aid to the Kosovars; and Israel took in 112 Kosovar Albanian refugees, none of whom were Jewish. Israeli aid to the Kosovars was completely disinterested; there had been no significant Jewish presence in Kosovo since the Holocaust. This did not prevent one bumptious Saudi "relief official" from denigrating the Jewish-sponsored refugee effort, which he asserted was established to aid "the Jews" in Kosovo.

Wahhabis likewise did immense damage by making the false claim that the KLA was fighting for an Islamic state. In fact, the Kosovo Albanian struggle was ethnic, not religious, and the KLA included Catholic commanders as well as Muslims and persons with no strong religious affinities. But foreign Islamists wrote that the struggle was a fundamentalist "*jihad*," a claim previously advanced by Milošević, his government, and his apologists to label the Albanians religious extremists. Of course, supporters of bin Laden did all they could to provoke hostility to the U.S. role in Kosovo, even after U.S. power ended the mass slaying of Muslims. In January 2000, a bin Ladenite Web site in the United States posted articles falsely claiming that NATO troops had introduced prostitution into Kosovo, and attempting to exploit a fatal sexual assault on an 11-year-old Albanian girl by a deranged U.S. soldier. Other Wahhabi Web sites purveyed the anti-NATO arguments that use of depleted uranium had polluted the soil in Kosovo, and that the real aim of the NATO intervention in Kosovo was to secure control of the Trepca mining complex (a facility that was a decade behind the rest of the world in extractive technology, while the commodities it produced are subject to a world glut).

Wahhabi contempt for the horrors inflicted on Balkan Muslims was also introduced into the American debate over Islam before September 11. Paul Findley, a former U.S. congressman (Republican) turned visceral foe of Israel, published a whitewash of the Taliban early in 2001. He wrote, "Human slaughter was far greater in Afghanistan than the well-publicized massacres carried out in the early and late 1990s by Serb forces against Bosnian and Kosovar Muslims in Yugoslavia." Here was a particularly compact example of the political corruption of language identified in the past by George Orwell. In Afghanistan there had been little "human slaughter," in the sense of mass executions such as that of Srebrenica, in which 8,000 Muslim males were liquidated. Such incidents were much commoner in the Balkans, but they were by no means "well-publicized." To cite a single example, the slaying of thousands of Muslim hostages by Serb troops in the north Bosnian town of Sanski Most was never reported in Western media. In addition, the Bosnian war lasted only three years, while the Afghan-Russian combat endured four times that long. Had the Bosnian war gone on for a dozen years, losses might conceivably have been far higher. There were only 2.5 million Bosnian Muslims—a tenth of the population of Afghanistan—and a long war might have resulted in their complete disappearance. Finally, the intention of the Russians had been to absorb and exploit the Afghans, not to exterminate them and replace them with Russian colonists. By contrast, the Serbs attempted genocide, the crime for which Slobodan Milošević was tried at The Hague.

Wahhabism was as inimical as Serbian imperialism to the interests of Balkan Muslims and non-Muslim Albanians. The KLA had to work very hard to counter the misinformation regularly disseminated about its objectives. The problem has not gone away; in the aftermath of September 11 disinformation agents and rumormongers have revived a series of lurid claims against the Kosovar Albanians, including assertions that numbers of *mujahidin* had fought in the KLA. Milošević tried to recycle these hallucinations in his trial, but they were only believable by the mentally and morally deficient. Of course, such folk were not lacking in Western politics and media. In Washington, one could commonly hear such fantasies as the claim that Chechens had fought in Kosovo. Notwithstanding assiduous Wahhabi-Saudi infiltration in Kosovo *after* the NATO intervention, nobody ever produced serious evidence of significant *mujahid* activity during the Kosovo fighting.

Indeed, the 1999 Egyptian investigation of the Albanian Returnees revealed, in the disclosures of defendant Ahmad Uthman Ismail, that after four years of activity in Albania proper, the Wahhabis were warned not to go to Kosovo while the war with the Serbs was underway. This advice reflected caution after the subversives' experience in Bosnia-Hercegovina, where their operatives were exposed to the sanctions of the U.S. and European authorities. Drawing on the documents of the inquiry, the Arabic newspaper *Al-Asharq al-Awsat* stated, "Bosnia was an open field for the arrest of Egyptian Islamic Jihad and Islamic Group members when they tried to turn Bosnia into another Afghanistan in the heart of Europe and to move the 'Afghan Arabs' there." Similarly, the "Afghan Arab" and Albanian Returnee Sabri al-Attar recalled that in 1994 when he first expressed an interest in going to Bosnia to fight, the *Gamaa* leader Mustafa Hamzah, a.k.a. Abu Hazim, argued against it, proposing that he go to Sudan instead.

It would be a colossal mistake to think that all international Islamic efforts for the relief of Balkan Muslims were tainted with terrorism. The government and local Islamic scholars in Malaysia, for example, raised large amounts of money that were handed over to Muslim authorities in the Balkans with no strings attached. But while the rest of the world regarded the sufferings of Bosnian Muslims and Albanians as a great moral challenge to global policymakers, Arab states and Islamic extremists took a different view. They seemed to consider "ethnic cleansing" in the Balkans as a problem secondary to their schemes for more ambitious attacks on Israel and the West, and they viewed NATO's military response to Serb atrocities as part of a Western conspiracy to infiltrate the Balkans. But their posture cannot be explained only by their obsession with Israel and their anti-Americanism. It owed much to Wahhabism. Arab indifference to the fate of Balkan Muslims cannot be understood without an appreciation of Wahhabi hostility to Balkan Islam—a very acute clash within Islamic civilization.

And there remains the overall issue of Wahhabism's historical compromises with the Christian powers: Wahhabis not only cannot admit that the United States helped Afghan Muslims topple Soviet imperialism, guards the Saudi kingdom, and saved Balkan Muslims and Iraqi Kurds—the entire vertiginous rush into terror pursued by Wahhabism over the past decade has been dedicated to blotting these insistent facts out of the minds of the world's Muslims. Recent American conduct has increased in drama as well as morality—the intervention in favor of the Kosovar Albanians engaged the hearts and minds of the world much more than the defense of Kuwait, but was also carried out for more clearly humanitarian ends, since Kosovo has no oil. All that was at stake in the Balkans was the principle enunciated by Orwell during the Spanish civil war: the defense of essential human decency. It is this undeniable reality that confounds, maddens, and impels the Wahhabis to ever more extreme acts of violence.

Some marginal types and fanatical Islamophobes in the West sought to exploit the struggle against Wahhabi terror in the aftermath of September 11 to justify a defense of Milošević—in line with Putin's efforts to similarly whitewash his forces' abuses in Chechnya. But as the antiterror war continued, a growing number of Westerners perceived that U.S. actions in the Balkans had changed the course of Western policy in a way beneficial for the global cause of democracy. The martyrdom of the Bosnian Muslims and Kosovars caused the United States to assume a new posture of international intervention. The punishment inflicted on Milošević in Kosovo facilitated the later application of similar lessons in dealing with Islamist extremism. In a sense, this was the ultimate gift of the Balkan victims to the *ummah* and to the world: an opportunity for America to reassert its proper international role.

Bin Laden was the 21st-century Wahhabi hero *par excellence*. But he was never an original thinker. His sole assets as an ideological leader were financial—his personal fortune as well as his links with others in the Saudi elite. He was always dependent on mentors for guidance. Abdullah

Azzam had been one. But an even more destructive role model for the terror chief was the Egyptian doctor identified during the Afghan war of 2001–02 as bin Laden's second in command: Ayman al-Zawahiri. Zawahiri was a crucial figure in the broadening of the Wahhabi offensive after the fall of the Soviet Union. Understanding of the Wahhabi international—the coalition of extremist groups funded by the Saudis, organized by Azzam, and launched globally by the Palestinian's successors—must comprise events in Egypt, mainly the emergence from the Muslim Brotherhood of the conspiratorial group that murdered President Anwar Sadat in 1981.

Zawahiri is an archetypal extremist, even more than Azzam or bin Laden. Unlike Azzam, who lived through the typical contemporary experiences of the Palestinian middle class before arriving in the milieu of the Afghan *mujahidin*, and bin Laden, who had been a rich dilettante, Zawahiri was only 15 years old in 1966 when he joined the first cell of the Al-Jihad movement (usually referred to in Western media as Egyptian Islamic Jihad). His family was better than well-off, although he is no bin Laden; his father was a religious scholar, he himself is a physician, and his brother, who shares his extremism, is an engineer. Zawahiri had no life outside the subculture of Islamic radicalism; he never outgrew the mental environment of his adolescence. Because of his constricted worldview, it is unsurprising that he is also deeply cruel and sadistic.

In an autobiographical work written during the Afghan war of 2001–02, Zawahiri described his induction into the group that murdered Sadat. He was among those charged in the crime, but received a sentence of only three years. During the trial he gave the appearance of a self-dramatizer, ranting at the public in a demented tone. In a typical case of projection, he would write indignantly that Western media "portrayed [the 'Afghan Arabs'] as obsessed half-mad people who rebelled against the United States that once trained and financed them." According to the more-than-half-mad Zawahiri, "the United States did not give one penny in aid to the *mujahidin*." His writings are replete with self-pity in addition to fabrications and fantasies.

The Egyptian doctor's milieu included other groups as well as the *Gamaa al-Islamiyya*, the Wahhabi group that killed Sadat, and whose atrocious nature was emphasized anew in the 1997 massacre of foreign tourists at Luxor. The Luxor incident was intended as an "homage" to the aforementioned Mustafa Hamzah, alias Abu Hazim. The *Gamaa* was led by the blind cleric Shaykh Omar Abdel-Rahman, imprisoned for the first attack on the World Trade Center in 1993. It included many military officers and attorneys. During the 1990s, more than 1,000 people were killed by the *Gamaa* and similar entities in Egypt. In addition to leaders like Zawahiri, these groups provided many footsoldiers for bin Laden's al-Qaida organization. The influence of Wahhabi separatism on the *Gamaa* was especially visible in its targeting of Egyptian Coptic Christians as well as foreign tourists.

Another major arena for recruitment of Wahhabi terrorists in the 1990s was Algeria, with a post-revolutionary regime that was militarist and statist. A brutal civil war between the state, moderate Islamists, and Wahhabis, the latter enlisted in the Armed Islamic Group (GIA), had its origin in a constitutional crisis beginning in 1991. The Islamic Front for Salvation or Front Islamique de Salut (FIS), which was Islamist but only partly Wahhabi-oriented, won a majority in the first round of parliamentary elections. The government was shaken and refused to concede power. A grotesque sequence of horrifying incidents ensued, with the revolutionary-militarist government murdering alleged radicals, the GIA responding with increasing viciousness, and the onset of general disorder and massacre. The GIA recruited numerous "soldiers" whose practices included kidnapping thousands of young women, who were forced to serve them sexually in tunnels and caves hidden in the country's mountains. The situation became so bizarre that *Le Monde Diplomatique* stated in 1998 that certain groups, "convinced that the Islamist cause is lost, are reputed to have banded together to form a kind of Satanist movement, denying God and reveling in acts that are completely contrary to the teachings of Islam." This was the political and psychological environment that marked the youth of the Algerian bin Ladenites caught by Western law enforcement in Bosnia, on the U.S. border, and elsewhere.

But neither the Egyptian nor the Algerian conflicts drew the participation of many foreign *mujahidin*. Rather, the inevitable turn of the public in both countries against the extremists drove the aspiring martyrs into exile, in search of other battlefields. Simultaneously with the Serb assault on Bosnia-Hercegovina, theaters of war for the Wahhabi international also opened up in the Central Asian Muslim societies that emerged after 1991 from the ruins of the former Soviet Union. Two countries have been particularly affected by the confrontation of fundamentalism and traditional Islam: Tajikistan and Uzbekistan. These cultures are almost completely unknown in the West. Aside from Tajikistan, which is Iranian in language (although Sunni in its Islam), the rest are Turkic.

Tajikistan was the first of the Central Asian countries to be attacked by the Wahhabi virus: A bloody civil war, underreported in Western media and therefore largely overlooked by the outside world, began in 1992, within a year of the country's independence. Unfortunately, the main cause of conflict, at least at the beginning, was a repetition of the Algerian experience. An anti-Communist coalition, including the moderate-Islamist Party of Islamic Rebirth, gained significant support in the country's first post-Communist presidential election. But the official result of the poll, in which the Communists retained power, was controversial, and polarization led to violence. Tajikistan became a testing ground for the general transition of the Central Asian states away from Communism, as well as for Islamism. According to Ahmed Rashid, Pakistani and Saudi "missionaries" soon arrived in neighboring, still-peaceful Uzbekistan, flush with cash. The Tajik Muslim movement was infiltrated by a Wahhabi fringe, but Tajikistan, like Bosnia-Hercegovina, would not prove fertile ground for Wahhabism.

As described by Rashid, Tajikistan's experience paralleled that of Bosnia-Hercegovina in seeing ethnic conflict (with the Russians) as well as the departure of thousands of refugees for Afghanistan, a bleak alternative to say the least. Russia and Uzbekistan backed the Communist government, while the Islamists sought help in Iran as well as Pakistan and the Saudi kingdom. But the local Muslims also eschewed Wahhabi separatism and blocked with the Tajik democratic opposition. Then something startling occurred. With the victory of the Taliban over ethnic Tajik rulers in Afghanistan in 1996, the Tajikistan government and their Muslim opponents suddenly saw themselves with a terroristic anti-Tajik regime on their border. Peace was negotiated in Tajikistan, and the establishment of a new civil society began under the leadership of the former Communist Emomali Rakhmonov. The Wahhabi disease had been cured, although the propagandists of terror continue to speak of a *"jihad"* there.

Unfortunately, neighboring Uzbekistan was not favored by so happy an outcome. In the aftermath of September 11 and the Afghan antiterror war the United States acquired, in Uzbekistan, an ally about which most Americans knew very little. The past mistakes of the State Department—and by supposedly friendly "nongovernmental organizations"—in relating to the Uzbeks were a foretaste of the challenges ahead. Undeniably, Uzbekistan had emerged after decades of tsarist and Soviet imperialist rule with its share of problems. Uzbek President Islam Karimov was widely condemned as a post-Communist authoritarian and the transition away from a statist economy has been slow. But Uzbekistan has also had to deal urgently with a virulent form of Wahhabism.

On September 15, four days after the horrors in New York and Washington, State Department spokesman Richard Boucher announced that the Islamic Movement of Uzbekistan (IMU) would be designated a foreign terrorist organization under U.S. law. The IMU thus appeared on Washington's first list of 28 entities supporting Osama bin Laden and his network. Boucher called the IMU, which declared war on the Uzbek government in 1999, "responsible for criminal acts of terrorism" and noted its involvement in the kidnapping of foreigners, bombings, bus hijackings, and the murder of ordinary citizens as well as police officers.

IMU militants fought in Afghanistan alongside the Taliban and bin Laden's forces, with IMU founder Jumaa Namangani reportedly killed there. But such clear evidence of the terrorist threat to Uzbekistan got an international airing only after a long period of utter obliviousness on the part of Westerners to the reality of Islamic fundamentalism in that country. The IMU is a classic Wahhabi combat organization—a murderous gang of fanatics bent on imposing Saudi-backed Islamofascism. Propaganda on its behalf distributed by the Azzam network seeks to target Uzbekistan's large and ancient Bukharan Jewish community for violence and denounces President Karimov as "a Zionist Jew." Traditional Uzbek Muslims, who are devoted Sufis, believe that with their unbroken 2,500-

year history in the country, the Bukharan Jews have more right to be considered as neighbors and friends than foreign colonialists posing as Muslim reformers. Recently, the Uzbek adherents of Wahhabi terror declared, "We ask the Muslims to support not only us, but their *mujahidin* brothers in East Turkestan (China), Tajikistan, Afghanistan, Kyrgyzstan, and Chechnya since we are all working together for the same goal, to liberate this region from *kufr* [unbelief]." Still, until September 11, the IMU did an amazing job of conning Westerners—both human rights groups and governments—into believing its followers were innocent victims of outrageous persecution by the Uzbek regime.

Consider the 2000 Annual Report on International Religious Freedom, issued by the State Department only a year before Boucher's denunciation of the IMU. The report complained that the Uzbek authorities' "respect for the rights of unauthorized Muslim groups worsened, as its harsh campaign against such groups, which it perceives as terrorist security threats, intensified." The report described groups like the IMU as "suspected of being 'Wahhabist,' a term used loosely to encompass both suspected terrorists and . . . former students of certain independent *imams* or foreign *medresas* (Islamic schools)." Thus was the problem of Wahhabism in Uzbekistan framed in the euphemisms typically employed at State. The groups' terrorist identity was a matter of suspicion rather than evident fact; their ideology was only loosely defined; their instruction came from independent rather than institutional sources, and these latter were possibly victims of discrimination for being foreign, not Uzbek. Unfortunately, the State Department failed entirely to note the parallels with the Taliban—another once-innocuous group of suspected terrorists and students, who left Afghanistan to study at *medresas* in Pakistan.

Meanwhile, in October 1999, Human Rights Watch issued a book-length report, "Uzbekistan: Class Dismissed: Discriminatory Expulsions of Muslim Students," that is a classic of liberal accommodation to terrorism. In a two-year period beginning in 1997, 28 students were expelled from schools in Uzbekistan at various levels, primary through university, for growing Wahhabi-style beards or, in the case of women, covering themselves. A number of teachers and administrators were fired for the same or similar practices. The students denied being Wahhabis (as Wahhabis typically do) and alleged arbitrary persecution. This issue, although it affected a minute portion of Uzbekistan's population, compelled Human Rights Watch to carry out an investigation. The report described the bearded and covered students as "adherents of independent Islam or particularly pious."

Such terminology represented a double falsehood. Wahhabi Islam, whether in Uzbekistan or Union City, California, is no more "independent" than was the Uzbek Communist party: Wahhabi Islam in Central Asia is an arm of Saudi religious imperialism. Indeed, it is the traditional Sufi Islam for which Uzbekistan is famous that is truly independent, based as it is on the autonomous and transnational spiritual orders. The suggestion that Central Asian Sufi Muslims are less pious than the Wahhabis is a slander comparable to calling Catholics less pious than Pentecostals.

Human Rights Watch heavies Jonathan Fanton, the organization's chairman, and Holly Cartner, its executive director for Europe and Central Asia, questioned the internationally respected head of the Uzbek Islamic scholars, *Mufti* Abdurashid Qori Bahromov, about the expulsion of the alleged Wahhabi students. *Mufti* Bahromov, who presumably knows a bit more about the situation of his country and Islam generally than these humanitarian tourists, was unsympathetic.

The expelled women students had come to him repeatedly, weeping and seeking his help in getting readmitted to their schools. The *mufti* had refused to assist them, as is his right given that he holds a religious rather than a political function. He condemned the dismissed students as Wahhabis and as provocative, undisciplined agitators. Undeterred, Human Rights Watch composed a list of peremptory demands, which it presented to the Uzbek state. In particular, the country should forthwith end surveillance of religious students and reinstate any fired or demoted teachers or administrators. The Uzbek government sensibly ignored the demands.

Even after Uzbekistan had joined the antiterror coalition, the U.S. State Department maintained confusion over Central Asia by its indiscriminate adoption of human-rights rhetoric on Uzbekistan. The department's latest country reports on human rights were released on March 4, 2002. The Uzbekistan survey included numerous allegations of abuses that remained allegations, with almost none actually proven or even documented. This is a battle in which the United States has no business interfering with Karimov's policies.

In the Uzbek case, rights-watchers distinguished Wahhabis from a general, more benign category of "militants." But at the same time they failed to discriminate between Wahhabism and traditional piety. The State Department accused Karimov of seeing only evil Wahhabis where there were merely pious Muslims. But rights monitors saw only innocent, faithful Muslims where there were, in fact, Wahhabis and other terrorists. The issue was not Muslim devotion, but radicalism versus religion. The human rights profession had never recognized the difference between traditional Uzbek Muslims and Arab-subsidized infiltrators whose "piety" was a cover for terrorist recruitment. Even with a war on in Afghanistan, the State Department referred to Wahhabi elements politely as "independent" and "particularly devout" Muslims. State had evidently decided that such people were "nonpolitical" Muslims abused for their "religious beliefs." No evidence was produced to sustain these claims.

The world is learning the hard way that toleration of Wahhabism is collective suicide. Naturally, human rights advocates cherish such illusions as the idea that Uzbekistan should be as constitutionally open as the United States. But even America is being forced, in the aftermath of September 11, to find ways to identify, isolate, and defeat Wahhabi Islamofascists within its own society as well as around the world—while maintaining, to the maximum extent possible, its guarantees of human rights.

The government of Uzbekistan shared the U.S. commitment to the war on terrorism. The West should help its people complete their transition to democracy and capitalism. But we should cease interfering with their resistance to Wahhabism; indeed, we should find ways to strengthen them in that cause. Opposition to Wahhabism in Uzbekistan, as well as in the Saudi kingdom and the rest of the world, would not deny religious freedom, but protect and advance it. Uzbekistan could not afford to assure liberty for the enemies of liberty; nor can many other Muslim societies.

The Central Asian states have also been a major battlefield for an extremist tendency that began under Wahhabi inspiration but developed differences with it. This is the Liberation Party or Hezb-ut-Tahrir (HT).

With public protestations that it favors nothing but religious study and peaceful preparation of the masses for an eventual revolution, HT has also mounted a serious campaign in the West, where it has become active among younger Muslims, to portray itself as the victim of human rights abuses under post-Communist regimes. This is, in a sense, paradoxical, because of HT's striking similarity with Communism: Originating in the Middle East, HT is a clandestine, conspiratorial movement organized on the apparent model of the Masonic and other revolutionary secret societies in 19th-century Europe and in the Ottoman Empire. It claims to defend the legacy of the Ottoman caliphate even though its antecedents are purely Arab, its doctrines would have been rejected outright by the Turkish sultans, and its methods resemble those of the Unionists who destroyed the empire much more than those of the Ottoman rulers. The Ottomans, who zealously protected their Jewish subjects, would have dealt harshly with HT, which seeks the physical liquidation of Sufis, Shi'a Muslims, and Jews and is illegal in many Arab states.

Rashid quotes an Uzbek adherent of the movement who insisted its program is peaceful and complained that "the Wahhabis . . . wanted guerrilla war and the creation of an Islamic army." In its account of the history of Wahhabism and the Ottoman caliphate, HT appears to defend Ibn Abd al-Wahhab himself while condemning Al Sa'ud for political opportunism and dependence on the Christian powers. A similar posture was assumed by the quasicomical Omar Bakri Muhammad, a flamboyant extremist agitator in Britain. The most interesting aspect of HT, however, is the marked resemblance between its vocabulary and argumentation and the rhetoric of Soviet Communism. It denounces capitalism in identical terms and attacks the United States for hegemonism in the wake of the Soviet collapse, as if nostalgic for the latter. Its appeal in Central Asia could be explained as a fantasy of the stable, universalist environment of the caliphate replacing the chaos that followed the breakdown of the Soviet system. HT's propaganda could respond to confused and frightened ex-Soviet citizens left adrift by the disintegration of the Communist state. The party also agitates against the World Trade Organization and globalization in a manner indistinguishable from that of Western radicals. Indeed, HT sometimes sounds like a Communist group attempting to recruit Muslims, or a Muslim group seeking influence with Communists, rather than a religious body.[4]

Rashid echoes HT itself, as well as Western human rights experts and commentators on Islamism, who assert that the Uzbek authorities have engaged in "crude labeling of all Islamic militants Wahhabis," which "fails to acknowledge the differences between the HT and the IMU." But he acknowledges the historical continuity between Wahhabism and the supporters of Mawdudi, the Muslim Brotherhood that inspired Sayyid Qutb, Saudi-controlled Afghans, and HT. While one should not confuse the distinction between Wahhabism and less extreme forms of Islamism, one should also not exaggerate the differences between the Wahhabis and similar phenomena, including the Muslim Brotherhood, Hamas, Deobandism, the Taliban, and Hezb-ut-Tahrir, that may be described as Wahhabized. The Wahhabi-Saudi power, in addition to its many other similarities to Soviet Communism, resembles it in drawing smaller, more heterodox extremist strains in Islam into its orbit.

With the coming of the antiterror war, various Arab and other Muslims declared that the United States was really waging a war against Islam, and that it even had a master plan to undermine Islam. Some Americans agonized that they had not done enough to placate Muslim opinion, and that U.S. policy was to blame for September 11. The argument was nonsensical. The United States had used its power repeatedly in the 1990s on behalf of besieged Muslims, who are grateful for its intervention to this day. Aside from Wahhabis, those who charged the United States with being intrinsically hostile to Islam displayed a willful ignorance of recent history—so willful that it is doubtful the United States could ever do anything to persuade them otherwise. The United States has every reason to be proud of its record of solicitude for Muslims who have been persecuted for their ethnic and religious identity. It has no reason to apologize for its refusal to kowtow to Arab radicals like Saddam Husayn, or to indulge a Palestinian leadership that abandoned diplomacy in order to foment Balkan-style chaos in the Middle East.

Yet the United States has not acknowledged the goodwill it did create in the Balkans. As it looks forward to the next stages in the antiterror war, it would do well to make the most of the solidarity shown by Balkan Muslims generally, and Albanians in particular. The same could be said of the Chechens who defended themselves against renewed Russian imperialism in the 1990s. Reflecting the living traditions of Shaykh Shamyl and the other Naqshbandi dervishes who directed the Caucasian Muslim resistance to tsardom in the 19th century, the new chapter in the tormented history of Russo-Chechen relations was mainly written by Naqshbandi and Qadiri Sufis organized and led by the second post-Communist Chechen president, Aslan Maskhadov. Nearly a century after the *jihad* of Shamyl, in 1944, Joseph Stalin had worked revenge on the Chechens, deporting them en masse to the deserts of Kazakhstan. This more recent history helps explain the Chechens' continuing restiveness under Russian rule. Beginning in the 1950s, the deportees were allowed to return to their homeland, but they remained outsiders in the eyes of Russians, who regarded them as "blacks" or *chyorny*. And when Communism began collapsing, the old conflict between Russians and Chechens reemerged, this time with a new pretext. There is nothing Russia needs in Chechnya except a symbolic foe standing for Muslims in general, a hereditary enemy to replace the Jews.

The most remarkable aspect of the first post-Communist Chechen war, in 1994–96, was the complete absence of Wahhabi interference. At the combat level the Chechen conflict was even more brutal than that in Bosnia-Hercegovina. Small parties of Chechen warriors, fortifying themselves with Sufi ceremonies, underwent a continuous, devastating pounding from Russian artillery and air forces. More than twice the number of civilians was killed in Grozny, the capital, as in Sarajevo, and the city was completely demolished. This was no place for callow Saudis seeking diversion or the strengthening of their religious dedication; Chechen fighters without a strong commitment to traditional Islam could not be expected to survive. In the years since the war for the independence of Chechnya began in 1994, at least one in seven in its population of a million has been killed.

A troubled peace was effected in Chechnya by Boris Yeltsin, and President Maskhadov and the majority of the Chechens sought its preservation. Their fervent desires were thwarted by two parties: Yeltsin's Russian rivals and the Saudis. After September 11 Vladimir Putin strove to convince the American leaders that the Russians have a special understanding of Islamic extremism. In making this case, Russians typically pointed to their conflict with the Chechens. It is certainly true that Russia's relations with Muslims have been more intimate, but as we have seen, they have not been benign. Russia now has at least 20 million Muslims within its borders. The quest for a cultural enemy, and this alone, explains the willingness of post-Communist leaders in Russia to commit blood and treasure — not to mention police provocation, disinformation, bribery, and the lives of countless innocents hideously tortured and slain — to wars in Chechnya.

Putin seems unable to walk away from this dance of death. During the antiterror war, he sought American backing for a continued occupation of Chechnya. And in this he was abetted by extremists from the Muslim world. Around 1996, Wahhabis began flooding the Caucasus with preachers, money, and arms. Soon an Aramco-educated Saudi called Khattab, his real name Samir Saleh Abdullah al-Suwailem, appeared on the scene, an agent of al-Qaida, sent from Afghanistan to try to do to Chechnya what Osama bin Laden and the Taliban were in the process of doing to that country. He had also fought in Tajikistan. Khattab's distinction among the monsters was his addiction to videotaping every incident of conflict. Atrocities committed against Russian soldiers have become a common item of Wahhabi death-pornography, for sale in extremist mosques around the world. Khattab was killed in 2002.

The recent history of Wahhabism in the Caucasus may also have reflected a geopolitical development unperceived abroad. In 1998–99, *mujahidin* who looked covetously upon the patriotic Albanian struggle in Kosovo as a cockpit of martyrdom and recruitment found themselves almost entirely excluded from that area of conflict. The Saudi authorities, interestingly enough, rebaptized their committee for Kosovo aid as "the Joint Committee for the Relief of Kosovo and Chechnya." This committee has operated camps and schools in Ingushetia, on Chechnya's western border. It may not have been coincidental that a new wave of Wahhabis arrived in Chechnya as soon as the NATO intervention, and armed combat in Kosovo, ended. We know of at least one such case: Uthman Karkush, alias Bilal al-Qaiseri, a 23-year-old from Turkey, was killed in

Chechnya in February 2000. According to the Azzam network, he had "fought for six months in Bosnia during 1995 from where he unsuccessfully attempted travel to Chechnya. He was engaged at the time so he returned to Turkey initially to get married, but travelled on to Ogaden, East Africa, instead. It was when he returned from there that he finally did get married. He went to fight for the *jihad* in Kosovo but returned after a month when the fighting ceased."

Wahhabism, which drew a young husband away from his bride, also split families and villages in the Caucasus, as the ultrapuritans from Arabia agitated for adoption of extreme *Shariah* punishments, a ban on music, the covering of women, and above all the rejection of Sufism. The Chechen national movement fractured. In 1999, Khattab and his Wahhabis—who may never have counted more than a couple of hundred volunteers, compared with 10,000 in the official Chechen and Maskhadov-led forces—launched incursions into neighboring Daghestan, which made resolution of the Chechen relationship with Russia ever more remote. In 2001, the Wahhabis coldly assassinated many local Chechen leaders—low-level state functionaries, Muslim clerics, and so on. The Russians disingenuously blamed these killings on Maskhadov, who loathes Wahhabis. He once commented, of Chechnya, "Arabs, Tajiks, and other rogues have nothing to do here." For their part, a great many Russians and Chechens believed Putin's secret police, the KGB in new uniforms, worked hand in glove with the Wahhabis to undermine the mainstream Chechen leadership. Curiously, the Wahhabis did not view the Chechen struggle as an anti-Russian *jihad*. Rather, the Azzam network's propaganda declared, "This is not a civil, internal conflict between Chechens and Russians, but rather it is a crusade of the forces of *kufr* (Christianity, Judaism, Communism, atheism, etc.) against Islam." To this dishonest claim was added the despicable lie that "the Russians are receiving financial and physical help from America." In reality, the United States took the lead in condemning Russian human rights violations in the Caucasus.

Putin does not come to the West with clean hands in dealing with Muslims, and in our new effort to gain Muslim allies and supporters Americans can only harm our cause by appearing to sign off on the continued mistreatment of a small, isolated people. For the sake of American credibility, the Bush administration should continue to keep a close watch on Russian mischief in the Caucasus and should protest every abuse. At the same time, it should dramatically improve its relationship with mainstream, traditional Chechens—who had repeatedly offered help in beating bin Laden, help that we scorned only to the democracies' detriment. The Chechens, along with Albanians and Uzbeks, might have been much more reliable allies in combating bin Laden than our putative friends, the Saudis.

Meanwhile, what of the claims advanced, in the face of all this, that bin Laden had become an enemy of the Saudis and sought the overthrow of the monarchy? Through much of the aftermath of the September 11 events, while the Saudis attempted to deflect Western media and government attention from the Wahhabism of the terrorists, many commentators in the West repeated that bin Laden had called for the Saudi monarchy to be deposed and therefore was "as much a threat to them as to us." In reality, he had not gone very far in his criticisms of the Saudi royal family, and whether or not he or others like him really threatened the kingdom, its rulers maintained a curious nonchalance about him. They were obviously much more upset by Western criticism of Wahhabism than by bin Laden's diatribes against Saudi hypocrisy. The Saudi rulers support extremists like bin Laden to quiet complaints about their relations with the West, and they cannot, in the final reckoning, sacrifice Wahhabism on the altar of their foreign policy.

Anyone needing to be disabused of two fantasies—that bin Laden was a serious enemy of the Saudi regime and that Iraq and Saddam Husayn were not intimate with the Islamofascist terror command—had only to read bin Laden's own political and pseudo-religious declarations. They are properly called "pseudo-religious" because they have no serious Islamic content and bin Laden himself has no significant religious training. The most important manifesto of bin Ladenism was the "Declaration of War Against the Americans Occupying the Land of the Two Holy Places," also known as the "Ladenese Epistle," dating from October 1996. The "Ladenese Epistle" was stuffed with Islamic verbiage, most of it perfunctory and hortatory, as if hastily put together.

To read this text, one might think that bin Laden was mainly concerned with rescuing Muslims through holy war. But after a laundry list of geographical citations ranging from Bosnia-Hercegovina to the Philippines, intended to portray an *ummah* everywhere under assault, the author turned to his main obsession: the justification by some Islamic scholars of the American military presence in Saudi Arabia. The style was courteous to the Saudi rulers, because bin Laden did not wish to abandon his connections with Riyadh, any more than his Saudi supporters wished them to be fully revealed. But bin Laden's complaints about Saudi Arabia were those of a critic, not a revolutionary enemy. The oil wealth has been concentrated in the hands of a single family, Al Sa'ud; bin Laden bemoaned the resulting inequality but skirted discussion of those responsible. Various other grievances, ranging from the unemployment of overeducated youths to a kind of general malaise, were cited with vague indignation.

Throughout bin Laden's writings, one had the sense of someone going out of his way not to say certain things. Those things involved the personalities of the Saudi rulers. Since bin Laden continued to draw on financial resources in the kingdom while living in Afghanistan and was in no physical danger from Saudi hands, he could only be observing a policy of discretion, not expressing fear. Bin Laden was not a major strategist; he was an opportunistic improviser in the style of Hitler or Stalin. Calling for action by the Saudi populace to expel U.S. troops, he advised murdering Americans. But when he summoned Saudi citizens to correct the policies of their government, he never called for killing or other forms of terror against the Saudi rulers. Rather, he praised the drafting of petitions to the king and recommended that Saudi women boycott American consumer goods. He was aggrieved by the failure of the Saudi Army to serve ably in the Gulf War, but also by the destruction inflicted on Iraq, which he exaggerated. Unlike the Saudi and other Arab governments, he called for lifting the U.N. sanctions on Saddam Husayn.

So much for the claim of former president Bill Clinton and others that bin Laden was anti-Saddam, or the Iraqis' own disclaimers that they are not Wahhabis (one may rather view them as Wahhabized). If an intolerant Wahhabi like bin Laden could embrace the propaganda of leftist Iraq, there was no reason they should not return the favor by cooperating with his terror schemes. The convergence of interests between the Wahhabis and Iraq became more obvious at the conclusion of the 2001–02 Afghan war when the Saudis lobbied Washington against serious Western action to remove Saddam. The rest of the "Ladenese Epistle" wandered between exaltation of Ibn Taymiyyah and superficial geopolitical sloganeering. Bin Laden jeered at the United States for fleeing Lebanon, Somalia, and Yemen. He seemed to want to flatter the Japanese (who, as he noted, are the main consumers of Saudi oil) as possible adversaries of the United States. Still, he insisted on distinctions: "The [Saudi] regime is fully responsible for what has been imposed on the country and the nation; however, the occupying American enemy is the principal and main cause of the situation."

This seemed, if anything, a strategy to help keep the Saudi regime in power by concentrating attacks on the United States. Still, in the last spasms of his diatribe, the author switched back to sympathy for Saddam's Iraq. Bin Laden recycled the phraseology peddled in the West by Saddam's leftist apologists, blaming America and the Saudis for allegedly killing more than half a million Iraqi children. The overall effect is more that of an article from *The Nation* than that of an Islamic religious text, as if it had been lifted from Noam Chomsky or Edward Said. But that was consistent with reports that some of bin Laden's cadres, although exploiting Islam, were former leftists. The Wahhabi ideology has always been about power first.

A similar text is "The New Powder Keg in the Middle East," an interview bin Laden gave in 1996. Here again, bin Laden bemoaned various aspects of Saudi rule, but in surprisingly circumspect terms. The regime, he said, faced two choices: compliance with the demands of the extremists or an escalation of violence against Americans. Bin Laden was obviously a vain figure, intoxicated by his capacity to wreak havoc in the West. But he had no such nihilistic inclinations when it came to his homeland, Saudi Arabia. His Saudi patrons continued to play a double game with the West. They smiled in our faces and begged for healing and trust. Meanwhile, they sent money to bin Laden, and dispatched their unemployable sons around the Muslim world to serve as Wahhabi missionaries before they joined the terror networks. How long would Western political and business leaders continue pretending this was not the reality of the Saudi relationship with the West?

The frontline of the Wahhabi terror war is a long and sinuous one. Even after the defeat it suffered in Afghanistan, Wahhabism continues its atrocities in Kashmir, where Pakistani president Pervez Musharraf claims his intention to rein it in. This will not be a small task. Until recently, Kashmir has been a Pakistani rather than a Saudi cause, much as the terrorist effort mounted in the Philippines by the Abu Sayyaf terror network originally had more to do with local issues. But in both places, Wahhabi influence was visible in the sadism of terror crimes, as well as targeting of Hindus and Christians. Funding of local terror, along with recruitment of combatants, is supported from Saudi Arabia.

Of course, notwithstanding heavy Iranian propaganda and funding for groups like Hezbollah and Palestinian Islamic Jihad, the Wahhabi-Saudi regime played a much greater role in supporting suicide bombings in Israel. On March 26, 2002, Charles Krauthammer correctly noted in the *Washington Post*, "Before the Oslo peace accords of 1993, suicide bombing was a practice almost unheard of among Palestinians." While Krauthammer ascribed the novelty of suicide terrorism to indoctrination in hatred foisted on Palestinian youth by Yasir Arafat, in a period of Israeli peaceseeking, others blamed it on general alienation and hopelessness, as well as Israeli policies. Non-Muslims failed to notice that the emergence of suicide terrorism in Israel coincided with the intensification of the Wahhabi-Saudi campaign for global colonization of Islam.

Until very recently, suicide bombings were rare everywhere in the Muslim world except Israel, where they were encouraged by Wahhabi clerics that seek to dominate Palestinian Islam. With the onset of a new wave of terror and retaliation in Israel after September 11, bombings were blamed on the familiar enemies, Iraq, Iran, and Syria. Disclosure that Saddam Husayn's regime paid $25,000 to the family of each terror martyr supplemented other evidence in making the case against Baghdad. Charges against Iran and Syria were seemingly reinforced by the murky news accounts about the *Karine A*, a ship full of heavy weapons sent to the Palestinians, and a brief rocket campaign on the northern border of Israel. Unfortunately, even the Israelis themselves were reluctant to find the source of heightened terrorism in Saudi Arabia and in the Wahhabi ideology. The Al-Aqsa Martyrs' Brigades, the terrorist formation that emerged from the ranks of Yasir Arafat's followers, could be described as a Wahhabized tendency drawn into the Saudi-Hamas orbit.

On October 12, 2000, the Saudi-based International Islamic Relief Organization, later compromised by its association with al-Qaida, had ponied up a first installment of $500,000 to support the revived Palestinian *intifada*. IIRO director Adnan bin Khalil Basha recommended a subsidy of $1,000 to the family of each "martyr." A flurry of decrees and speeches resulted in the establishment of a gigantic Saudi solidarity fund for the Palestinians. On October 20, Crown Prince Abdullah called for $200 million more for the families of "martyrs" and the care and education of "martyrs' sons." All comment on fundraising for the Palestinians focused on support for "martyrdom." Wahhabism had created a welfare system for the production of suicide terror. In 2001, the Saudi authorities budgeted almost $2 billion for the operating expenses of Arafat's Palestinian Authority. At the same time, repeated pledges for the families and sons of "martyrs" were reported, in addition to the $250 million finally committed for 2000. The sums comprised $33 million, including outlays for 358 "martyrs," disbursed in January 2001; $33.7 million for "martyrs" in March 2001, at a rate of $5,333 per family; $50 million donated, also in March, by Crown Prince Abdullah for the education of "martyrs' sons"; and $40 million in private donations for "martyrs" in April. Doing the math could be frightening: $33.7 million at $5,333 per family meant the Saudis anticipated at least 6,000 "martyrs."

The convoluted Wahhabi theology occasionally created impediments for their Palestinian acolytes. A Wahhabi ideologue of Albanian ethnicity and virtually no authentic Islamic scholarship, Nasr ad-Din al-Albani, became an idol of the Saudi regime. He was a watchmaker by trade who had been brought up in Jordan and repudiated for his extremism by his own father, who was a distinguished Muslim scholar from northern Albania. Al-Albani carried Wahhabi separatism so far as to issue a *fatwa* recommending that Muslims leave the territory of Israel and the West Bank. This hardly suited the attitude of Hamas, which had previously worshipped al-Albani, but which was also committed to driving the Jews out of the land. But these curious controversies were ignored outside the *ummah*.

More serious problems were created in spring 2002 when the disclosure in Western media of Saudi subsidies for "martyrs" in Israel and the West Bank stirred considerable controversy. The bad publicity coincided with the new round of bloody bombings in Israel as well as a Saudi "peace offer" to the Israelis. The Saudis at first denied that any of their funds had gone to subsidize terror. But rhetoric defending terror "martyrdom" by prominent figures in the kingdom discredited these disclaimers. Then the Israelis announced that in their occupation of the West Bank they had found documents corroborating the direct disbursement of Saudi funds to terrorists. The bookkeeping loop between the financing and fulfillment of terrorist orders had been closed.

But after one round of Middle Eastern bloodshed seemed to have ended, in April 2002, a silly season seemed to have begun—at least as far as Western reporting on Saudi Arabia and its involvement with terrorism went. The worst form of journalistic ineptitude is obliviousness. U.S. media assumed a policy of heedless disregard about the documents captured by the Israelis, which revealed more extremely interesting information about the Saudis, Hamas, and the Palestinian Authority. Cable News Network correspondent Wolf Blitzer flew right over this juicy topic in a May 12 interview with Yasir Arafat.

Arafat, his demeanor that of someone who might prefer to rid himself of a compromising affiliation, commented, in reference to suicide terrorism, "there are some—I don't want to say their names—some international powers supporting this." Blitzer asked about the usual suspects: Iraq and Iran. However, since Arafat had already said that he would not identify the culprits by name, the Palestinian leader had no incentive to spell things out. This ill-informed colloquy echoed an earlier exchange on CNN's *Crossfire*, in which Clintonite commentator Paul Begala questioned Saudi spin-shaykh Adel al-Jubeir about Saudi funding of Hezbollah. But Saudi Arabia funded Hamas, not Hezbollah. Western confusion on these issues sent a message to Middle East extremists: The democratic governments had no idea what was really happening.

What did the documents captured by the Israeli Defense Forces add to this picture? First, they confirmed a rumor long circulating among Arabs and Muslims, which held that Saudi Arabia and Hamas wanted Arafat dealt out of the Middle East game and were using their financial and political resources to that end. The reason: to supplant the secular nationalist politics of Arafat with the ideology of the Wahhabi death cult.

The IDF cover materials on the captured documents summarized these intrigues as follows: "Strengthening the Hamas' status among the Palestinian population and weakening the Palestinian Authority . . . attempts by Arafat and the PA in the first months of the 'intifada' to change this problematic situation (including by a personal request of Arafat to senior Saudi Arabian officials who supervise money transfers) were in vain." In the accompanying, more detailed commentary, the Israelis noted, "the PA and Arafat at its head . . . were especially concerned with the strengthening of the status of the Hamas vis-à-vis the PA . . . the Saudis, for their own reasons, preferred to send the funds to Islamic entities."

Referring to correspondence between the PA and the Saudis, in December 2000–January 2001, the Israelis pointed out, "In these documents, Arafat complains about the fact that the Saudi aid is not transferred to the PA areas via the PA, and it does not reach the Fatah, but is given to Hamas and radical Islamic groups associated with Hamas, thus weakening the PA. The documents concern discussions held in Riyadh between the Palestinians and the Saudis on this issue. In hindsight, it can be stated that Arafat failed in his attempt to persuade the Saudis to channel the financial aid via the PA, and the phenomenon of transferring Saudi funds to Hamas elements continued and continues until the present."

Finally, the Israelis indicated, "The Saudis, for their own reasons (apprehension [about] PA corruption, hostility to Arafat, ideological proximity to Hamas) preferred to transfer the money to Hamas." And "in conclusion . . . the PA did not succeed in effective supervision of the use of [this] money and in blocking [its] use as a lever for strengthening the Hamas."

The captured documents also reinforced past observations about links between Hamas in Israel and funding of it by Wahhabi institutions in the United States and elsewhere around the world. One such was the Holy Land Foundation for Relief and Development, under investigation by U.S. federal authorities. Another was a network headed by Qatar-based Yusuf al-Qaradawi, a Wahhabi cleric who was consulted by Islamic chaplains in the U.S. military about the religious duties of Muslims serving under the Stars and Stripes (both these matters are discussed in the following chapter).

In addition, the Israelis seized materials showing that in the ranks of Hamas, the memory of Osama bin Laden's mentor Abdullah Azzam remained a powerful source of inspiration ("posters, leaflets, and quotes").

Did Saudi maneuvers against Arafat make the latter a moderate? That is a silly question—about as silly as asking if Binyamin Netanyahu's speechifying against a Palestinian state made Ariel Sharon a sellout to the Arabs. On the other hand, it was doubtful that many people on either side of the Israeli-Palestinian divide would have liked to see the battle between Sharon and Arafat turn into a conflict between Netanyahu and Hamas.

If there was anything to be learned from the captured documents, it was that the Saudis must remain suspect as partners for either the Israelis or the Palestinians, in any resumption of peace negotiations. If their funding of Hamas made their peace gestures to the Israelis questionable, it made their standing as supporters of non-Wahhabi Palestinians—the majority, given local traditions of secularism, as well as the influence of Arab Christians in the nationalist movement—even more dubious. Indeed, it had to fortify suspicions that the entire Saudi gambit in publicly injecting themselves into the Israeli-Palestinian confrontation had a sole aim: to shift attention from their citizens' involvement in the events of September 11.

In these circumstances, for the Saudis to claim they wanted "peace" appeared a ridiculous imposture. The Bosnian Muslims and the mainstream leadership of the Chechens had undergone unspeakable atrocities and horrors, yet they sincerely sought peace, and when given the opportunity, made peace. The Saudis and other Wahhabized Arabs needed war, not peace—to keep the attention of their restive subjects under their control and to feed the terrorist monster they had created. The terrible outcome of Wahhabi involvement in the Middle East conflict was eloquently expressed when the father of Andaleeb Takafka, a 20-year-old Palestinian woman who blew herself up at a Jerusalem bus stop in April 2002, declared, "I am happy. . . . All the girls should do it."

A question that must occur to those observing the activities of the Saudi-Wahhabi network is: How did they so successfully conceal their activities and aims for so long? As previously described, willful ignorance or obfuscation on the part of the Western oil industry and academy played a major role. In addition, Western media were extremely susceptible to diversion of their attention away from the Saudis to the Iraqis and Iranians. For example, an influential Australian daily, the *Sydney Morning Herald*, in March 2002 described Palestinian leader Hassan Khraisheh praising Iraq as "the only Arab country officially donating to the Palestinian cause." The newspaper quoted Khraisheh's claim that "the Saudis used to give US$4,000 to the martyrs, but now it depends on public donations." This can only be considered deliberate disinformation. But the Saudis had also learned how to charm their victims into obliviousness. In February 2001, the King Faisal Foundation presented its annual King Faisal International Prizes. Intended to honor contributions to humanity, the prizes are typically given to a mix of Western medical researchers and Arab intellectuals. The award for "service to Islam" was presented to the governor of Riyadh province, Prince Salman, in the name of the Saudi High Commission for Relief to Bosnia-Hercegovina. Predictably, it was said the prize money would be sent to the Balkans for mosque reconstruction, cultural centers, schools, Islamic colleges, health care, and housing. In reality, much of it may have ended up in the coffers of al-Qaida. But more remarkably, the prize ceremony in Riyadh was attended by Charles, Prince of Wales. Following that event, Prince Charles met with Saudi businessmen and officials to advise them on setting up a fund to encourage private enterprise among young people, financed by the Saudi Arabian Monetary Agency.

Saudi-Wahhabi outreach to the Christian world has operated at an even higher profile, at times, than in the *ummah*. Annual cultural forums under royal patronage have been held in Gibraltar (1998), Edinburgh (1998), Brussels (1999), Budapest (2000), and Copenhagen (2001). The kingdom has founded and contributed funds to 210 Islamic centers (i.e., mosque complexes) in Europe, the Americas, Africa, and Asia. Major Islamic institutions have been established, with personal grants from the monarch, in Malaga, Spain, Toronto, Buenos Aires, the Maldive Islands, Chad, and Edinburgh. The Saudi authorities have also paid to create such centers in Geneva, New York, Tokyo, Zagreb, London, and Nigeria. Academic endowments have been provided for major universities, including U.C.-Berkeley, Harvard, the University of London, and Moscow University. In their program for schoolchildren, the kingdom created the Islamic Saudi Academy in Washington, D.C., which became controversial for the harshness of its Wahhabi curriculum. The ISA spent $27 million in the decade 1984–94, and reported a student body of 1,300 in 1999. At the beginning of the recent Afghan war, the ISA raised funds for Afghan families and children, ignoring that the latter then remained under Taliban control. Not far away, Fairfax, Virginia, is host to the Institute for Islamic and Arabic Sciences in America, also subsidized by the kingdom.

Indeed, until September 11 one of the most significant Wahhabi war fronts was located in the United States, to which we now turn.

CHAPTER 8

Religious Colonialism

WAHHABISM AND AMERICAN ISLAM

On September 17, 2001, President George W. Bush stood in the Islamic Center of Washington, the capital's most important mosque. Following the horror six days before, he sought to calm the fears of Americans about terrorism. "The face of terror is not the true face of Islam," he said. "Acts of violence against innocents violate the fundamental tenets of the Islamic faith and it's important for my fellow Americans to understand that."

The president's intention, in seeking to dampen anxieties about and among Muslims living in America, was laudable. But when he stood up in the mosque, he was accompanied by a group of men and women unfamiliar to the wider public. These were the self-appointed representatives of American Islam, and in allowing them this photo opportunity, Bush unintentionally undermined the positive message he delivered. Far from being firm friends of America, the most prominent of these figures were ringleaders in the Wahhabi takeover of American Islam. As non-Muslim Americans would soon learn, it was a measure of their astonishing success that they, and their Saudi-patronized colleagues, had managed to enlist

Americans, including a troubled teenager from Marin County, California, named John Walker Lindh, in their war against the West, just as they recruited young Saudis and other Arabs.

The Wahhabis had imposed the Saudi monarchy by bloodshed; but they had carried out a bloodless coup within the American Muslim community thanks to American constitutional protections, which they exploited, as well as the ignorance and accommodating attitude of the non-Muslim majority and the timidity of non-Wahhabi Muslims in the face of a careful and well-crafted Wahhabi campaign.

The story of the Wahhabi conquest of American Islam is a complicated one. To begin with, as a religious community Muslims were, in great part, new to the country. Even counting them has been difficult, with estimates ranging from 3 to 10 million in the year 2000. The first Muslims to immigrate in any significant numbers began to come in the 1960s and 1970s from Pakistan, India, and Bangladesh. Although it remains difficult to gauge their total, they were mainly professionals—including many doctors, engineers, and computer experts. They accounted for a majority, and then a plurality—up to 40 percent. Considerable Arab Muslims began arriving a bit later, most of them working-class or involved in small business. Although they did not at first bring a significant body of scholars with them, they did significantly alter the demography of American Islam, rising to a position equal to or exceeding the subcontinentals. Moreover, the Arab Muslims were highly politicized. While the subcontinental Muslims typically left politics behind when they came to America, many Arabs had been radicalized by the confrontation with Israel—and, by extension, with U.S. support for the Jewish state. Small but significant Slavic and Albanian Muslim groups also established a presence in the country. Nevertheless, both Indo-Pakistani-Bengali and Arab Muslims were exceeded by African Americans.

In short, by the end of the 20th century there was to all outward appearances a flourishing and diverse American Muslim community. Indeed, before September 11, Islam was often described as the fastest growing faith in America. However, the great weakness of American Islam was its lack of tradition—the continuity of scholars that, elsewhere in the *ummah*, has stabilized the community and, with varying results, has guarded it from excesses and extremism. In addition, its public religious institutions were underdeveloped, if only because the community had been so small and scattered.

Some time before the attacks on New York and Washington, a representative of the Muslims of the United States visited the *Mufti* of Uzbekistan, Abdurashid Qori Bahromov. When the latter asked the American if Wahhabism had arrived in the United States, the American replied, "In the United States we have all forms of Islam, including Wahhabis, Salafis, the Muslim Brotherhood, and the Sufis. Thanks be to Allah, we meet together and have an excellent situation."

Mufti Bahromov replied reprovingly, "You are wrong, because you are telling me that a group of people are sitting in a room, and someone has put a gun on the table between them. You tell me you are sure the gun will never be used. But I tell you that when a gun is put on the table, it will be used. The gun is Islamic extremism—whether you call it Wahhabi, Salafi, or the ideology of the so-called Muslim Brothers. You have allowed the gun to be put on the table in America—and it will be used against America. I cannot agree with you that the situation is excellent. Rather, it is extremely dangerous for America and for the Muslims."

A "Muslim establishment" did not exist in America until the mid-1980s when Hamas, the Wahhabi organization fighting Israel, decided to open a political front on U.S. territory: a "Wahhabi lobby." A constellation of carefully designed entities, funded from the same source, suddenly appeared, radiating ideological aggression in all directions. Like the front organizations fostered in the past by Communism, they each had specific tasks and were designed to appeal to various constituencies. But they had a single program: to create a secure base for planning terrorist operations in Israel, to amass funds and recruits, and finally to control all discussion of Islam and Muslim societies in American media and government. No such aim had ever before been put forward by a Muslim group in America, and no single Christian or Jewish institution had ever staked an exclusivist claim of this kind.

In typical Wahhabi style, the creators of the lobby sought to have it both ways. They wanted all the benefits and guarantees of American society while, at the same time, rejecting the foundation of American reli-

gious liberty: tolerance of differences. The lobby sought to subordinate
American Muslims to their orders and direction and to set up Wahhabism
as the single recognized Islamic dispensation. This intent was plainly visible in their approaches to both Muslims and non-Muslims. The representatives of these organizations insisted on defining Islam in purely Wahhabi
terms. They excluded Sufis and Shi'as from their councils and delibera-
tions. They told reporters from the mainstream media that such customs
as celebration of the Prophet's birthday were non-Islamic and attacked the
use of the term "Muhammadan" as supposedly inferring the worship of
the Prophet as a divine being. They similarly condemned the description
of their outlook as "fundamentalist" by arguing that "all Muslims agree on
the fundamentals of the faith." While this is correct in a general sense, it is
no less true that the Wahhabi rejection of all historical and cultural developments in Islam after its first two generations, including Sufi mysticism,
the four established schools of Islamic jurisprudence, and Ottoman traditions of pluralism and tolerance, could only be described as fundamentalist.

Above all, their Wahhabism was visible in their central, obsessive promotion of a rejectionist stance against Israel and their unwavering apologetics for suicide terrorism. Indeed, these were their essential and ultimate
principles; they were committed to defending extremism on American
soil, and thus they sought ideological control over the field of operations.
To do this they coldly and boldly manipulated the susceptibility of American politicians, academics, and journalists, demanding a special place at
the multicultural table, while at the same time actively seeking to reduce
the space occupied by Jews and to ensure that there would be no place
whatever for Sufis, Shi'as, or Arab peace advocates.

This was accomplished by refusing all discussion or recognition of Sufi
traditions, excluding and expelling Shi'as from mosques, and marginaliz-
ing Arab voices for conciliation with Israel. They would not even engage
in dialogue with such elements, much less recognize them as partners in
Muslim public activities. One searches their publications, press releases,
and Web sites in vain for the slightest recognition that such aspects of
Islamic civilization had any presence or legitimacy whatever in the
United States. Moreover, their nominal religious and cultural concerns

were window dressing for their core political activities. Teaching Islamic history, theology, or culture was merely a means to gain standing in the academy; organizationally, they completely ignored these topics. Instead, they concentrated on organizing demonstrations, registering voters, pressuring elected officials, confronting Jewish groups, and issuing propaganda supporting the regimes of Saudi Arabia, Sudan, and, formerly, Afghanistan. In addition, they defended successive suicide terror campaigns in Israel, while also apologizing for the Muslim Brotherhood and al-Qaida, and opposing Western action against Saddam Husayn. (Occasional flings into support for Iran or Hezbollah were a secondary phenomenon at most.)

Their ideological rigidity was especially visible in their public response to threats facing the Iraqi Kurds, Bosnian Muslims, Kosovar Albanians, and Chechens. They rejected many appeals from Jewish advocates for common action to defend the victims of Serbian imperialism. Indeed, the campaign for American intervention in the Balkans was overwhelmingly carried by Jews, not by Muslims, notwithstanding the fabrication of letterhead organizations by the Wahhabis. Among Muslims, they professed to weep for Bosnia and Kosovo, but these topics never replaced Israel at the head of their agenda. For them the Iraqi Kurds simply did not exist, and the Chechens were an item for occasional commentary and no more.

We may begin a review of such activities with a somewhat heterodox entity: the Muslim Public Affairs Council (MPAC), which occasionally presents itself as more inclusive and more open to real dialogue with Jews and Christians, but which nonetheless typically defends extremist violence and the aim of destroying Israel and undermining American power. The leadership of MPAC includes Maher Hathout. In a Friday sermon at the Islamic Center of Southern California on August 21, 1998, Hathout condemned U.S. retaliation in Afghanistan, after the bombing of American embassies in Kenya and Tanzania, as "illegal, immoral, unhuman, unacceptable, stupid, and un-American." When a bomber blew up a pizzeria in Israel on August 9, 2001, MPAC declared that Israel itself was "responsible for this pattern of violence."

In addition, the Islamic Institute (which enjoys the backing of consultant Grover Norquist) serves as a bridge to conservative Republicans.

Indeed, Norquist, founder of Americans for Tax Reform, was responsible for bringing President Bush together with the Wahhabi leaders at the Washington mosque in the aftermath of September 11. Describing himself as "a longtime advocate of outreach to the Muslim community," Norquist argued that Muslims had strong conservative and family values that made them a natural Republican constituency and declared that Bush had been elected "because of the Muslim vote," which Norquist had allegedly summoned. Unfortunately, Norquist has found it difficult to distinguish between ordinary and normal political activities by Muslims and the defense of extremism. After September 11, he repeatedly echoed hysterical charges by Arab and Muslim advocates who claimed that their communities were under siege and faced a wholesale curtailment of their civil rights. Norquist and the Islamic Institute have also served as lobbyists in the United States for the Wahhabi-dominated Gulf state of Qatar.

But the core of the Wahhabi lobby is composed of a number of interlocking groups, which are centrally funded and directed by America's foreign enemies, though they serve different aims and constituencies. To begin with those based in Washington: The Council on American-Islamic Relations (CAIR) is dedicated to pressuring government and media to accept its definition of Islamic issues and sensitivity thereto; while the American Muslim Council (AMC) is an advocacy group aimed at the wider American public through political, community, and "interfaith" activism. When President Bush stood up in the Washington mosque in the days after September 11, CAIR's national director, Nihad Awad, an inexhaustible agitator for Hamas, stood beside him. In the same group, AMC president Yahya Basha and representatives of MPAC were also to be found. Related organizations include the American Muslim Alliance (AMA), which has conducted targeted political lobbying to advance the Arab Muslim agenda and distributes Holocaust denial literature at its annual convention; and the Islamic Society of North America (ISNA), which enforces Wahhabi theological writ in the country's 1,200 officially recognized mosques (out of a possible total of 4,000, including unrecognized and small congregations).

ISNA president Muzammil Siddiqi, described by many of his critics as a power-hungry fanatic, appeared in the interfaith prayer ceremony at the

National Cathedral in Washington directly following September 11. On October 28, 2000, at an anti-Israel "Jerusalem Day" rally sponsored by Norquist's Islamic Institute, AMC, and other groups, Siddiqi asserted, "America has to learn . . . if you remain on the side of injustice, the wrath of God will come. Please, all Americans. Do you remember that? . . . If you continue doing injustice, and tolerate injustice, the wrath of God will come." Many of the main mosques in the United States were recently built with Saudi money and saddled with a requirement that they follow Wahhabi *imams* and Wahhabi dictates. Testimony to this effect comes from (among many others) Kaukab Siddique, the editor of *New Trend*, an Islamic periodical of extremist but nonconforming views, who charged: "ISNA controls most mosques in America and thus also controls: 1. Who will speak at EVERY [Friday prayer]. 2. Which literature will be distributed there. . . . *New Trend* tried right from 1977 to warn the people about this danger of monopoly created by funds coming in from Saudi Arabia . . . the *Ikhwan* mafia, a group of six . . . were bringing in funds from Saudi Arabia and the Gulf states. The movement for reform was quashed by the mafia (who are the revered 'elders' of ISNA) who went from city to city."

Subsidiary groups within the Wahhabi lobby include the Islamic Circle of North America (ICNA), aligned with "Salafi" extremists in Pakistan, and a cluster of Hamas operational groups comprising the Islamic Association for Palestine (IAP), the American Muslims for Jerusalem, and the Holy Land Foundation for Relief and Development (HLF), which constitute the nerve center of the radical Islamic institutional network. These groups appear independent of one another, but nearly all of them draw from the common financial and technical pool at HLF. They do not disagree or compete; they are diverse "shops" offering identical ideological content.

The network has also infiltrated the Muslim Students Association (MSA), which targeted campuses, serving as a predecessor of ISNA. The MSA was created in 1963 in close coordination with the Muslim World League. As noted by Khomeini biographer Hamid Algar, "Particularly in the 1960s and 1970s, no criticism of Saudi Arabia would be tolerated at the annual conventions of the MSA." Within its ranks, Algar writes, "official approval of Wahhabism remained strong," and in 1980 it produced an English translation of Ibn Abd al-Wahhab's own writings. *New Trend*'s Siddique emphasized, "These well-funded groups will not allow any Islamic material other than their own to be distributed."

These were the main groups whose representatives took to the airwaves after September 11, during the war in Afghanistan, and more intensively than ever during the March–April 2002 Israeli incursions into the West Bank, to provide the "Muslim view" of these events. As self-appointed Muslim spokesmen, they typically refused to "simplify the situation" by blaming Osama bin Laden for the horrific attacks on America, following the Wahhabi line that no compelling proof had been offered by U.S. authorities. While they were eventually induced by wheedling journalists to condemn suicide terror in a pro forma manner, they hedged their disavowals by describing them as an understandable response to Israeli brutality. But their loudest noise was made in their assertions that American Muslims faced widespread bias attacks and restrictions on civil liberties after September 11. They were also full-throated in their opposition to the investigation and closure of Hamas- and al-Qaida–linked "charities" and other Islamic institutions.

Though the words "Islam" and "Muslim" appear in most of their titles, authentic religious ends were clearly absent from their programs. Rather than working to improve the training of *imams*, they mobilized them for political goals. In this way, they sought to introduce extremist activities based in the Middle East into the American heartland. Indeed, the functional center of the system was located in Richardson, Texas, in the form of the Holy Land Foundation. But they did not run candidates in U.S. elections on a pro-Hamas ticket. Rather, they worked behind the scenes to demand special consideration for their agenda. They often did not make open claims for Muslim causes. Rather, they stressed "sensitivity" to "Muslim feelings." They did not propose meaningful political discussion or interfaith dialogue. Rather, they complained about injuries allegedly done to Muslims, which must be recognized and apologized for before any dialogue takes place. They purported to know the feelings and opinions of all Muslims and arrogated to themselves the right to speak for all Muslims.

To experienced Washington journalists and political insiders, one thing was immediately clear about the Wahhabi lobby: It had been crafted in direct imitation of the leading American Jewish organizations. CAIR was modeled on the highly effective Anti-Defamation League (ADL), AMC on the American Jewish Committee (AJC), ISNA on the Union of Orthodox Jewish Congregations, and MPAC on the American Israel Public Affairs Committee (AIPAC). But the imitation embodied certain intrinsic flaws in Wahhabi and Hamas politics, caused by their ideology. With their primitive, conspiratorial mentality, the Wahhabis assumed that the various American Jewish groups were all controlled and coordinated by a single, commanding power, i.e., the Israeli embassy. They had no conception of the considerable competition, and fundamental diversity in vision and practical affairs, between the Jewish groups. Nor could they permit the flowering of such differences within their own community. Their mentality was monopolistic and totalitarian, and they could only function in a rigidly disciplined structure.[1]

None of these groups had behind them the hard work of political organizing and domestic activism pursued by other recently arrived immigrant communities, such as Cuban Americans or Korean Americans. But Saudi money gave the Wahhabi lobby an artificially high level of influence and access. In addition, they had learned a crucial lesson from the activities of Irish Americans, even if they lacked their long history or large numbers in the country. The Irish Republican movement had long been financed and even directed from the United States, and domestic political influence had given Irish extremists virtual impunity to operate on U.S. soil against America's most important historic ally, Britain. Wahhabis have tried to create the same kind of operation, raising funds and coordinating their international operations largely from the United States. In defending themselves against charges of terrorism, the Wahhabi lobby, as well as Osama bin Laden himself, frequently cite the Irish precedent. In addition, Arab terror suspects prosecuted in the United States have called on Irish radical groups for legal support.

The effectiveness of the Wahhabi lobby in intimidating mainstream American opinion may be illustrated by a fawning letter issued in 1996 endorsing the AMC, signed by the American Friends Service Committee, along with a leading body of the Methodist Church, the National Conference of Catholic Bishops (NCCB), the National Council of the Churches of Christ, the Presbyterian Church, and the United Church of Christ. The occasion of this letter was a protest over alleged unfair media scrutiny of AMC's activities. The absence of even the most peace-oriented or leftist Jews from this roster was noticeable; but far more eloquent was the very first line of the letter, which endorsed AMC as "the premier, mainstream Muslim group in Washington." Can one imagine such a coalition conferring this title on any Jewish group? Such an action would be enormously divisive. Similarly, can one imagine a roster of Jewish groups conferring the same status on, say, Evangelical Protestants? Obviously not. In this respect, notwithstanding the endless whining of Arab advocates about Jewish and Israeli power in America, it may be argued that both the Wahhabi lobby in American Islam and the Saudi influence in U.S. foreign policy benefited from a "blank check." American Jews and Israelis were required to remain constantly active and vigilant, because they had to argue for their demands and see them through the judicial and legislative process, while the Wahhabis and Saudis were repeatedly granted a privileged position without public discussion.

American Christian leaders clearly had no idea of how to approach Muslims, how to distinguish among Muslims, or how to assist Muslims in finding a legitimate and proper place in American religious life. They implied in a patronizing manner that Muslims, rather than being fellow believers in an Abrahamic revelation, were members of a persecuted "minority" requiring political certification of their advocates. But the 1996 letter also reveals the naked power politics driving AMC's agenda, for on what basis could any Christian or Jewish group extend such an honor to a Muslim institution? Deciding who, if anybody, is premier among American Muslims is a responsibility of Muslims. AMC, obviously, considered itself as premier, and by appealing to the conscience of politically correct Christian leaders, they arranged for their narcissism to be validated. Christians who questioned this practice were told by the NCCB to take their complaints up with Abdulrahman Alamoudi, the godfather of AMC and a man with a well-known history of extremist incitements, including the statement: "O Allah, destroy America!"

Of these groups, CAIR was the most adroit, and therefore the worst. CAIR is also, without doubt, the most obnoxious front for terrorist apologetics to be found in the United States. CAIR's methods are anything but subtle, usually featuring peremptory demands and even threats, and even after September 11, it remains notably successful. Although its Islam is Wahhabi, it sought to represent all Muslims in their relations with America as if practicing religious diplomacy.

In 1998, CAIR and AMC cosponsored a rally at Brooklyn College, which included an anti-Jewish diatribe by Wagdi Ghuniem, an Egyptian extremist. Ghuniem led 500 people in singing a ditty with the chorus: "No to the Jews, descendants of the apes." Yet before September 11, CAIR was amazingly good at intimidating American media from even using such terms as "Islamic fundamentalism." CAIR and their associates understood that Americans wanted to be liked and that our journalists want or need to be politically correct. Therefore they cleverly framed their assault on American public opinion in terms of sensitivity: It is hurtful to Muslims for American media to describe anybody among them as fundamentalists and terrorists.

CAIR's methods were exposed early in June 2001, when Khalid Durán, a shy, sensitive 61-year-old man living in Bethesda, Maryland, was threatened with death by a Jordanian Muslim cleric. According to Shaykh Abd al-Mun'im Abu Zant, Durán had offended Muslims by writing a book seeking to introduce the essentials of Islamic faith to American Jewish readers. The book, along with a companion volume written by a rabbi to introduce Judaism to Muslims, had been published by the American Jewish Committee (AJC). Abu Zant was echoing polemics by CAIR, which had assailed Durán's book and the AJC for "stereotyping" Muslims; but the group's stated objections to the book were perfunctory and flimsy. CAIR made the egregiously un-American demand that the manuscript be submitted—before publication—to a group of Muslim experts of the group's own choosing, and echoed Abu Zant's assertion that Durán's blood could rightfully "be shed."

Although CAIR asserted that its objective was to prevent "stereotyping and inaccuracy" in the depiction of Muslims, its real aim was not to protect American Muslims from harmful prejudice but to prevent Islamic moderates like Durán from conducting an open religious dialogue with American Christians and Jews. The reason is simple: Such a dialogue would reveal to the American public the important truth that the great majority of the world's more than one billion Muslims do not support Wahhabism.

To most sensible Americans, this AJC-inspired project would appear at first glance to be simply an example of Jewish liberalism seeking peace through understanding. It is extremely difficult to imagine that the AJC provided funds for this project with the objective of making life difficult for Muslims anywhere. Nevertheless, the reaction Durán's book provoked revealed the depth of the fracture within the Islamic world. The threat against Durán was just a single incident in the long-running war between Wahhabis and Muslim moderates.

Durán detailed the striking contrast between the harsh, rigid, and violent universe of the fundamentalists and the passionate, welcoming, and pluralistic culture of Sufi spirituality. The fundamentalist scholar, he wrote, "insists on separate identities: A Muslim is not a Jew, a Jew is not a Muslim. The sufi . . . seeks to merge identities: A Muslim is a Jew too; and a Jew can also be a Muslim." Such notions are anathema to Wahhabis.

The Wahhabi lobby understood and exploited the fact that the gullibility and ignorance of ordinary Americans, the generally pro-Palestinian bias of our academia, and the essential openness of American democracy could all be manipulated for ends totally at odds with the traditions, laws, and policies of the United States. The lobby supported terror against Israel, assisted the funders and organizers of terror to operate in the United States, and promoted the ideology of terror in American mosques. In the most infamous, and oft-cited examples, CAIR national spokesman Nihad Awad declared in 1996, "I am in support of the Hamas movement." Similarly, AMC's Alamoudi proclaimed at a White House demonstration in 2000, "We are ALL supporters of Hamas!" Such declarations did not involve mere support for Hamas social service networks in the West Bank and Gaza, as their apologists occasionally argued. In November 1999, CAIR board chairman Omar Ahmad told an audience in Chicago, "Fighting for freedom, fighting for Islam—that is not suicide. They kill themselves for Islam." At a meeting of the Islamic Association for Palestine

(IAP), a Muslim cleric from Kuwait, Tariq Suweidan, preached, "Nothing can be achieved without sacrificing blood."

These radical Islamic activists were convinced, with perfect confidence, that the First Amendment of the U.S. Constitution protected them fully in their inciting language, and they were assisted in this presumption by numerous attorneys and judges who insisted on enforcing the letter, rather than the spirit, of the law. They believed, and far too many Americans agreed with them, that the presumption of innocence before the law meant absolute, unchallengeable innocence unless the very worst crimes could be proven beyond any doubt.

When the Wahhabi lobby came under American investigative scrutiny in the 1990s, their response and that of their defenders (including a considerable number of ultrasecularist and leftist Jews) reproduced the effort mounted earlier in American history by Stalinist Communists and their protectors. Like the Communists of the 1940s, the Wahhabis claimed to be victims of slander while practicing it against their critics. Detailed, factual charges against them were denounced as mere allegations, when they were, without exception, based on publicly recorded, voluntary statements made before thousands of witnesses. When the Wahhabis were shown, by their own public declarations, to be terrorists and terror advocates, they insisted that their activities were benign and innocuous, involving only fund-raising for the relief of children and refugees.

The Communists had used the same methods with extraordinary success. They claimed to be "progressives," not Stalinists; they denounced their critics, including anti-Stalinist socialists and liberals, as "fascists" and "witch-hunters," and when it was demonstrated that they did belong to Soviet-controlled organizations, argued that they had only been engaged in programs of social uplift, defense of labor rights, and fighting against racism. In reality, their main tasks had not been in the field of trade unionism or civil rights, but rather involved the propagandistic defense of Stalin's purges, pact with Hitler, and other atrocities.

Furthermore, years of wrongheaded decisions were handed down by the U.S. Supreme Court, which seemed to want to overlook Communist espionage and terrorism in America (the assassination of Leon Trotsky in Mexico in 1940—the most famous terrorist act of the 20th century—was almost entirely organized in the United States by members of the domestic Communist Party). The Court held to the philosophy that suppression of Stalinism was only appropriate if it could be shown that the republic was in danger of immediate overthrow. That the American Communist party was an arm of the Soviet secret police, controlled in its entirety by Moscow, remains, to many, "unproven," even though it was self-evident, because the Central Intelligence Agency and the Federal Bureau of Investigation were unwilling to produce testimony that would reveal to the Russians the extent of American success in decrypting secret KGB and related communications. So the courts, the lawyerly establishment, civil liberties lobbies, and assorted other sectors of the public adopted a hard-line attitude: If treason, espionage, and terrorism could not be proven in open court, with full right of cross-examination by attorneys hired with Soviet money and intent on assisting the Soviet government, it did not exist. It was for this reason that so many potential codefendants in the infamous case of the Rosenberg couple were never even indicted, and some made their escape from the United States altogether.

Until September 11, the Wahhabis in America enjoyed similar success in convincing American investigative agencies, judges, lawyers, civil liberties advocates, journalists, academics, and others that they were, in effect, prosecution-proof. Ludicrous mistakes were made because Americans were concerned to protect the freedom of the enemies of freedom. Sayyid Nosair, assassin in 1990 of Jewish extremist Meir Kahane, was only found guilty on a firearms charge. The FBI impeded the investigation of Zacharias Moussaoui, who was arrested before September 11 and later charged as a member of the conspiracy, because it lacked "sufficient" probable cause. The list of such errors could be greatly lengthened. But the traps of moral equivalence were deeper and more dangerous. America's capacity to defend itself spiritually and intellectually had been deeply harmed by "anti-anti-Communism."

The legacy of this deviation in American political life was audible whenever the claim was made that firm measures against terrorists—the use before September 11 of "secret evidence," or, after that date, denying terror troopers status as prisoners of war, investigating extremist activities that sheltered under the cover of religion, more efficient standards for wiretapping, detention of aliens, higher levels of transportation and communications security, or the failure to provide "American Taliban" John Walker Lindh with a "dream team" of lawyers in the Afghan hinterland — threatened to put America on the terrorists' level. America was told repeatedly it must fight for protection of the rights of its enemies if it was not to become indistinguishable from them. Similarly, apologists for bin Laden and his accomplices insisted that evidence of his terrorist activities, satisfying absurdly high standards, must be produced before action could be taken against him.

Some of this babble was heard again after disclosure of the arrest of José Padilla, a violent criminal from the Chicago area who had been introduced to Islam while incarcerated and was then identified as an agent of al-Qaida interested in exploding a "dirty bomb," combining regular explosives and radiological material, in an urban environment. Padilla had links through a South Florida mosque to the Benevolence International Foundation, exposed as a major bin Laden front mainly thanks to Bosnian investigators. He was held as an enemy combatant, much to the dismay of civil liberties lawyers. But the Padilla case revealed another problem: that of Wahhabi influence in the American prison system. With the growth of Islam among African Americans, the faith was viewed as a major source of personal reform and redemption for those who found themselves in conflict with the law.

But as part of the general strategy of the Wahhabi lobby, Islamic prison outreach — including prison *imams* employed by federal and state authorities — was brought under Wahhabi-Saudi control. The *imams* were granted religious credentials by Wahhabi institutions under Saudi supervision, an extraordinary intrusion by a foreign government into one of the most sensitive areas of American society. Mahdi Bray, head of the National Islamic Prison Foundation, is also national political director of MPAC and an AMC advisory board member.

Because of religious and other constitutional issues involved in the controversy over Islam in American prisons, as well as the need to avoid provocative actions that may subvert the good order of the judicial system, it is necessary to proceed with great caution and care in addressing this problem. Wahhabi *imams* have allegedly sought to prevent new Muslims in prison from encountering the full complexity of Islamic civilization, including Sufism, which teaches peace, cooperation with other believers, and psychologically stabilizing practices. Some prisoners say that non-Wahhabi literature may be confiscated from them. Prison authorities, who would naturally monitor the distribution of overtly extremist materials, should also guarantee that Muslims in prison have access to a diverse range of educational and religious materials and advocates. Prison libraries must include Sufi as well as other Muslim books and publications, and Sufis and other mainstream and moderate Muslims should be encouraged and assisted to develop their own programs of outreach to prisoners.

There are many critics of Wahhabism among American Muslims, but few are willing to speak out for the record. Most have been intimidated into silence. In addition, among the enemies of the Wahhabi-Saudi conspiracy, some of the angriest, most knowledgable, and most forthcoming with information, like the previously mentioned Kaukab Siddique, are not pro-American; they are angry at Riyadh for its compromises with the West. Yet their rage at Wahhabi-Saudi duplicity leads them to publicize damaging and verifiable information about Wahhabi-Saudi mischief.

Shaykh Hisham Kabbani of the Islamic Supreme Council of America is one critic of the Wahhabis who falls into neither of these problematic categories. He is an eloquent public opponent of Wahhabi efforts to regiment American Muslims; and he fully supports American democratic values, as well as a peaceful resolution of the Israeli-Arab conflict. Recently he described the spreading influence of the Wahhabis, under the cover name "Salafis": "Supported by certain regimes pursuing specific ideologies, 'Salafis' are taking over the mosques built in Europe and North America, mostly by Indian and Pakistani immigrants, by means of elections and funding."

According to Kabbani and other dissenters, 80 percent of American mosques are run by Wahhabi *imams* directly subsidized by Saudi Arabia. This, however, does not imply that ordinary Muslims are enthusiasts of Wahhabism. Khalid Durán is doubtless correct in arguing that no more than 20 percent of American Muslim congregants support Wahhabism.

But such groups as CAIR, AMC, and ISNA are comparable to the Saudi religious militia, or their now-defunct Taliban imitators, in seeking to establish ideological control over the American Muslims. In the furtherance of this goal, which did not diminish after September 11, they imported the methods, rhetoric, and characteristic deceit of Islamic fundamentalism into the American public square.

Kabbani, for his part, has been viciously attacked by the Wahhabis in a manner remarkably similar to that used by the Stalinists and their supporters, by stigmatizing him as a "marginal" allegedly attempting to introduce Middle Eastern quarrels—in this case, the battle between Sufis and Wahhabis for the soul of Islam—into the American public square. According to the lobby and its allies, importing Hamas into America is an acceptable form of intellectual activity, while importing Sufism represents a menace.

But Wahhabi domination of American Islam involves much more than control over money and the elected governing assemblies of mosques; it also means dictating the curriculum for the training of *imams* and setting the tone and content of sermons.

Various examples of intolerance and incitement in Friday sermons were publicized after September 11. Hassan Hathout, brother of MPAC's Maher Hathout, confessed, "Some people for example said America is evil." San Francisco Bay Area Islamic preacher Hamza Yusuf had become notorious for his extremist sermons, which were widely circulated on video. Two days before the terror attacks, on September 9, 2001, he declared that the United States "has a great, great tribulation coming to it." He went on, "This country is facing a very terrible fate . . . this country stands condemned." After the attacks on New York and Washington, Yusuf sought to dissociate himself from these incriminating statements. However, AMA's founder-chairman, Agha Saeed, even after September 11, brushed off controversies about such rhetoric. He added that while he rejected bin Laden, it was "simplistic" to condemn him. Saeed insisted, "Who trained him? Who taught him how to make these bombs?" This deliberate obfuscation sought to falsely blame U.S. involvement in the Afghan struggle against Russian imperialism for bin Laden's terrorism.

Extremist claims were still to be heard in reaction to September 11 and the investigative efforts of the federal authorities. On October 20, 2001,

Siraj Wahhaj, a New York *imam*, CAIR board member, and character witness for Omar Abdel Rahman in his trial for the 1993 World Trade Center bombing, told a meeting of Muslim activists in Houston, "This government has already sent in every major [mosque], agent provocateurs. Most of you don't know what that is. All you know is about spies. The government has spies, they have infiltrators. But there's some difference from being a spy and an agent provocateur. What an agent provocateur does, he goes to a [mosque], he looks just like you. He's got a beard just like your beard. . . . And their job is to entrap you no different than the prostitute, the policewoman dressed as a prostitute, whereas he's coming to the [mosque], dressed as a Muslim. And when they talk, their rhetoric, they are stronger than anyone else." Thus, while the officials of Wahhabi lobby organizations claimed to support federal law-enforcement action against extremists, Wahhaj tried to argue that extremism was a fabrication by the authorities. In 1995, Wahhaj was named by U.S. Attorney Mary Jo White among "unindicted persons who may be alleged as co-conspirators" in a plot to blow up New York City monuments.

Wahhabism is based on the justification and promotion of violence against all "unbelievers," beginning with traditional Muslims who do not share the "reformed" Wahhabi outlook. Kabbani has called this Wahhabism's "most harmful legacy." Pious youths from Muslim countries, sent to be educated in the Gulf states, are brainwashed. On returning to their homes, they brusquely reject the traditional Islam of their parents. Further, they are taught to abstain from all participation in society outside Wahhabi mosques and organizations. For American Muslims this means, Kabbani notes, that they must not vote, serve on juries, or join in interfaith activities. Such strictures prevented the numerous *imams* and activists associated with Wahhabi mosques in the United States from joining forces with Jews, Christians, and others in behalf of the Muslim victims of the Balkan wars.

The Wahhabi worldwide offensive does not end with such manipulations. Rather, it comprises, in Kabbani's words, "heavy financing, deviant teaching, Internet and book publishing, and biased editing." The Wahhabis are particularly known for the free distribution and dumping on the book market of their literature, including tendentious translations of

Qur'an that support their doctrinal claims. Such materials have included the writings of a Wahhabi bigot, Hamd ibn ʿAbd al-Muhsin, who demanded that women who drive automobiles in Saudi Arabia be charged as prostitutes and punished by flogging.

Nearly the whole Islamic establishment in America and other Western countries may be placed on the roster of Saudi-subsidized propagandists. This includes the functionaries who stood alongside President Bush at the Washington Islamic Center soon after September 11, and encompasses ISNA, ICNA, the World Assembly of Muslim Youth, and numerous other incarnations of this hydra-headed beast. According to one informant who requested anonymity, Wahhabi *imams* in American mosques until recently received salaries of between $2,000 and $4,000 a month from the Gulf states.

Indeed, the multifarious Wahhabi entities spend money like, well, a Saudi oil prince—some of it on direct political lobbying. In 1999, the Saudi embassy in Washington announced a grant by the Islamic Development Bank of $250,000 to CAIR for the purchase of land in Washington, to be used in the construction of "an education and research center." (CAIR is but a minor line item in the Wahhabi budget. The Saudi embassy statement announcing the grant to CAIR also reported gifts of $395,000 for the construction of a school in Tanzania and $30 million for "Islamic associations in India.") The Saudis also use their control over Mecca and Medina as an opportunity for political shenanigans. In their hands, the *hajj* required of Muslims who can afford to perform it has frequently become a paid junket useful for recruitment purposes. In 2000, the Muslim World League (a provider of funds to Osama bin Laden) hosted 100 prominent American Islamic personalities on *hajj*. They were accompanied by a delegation of 60 Latin American "academics and specialists." All expenses for the latter were paid by Prince Bandar, Saudi ambassador to the United States. The same year the Saudis advertised their subsidy of 1,500 pilgrims from Europe, Asia, Africa, and North America. In 1999, the Saudis paid for 100 influential American Muslims to make *hajj*. The list of such expenditures seems limitless.

Resentment of this religious colonialism is rife among American Muslims, however subdued its expression. One authoritative source who asked to remain nameless but who was long courted by the Islamic Society of North America said, "American Muslims are getting real sick of Wahhabi domination." Others, however, note that ISNA has recently feigned openness to non-Wahhabi Muslims, just as its leaders portrayed themselves as "anti-terrorist" to President Bush. For Wahhabis everywhere, the party line is laid down in Riyadh, which simultaneously foments terrorist teaching and disclaims any responsibility for Wahhabi atrocities, as in the case of bin Laden. Friday sermons in American mosques have frequently been faxed directly from the kingdom. Saudis corrupt Muslims abroad in exactly the way that the Soviet Union once bought the loyalty of foreign intellectuals, labor leaders, and guerrilla fighters, and for the same ends. This worldwide subversion can be combated only as fascist and Communist sedition were once fought: with courage and determination, and in full solidarity with the Muslim heroes in the forefront of resistance to it.

The entrenchment of foreign Wahhabis in American Islamic affairs was more vividly demonstrated soon after September 11, when a group of Islamic scholars in the Middle East issued a *fatwa* on the duties of Muslims serving in the U.S. armed forces. The story of this *fatwa* shows both the confused state of relations between American society and Islam and the nature of Muslim fundamentalism. It all began when the first-ever Muslim chaplain to American military personnel, U.S. Army Captain Abdul-Rashid Muhammad, sought an authoritative opinion as to whether Muslims could serve in a war against a Muslim enemy. By official count, there were some 4,100 Muslims in the U.S. armed forces (although Captain Muhammad has been quoted claiming 12,000) out of a total force of a million and a half.

Captain Muhammad turned for help to the head of the Graduate School of Islamic and Social Sciences in Leesburg, Virginia, one Taha Jabir Alwani. Alwani conveyed the request to the Qatar-based Wahhabi cleric Yusuf al-Qaradawi, who drafted the resulting document. Although he was presented as a mainstream and moderate figure, Qaradawi is best known for his *fatwa* legitimating terrorist attacks in Israel; in April 2001, he defined suicide bombings as "martyrdom, not suicide," suicide being forbidden by Islam. How such an individual could have been consulted officially about the religious life of American citizens is questionable to say the least.

However, the content of the *fatwa* was benevolent. Qaradawi and his cosignatories (three Egyptians, a Syrian, and Alwani) held that, in the face of the recent attacks, American Muslims were obliged to support the United States, since Islamic law prohibits "terrorizing the innocent, killing noncombatants, and the destruction of property." Further, the *fatwa* declared that American Muslims must fulfill the duties of citizenship, including conscientious service in the armed forces, lest their loyalty be doubted. Some American media seized on the *fatwa* to prove that all Muslims abhor terrorism. Sam Jaffe, for instance, writing in *Business Week Online*, characterized Qaradawi as one of those "Islamic thinkers . . . that will defeat bin Laden."

But the honeymoon was brief. The September 27 *fatwa* set off a firestorm in the Arab world, and Qaradawi changed course. For example, a professor of Islamic law at Al-Azhar University in Cairo argued, "It is not allowed for a Muslim who is currently recruited in the American army to fight against Muslims, either in Afghanistan nor anywhere else." Curiously, a Hamas figure named Bassam Jarar noted in the Palestinian daily *Al-Quds* that soldiers refusing to serve in the U.S. forces in Afghanistan on Islamic religious grounds would be in a strong position before American law.

On October 11, Qaradawi held a press conference in Qatar where he condemned American military action against Afghanistan. His wording was anything but mild: "We support the Afghans who stand firm against the American invasion," he proclaimed, likening the U.S. campaign to the Russian occupation. He blamed the United States for September 11 because of American support for Israel and threatened that a thousand bin Ladens would rise up unless U.S. policy changes. He incited the Pakistanis against their government and concluded with the claim that bin Laden's videotaped self-justifications could not be considered a confession of wrongdoing. He praised the terrorist chieftain as "a symbol of the world uprising against American hegemony." Some Islamic Web sites reported that the original *fatwa* had been "misattributed," others that it had been superseded. Qaradawi's outburst of hatred, and his manifest self-contradiction, prompted inquiries from the media, but he declined to elaborate. On October 30 he brushed off the Associated Press, saying, "I wrote an explanation. I can't tell you anything more."

Many Wahhabi functionaries in the United States maintained an attitude of truculence toward American society, even after September 11, encouraging the more backward elements that blamed the events on Israel or repeated the paranoid claims that 3,000 American Jews had been warned to stay away from the World Trade Center the day the terrorists struck. None of them indicated the slightest sense that American Islam had been compromised by the attacks; only that Muslims were now victimized by non-Muslim opinion and American law enforcement. Some of them appeared rattled; thus, CAIR expressed condolences after the massacre of 16 Christians during a worship service in Pakistan on October 28, 2001, although the organization had never expressed regret over killings by suicide bombers in Israel. At the same time, CAIR and partner groups like the AMC and ISNA incessantly complained of purported hate crimes and civil liberties violations to keep American society on the defensive.

Yusuf al-Qaradawi embodies the fantasy that there are "moderate" fundamentalists who can be our allies in the antiterror fight. Qaradawi, to be sure, has expounded a "liberal" approach to music, which Wahhabis typically abhor. But he also defended the Taliban's demolition of ancient Buddhist statues in Afghanistan. In reality, there is no "moderate" Wahhabism, for it is an amoral power ideology that cannot accept the coexistence of Muslim and non-Muslim civilizations. American Muslims who wish to dissociate themselves from these extremists have their work cut out for them.

President Bush did not long suffer the questionable attentions of the Wahhabi lobby. During the Afghan campaign he ordered the closing of the Holy Land Foundation for Relief and Development (HLF). The Holy War Foundation would be more like it. HLF is the central node of the Hamas front in the United States, headquartered in Texas, with branch offices in Paterson, New Jersey; Bridgeview, Illinois; and San Diego. Established in 1989, HLF took off when it received a $200,000 cash infusion from Musa Abu Marzook, the external director of Hamas, who lived in the United States until he was deported in 1997. Marzook, brother-in-law of Ghassan Elashi, chairman of HLF, financed six terrorist attacks in Israel from his home in Falls Church, Virginia. In 1995, the U.S. authorities asked for the arrest and deportation of Marzook to Israel, where he had been indicted for involvement in terror attacks carried out while he resided in the United States, and in which 47 people were killed. Although Israel then dropped its demand, because of "security concerns," the United States deported Marzook to Jordan.[2] His chief of military affairs was another U.S. resident, Muhammad Salah, of Bridgeview, Illinois. Ordinary Americans would have been shocked and outraged to learn that Hamas was running its terror campaign from a sanctuary in the United States.

Federal authorities had been watching the foundation since 1996, and concerned American Muslims had denounced its activities on numerous occasions. On September 5, 2001, less than a week before the World Trade Center atrocities, federal antiterrorism agents raided InfoCom Corporation, the company that ran the HLF Web site. The InfoCom connection is crucial to understanding relations between the various components of the Islamic extremist conspiracy. According to defectors from Hamas, the HLF Web server was also used by CAIR, ISNA, MSA, the Islamic Association for Palestine (IAP), and other terrorist apologists on our soil. All of these groups shared a single administrative and technical contact for the maintenance of the server. They had been erected as political shells around the Hamas hydra-head represented by HLF.

Even after the horrors unleashed in Israel in the aftermath of September 11, few Americans fully recognized what HLF represented. In addition to defending suicide bombers, the foundation paid annuities to the children of Palestinian "martyrs." It also supported the Wahhabi clerics whose *fatwas* declared that, since all children are, by Islamic legal definition, innocent, Jewish children slain at the hands of the bombers are guaranteed entry into Paradise. These *fatwas* advance the same claim for other innocents, Muslim or Christian, accidentally killed in the September 11 attacks: These too are "involuntary martyrs" headed for Paradise. This hideous doctrine rationalizing the murder of children is a pure expression of the Wahhabi totalitarianism emanating from Saudi Arabia.

The foundation embraced the identity of an Islamic charity; this religious cover has given the group and its satellites a fund-raising appeal far exceeding that of any earlier Arab advocacy group. As we know, purported charitable or relief organizations based in Saudi Arabia funded Osama bin Laden's al-Qaida cadres. The same cover is used by those who recruit American Muslims like the ill-fated "American Taliban" John Walker Lindh, the *"jihad"* fighter from California found in a ratlike condition in the cellar at the Qalaj-i-Janghi prison in northern Afghanistan.

The Bush administration took a major step in moving against HLF, one of the central components of an extremist conspiracy that deserved to be fully investigated and unmasked. Soon thereafter, federal law enforcement kicked over quite an anthill in Northern Virginia. A U.S. Treasury task force, Operation Green Quest, had been investigating the funding of Islamic terror. Raids on March 20, 2002, struck an extraordinary array of financial, charitable, and ostensibly religious entities identified with Muslim and Arab concerns in this country.

Reaction to the raids suggested that the Feds had inflicted serious injury on the Wahhabi lobby. Officials of the targeted groups as well as their non-Muslim apologists—notably GOP operative Norquist, the chief enabler of Islamic extremists seeking access to the White House—condemned the raids as civil rights violations. Norquist declared, "There's a great deal of disappointment that the raids happened the way they did. And I don't think the Muslim community is overreacting."

The convoluted system of interlocking directorates, global banking transactions, and ideological activities exposed in Northern Virginia would take time to sort out. Meanwhile, however, Operation Green Quest drew attention to a previously overlooked aspect of support for Islamic extremism in this country: The principal threat comes not from the thousands of working-class Arab immigrants in places like New Jersey and Michigan who contribute modest sums to Islamic charities, but from the Arab elite, most notably Saudis. The keystone of the Saudi-sponsored Northern Virginia network was the Saar Foundation, created by Suleiman

Abdul Al-Aziz al-Rajhi, a scion of one of the richest Saudi families. The Saar Foundation is connected to Al-Taqwa, a shell company formerly based in Switzerland, where its leading figures included a notorious neo-Nazi and Islamist, Ahmed Huber. Subsequently moving to the United States, Al-Taqwa was shut down after September 11 and its assets frozen by U.S. presidential order. But operations continued, as the Wahhabi lobby shifted to its backup institutions here.

Saar has also been linked to Khalid bin Mahfouz, former lead financial adviser to the Saudi royal family and ex-head of the National Commercial Bank of Saudi Arabia. Mahfouz has been named by French intelligence as a backer of Osama bin Laden; Mahfouz endowed the Muwafaq Foundation, which U.S. authorities confirm was an arm of bin Laden's terror organization. Muwafaq's former chief, Yasin al-Qadi, oversaw the financial penetration of Bosnia-Hercegovina and Albania by Wahhabi terrorists in the late 1990s.

Men like al-Rajhi, Mahfouz, and al-Qadi are big players in the financing of Islamic extremism. And their paths repeatedly led back to northern Virginia. They don't play for small stakes: Saar received $1.7 billion in donations in 1998, although this was left out of the foundation's tax filings until 2000. No explanation has been offered for this bit of accounting sorcery, although many details of these operations were exposed in the main American media.

A major figure in the Virginia operation is an individual named Jamal Barzinji, whose office in Herndon was a target of the raids. In 1980, he was listed in local public records as a representative of the World Assembly of Muslim Youth (WAMY), an arm of the Saudi regime. WAMY has been deeply involved in providing cover for Wahhabi terrorism. The 2002 entry in the U.S. Business Directory listed the president of the WAMY office in Annandale, Virginia, as Abdula bin Laden—the terrorist's younger brother.

Barzinji served as a trustee and officer of the Amana Mutual Funds Trust, a growth and income mutual fund headquartered in Bellingham, Washington, conveniently near the Canadian border. Amana's board also included Yaqub Mirza, a Pakistani physicist who shares Barzinji's Herndon office address and who is widely described as a financial genius. Another board member and tenant in the Herndon office was Samir Salah. He formerly ran a branch of Al-Taqwa in the Caribbean, heads a financial firm linked to Saar, and directed Dar al-Hijra, a mosque in Falls Church, Virginia, notable for hard-line Wahhabi preaching. Salah was also deeply involved with Taibah International Aid Association, a Virginia charity with a Bosnian branch investigated by authorities in Sarajevo.

Front groups interfacing between the Wahhabi-Saudi money movers under federal suspicion and the broader American public included two institutions active in the religious field: the International Institute of Islamic Thought (IIIT) and the Graduate School of Islamic and Social Sciences (GSISS). The involvement of GSISS with the financing of extremism was especially startling in that it alone is credentialed by the Department of Defense to certify Muslim chaplains for the U.S. armed forces, and was previously noted in the matter of the Qaradawi *fatwa*. Barzinji has appeared on the boards of both.

The day of the raids, Barzinji appeared on television insisting he knew of no questionable behavior by the groups under scrutiny and promising full cooperation with the authorities. But he expressed himself quite differently in the Islamic media. Barzinji told the Internet news service Islam Online he believed the investigations fulfilled the will not of the Bush administration, but of "elements within the government, media, and [academia] who were unhappy with the positive attention being given to Muslims." Barzinji further alleged that the real powers behind the raids were "self-styled Middle East 'experts,' " individuals "who do not want to see Muslims develop such excellent relations with the government, assuming political rights."

Barzinji and his cohort gave the impression of living in their own conspiratorial world, divorced from reality. For them to imagine that the aftermath of September 11 has been anything but disastrous for the image and credibility of American Muslims is absurd, notwithstanding Barzinji's claims about "positive attention." The presumption that anybody outside government dictated policy to the Treasury, however, was only the classic supposition about alleged Israeli influence that preoccupies the Arab mind.

During the American offensive in Afghanistan, a young Taliban soldier was seized early in December 2001. He turned out to be, under layers of filth and matted hair, an American citizen from Marin County, California, named John Walker Lindh. The American and international media exploded with amazed speculation as to why this affluent teenager from the suburbs of San Francisco found his way to Afghanistan and service in the perverted "*jihad*" of the Taliban and al-Qaida.

For Americans unfamiliar with the permissive culture of Marin County, bafflement is justified, because in a very real sense, Lindh has no story. He stares blankly and dumbly from his photographs or appears in videos affecting an Arabic accent and Muslim rhetoric; but his eyes are empty, and to look into them is to peer into illimitable nothingness. Lindh is a cipher, lacking the intellectual cultivation or the passion of ideal-driven warriors in the past, exemplified by the Sufis who resisted Russian imperialism and previous generations of Western social revolutionaries. Wahhabism filled the emptiness in Lindh exactly as "militia" paranoia filled the void in homegrown American terrorist Timothy McVeigh. McVeigh was a practitioner of what might be called "junk terrorism" comparable to junk food—a content-free McTerror. Lindh represents Islam reduced to a similar banality: McJihad.

Marin County exists in a lush natural environment almost unimaginable for those away from the Pacific slope—a kind of untrimmed park of redwoods, creeks, secluded beaches, and cozy homes. San Francisco is nearby, but separated from Marin by the relatively narrow Golden Gate Bridge. Driving back and forth across the bridge is tedious, and young people from "the county," as the hippies called it long ago, travel to the city much less than might be imagined. Unlike kids from Berkeley or the San Francisco Peninsula, they do not hang out in the coffee houses and clubs of San Francisco. They become mall rats of a distinctive type. San Francisco operates at an international level of pretension in politics and the arts, and although it produces little of lasting importance, one can get the heady feeling as a San Franciscan, young or old, of a connection with Manhattan, Paris, Berlin, and, in the legendary past, Moscow. Young Marinites, although stimulated by big notions, do not connect with them in practical terms. They hang out and fantasize and b.s. each other and then go to their homes like suburban kids everywhere else in the country. But they still have much bigger ideas than the average bored, suburban American teenager.

In the superficiality of their existence, these middle class children have much in common with their counterparts in the Saudi kingdom. A combination of naivete and self-loathing has always been visible in Marin youth. In the 1960s they wanted to be Woody Guthrie; in the 1990s, the same search for moral authenticity caused liberal/left teens like Lindh to identify themselves with ghetto blacks. But San Anselmo, where Lindh lived, is not the 'hood.

In the 1960s, when Marin kids became radicalized, a few went to San Francisco, Berkeley, and Oakland, where they were welcomed into the "movement." Nobody, at first, challenged their *bona fides* as aspiring revolutionaries. Things were different for Lindh. He was a fan of hip-hop music, but he could not make himself into an inner-city African American, and he could not escape the taunts of those who found his posturings ludicrous. During the 1980s and 1990s, millions of white American youths adopted the trappings of the rap subculture: the gangster vocabulary, the weird outfits, the adulation of crime and degeneracy, the misogyny. Few of them demanded of themselves that they truly live out such a nonsensical pose. But Lindh needed to prove that he did not have to go home to a comfortable bed each night. He needed to show, in effect, that he could be "black" in the African American manner. He was successful in "blackening" himself, but not in an ethnic sense. Instead he showed the youth of Marin that he could be more radical in his rejection of American society than Malcolm X; but unlike the famous black nationalist, who had a complex personality, Lindh was truly a nonentity.

The friendless Lindh, driven to present himself falsely on the Internet as an African American, parading the streets of Marin in Islamic dress, became America's most infamous miscreant since Lee Harvey Oswald. The means to this end was provided by Wahhabi Islam and the call to the fake *"jihad"* of bin Laden, a call Lindh must have heard almost immediately after he began visiting mosques in Mill Valley and San Francisco. The speed with which he succumbed to Wahhabi conditioning is seen in his peremptory rejection of music almost as soon as he began praying and studying—not just hip-hop music, with its negative and arguably destructive character, but all music. Traditional Muslims would have told Lindh that since he had learned about Islam through music he should not reject it, but recognize it as part of God's plan for him. The presumptuous air he assumed in claiming a proper knowledge of Islamic jurisprudence at the age of 17 offers a pure example of the globalization of the Wahhabi mentality.

Lindh could not be a real African American like Malcolm X, but he could follow him in making the Muslim profession of faith. But Malcolm made the journey from the fake-Masonic mummery of the so-called Nation of Islam to a universalist and humanist vision of Islam after his eye-opening visit to Mecca. For Lindh the Islamic profession of faith was merely a pretext for rejecting the universalist humanism of his Marin County background in favor of sectarian extremism.[3]

Unfortunately, Lindh never had an opportunity to encounter the authentic Islamic intellect. Recruiters for the Wahhabi "*jihad*" in San Francisco were prepared to take control of his life. Lindh is part of a new Islamic "international brigade" whose numbers remain unknown, although the arrests of "shoe-bomber" Richard Reid and "dirty-bomb" plotter José Padilla indicate its extent.

Lindh's case must have broader consequences than many Americans imagine, for as important as he may be for the investigation of al-Qaida and related terrorist activities in Afghanistan, his prosecution should also make it possible to trace, identify, and shut down Wahhabi recruiting networks in the United States and Britain. According to Lindh's own disclosures, he was trained by the Pakistani-based Movement of Jihad Fighters or *Harakat ul-Mujahidin* (HUM). HUM has been identified as a terrorist organization by the U.S. State Department. Its main target area has been Kashmir. How did Lindh find his way to HUM? The intermediary was a secretive international Islamic group that both Lindh and Reid joined, *Tabligh-i Jamaat* (TIJ), or Call to the Community.

TIJ was founded in India in the 1920s at a time of aggravated conflict between Muslims and Hindus, which has always been a pretext for the spread of Wahhabism in the subcontinent. In the past, TIJ rejected the Wahhabi label while also claiming to stay out of politics. But in recent years it has undergone a transformation. It infiltrated the Pakistani government and was left off President Musharraf's recent list of banned extremist organizations. However, Indian sources claim that it was a major supplier of recruits for the terrorist groups Musharraf has suppressed—groups that also supported *Harakat ul-Mujahidin*, which planned to send Lindh to Kashmir. American Muslim sources say TIJ indoctrinated its followers to fight for the Taliban and al-Qaida as well.

According to Bay Area media, John Walker Lindh attended a small mosque in San Francisco run by TIJ. *Tabligh-i Jamaat* presents itself as nothing more than a prayer and study circle. Published accounts of Lindh's involvement with TIJ quoted University of California specialist Barbara D. Metcalf, who recycles the movement's claim that its obsessive rhetoric about *jihad* refers only to "the *jihad* of personal improvement." Yet Metcalf herself acknowledged having heard that the group was also committed to military action.

U.S. government investigators did not seem to have taken much interest in TIJ's activities, perhaps fearful that agents would be seen as persecuting a religious group. However, American authorities repeatedly betrayed a misunderstanding of recruiting practices in the Islamic milieu. Joining the worldwide Wahhabi *"jihad"* is not a matter of filling out a form. One does not have to go to a recruiting office to sign up. Mosques in Western countries are permeated with Wahhabi *"jihad"* rhetoric, encountered the minute one walks in the door. Some *imams* preach *"jihad"*; some tolerate it sympathetically; some oppose it privately but are intimidated into permitting it. But it is everywhere. If the *imam* does not advocate *"jihad,"* activists hang out on the premises or on the sidewalks and in the parking lots nearby, spreading the word.

The sense of impunity enjoyed by Wahhabi terror recruiters in the West is epitomized by advice published on the Internet by supporters of bin Ladenite agents in Chechnya: Answering the question "How can we help the *mujahidin* in Chechnya?" the acolytes of Abdullah Azzam recommend actions to be carried out in Western countries, including:

By printing the website addresses on paper and putting it up in mosques, centers, and university prayer rooms (obtain the proper permission before doing so).

By announcing the website addresses after Friday Prayers in mosques, centers, and universities.

By printing out the latest news each day and putting it up on mosque, centers, and university prayer room notice boards.

By printing out the latest news each day and giving it to your local imams and leaders, if they do not have Internet access.

By collecting as much money as possible from friends, families, relatives, and contacts, in mosques, centers, everywhere.

Unfortunately, there is no indication that terror agitators would fear any sanction by mosque authorities against these activities.

Another medium for recruitment to the Wahhabi *"jihad"* comprised propaganda videotapes, many of them extremely violent in content, produced in tormented places like Chechnya. The most infamous such production was that depicting the murder of *Wall Street Journal* reporter Daniel Pearl in Pakistan. With the recovery of Pearl's corpse, in May 2002, the Pakistani Wahhabi terror group *Lashkar-i-Janghvi* (Janghvi's Army) was identified as the journalist's probable killers. *Lashkar-i-Janghvi* is named after Maulana Janghvi, an extremist who declared Pakistani leader Benazir Bhutto an unbeliever and was then killed. *Lashkar-i-Janghvi* had previously been involved in murdering Pakistani Shi'a Muslims and Iranian diplomats serving in the country.

The group's violence against Pearl, an American Jew, fit in macabre fashion with Wahhabi ideology, which condemns Shi'a Islam as an alleged invention of an imaginary Jew, "Abdullah ibn Sabaa." At the time of Pearl's slaying, the World Assembly of Muslim Youth, the Saudi-funded body with an office in Falls Church, Virginia, was distributing a hateful pamphlet, repeating these anti-Jewish and anti-Shi'a smears. Titled *The*

Difference Between the Shi'ites and the Majority of Muslim Scholars, it had been prescribed for use in Saudi-controlled educational institutions, including Islamic schools in the United States. Ever on top of new developments, WAMY's U.S. office announced in June 1999 a competition, with three prizes of $6,400, for the best Islamic Web sites. At the same time, it inaugurated a program on public television in Fairfax County, Virginia, aimed at the local Arab community.

Young Muslims in the mosques of Western countries generally fall into two categories: children of immigrants uncertain about their identity and new Muslims, who tend to be either middle-class whites attracted by Sufism or upwardly mobile African Americans. To both, the Wahhabi message is simple and, for many, dazzling: If you want to be good Muslims, you must support armed combatants in Chechnya, Israel, Kashmir, and more obscure places that have yet to make it into the media, like Burma.

The case of John Walker Lindh strongly suggests that it is not enough to declare that the war on terrorism will be a long one, fought in many places around the world. There is also an internal battlefield in the United States that has remained out of the limelight. That terrain consists of numerous groups, like TIJ, that the U.S. authorities seem to have overlooked, even after September 11, out of the fear that they may seem to be meddling in the protected area of purely religious endeavors. The time has come to end such hesitations, at home as well as abroad.

CHAPTER 9

Whither Saudi Arabia?

In the aftermath of September 11, the Saudi authorities were asked, as allies of the United States in the antiterror war, to investigate, freeze, and seize the bank accounts of participants in and contributors to terrorist activities. In addition, like other foreign carriers, Saudi airlines were asked to provide advance passenger lists for flights to the United States. These requests were not specifically prompted by the discovery that 15 out of the 19 terrorists involved in the attacks on New York and Washington were Saudi citizens and the long-standing awareness that most of Osama bin Laden's funds also came from the kingdom. Rather, they were viewed as almost perfunctory measures necessary for a coordinated response to bin Laden's terrorism. But in both cases, the Saudis refused compliance.

Revelations of these disturbing facts were followed by others. The Saudi Embassy's official Web site in Washington turned out to have advertised the outlay of hundreds of millions of dollars for the families of "martyrs," i.e., suicide terrorists, in Israel. A Saudi telethon collected $109 million more for the "martyrs" in April 2002. The Wahhabi cleric who hosted the telethon, Shaykh Saad al-Buraik, preached in a mosque in

Riyadh, calling for the enslavement of the Jewish women of Israel, once Palestinian victory was achieved. Referring to Jews as "monkeys," al-Buraik declared, "Muslim Brothers in Palestine, do not have mercy or compassion toward the Jews, their blood, their money, their flesh. Their women are yours to take, legitimately. God made them yours. Why don't you enslave their women? Why don't you wage *jihad*? Why don't you pillage them?" Al-Buraik, a leading figure in the Wahhabi-Saudi order, was a mentor of the Saudi delegation that accompanied Crown Prince Abdullah to visit with President George W. Bush in Crawford, Texas, at the end of April 2002. He is a close associate of Prince Abdul-Aziz bin Fahd, the youngest son of King Fahd.

While much of the world joined in condemning the incitement of Palestinian youths to murder civilians in suicide bombings, verses were published by the Saudi ambassador to Britain, Ghazi Alghosaibi, praising a suicide terror bombing by a teenaged Palestinian girl, and endorsing the continued hideous use of this strategy against the Jewish state. Despite official Saudi denials, documents seized by Israeli troops in the West Bank revealed the final destination of the funds allocated from the Saudi state budget—their payment to the families of terrorists. While Yasir Arafat condemned suicide terrorism as an impediment to the Palestinian cause, Saudi television beamed how-to instructions to potential bombers among Israeli Arabs. Nor did the Saudis cease their support for bin Laden and his network.

This could hardly be described as the behavior of an antiterror ally, and questions multiplied in the minds of ordinary Americans. Why had the Saudis refused to comply with our reasonable and necessary requests? Didn't they appreciate the long history of U.S. protection of their security, economic generosity, and general accommodation? In light of these developments, moreover, it seemed particularly strange that the U.S. government was giving the Saudis a pass. Why did the Bush administration's State Department refuse to list Saudi Arabia among the nations charged with state support for terrorism? Why, for that matter, had President George W. Bush allowed Crown Prince Abdullah to lecture him about U.S. support for Israel during the trip to Crawford?

Little of substance had emerged from the ostensible summit. The Arabian oil prince had nothing new to say after the meeting, and nothing was achieved by the American side in the quest for wider Arab assistance in dealing with Saddam Husayn. Prior to the Crawford visit, a remarkable article had, it was said, been planted in the *New York Times* by elements in the State Department pressing for accommodation with the Saudis. In it, a "person familiar with the Crown Prince's thinking" was cited, offering a list of "blunt messages." The bottom line: Once in Texas, Abdullah would take charge. He would compel Bush to call Ariel Sharon, then occupying West Bank cities, to account. The alternative to compliance with these demands: a new oil embargo, no further Saudi assistance to the U.S. military, and an open alignment between the most obscurantist and backward regime in the world and the terror master of Baghdad.

The United States was apparently required to refrain from issuing any such ultimatum to the Saudis. Why? If Bush could pressure Israel and Sharon, why not Saudi Arabia and Crown Prince Abdullah? How could Riyadh presume to present supposed grievances to us? The September 11 atrocities were perpetrated by Saudis, not Americans. The Saudis only spoke for the Hamas wing of the Palestinian movement, not for the Arabs as a whole. How, then, could Crown Prince Abdullah's trip to Texas be accompanied by such outrageous threats? Were the Saudis friends or foes?

In any event, the Saudi gambit succeeded. President Bush, carrying water for the desert chieftain, reassured Americans that he had been told no "oil weapon" would be used against us, that Crown Prince Abdullah opposed terror against Americans, and that the Saudi regime hated bin Laden as much as we did. Nevertheless, Abdullah failed to disavow the preaching on his soil and in his media of terror against Americans, as well as against the Israeli Jews and Arabs.

There were precedents for these absurdities. The Saudis had never committed to a full and transparent investigation of the Khobar Towers bombing of 1996. Nineteen Americans had been killed and 372 injured in an assault on a U.S. military residential complex in the kingdom. With the apparent acquiescence of U.S. intelligence and law enforcement, the Saudis blamed this atrocity on Iranian sympathizers. But Saudi dissidents claimed it had been the work of bin Laden's supporters, an involvement concealed by the Saudis to hide their overall association with his extremist cadres.

Khobar was the second such incident in recent times. In 1995, five Americans and an Indian citizen were killed by a bomb in Riyadh. A month before the Khobar blast, the Saudi government announced that four Saudis, three of them reportedly "Afghan Arabs," had been executed for the Riyadh explosion. American investigators were prevented from interviewing the suspects. In that proceeding as well, there were claims from within the kingdom that the Saudis had worked a cover-up.

Bizarrely, American authorities handed over Hani al-Sayegh, a suspect in the Khobar affair who had come to the United States, to the Saudis, and he remained in their hands six years after the crime, on June 21, 2001, when U.S. Attorney General John Ashcroft announced the indictment of al-Sayegh and 13 other people in the case. The Saudis were said to be displeased by Ashcroft's action, arguing that the matter belonged exclusively in their jurisdiction. In June 2002, the Saudis announced that the Khobar defendants had been tried, without offering further details.

In 1999, after al-Sayegh was unwisely extradited to Saudi territory, Prince Nayef, the Interior Minister, blandly stated that bin Laden "is not a Saudi, since his Saudi nationality was withdrawn from him." Nayef "criticized those who try to exaggerate the issue of bin Laden, who is no longer a source of concern to the kingdom, and whose file has been closed." These words rang hollow after September 11, and it soon became clear that the special relationship between the United States and Saudi Arabia had become an obstacle to American security interests. The Saudi reputation as a "moderate Arab state" had finally come into question.

However, the reluctance of the American leadership to exercise pressure against the Wahhabi demagogues and the petro-kleptocracy reflected something unreported in media: An awareness that, however often it might be denied, the regime was in trouble. In the aftermath of September 11, Saudi Arabia had entered a profound crisis.

So far the Saudi crisis has yet to become a political or social crisis in the usual sense: That is to say, it is not yet a crisis of the internal political system or of conflicting social interests. Rather it is a moral crisis, a crisis of legitimacy. Above all, it is a crisis of Saudi Arabia's standing in the world, caused by its association with September 11.

In the history of states, moral crises typically lead to political and social crises, not vice versa. Saudi Arabia has begun a period in which it is increasingly difficult for the ruling power to govern in the way it previously did. As the world learned in Eastern Europe in 1989, there are only a few short steps from the moral crisis of a regime to a situation in which the ruling power can no longer govern in the old way, and from there to a situation in which the populace refuses to live in the old way. The combination of the two would create a revolutionary situation.

Unfortunately, because the Saudi kingdom is a closed society whose media are state-controlled and from which most foreign journalists are barred, the nature and development of the Saudi crisis has remained hidden from the world. In this respect Saudi Arabia resembles the Soviet Union at the height of Stalin's forced collectivizations and famines in the early 1930s; outsiders see only what the regime wants them to see. Even the few Western journalists who penetrate the kingdom seldom know what questions to ask or whom to ask them of.

Nevertheless, astute foreign observers may gain information from two sources. The first is the stream of pilgrims performing the annual *hajj*, along with Muslims traveling to the kingdom for the lesser *hajj* or *umra*, a ceremony limited to circumambulation of the Ka'bah, outside the regular pilgrimage calendar and without the other ritual observances included in the main *hajj*. Wealthy Muslims from around the world make the full *hajj* repeatedly, and some go for *umra* visits several times a year. Although the Wahhabi religious bureaucracy and the Saudi security bodies control (and restrict) participation in the full *hajj* to those in whom they have ideological confidence—which is why less than a million foreign Muslims out of at least a billion worldwide complete the full *hajj* each year—many *umra* pilgrims are heterodox individuals, including Sufis, from countries like Malaysia. These Muslim "dissidents" despise Wahhabism, and they are sharp observers of the society's contradictions.

The second source of reliable intelligence on conflicts within the kingdom, and especially within its ruling families—the Al Sa'ud and the Al Shaykh, descendants of Ibn Abd al-Wahhab—consists of expatriate Saudi subjects. Many of them adopt nonconforming attitudes once they have escaped the close scrutiny of the religious militia. Some become Sufis while studying or working abroad. And some have become eloquent adherents of a transition to a new political system in the kingdom. These developments, rather than fear that young Saudis outside the royal family will adopt the sybaritic, decadent manners displayed by the monarchical caste on their visits to the West, have led to Wahhabi strictures against travel by Saudi citizens to "the lands of the unbelievers," as a threat to public morals.

From such informants one learns of growing discontent in the three peripheral regions that, in the ironic form of a crescent, surround Najd, the home base of Wahhabism and Al Sa'ud. These regions are Hejaz, the former kingdom including Mecca and Medina; the Eastern Province, in which the precious oil fields are located; and the southern province centered in the city of Najran. All three are characterized by abiding grievances against the Wahhabi-Saudi power structure.

Westerners perceive Saudi Arabia as a compact whole, a nation like those of Europe and North America. Ibn Sa'ud himself, and his legions of Western flatterers led by the publicity officers at Aramco, fostered this misleading impression. In an American magazine profile in 1947, Ibn Sa'ud described himself as having "forged a nation" in the desert. In reality, Ibn Sa'ud subjugated the other regions by bloody conquest—in the cases of the Eastern Province and Hejaz—and by diplomatic dishonesty, in Najran and the Yemeni borderland. However, the occupied provinces have never given up their sense of their own identities.

In the Saudi kingdom, there is no separation of powers. Al Sa'ud, the royal family, is the state; the royal family is the owner of the energy resources; the royal family's partner for 250 years, the Al Shaykh or descendants of Ibn Abd al-Wahhab, are indistinguishable from the institutions of religion, justice, and education. Both families are made up of Najdis, born in the central Arabian wastelands from which Al Sa'ud and Wahhabism emerged. Najdis are the sole holders of power in Saudi Arabia, occupying all administrative and decision-making posts.

Although no more than 40 percent of the Saudi population are Wah-habi, the cult holds a monopoly on religious life in the kingdom. The entire judiciary is Wahhabi, made up of graduates of the sect's religious schools. There are no judges representing Hanafi, Maliki, Shafi'i, or Shi'a jurisprudence. Shi'a Muslims must therefore be tried by judges who consider them "heretics," and their testimony may not be heard against Sunni Muslims or even in cases affecting Sunnis. In any event, until very recently no defendants had the right to representation by lawyers. Late in 2001 a law was promulgated under which criminal defendants could appoint lawyers for their defense. However, the right of representation was limited in practice to proceedings against foreigners—specifically, Europeans.

In addition, the government decreed a ban on physical and psychological torture by the authorities and ordered that suspects could only be held for five days unless charges were filed against them. But at the same time, the law allowed the Interior Minister, Prince Nayef, an unlimited right to hold suspects in indefinite periods of detention, without specifying the basis for such exceptions. Secret trials and punishment by flogging remained in force. Torture is widespread and there is no means of redress for its victims.

Prince Nayef is one of the "Sudairi Seven"—sons of Ibn Sa'ud and full brothers of King Fahd. The group is named for their mother, the favorite wife of Ibn Sa'ud, Hussah bint Ahmad Sudair, a member of a powerful Najdi family that rose to prominence in the 19th century. (Ibn Sa'ud had 17 wives and hundreds of concubines, and his male offspring totaled 36.) Aside from his affection for Hussah, Ibn Sa'ud's marriage to her strengthened his power in Najd, while reinforcing the grip of the Najdis on the whole of Saudi Arabia. The "Sudairi Seven" also include Prince Sultan, Minister of Defense and father of Prince Bandar, Saudi ambassador to the United States.

Understanding, from outside, the politics of the Saudi royal family is difficult. Much speculation surrounds the histories of King Fahd, his Sudairi brothers, and his designated heir, Crown Prince Abdullah. In some respects, analyzing the Saudi ruling elite resembles the old methods of "Kremlinology" that were applied to the secretive and unpredictable

Communist rulers of the Soviet Union. In the absence of normal reporting in the Saudi kingdom's controlled media, complicated by the exclusion of foreign journalists, speculation must often be the only basis for predicting the future of Saudi society.

The open question of succession provides an example of the difficulties involved in penetrating the mysteries of the Saudi elite. In 1992, Fahd issued a decree on succession. The decree greatly complicated the future of the Saudi kingdom. Until it was promulgated, Crown Prince Abdullah, although not a Sudairi, was considered the unchallengeable heir to the throne.

The Saudi monarchy is a gerontocracy—a dictatorship of the old, again like the former Soviet Union. King Fahd was born in 1921 and has been medically incapacitated since 1995. Crown Prince Abdullah was born in 1923 and, even if he inherits the throne, may not last much longer than his predecessor. Of the rest of the "Sudairi Seven," Prince Sultan was born in 1924 and Prince Nayef in 1933. The 1992 decree seemed to account for difficulties caused by age in allowing for a succession based on ability rather than seniority, but it also granted the sons of the princes, i.e., grandsons of Ibn Sa'ud, totaling as many as 20, the right of succession. The main such figures include Prince Bandar, who was born in 1950, and Prince Turki, a son of King Faisal, born in 1945, who was chief of foreign intelligence until his abrupt departure from that post on August 31, 2001. Prince Turki is said to have been close to bin Laden, and many claim his "purge" resulted from this relationship. The 1992 decree gave this new generation of princes hope that power might be handed to them before they became old men.

The perplexing nature of the Saudi royal power is also reflected in external perceptions of the princes' attitudes. The "Sudairi Seven" were long considered the most "modern" of the ruling elite because of their close association with the United States, thanks especially to Prince Sultan's business deals with American arms manufacturers. In this perspective, Crown Prince Abdullah was seen as a pious Muslim with strong anti-American tendencies. More recently, however, opinion among Saudi dissidents and Muslim visitors to the kingdom presents an apparent reversal: The "Sudairi Seven" are considered to cleave to the United States, not from friendship but as an expression of the historical Wahhabi strategy of dependence on the Christian powers. By contrast, Crown Prince Abdullah is now viewed as a non-Wahhabi traditionalist who would prefer to extricate the kingdom from the Wahhabi grasp, and as a Pan-Arab nationalist favoring a pluralistic vision of Islam in the interest of Arab unity.

Further complicating the mix is the reputation of Abdullah's circle as favoring some kind of accommodation with Israel. Even before the emergence of the 2002 "peace offer," his associates promoted visits by American Jewish leaders to Saudi Arabia and in other ways indicated acceptance of Israel's legitimate existence as a state. Unarguably, Abdullah has expended much rhetoric in praise of the stop-start "peace process" that began at Oslo in 1993. Paradoxically, he remains a firm supporter of Yasir Arafat, Hamas, and other proponents of Arab resistance in Israel, at the same time as he improved relations with kings Husayn and Abdullah of Jordan, who recognized the Jewish state. In general, it may be said that while the "Sudairi Seven" hold to the well-established Wahhabi-Saudi technique of allying externally with the strongest Christian power while depending internally on harsh clerical repression, Crown Prince Abdullah has a pragmatic view of power in the Middle East and a tolerant conception of Islam.

The 1992 succession decree injected considerable uncertainty into relations between the princes, touching off a hidden struggle for dominance between Crown Prince Abdullah and Prince Sultan, who is considered his main rival to follow King Fahd. Abdullah triumphed in this intrigue, and by the middle of the 1990s had emerged as effective ruler of the kingdom. Still, until September 11 and the Israeli-Palestinian crisis of 2002, Prince Sultan and his son Bandar were the Saudi personalities best known to the American public. This was largely thanks to their many appearances on American television during the Gulf War—when Prince Sultan, as Minister of Defense, served as the main Saudi liaison to U.S. political and military leaders.

Sultan enriched himself immensely through his deals with American arms suppliers, but aside from such personal corruption, the arbitrary cruelties meted out by the "Sudairi Seven" have made them deeply hated and feared. Prince Nayef, along with other members of the royal family, has become known for his habit of ordering exemplary floggings. An incident in 1980 was characteristic: Prisoners in the Dammam prison sang in celebration of the Muslim feast of *Eid al-Fitr*. Prison authorities, offended as Wahhabi enemies of song, tried to halt the music by segregating, then beating prisoners. Prince Nayef ordered that 100 lashes be administered to every inmate of the facility, without trial. Prince Salman, governor of Riyadh and another of the "Sudairi Seven," is also known for decreeing lashings without due process. In an incident involving Shi'a teenagers who resented insults directed against their faith by their teachers, Prince Meqran of Medina ordered that a dozen of them be whipped 300 times each. Four more Shi'a high school students suffered similar brutal punishments at the pleasure of another prince, Meshael.

A report by the Virginia-based Saudi Institute on torture in the kingdom points out that *Qur'an* prescribes flogging as an Islamic punishment for only two crimes: adultery—which requires four credible eyewitnesses—and libel against the honor of a woman. For adultery, no more than 100 lashes, and for libel, only 80 are mandated. In addition, Islamic law calls for 40 to 80 lashes for drinking alcohol. But under traditional Islam, no more than 100 lashes could be administered, and only for these three violations. Further, flogging was to be carried out with soft straps, cloths, or small branches, with the intention of humiliation rather than infliction of pain or injury. In addition, the individual imposing the punishment was barred from striking with the full force of his arm, which was not to be extended above his own waist.

Yet the Saudi kingdom has routinely delivered sentences totaling thousands of lashes; at the beginning of 2002 a man in Jeddah was whipped 4,750 times for sexual relations with his sister-in-law. Flogging is carried out in the kingdom using wooden rods and metal cables, which cause extraordinary suffering. No other Islamic society in the world imposes such punishments.

The regime's benighted cruelty in the judicial field is matched by its obscurantism and bigotry in education. All students are taught religion beginning in primary school. The curriculum is exclusively based on Wahhabism. Shi'a Muslim doctrines are condemned, from the beginning of the child's education, as heretical and sinful. Shi'a clerics must travel outside the kingdom, to Iran, Yemen, Iraq, and Syria, for training in their creed. As noted in an earlier chapter, Shi'a Islam is described in the Wahhabi-Saudi curriculum as a Jewish conspiracy; in addition, the inevitability of war against the Jews is taught to all students. There is no room for doubt that the 15 Saudis of 19 suicide terrorists on September 11 did what they did because of the instruction they received in Saudi schools.

The Saudi educational system is more than a school for intolerance and a breeding ground for resentment and discrimination. Exactly six months after September 11, the viciousness of Wahhabi-Saudi rule was again dramatized, this time inside the kingdom: on March 11, 2002, a fire at Girls' Intermediate School Number 31 in Mecca took the lives of four-teen young women, leaving dozens more badly burned.

The March 11 tragedy could not be blamed on fire alone. Like many more educational facilities in Saudi Arabia, the girls' school occupied a substandard apartment building. But soon after the blaze broke out, reli-gious militia (*mutawiyin*) arrived at the scene. The *mutawiyin* forced girls who had escaped the burning building back into it, because, fleeing the flames, they had not fully covered up. The militia attacked other adults who tried to save the "immodestly clad" girls.

Crown Prince Abdullah, recognizing the gravity of the scandal, quickly removed jurisdiction over girls' education from the Wahhabi cler-ics and gave it to the state. The Wahhabis lashed back, allegedly supported by Sudairi princes Sultan and Nayef. Meanwhile, although unreported in Saudi and, therefore, Western media, demonstrations swept the kingdom, protesting the deaths. Aggrieved folk, including pro-Palestinian elements and Shi'as, joined in.

According to a later report in the London *Observer,* Shi'a towns in the Eastern Province saw massive protests. The regime responded with beat-ings and arrests throughout the country, and a blockade around the U.S. consulate in Dhahran, to prevent demonstrations being held there. Sup-porters of bin Laden used the opportunity to condemn the internal confu-sion of the monarchy, while taking care to attack Crown Prince Abdullah for cutting back on Wahhabi clerical authority.

Was it the beginning of the end? Certainly Saudi students and intellec-tuals have many reasons to despise Wahhabi control. Libraries are restricted to Wahhabi volumes. Shi'a and non-Wahhabi Sunni texts are regularly confiscated and burned; many Shi'a works are smuggled into the country or circulate only in manuscript, and their possession is a criminal offense. The register of banned Islamic works is extensive and includes the writings of extremist Wahhabi clerics who criticize the Saudi regime for its Western alliances, as well as Sufi and other classics. Religious commentaries on state electronic media are limited to official Wahhabi arguments.

The Wahhabi obsession with control also extends to the Internet. In one of the most bizarre of the many weird incidents in Saudi society, Grand *Mufti* Shaykh Abd al-Aziz al-Alshaikh issued a *fatwa* authorizing a "cyberjihad" that encouraged Wahhabi fanatics to hack into and disable Shi'a and non-Wahhabi Web sites. On the other hand, the regime encourages the establishment of Web sites promoting hatred of non-Wahhabi Islam.

Far from being a successful nation-state, Saudi Arabia bears a striking resemblance to the old Soviet Union and the former Yugoslavia. Like the Russians and the Serbs, the Najdis have created a society in which deep discontinuities between constituent groups have never been resolved, a mini-empire ruled by a single privileged regional and ethnic group. While the role of the Russians and Serbs in the fallen Slav dominions is comparable to that of the Najdis, the function of the Soviet and Yugoslav Communist cadres is fulfilled by the Wahhabi clerics.

Like the subject peoples of the Baltic states and Croatia, the Hejazis look back to a tradition of independent statehood. Like the Ukrainians and Bosnian Muslims, the Shi'a residents of the Eastern Province represent a culture that cannot be assimilated by the ruling national group. And like the Chechens in the Soviet Union and the Albanians in Kosovo, the people of Najran and the south are profoundly alienated from Saudi authority and drawn into the orbit of their Yemeni neighbors.

In discussing the Saudi crisis, American government officials, policy experts, academics, and journalists have given the impression of attempting, at all costs, to pretend no such crisis existed, or would exist, in the near future. In the wake of September 11, questions about Saudi Arabia in

State Department and Pentagon press briefings were waved off. U.S. Secretary of State Colin Powell repeated the mantra of full Saudi cooperation in the war against terror; Defense Secretary Donald Rumsfeld and his assistant, the beetle-browed Torie Clarke, whose mien was that of someone trying out for a film role as a serious expert, denied any knowledge of Saudi funding of "martyrs" in Israel. Debate over a Saudi crisis was restricted to closed-door sessions in elite think tanks like the Washington Institute for Near East Policy, where everything was cast as a possible outcome—one among many. Experts were assembled to chew over whether the world would remain dependent on Middle East oil and whether the Saudis would disrupt the energy markets.

There was controversy over the impact of political instability in the Saudi kingdom, "if that were to occur"—as if September 11 had not already provided dramatic evidence of its existence. Saudi dissidents were tarred in such colloquies, without exception, as religious radicals angry over "failures to adhere to Islam," without any attempt to distinguish between varieties of Islam. Almost nobody in the West was aware that religious discontent in the Saudi kingdom mainly involved resentment of Wahhabi rigidity, not its insufficient application. But the bottom line for most Western "experts" was the same: Public confrontation with the Saudi royals would only bring about defiance; quiet diplomacy without the glare of media would achieve results. In other words, business as usual, as practiced for 70 years, as if September 11 had never taken place.

Western policy discussions of a Saudi crisis seemed to be enacted in a dreamworld. Iran was viewed as the main threat to internal Saudi stability; the financial problems of the kingdom were cited as threatening the royal family's primitive systems of patronage, and none of the Westerners wanted to see the royal family divided, since its unity has been considered the main guarantee of continued stability, and, above all, an orderly succession to King Fahd. In reality, Wahhabi-Saudi hypocrisy was a greater threat than Iran. Saudi society has outgrown the royal patronage systems, which once served as the backbone of the regime, and which continue to play a role in many Third World countries. Today, they are only a major factor for the most backward Bedouins living in the farthest reaches of the deserts—but, being folklorically appealing, are treated by Western reporters like Barbara Walters as the foundation of the Saudi order. Saudi Arabia had long since entered the path of a middle-class society without middle-class opportunities, which was far more dangerous than the limitation on generous personal gifts by egotistical princes. And the divisions in the royal family, between the Sudairis, the supporters of Crown Prince Abdullah, and the new generation of princes, have existed for a decade, and were obvious to all who were not blinded by the fog emitted by generations of Aramco stooges and American diplomatic errand boys.

American diplomats were among the worst offenders in this regard. Second-rate politicians like Wyche Fowler, Jr,. exemplified the pattern. Fowler and others returned from Riyadh acting like honorary Saudi ambassadors to the United States, where they joined hands with a thick stratum of former and present Aramco officials, advisers, and technicians, to express their admiration of the princes and their support for the Saudi status quo. As noted in Chapter 4, Fowler and other ex-ambassadors, as well as characters like the former *Washington Post* Wahhabophile, Thomas Lippman, ended up on the roster of the Middle East Institute (MEI), the Saudi advocacy arm functioning as a Washington think tank. Fowler was appointed MEI board chairman within six weeks of September 11, succeeding ex-ambassador Richard W. Murphy, Jr., and serving alongside MEI's president, ex-ambassador Edward S. Walker, Jr. Other former U.S. officials affiliated with MEI included ex-ambassador David L. Mack, former defense secretary James Schlesinger, former FBI head William Webster, and former CIA chief Richard Helms.

MEI's activities are, on the surface, respectable, including numerous conferences, publications of papers, and events such as a promotion for John L. Esposito, head of the Center for Muslim-Christian Understanding at Georgetown University. (The event was held to publicize Esposito's 2002 book, *Unholy War: Terror in the Name of Islam.*) Esposito had been somewhat embarrassed by his previous enthusiastic advocacy for the view that Islamic extremism represented an understandable response to the errors of American policy, which fostered social injustice and other grievances in the Muslim world. Such an attitude was predictable given that Esposito had previously occupied the post of president of the Middle East Studies Association, an organization firmly located on the left, anti-Western side of the academy. But Esposito was more embarrassed by the unfortunate fact that when bin Laden's agents slammed jets into the World Trade Center, the Pentagon, and Pennsylvania on September 11, the *Fletcher Forum* magazine remained on the newsstands with an article by him, titled "The Future of Islam," decrying the obsession with bin Laden on the part of American political leaders. With the publication of *Unholy War*, he somewhat clumsily attempted to rectify his mistakes while holding to his original theses.

Other affiliates of Esposito's Center had offered grotesque distortions of the situation of American Islam to the wider media after September 11. Dr. Zahid Bukhari, a fellow of the Center, declared, "Muslims in this country are blending with each other. There is more convergence and more acceptance of each other's opinion." This nonsense was emitted at a time when Sufism and Shi'a Islam were completely excluded from most mosques as well as the dominant Islamic advocacy groups, as described in Chapter 8. Professor Yvonne Y. Haddad, a specialist in Islamic history at the Center, put forward the claim that Wahhabism in America was "very insignificant," adding, "The Saudi influence weakened considerably in the 1990's, as many believers stopped being Muslims living in America and became American Muslims." This was either fantasy or deliberate deceit.

Ambassador Wyche Fowler brought no discernible expertise or wisdom to the job of representing American interests to our most important Arab ally. But once ensconced at MEI, he showed a remarkable capacity for rage and invective when faced with criticisms of the Saudi kingdom. Calling on Aramco's retired professional personnel for support, he railed at those whose disregard for American strategic commitments led them to express concern for the difficulties encountered by U.S citizens in conflict with Saudi authority.

Supplementing the activities of Fowler and others at MEI, after September 11 the Saudis hired public-relations experts to burnish their image. These included executives at Burson-Marsteller, who were retained immediately after the attacks on New York and Washington and who spent $2.5 million on a national print campaign intended to dissociate the

Saudi kingdom from the suicide terror operation. In addition, another firm, Sandler-Innocenzi, produced a series of smarmy television spots, turned down by some cable outlets, which were insulting to American journalists who questioned Saudi behavior. In March 2002, Qorvis Communications, based in Washington, registered as a foreign agent of the Saudi government, with managing partner Michael Petruzzello offering official disclaimers against evidence that Saudi funds had gone to support "martyr" terror operations in Israel. Qorvis was joined in this effort by a leading law firm, Patton Boggs.

Much of this sequence of events possessed an unmistakable echo of earlier phases in the U.S.-Saudi relationship. In 1980, David Long, a leading State Department expert on the Saudi kingdom, had written an extensive classified study describing the contradictions of the regime: the rigid nature of Wahhabism, hypocrisy and decadence in the royal family, distrust of the military, and deep resentments within the Shi'a community. But Long's study was effectively suppressed, with sections of it lifted and then published after being edited to present an image of stability in Saudi Arabia. Journalist Steven Emerson, later known for his exposure of Hamas terrorist activities in the United States, described the incident as "the State Department hoax" in his 1985 volume, *The American House of Saud*. But Emerson could not anticipate that the concealment of the true nature of the Saudi monarchy would lead America into support for Wahhabism in Afghanistan, then to blind engagement with the princes during the Gulf War, and finally to the gross failure to anticipate the horrors of September 11.

Aside from President George W. Bush himself, who appears intent to do right in dealing with the Saudis, three men at the summits of power have been involved with the Saudi problem since the assaults on New York and Washington: Vice President Dick Cheney, Secretary of State Colin Powell, and Defense Secretary Donald Rumsfeld. In the chapter of the Saudi seduction of America that began with the Gulf War and continues today, Cheney has played a special role.

Cheney is famous, or infamous, for his comment that "The good Lord didn't see fit to put oil and gas only where there are democratically elected regimes friendly to the United States." Having been an executive of companies that do significant business in the Saudi kingdom, he appears to have clear conflicts of interest. His former employer, Halliburton, an oil-field technology firm, recently gained a $140 million contract from the Saudis; Halliburton subsidiary Kellogg Brown & Root formed a consortium with two Japanese firms to build a $40 million ethylene plant in the kingdom.

But Cheney's relationship with the Saudis has been military and sentimental as well as political and financial. In 1990, as defense secretary, Cheney went to the kingdom to convince the Saudi rulers of the wisdom of letting their country be used as a base against Saddam Husayn. As is always the case with the Saudis, a useful relationship became a permanent one, and then a lucrative one.

Inside the administration, Cheney is viewed as the most active in diverting the president from any actions detrimental to Saudi interests. Cheney argues against pressing the Saudis on their involvement in September 11; he advocates for the importance of the so-called Saudi peace plan; he insists that they are our firmest allies, and seems to believe they must not be challenged on any grounds. When bombs go off in Israel, Cheney goes on national TV to blame Hezbollah, which does not even have a base in Israel, but which is Iranian-backed, and therefore can be used to divert attention from the Saudis. When bin Laden financier Yasin al-Qadi is questioned about his terrorist associations, he claims to be a friend of Cheney. One should ask why it was that when Crown Prince Abdullah went to Crawford he stopped first to see Cheney; was Cheney briefing him on the president's state of mind? Is this appropriate?

President Bush himself seems to be too honest to fall for 100 percent of these manipulations. His own father, former president George H. W. Bush, is involved in Saudi affairs through the Carlyle Group, which has immense business interests in the kingdom, but the sins of the father cannot be facilely transferred to the son. Bush Jr. is his own man. Nevertheless, enormous pressures are brought to bear on him. Crown Prince Abdullah went straight from Crawford to a "friendlier" dinner with Bush Sr., whose associates at Carlyle include former defense secretary James Baker, former CIA head Frank Carlucci, former budget chief Richard

Darman, former CIA head Robert Gates, and former U.S. ambassador to Japan Michael Armacost.

In this context, few escape the embrace of the desert chiefs. For example, ChevronTexaco named a tanker for Condoleezza Rice, although it was renamed after she was appointed National Security Adviser. Powell plays a junior role to Cheney. While Cheney directly and aggressively advocates for the Saudis, Powell assumes his "I love everybody" role. For Powell, the Saudis have problems, but they are still our friends. For Cheney, they are spotless and indispensable. But sources inside the State Department pointed out that Powell's public profile was reduced as spring 2002 wound down, because President Bush did not support Powell's endless cheerleading for the man Powell always called "Chairman Arafat," in a manner reminiscent of Chinese obsequiousness toward Mao Zedong, but for whom Bush reserved the somewhat distant title "Mr. Arafat."

Rumsfeld was something of a cipher in all this: He was reluctant to go after the Saudis, viewing them as a major military ally, but he did not engage with the issue enough to really advocate for them. On the other hand, he contributed to confusion on their support of Hamas, with his denial of knowledge of Saudi "martyr" funding.

In spring and summer 2002, the crisis of Saudi-American relations unavoidably grew more acute from both directions. Hearings were held on the Hill to examine the future of the relationship, human rights in Saudi Arabia, and related matters. Several voices called for hearings into the Saudi connection to September 11. Pressure on Bush to alter the American relationship with Saudi Arabia is growing. The role of the Saudis in the Middle Eastern peace process has grown ever shakier.

Notwithstanding their attempts at damage control, there was absolutely nothing to be gained either by the United States or by the rulers and subjects of the kingdom itself pretending that there was no crisis, or reassuring themselves that the royal family is in control, or taking refuge in the belief that a crisis is only "possible," or arguing that the United States has no standing to make demands on the kingdom. The crisis is here. These issues will not go away.

The question is therefore not whether Saudi Arabia is a friend or a foe, but whether the Saudi regime can survive, and whether we should conspire with the Wahhabi-Saudi establishment to continue propping it up. Saudi Arabia is still viewed by many in the West—however wrongly—as a force for stability in its region; but so was Yugoslavia once upon a time. And it is with the horrors of the Yugoslav collapse in mind, rather than the Iranian revolution, that Western policymakers must ponder the question: Whither Saudi Arabia?

Western reporting uniformly treats opponents of the Saudi regime as fanatical, anti-Western theological extremists bent on replacing the existing order with one inspired by bin Laden or Khomeini, and therefore inconceivably worse. Some prominent opposition elements are clearly aligned with extreme Wahhabism and even serve as apologists for bin Laden—the most notable being the Movement for Islamic Reform in Arabia, headquartered in Britain. In reality, while religious dissidence will doubtless be the source of future upheavals in all three peripheral provinces, none of these communities are extremist in their outlook or their probable demands. All of them mainly seek to replace Wahhabi rigidity with the pluralism and spirituality of traditional Islam.

In Hejaz, home of the Two Holy Places, young people have begun expressing a yearning for the old way in which Mecca and Medina were administered—with representation of all the Muslim legal schools, not simply the Hanbali-Wahhabi interpretation. Before the imposition of Wahhabi dominance, the Two Holy Places were known for rich intellectual interchanges among Hanafis, Malikis, Shafi'is, and Hanbalis, as well as the Shi'a legal scholars of the Jafari school of jurisprudence. Each of the schools had its institutions in the holy cities. Each welcomed its members to the *hajj*. Each had a voice in all the major issues confronting the residents of Hejaz and the Muslims of the world. Wahhabism wiped this tolerant mode of existence off the map of the Arabian Peninsula, at least as far as external appearances went.

The same was true of the Sufi orders: Before the establishment of the Wahhabi dictatorship, each had a *han* or lodge system in Mecca and Medina, where pilgrims affiliated with them could stay during their visit. The orders—including the Bektashi community with its panoply of heterodox practices—were free to teach their doctrines, and recruited many local followers.

With the coming of the Wahhabi tyranny in Hejaz these aspects of Islamic culture were forced underground. But aside from the Hanafi school of law, which has nearly disappeared and no longer has any clerics in the country, they were never completely suppressed. (The few Hanafis remaining in the country gain religious instruction from Malikis and Shafi'is.) Their memory is regaining vitality in the minds of the Hejazi young. And the traditional pluralism of the old Arabia extended beyond Islam, as noted in Chapter 2; until the Wahhabi conquest, an indigenous Christian church functioned in Jeddah, and Najran had a Jewish community.

A case study in religious persecution involves the fate of the Maliki sect and its leader, Syed Mohamed Alawi Al-Maliki, son and grandson of teachers at the Great Mosque in Mecca. Unlike his pre-Wahhabi forebears, he, along with other Malikis, is barred from preaching in the Great Mosque or at the Prophet's Mosque in Medina—a privilege extended to the Maliki school for more than 1,000 years until the 20th-century Saudi reconquest of Mecca and Medina. Al-Maliki has suffered extraordinary attacks from the regime and its adherents, who accuse him of Sufism and apostasy. The former oil minister, Ahmed Zaki Yamani, was a Maliki who reached a position of high authority notwithstanding his loyalty to that school. But he represented a notable exception.

Shafi'i Islam was once dominant among Sunnis in the Arabian Peninsula and its adherents still comprise the majority in Hejaz, but they also are barred (since 1925) from leading prayers in the Great Mosque at Mecca, as they traditionally did. Like the Malikis, they are alleged to be Sufis, and Sufism is rigorously prohibited in the kingdom.

Protest in Najran and the Eastern Province is based on Shi'ism, which, notwithstanding Saudi propaganda, is neither radical nor anti-Western in the Arabian Peninsula. Nevertheless, it is brutally repressed. Among the more than 200 religious prisoners held in Saudi Arabia in February 2002 were 17 who faced execution or life sentences. They were arrested on no charges other than the heresy of being Shi'as, as an example to the others. Shi'a Muslims are also forced to accept state-dictated names (as were Jews in Nazi Germany, Koreans under Japanese imperialism, and Albanians ruled by the Serbs). Further, thousands of Shi'a Muslims are barred from leaving the kingdom.

A dissident living in the Saudi kingdom, Dr. Mohammed J. Al-Hassan, who is also a Washington State University graduate in veterinary medicine, has recently shown great courage in releasing a public denunciation of the official persecution of Shi'a Muslims. He writes: "Discrimination against Shi'a Islam in Saudi Arabia is a really sensitive issue, and not many want to discuss it publicly, because there is no clear governmental policy regarding it. Books that insult Shi'a Islam are published by government agencies and distributed everywhere in the country. In addition, religious texts taught in the universities insult Shi'as, using demeaning and derogatory words when decribing them, especially *rafida*, which means 'rejectionists in religion.' This is an insult equal to the word 'nigger.' Decrees from government religious agencies insult Shi'as and promote hatred, violence, and discrimination against them. These decrees are made available via print and audiocassettes, and are promoted on the Internet. Decrees bar Shi'as from teaching in schools, claiming that as Shi'as they are not Muslims. These decrees are not new; they were imposed years ago but additional decrees of this kind come out every now and then."

Saudi government cleric Abd al-Qader Shaibat Al-hamd recently went on the Middle East Broadcasting Corporation (MBC)—the same network that presented the infamous terror-funding telethon. He said, of the Shi'as, "we should not eat their food, marry them, or bury their dead in Muslim graveyards," even though *Qur'an* holds that marrying women from among Jews and the Christians, as People of the Book, as well as eating food prepared by Jews, are acceptable. Another government cleric, Abdullah Ibn Jabreen, called for a *"jihad"* against the Shi'a on grounds of their "bad faith."

The worst aspect of this situation, according to Dr. Al-Hassan, is the indoctrination of children in hatred of Shi'a Islam by Wahhabi clerics who alone are permitted to teach religious subjects in the schools. Shi'a children are especially harmed by this practice. As Dr. Al-Hassan notes, "These are not individual incidents that happen on rare occasions, it happens systematically in almost all schools and almost every child (male or female) has a story." But such discrimination is not exclusively ideological. Saudi authorities have also forbidden the establishment of private day care programs and schools for girls in the Shi'a majority areas of the Eastern Province of Saudi Arabia, even though private day care is permitted throughout the rest of the kingdom. For these reasons, many Shi'as hide their faith, and even join Sunnis, who do not know their real identity, in personal attacks on Shi'as.

Shi'as in Najran presently face a campaign to force their conversion to Wahhabism. (This campaign went on in the Eastern Province for decades but has lately been stepped up by the regime in the south.) As a report by the Saudi Institute has noted, the history of Shi'ism in Najran is as old as Shi'ism itself. Nevertheless, a Saudi state religious commissar, Shaykh Ali Khursan, has denounced the Shi'as to Western media as "unbelievers." Shi'a clerics have been arrested on charges of "sorcery," and Shi'a Muslims are accused of conducting orgies in their meeting places.

One Shi'a divine, Shaykh Mahdi Theab al-Mahaan, was released from jail in January 2002. He had been imprisoned for three years and received 3,000 lashes, a common punishment for religious nonconformity. In 2001, four Shi'a high school students in Najran, aged 16 and 17, were arrested after a fight with a Wahhabi instructor who insulted their faith: They received two to four years in jail and 500 to 800 lashes. Shaykh Ahmed Turki al-Sa'ab, who was quoted in the *Wall Street Journal* on the difficulties facing Shi'a Muslims in the Saudi kingdom, was arrested on January 15, 2002, six days after his comments appeared. On April 23, 2002, following a "trial" in which he was denied the right to counsel, and after a perfunctory colloquy between a security officer and the judge, he was sentenced to seven years in prison and 1,200 lashes.

A preview of the kind of aggravated civil conflict that may be in store for the Saudis occurred in Najran in April 2000 when Saudi intelligence agents and religious militia stormed al-Mansoura, the main Shi'a mosque in the city, following a typical campaign of violent incitement by the city's lead judge, Shaykh Muhammad al-Askari. Officers arrested a Shi'a religious teacher in the mosque, confiscated religious manuscripts, and shot one Shi'a worshipper. About 60 Shi'as gathered at the residence of the regional governor (located in a Holiday Inn) to protest the arrest of the teacher. Trucks mounted with machine guns were posted outside the hotel, and two Shi'a protesters were shot dead and dozens wounded. The injured were taken from the hospital to prison (where they remained two years later).

Authorities sent emergency forces to the town, but they could not enter the neighborhood of the al-Mansoura mosque; some Shi'as armed themselves to guard the home of their local leader, Shaykh Husayn Ismail al-Makrami. The government sent troops to the city, accompanied by 20 American-made tanks and other combat vehicles. The military occupation lasted a week, during which 600 Shi'as were arrested on the streets, some of them beaten. The use of our tanks and weapons in such incidents does far more damage to the reputation of the United States among Saudi citizens than the pseudo-religious ranting of bin Laden about American pollution of holy soil.

The split between the "Sudairi Seven" and the rest of the princes remains the key division in the Saudi ruling strata. As previously noted, while the Sudairis, exemplified by Prince Sultan and his son Bandar, court Western leaders, they remain attached to the Wahhabi clerisy. There is nothing strange in this; it merely reproduces the archetypal dual strategy of the Wahhabi-Saudi alliance, accommodating the Christian powers for security purposes while preaching fundamentalism, fanaticism, and intolerance. In contrast, Abdullah—the designated heir of his half-brother Fahd—is known for his dislike of Wahhabism and for encouraging such practices as *mawlid*, the celebration of the Prophet's birthday. With Prince Sultan and Crown Prince Abdullah viewed as the sole contenders to succeed King Fahd, much hope for an opening to reform is increasingly invested in Abdullah. The divisions between the "Sudairi Seven," Crown Prince Abdullah, and the younger generation of princes make a serious, and even a bloody, conflict possible. Both Prince Sultan and Crown Prince Abdullah have control over bodies of armed men. Sultan, as defense minister, remains head of the army. Crown Prince Abdullah, on the other hand, controls the National Guard, a domestic security body. As in other Arab countries, the army is feared as a source of a possible coup, and the National Guard serves as a counterbalance to such a threat. How the army and the National Guard might behave in a severe crisis simply cannot be predicted.

The peace deal offered to Israel and the West by Abdullah in 2002 had a contradictory character. On the one hand, it was clearly intended to divert attention from U.S. concerns about September 11. On the other, it may also have reflected Abdullah's need to reinforce his position in anticipation of the passing of Fahd. It is in the interest of both Saudi Arabia and the United States for President Bush to assist Abdullah in finding a way out of this crisis, and it is to be hoped that this, and not the Israeli occupation of Palestinian cities, was the real subject of their discussions in Crawford, Texas. Indeed, from the U.S. perspective, helping to craft a transition for Saudi Arabia, and finding a new basis for stability in the wider Middle East and Gulf, are as important as securing a Saudi commitment to an Israeli-Palestinian peace. The influence of Wahhabism aggravates hostility to Israel beyond the intrinsic challenges of the Israeli-Palestinian conflict. A successful transition in Saudi Arabia can solidify a peace agreement. A peace agreement without a transformation in Saudi Arabia will always be subject to strains perpetuated by the Saudi situation.

The United States remains directly and deeply implicated in this crisis, first because of our unique economic and strategic relationship with the Saudi monarchy, and second because September 11 was an attack on the United States. Western media, reflecting ignorance about Islam, have recycled bin Ladenite charges that our military protection of the kingdom undermines the Saudi regime. In reality, our support for the monarchy more deeply compromises *us*, in the eyes of the world's mainstream and traditional Muslims, who resent Wahhabi-Saudi usurpation of control over the Two Holy Places.

Many observers have argued that rising unemployment among the overeducated young, the growth of an immigrant labor force—mostly South Koreans, Filipinos, and Pakistanis—and the backward status of women spell an inevitable breakdown of the Saudi social order. Saudi Arabia urgently needs to turn a new page in its history, comparable to Spanish king Juan Carlos's break with the legacy of Franco. There is simply no other way forward. A complete and thorough investigation into the involvement of Saudi citizens in the atrocities of September 11 would mark the beginning of such a new phase. This would continue with further dialogue between the two countries and encouragement of the growth of civil society.

Saudi dissidents say there are three kinds of Muslims in the kingdom: Those who want to kill everybody (the most extreme Wahhabis); those who wish to kill all non-Wahhabi Muslims but also seek to maintain good relations with the Christian powers (the royals); and the rest, who are traditional Muslims and do not want to kill anybody. The way out of this nightmare can only be found by Muslim believers.

Such a possibility has already been envisioned by moderate Muslims themselves. As an anti-Wahhabi *imam* recently expressed it,

> Saudi society under Wahhabism has thrown away its ancient traditions of tolerance, most embodied in the *hajj*, where Muslims from around the world, of varying aspects of faith and adherence, and of multifarious linguistic ethnic and cultural additions to "basic" Islam, converge. The *hajj* was, until the advent of the Wahhabi-Saudi alliance, an event where the subtle nuances of faith were brought out and where differences were tolerated. Reviving that tradition, far from being difficult, under the regime of Crown Prince Abdullah, should he become king, would be easy. The scholars of the tradition are still there, living quietly and secretly observing the religious precepts that have been passed down to them from their traditional forefathers. The religious element in Hejazi society is dominated by traditional Muslims and Sufis, biding their time for a "sea change." This could be effected by transferring the religious authority from Najd to Mecca, and from the descendants of Ibn Abd al-Wahhab to those of the Prophet. While the tree has been cut, the roots remain, healthy, ready to sprout forth new vegetation and flowers in the spring of a new regime. Almost all Saudis would welcome such a change and the admission that the Wahhabis' strict and rigid interpretation is the source of the hypocrisy rampant throughout Saudi society, most particularly among the princes.[1]

Resentment of the Wahhabi-Saudi dictatorship over the Two Holy Places is growing in many Muslim countries. Early in 2002, the Turkish journalist Semih Idiz wrote in the *Star*, an Istanbul daily, "The West is only two notches away from accusing the [Saudi] government for its indirect support of the worst kind of Islamic radicalism . . . No doubt what bothers the Saudi regime the most is that the world is also beginning to understand what Wahhabism represents, and how this ultra-ultra-fundamentalist approach to Islam . . . has been successfully hidden from international attention for decades. But now the Pandora's Box has been opened and it looks like it is going to cause major headaches for the Fahd regime." Idiz also noted that the Riyadh authorities had recently demolished the historic Ottoman fortress of Ajyad at Mecca, to much anger in "many Islamic nations, for example Pakistan, [that] revere the Ottomans and all they represented."

Idiz further warned of what he called the worst possible outcome for the Saudis. Certain Turkish Islamists have begun arguing that Mecca should not be subject to the sovereignty of any single country, but rather should become an international city-state comparable to the Vatican. Such a city would be open to all believers, "regardless of nationality or race." A formal proposal for such a change would gain considerable support in the global Islamic community.

The Saudi regime finds itself in these difficulties because of its inability to bridge the gaps between its self-image and its reality: the contradiction between Wahhabism and the lifestyle of the 4,000 princes, and the conflict between Saudi dependence on U.S. military aid and Wahhabi hostility to Islamic pluralism, to other religions, and to the West in general. These problems are further increased by the continuing Iranian challenge.

This returns us to the most common question asked about the future of the Saudi monarchy—isn't the alternative worse? Wouldn't an end to the monarchy bring a more extreme, more rigid, and more anti-Western regime to power? Many Westerners remain haunted by the Iranian example and fear the rise of a new and more fearsome fundamentalism in Saudi Arabia.

It is highly doubtful that Saudi rule could be replaced by an Iranian-style regime. To begin with, the Iranian people had never lived under a strict Islamic order when the shah fell and were willing to experiment with a radical alternative to secularism. By contrast, the subjects of the

Saudi kingdom—like the peoples of Russia and Eastern Europe under Communism—have suffered under Wahhabi rule for three-quarters of a century. A more extreme Wahhabi regime would not only be extremely unpopular, its chances would be limited by the very nature of the Wahhabi clerisy, especially compared with the Shi'a scholars who took power in Iran. Unlike the Iranian Shi'as, the Wahhabis never opposed the Saudi monarchy, and if it were to fall, they would fall with it. Furthermore, the Wahhabis have no tradition of collective action comparable to that of the Iranians, have never studied the arts of revolution as had been taught and discussed in Iranian society for 30 years prior to the triumph of Khomeini, and, most important, lack a charismatic leader. While bin Ladenites or other extreme Wahhabis could cause short-term disorder in a collapsing Saudi state, it is highly doubtful that they could supplant it.

The other question—what about the oil?—has repeatedly been brandished as an item of blackmail by the Saudis and their apologists. But the realities of the international petroleum market, and the relationship to it of radical Arab and Islamic regimes, suggest that while a Saudi crisis might cause a temporary disruption in oil supplies, a long-term cutoff is unlikely. Neither Iran nor Iraq nor Sudan, which has a Wahhabi-oriented regime, withdrew their oil from global sale. Indeed, their dependence on the world market increased along with their diplomatic and political isolation. But in the oil markets, the behavior of the oil companies, which are mainly Western, is finally more important than that of the national producers. It is the oil companies that determine where to extract oil, not governments, and U.S. leaders' commitments to diversification of supply repeatedly run aground on business realities. Thus, even as the need for a U.S. congressional investigation of the "Saudi connection" to September 11 was posed, a similar inquiry into the activities and involvement of the Aramco partners with the Saudi regime also appeared appropriate, if not urgent.

How would a domestic Saudi revolution affect the U.S.-led war on terrorism? Although President Bush, Cheney, Powell, and Rumsfeld repeatedly assured the public that the Saudi monarchy was a firm ally of the West in the antiterror effort, Americans proved increasingly skeptical, and with good reason. The Saudis remained opaque about the involvement of their citizens in September 11; they quarreled about the use of "their" military facilities, built and maintained by the United States, in the Afghanistan campaign, and they offered continuous objections to a resolution of the problem of Saddam Husayn, who, after all, had served as their weapon against Iran during the 1980s.

The success of the 70-year campaign of disinformation in the West to protect Saudi power has reached its end. Difficult as it may be for our leaders to say so in public, it is clear that Wahhabism-Saudism is part of the "axis of evil"—and possibly the most dangerous part. For these reasons, there was little hope that the Saudi rulers would carry out a serious investigation of their citizens' complicity in the attacks on New York and Washington, even though such an inquiry offered the regime perhaps the only possibility of an exit from its growing crisis.

Self-described "realists" may say that as bad as the Saudis are, they remain our friends, and that in the Islamic world we have to stay loyal to our friends. This paradigm has dominated American policy for three generations, but it has outlived its historical relevance and the time has come for its abandonment. In contrast with the Islamophobic view that sees all Muslims as our enemies, we have many friends in the Islamic world who would stand with us loyally and who need our help in defeating Wahhabism on their own soil.

How would dispelling the mental fog caused by the myth of Saudi moderation affect the American approach to the Islamic world?

To begin with, the Saudis are the main obstacle to decisive action against Saddam Husayn. With the recognition of this reality, little would stand in the way of forming an effective international consensus for his swift removal. In addition, realism about the Saudi regime would generally free America's hands in pursuing our security ends in the region. Since Saddam and the Saudis together constitute the main sources of support and encouragement for radical rejectionists among the Palestinians, such a change would go far toward resolving the Arab-Israeli conflict.

Removal of the Saudis from the picture would also strengthen the position of Turkey, our oldest and most reliable Muslim ally, and provide opportunities to craft a global alliance with other progressive Muslim nations. It has become a cliché for Turkey to be held out as the sole example of a modern, developed Muslim state, because of its militant secularism. In reality, there are other secular Muslim societies, and some that are not necessarily secular at all, that are prepared to stand alongside the United States in the antiterror struggle, and to contribute to a reorientation of the *ummah* toward pluralism within Islam and cooperation with the other faiths.

The United States should begin by reaching out to the Muslims of Bosnia-Hercegovina, Kosovo, and the other Balkan Muslim societies, which represent an authentically indigenous European Islam that is fully Westernized in its social norms while often permeated with a profound Islamic spirituality. In the Balkans, the more prosperous European states can show whether they are prepared to allow a genuine Islam to flower on European territory for the first time since the tragedy of 1492, or whether they are doomed to sink into prejudicial and violent attitudes.

A similar approach is due the majority of the Chechens and the people of Uzbekistan, who desperately need our help in turning back the assaults of Wahhabism. Russian disinformation and Western journalistic passivity have induced us to keep the Chechens at arm's length, when not demonizing them as terrorists. In reality, most Chechens urgently seek U.S. involvement in the Caucasus as the only means for them to gain justice in their demand for national freedom and dignity. When President Bush visited Vladimir Putin in Moscow in May 2002, Chechen President Aslan Maskhadov addressed an appeal to the American leader, declaring that his people welcomed the international campaign against terrorism and fervently wished to join the antiterror coalition. Experts on the Chechens in Washington vividly recalled offers by Maskhadov in the late 1990s to become the eyes and ears of the United States in combating bin Laden and other extremists. But his entreaties then were ignored. With the Bush-Putin meeting Maskhadov also called on the United States to lead Russia and Chechnya to peace and democracy by facilitating a peace agreement between the two parties.

The Uzbeks, who were welcomed into the antiterror coalition during the 2001–02 Afghan war, continue to face the dual challenge of Wahhabi terrorism and propaganda aimed at portraying their government as unfairly repressing "pious" Muslims. The Wahhabi threat to Central Asia remains a serious one, requiring more than military and political support; an Uzbek effort to strengthen an alternative to Wahhabism through reinforcement of local Sufi traditions also merits our full backing.

Chechnya and Uzbekistan are joined as current targets of Wahhabi terrorism by the Philippines and Kashmir. Washington and Manila quickly arrived at a necessary agreement for military assistance to the Philippine government in combating terror. Kashmir represents a much larger problem; Wahhabi terrorists based in South Asia have long viewed the war against India as a second front in addition to that pursued by the Taliban in Afghanistan, and with the defeat of Taliban rule in Kabul, terrorists moved quickly into Kashmir. Because of its long duration, the Kashmir conflict has become a central element in Pakistani foreign policy, with extremist activities enjoying extensive backing by Islamabad. The Wahhabi legacy in South Asia encompasses genocidal attacks on Shi'a Muslims as well as Sikhs, Hindus, and others. But Muslims are also massacred by Hindu extremists in India. Pakistan's—and India's—status as allies in the antiterror coalition therefore must remain problematic.

Above all, a new strategy should be applied to Malaysia, a traditional Muslim society that has succeeded in attaining a modern, capitalist level of development, with the emergence of a large and prosperous middle class. Malaysia is a key power in many respects. Geopolitically, it is a stable base to reinforce the antiterror campaign in the Philippines as well as resistance to Wahhabi infiltration in Indonesia. But more important, Malaysia offers a positive example of the transformation of an Islamic society, which has lost none of its Muslim culture on its road of achievement and progress. Its leaders, also, are ready to stand side-by-side with the Western powers in the defense of civilization.

Another positive result might come from a new approach to U.S. dealings with Iran. Although some hard-line American conservatives refuse to give up their obsessive hatred of the Tehran regime, a gradual process of democratization is increasingly evident in Iranian life. As Israeli political scientist Shlomo Avineri wrote early in 2002, "Paradoxically, compared to Saudi Arabia, Iran appears to be a much more open society: There is a parliament, albeit elected within a limited Islamic discourse, yet elections are contested; women, despite discrimination, are active in public life (the deputy speaker of the Majlis [parliament] is a woman); there is limited freedom of the press—the fact that some dissenting journalists are occasionally jailed suggests that the limits of control are flexible. In Saudi Arabia, no dissident journalist is in jail, as no dissident journals exist."

The contrast between Saudi Arabia and Iran resembles that between the Soviet Union and China in the early 1960s. At that time, Moscow was viewed as a force for stability, committed to coexistence with the West, while China was seen as ruled by fanatical ideologues willing to risk nuclear war with the dominant powers. If a war was to take place it was assumed that Russia and the West would join in fighting the Chinese. Had any expert argued in 1967 that the United States would shortly reconcile with China, whose forces had killed American soldiers in the Korean War, contemptuous disregard would have been the mildest reaction. Yet as the decade drew to a close, Mao Zedong and Richard Nixon turned this paradigm on its head. Mao withdrew Chinese support from North Vietnam to concentrate on the "cultural revolution," his internal social experiment, and arrived at a diplomatic accommodation with the United States. Meanwhile, Russia continued fomenting global disorder, from the Middle East to Africa and Latin America, and eventually Afghanistan.

The same situation exists today in the Gulf. Iran is more concerned with the development of its Islamic model of governance than with international troublemaking, while Saudi Arabia, which was able to assume such a posture at the end of the 1920s, when the Saudi *Ikhwan* were repressed, cannot today divorce itself from worldwide Wahhabi extremism. One might state as a law of history that hypocritical extremists are always more disruptive and dangerous than those who, untroubled by a credibility gap, are not driven to prove their authenticity. Soviet Russia could no more live by its professed socialist ideals than the corrupt Saudi princes can fulfill the puritanical demands of Wahhabism. Maoist China, by contrast, had established a harsh but egalitarian order, as Iran has created a severe but complete Islamic polity. From such a position of ideological strength, Iran, like China, could sit down with the West. Further, the

West might recruit the Iranians as consistent allies in dealing with Saddam Husayn and with Wahhabi extremism elsewhere in the world.

New orientations in the Middle East could also help the United States pursue its own interests in the region with a policy undistorted by constant concerns over the security of Israel. The disestablishment of Wahhabism would be a key contribution to this end. Reform of the ideological life of the Saudi kingdom would require a creative coalition of informed Western leaders with traditional Muslim believers—similar to those which the United States assembled in Kuwait, among the Iraqi Kurds, in Bosnia-Hercegovina, in Kosovo, and in Afghanistan after 2001. Such a coalition would offer public endorsement of Islamic pluralism in Mecca and Medina and would support the human rights demands of the large Shi'a community in the Saudi kingdom. In addition, however, it would require that the Saudis recognize the Wahhabi role in the campaigns of incitement that led to September 11.

Currently the world views the Israeli-Palestinian conflict as a religious one, and therefore despairs of a solution. But the conventional wisdom is wrong. These conflicts are not ageless or irresolvable. Nor are they religious in character. They are recent and historical. It is at bottom a political conflict that has eluded resolution because of Arab intransigeance and interference by Wahhabi and other outside powers.

But even if peace does come in the Middle East, the wounds between the religious traditions must be healed. The fall of Wahhabism could help foster new relations between Jews, Christians, and Muslims—all believers in the monotheism of Abraham—leading to a renewed study and appreciation of their common historical and spiritual ancestry, rather than their differences. Far from being a utopian idea, the possibility of such a reconciliation has important antecedents—especially the examples of coexistence between Muslims, Jews, and Christians in medieval Spain and the Ottoman dominions.

A major step in this direction would be the foundation of a multireligious university in Jerusalem. Such an institution could provide training for professors of comparative religion around the world, while supporting original research in the history of the Abrahamic faiths, monotheistic spirituality, and similar topics. It could also provide funds for the preservation of religious archives and structures, and related research. Finally, it could host seminars and similar encounters aimed at promoting interfaith solutions to human conflicts. Another step forward might be the creation of a permanent interfaith council in the Holy Land. Such an initiative came in Alexandria, Egypt, in January 2002, at a meeting held with the participation of the Sephardic Chief Rabbi of Israel, Ha-rav Eliyahu Bakshi-Doron, one of the outstanding Jewish religious thinkers of modern times, along with the head of Al-Azhar University in Cairo, Shaykh Muhammad Sayyid Tantawi, and the Latin Patriarch of Jerusalem, Michel Sabbah. The encounter, which was endorsed by Ariel Sharon, Hosni Mubarak, and Yasir Arafat, produced the "Alexandria Declaration" calling for a "religiously sanctioned cease-fire" between Israelis and Arabs.

The legacies of Abraham, Ishmael, and Isaac summon all believers to attempt such a reconciliation. For the Islamic world community, the liberation of Mecca and Medina from the dictatorship of Wahhabism would doubtless be greeted as a positive event. But the moment must come when the children of Abraham at last recognize their common birthright. To do so requires, once again, understanding the two faces of Islam.

After September 11, the people of the United States, and of the West in general, were deluged with images of the evil face of Islam—the face of Wahhabism. Hate-filled spectators in the "Arab street" cackled in glee as flames consumed the Twin Towers; the mug shots of the 19 hijackers projected incomprehensible malice; bin Laden and Zawahiri grinned with pleasure as they promised new attacks in their fatuous videos; John Walker Lindh peered with an evil glare from behind his tangled hair in an Afghan prison; Richard Reid stared out glassy-eyed and José Padilla possessed the typical sneer of the common thug. Deluded Palestinian mothers danced while sending their children out to commit mass murder, and rich Saudis, as so often before, smiled lovingly at Americans while measuring our heads for the cut of the terrorist's blade.

But the other face of Islam waited patiently, seemingly hidden, but no less present: the face of pluralism and coexistence, of Sufis preaching love and healing, of scholars seeking new routes for the Islamic imagination, and of millions upon millions of ordinary Muslims around the world looking confidently toward a world of prosperity and stability. In tearing the benign mask away from Wahhabi-Saudi hypocrisy, paradoxically, the democratic powers and traditional Muslims had the opportunity to reveal anew, at the same time, the inspiring and inviting face of an Islamic civilization that could offer fresh and valuable contributions to humanity. For Westerners to miss such an opportunity would be worse than folly; it would be suicide. In defeating terror, let us therefore clasp the hands of traditional Muslims, and recognize in them our cousins, our sisters, our brothers.

AFTERWORD TO THE
ANCHOR EDITION

In the months that followed the first anniversary of the atrocities of September 11, 2001, the visible crisis of Wahhabism and the Saudi state grew more acute. At the end of 2002, news broke in the United States regarding Princess Haifa, wife of the Saudi ambassador to Washington, the Sudairi Prince Bandar bin Sultan Abd al-Aziz. The princess had made a personal cash donation that ended up in the hands of two of the September 11 hijackers, Khalid al-Midbar and Nawaf Alhazmi. The royal family's spin doctor, the oleaginous Adel Al-Jubeir, became a leading media personality as he appeared on the American television networks seeking to absolve the Saudi regime of any involvement in terrorist conspiracies. Unfortunately, he was abetted in this activity by the failure of the American political leadership, which still had not gotten around to demanding a necessary, full, and transparent accounting of Saudi involvement in al-Qaida.

In contrast with impoverished Bosnia-Hercegovina, which could not afford to install new computers in its war-wrecked university system, but which acted immediately to arrest and investigate Arab terrorists within its borders, the Saudi kingdom remained passive, if not indifferent about its responsibilities to the United States, its historic partner. The authorities of the kingdom insisted that the presence of 15 out of 19 Saudis among the suicide pilots of September 11 was a mere gambit by Osama bin Laden to increase friction between the two powerful countries.

It was not. Al-Qaida and its foot soldiers were, simply put, quintessential products of the Wahhabi ideology and the Saudi order. Of the 9/11 murderers:

- Wael Muhammad al-Shehri, 25, was a physical education teacher at an elementary school in the Kamis Mushayat airbase in Saudi Arabia.

- Waleed al-Shehri, 21, was a dropout from a teachers' college. His brothers included professional officers in the Saudi military, among them an air force pilot.

- Abd' al-Aziz Abd' al-Rahman al-Omari, 23, was a graduate of the Imam Muhammad Bin Sa'ud University, a prestigious religious institution in Saudi Arabia, and was a disciple of a senior Saudi cleric.

- Fa'iz Muhammad al-Shehri, was an employee of an official Saudi relief agency.

- Mohned Muhammad al-Shehri, 24, was a student at the Imam Muhammad Bin Sa'ud University.

- Hamza Saleh al-Ghamdi, 21, traveled extensively, using his family's money, in Pakistan and Afghanistan, before coming to the United States.

- Ahmed Ibrahim al-Haznawi al-Ghamdi, 24, was the son of a leading imam, or mosque leader.

- Ahmed Abd' Allah al-Nami, 23, was also a student at Imam Muhammad Bin Sa'ud University, and served as an imam in the southwestern city of Abha in Saudi Arabia.

- Majid Mishaan Moqed al-Qufi al-Harbi, 22, was a student at the elite King Sa'ud University in Riyadh.

- Hani Saleh Hassan Hanjour was a pilot for Emirates Airlines, headquartered in the United Arab Emirates. His father was a military contractor.

- Satam M.A. al-Suqumi, 24, was also a student at King Sa'ud University in Riyadh.[1]

The great omission on the part of American politicians—the strange, invertebrate posture about Saudi responsibility for terror—persisted even as military intervention in Iraq came and went. For their part, the Saudi authorities undertook only minor actions to curb the more outrageous activities of terror funders on their soil. For example, after lawsuits by families of September 11 victims, and similar legal actions, shone attention on Saudi backing of al-Qaida, Riyadh moved to more seriously restrict the activities of the Al-Haramain Islamic Foundation, whose offices in Bosnia-Hercegovina and Somalia were ordered closed in March 2002 because of terrorist links. Thirteen months later, its accounts inside the kingdom were reported frozen. Al-Haramain was headed by Dr. Ali Al-Murshed, the former director of the Girls' Education Presidency, who had been removed after the school fire in Mecca, also in March 2002, when 14 schoolgirls died. The foundation's general director was the state Minister of Islamic Affairs, Saleh Al-Alshaikh, a scion of the family of Ibn Abd al-Wahhab.[2]

But Saudi/Wahhabi mischief, inside and outside the kingdom, continued even as coalition troops marched to liberate Baghdad. Naturally, the Wahhabi ruling class was less than enthusiastic about the possible emergence of a Western-oriented, protodemocratic society led by Shi'a Muslims in wealthy, educated Iraq on the long northern border of the kingdom. The April 2003 issue of *Future of Islam*, a periodical of the terror-promoting World Assembly of Muslim Youth (WAMY), headquartered in Riyadh with offices in northern Virginia, published a cover interview with Saudi cleric Ayed al-Qarni, an adviser to Prince Abd al-Aziz bin Fahd, youngest son of the elderly and ailing King Fahd. Al-Qarni authored a poem recorded and repeatedly broadcast on Saudi-subsidized television and radio during the Iraq conflict, in which he declared, "Slaughter the enemy infidels and say there is but one God." In the magazine interview, he stated that he prayed for the destruction of America, which he called the main source of global suffering, several times daily. He also urged Saudi subjects to go fight and die in Iraq and to contribute money to help defend Saddam. Numerous hapless fanatics did so.

Al-Qarni was not alone. Also in April, another Wahhabi cleric, Naser Al-Omar, preached in favor of suicide attacks on the coalition forces in Iraq. He was among the signers of a fatwa calling for defense of Saddam, distributed in Saudi government offices and hospitals. Al-Qarni was also joined, in the pages of *Future of Islam*, by the current U.S. ambassador to Saudi Arabia, Robert Jordan, who gave an uncritical interview to the terrorist magazine at the same time as he refused to meet with Shi'a and other human rights activists in the kingdom. (Jordan expressed derision toward critics of Saudi Arabia who, unlike him, had not spent time in the kingdom. One wonders whether a U.S. ambassador to the former Soviet Union would have been allowed to make similar comments, blasting anti-Communists for failing to visit Moscow before emitting their complaints, prior to 1989.)

Jordan, however, was forced to abandon the posture of happy courtesan to the Saudi monarchy in the aftermath of the Riyadh bombings on the night of May 12, 2003, in which nine Americans were killed, out of as many as thirty fatalities. He was compelled to denounce the refusal of the Saudi authorities to provide adequate security for compounds in which Americans and other foreigners resided. But the Riyadh bombings, followed by similar horrors in Morocco and Chechnya, represented atrocities foretold. The message was direct: the ultra-Wahhabi wing of the Saudi ruling class would not stand by while a Shi'a-majority democracy was installed in Iraq. A similar hand guided increased subversion inside Iraq. As American Shi'a leader Agha Shaukat Jafri put it, "the Arab street is the Wahhabi street, and when the Arabs demonstrate against the U.S. in Iraq, the Wahhabis are not far from the scene."

The Riyadh bombings had been preceded by a rise in Wahhabi incitement inside the kingdom, with the Shi'as as their most notable target. During the Iraq war, an introductory class in Islamic culture at King Sa'ud University focused on teaching students how, why, and where to fight Americans in the name of "jihad." Dr. Abdullah al-Rayess, who taught the course, called for new attacks on Americans in Iraq, the Philippines, Kashmir (where American military forces had never been present), and Bosnia-Hercegovina (where American troops protected Muslims from Serbian terror.) Al-Rayess also continually insulted Shi'as, calling to prayer for their death and devastation, and praising Saddam for killing Shi'as, whom al-Rayess described as "atheists." The campus of King Sa'ud University had long been polluted with hate literature attacking Shi'as as "the number one enemy," more dangerous than the Jews and Christians. Meanwhile, the arch-Wahhabi, interior minister Prince Nayef, was reported to have issued annual orders blacklisting Shi'a families from enrolling their children in the kingdom's institutions of higher education.[3] Nayef had distinguished himself by suggesting that the Jews had committed the terrorist attacks of September 11, and, in the wake of the Riyadh bombings, his message to the United States was arrogant: these things happen, they cannot be avoided or prevented, and the foreigners who come to the kingdom must get used to them.

Continuing attacks on Shi'as in the kingdom included floggings in the streets of the southern city of Najran. In the Shi'a majority areas, a real reign of terror was reported in weeks before and after the Riyadh atrocity, including the destruction of three Shi'a community centers in the Eastern Province, and the kidnapping of a blind Shi'a cleric, Shaykh Ibrahim al-Garaash, aged 65, from the city of Qatif.[4] The above-mentioned Wahhabi, Shaykh Naser al-Omar, had called for confiscation of Shi'a mosques and community centers, their forcible conversion to Wahhabism, and the arrest of all their religious leaders.

But Shi'as could not be seriously suspected in the Riyadh attack. The Shi'as under Saudi rule had reacted to the fall of Saddam by new peaceful initiatives demanding recognition and rights. On April 30, 2003, a petition signed by 450 Shi'a personalities was submitted to Saudi Crown Prince Abdullah, demanding an end to the Wahhabi monopoly over religious life in the kingdom, with respect for all Islamic sects, including the Shi'as, and their representation in all official bodies. The document said, "our country suffers from the activities of fanatical, sectarian tendencies that stimulate hatred and aversion against the other Islamic sects and their followers, particularly the Shi'as, and that call on believers to hate them. . . . These hateful tendencies benefit from their power and their official status.

The religious curricula in the schools insistently describe the followers of the other Islamic sects as unbelievers, idol-worshipers, deviants, and heretics. Religious programs and official media are exclusively controlled by one sect [Wahhabis], agitating for exclusion of other Muslims and insulting them. This is supported in other institutions, including the courts, the institutions of public morals, and centers of Islamic outreach and guidance." A major grievance was the continued hindrance to construction of new Shi'a mosques and community centers.

The Riyadh bombing was undeniably shocking to the Saudi elite. Crown Prince Abdullah, until then, was seen as the sole figure at the heights of power to comprehend the depth of the crisis, and the need to extricate the regime from Wahhabism. But Abdullah's path to reform has been tortuously slow. The daily *Arab News* editorialized on May 14 against "the fantasy that September 11 and all the other attacks laid at the doors of terrorists who happen to be Arab or Muslim were the work of the Israelis or the CIA. For too long we have ignored the truth. We did not want to admit that Saudis were involved in September 11. We can no longer ignore that we have a nest of vipers here. . . . The environment that produced such terrorism has to change. . . . We cannot say that suicide bombings in Israel and Russia are acceptable but not in Saudi Arabia."[5]

Perhaps predictably, the problem in Saudi Arabia was easier for Saudis to recognize than for American officials to understand. FBI and other investigators were dispatched to find out whether the Riyadh bombings were the product of al-Qaida. What they didn't comprehend was that the problem was not just that of al-Qaida; the problem was Wahhabism. This was much better understood by the majority of the world's Muslims than by Western experts and journalists. For the Islamic believers, there was nothing new about the Wahhabi menace. They knew that Wahhabism always found its first victims in Muslim ranks, having become infamous for violent repression of traditional Islamic practices within the precincts of the kingdom. However, with the deepening of the crisis that followed September 11, sudden concessions to popular feelings among Muslims residing in and visiting Saudi territory included permission to pray, under Wahhabi direction, at the Prophet's Shrine in Medina, but not inside it, and for Shi'a Muslims to pray in Jannat al-Baqi, the graveyard in Medina demolished under Wahhabi rule. Touching the Prophet's Shrine as a devotional act is still punished by arrests and beatings.

Ibn Abd al-Wahhab and his followers have consistently called for the nullification of the four established Sunni legal schools and their corpus of precedents and decisions. This aspect of Wahhabism has been a cornerstone of Wahhabi-Saudi rule. However, with the progress of the crisis inside the kingdom, Saudi subjects have reported that representatives of the classic Maliki and Shafi'i schools of Islamic jurisprudence, previously repressed, have begun demanding the right to preach and teach. At the same time, young people in large numbers now embrace Sufism, or Islamic spirituality, as a form of oppositional culture. Thus, the basis of religious protest grows.

One major point of contention is the Wahhabi argument that failure to pray makes one an unbeliever. This claim is found in the Hanbali school of jurisprudence, from which the Wahhabis claim descent, but only there; Wahhabi attempts to justify their murderous attitude toward all other forms of laxity place them outside the Hanbali legal school, according to anti-Wahhabi scholars. Mainstream Islam holds that those who fail to fully observe sacred duties may not be declared disbelievers so long as they do not deny the sacred nature of the obligation. For the traditional Muslim, believers are judged on their belief, not on their outward conduct. This seems obvious when so stated, and would seem to illustrate the deviant character of Wahhabism.

Wahhabism, although claiming precedent in the Hanbali legal school, also diverges from the Hanbali tradition in claiming that a Muslim must adhere, in a spirit of absolute obedience, to a single Islamic legal school. As described by the historian Itzchak Weismann,[6] Hasan al-Shatti (1790–1858), a leading Syrian Hanbali scholar and opponent of Wahhabism, defended cooperation among the varying schools and argued that "there is no obligation to emulate in all matters the rulings of one specific madhhab [legal school], and that in case of necessity it is permissible to apply those of other madhhabs as well. . . . Almost no one performs the commandments according to one legal school, and the common people cannot be expected to know all the details of the law when even the 'ulama' [scholars] fail to do so."

In a debate with Ibn Taymiyyah, who is the Hanbali figure claimed by the Wahhabis as a mentor, the Sufi and Maliki jurist Ibn Ata Allah al-Iskandari brilliantly scored the narrow outlook of Islamic Puritans, in terms that could well describe the mentality of the Saudi establishment today.[7] Ibn Ata Allah commented on the Hanbali legacy in a manner even more notable in its anticipation of Saudi-Wahhabi habits. He pointed out that Ahmad bin Hanbal, founder of the school, "questioned the actions of some of his own followers who were in the habit of going on patrols, breaking open casks of wine (in the shops of their Christian vendors or wherever they found them), spilling their contents on the floor, beating up singing girls, and confronting people in the street. All of this they did in the name of enjoining good and prohibiting what is forbidden. However, [Ahmad bin Hanbal] had not given any fatwa that they should censure or rebuke all those people. Consequently, those followers of his were flogged, thrown into jail, and paraded mounted on assback facing the tail."

Ibn Ata Allah described such vigilance patrols as "bad behavior, which the worst and most vicious Hanbalis continue to perpetrate right down to our own day, in the name of enjoining good and prohibiting what is forbidden." Unfortunately, they are more prevalent than ever in Saudi Arabia, where, until the recent aggravation of the crisis, all public and private space was terrorized by a Wahhabi militia, the *mutawiyin* or "volunteers," bearing the precise title, "the League of Encouragement of Virtue," and operating through local units, or Public Morals Committees, acting as Wahhabi eyes and ears among the masses. With Saudi backing, a similar body was established in Afghanistan under the Taliban. In the wake of the Riyadh bombings of 2003, the figure of Ibn Taymiyyah symbolized, in public discourse, the inner rot of the Saudi regime. An article in the reformist daily *al-Watan* was headlined, "Who is More Important? The Nation or Ibn Taymiyyah"? Soon after it appeared, Jamal Khashoggi, editor of *al-Watan* and former deputy editor of *Arab News*, was dismissed from his post at the order of Prince Nayef.

Western media and academia were mistaken in their conceptions of Wahhabism. Both treated it as an ancient and conservative form of Islam, which it was not; rather, it was a form of extreme radicalism. Second, and paradoxically, those who had established careers as apologists for the Saudi order treated all discussion of Wahhabism as an invention or provocation emanating from illegitimate, if not Zionist circles. The latter attitude was unintentionally supported by the confusion of Western law enforcement bodies. But if, as demonstrated by the citations above, the debate over Wahhabism was anything but new among Muslims, there were also precedents for warning the rest of the world about the Wahhabi menace. In the first quarter of the nineteenth century, a now-forgotten English writer, Thomas Hope, composed an extraordinary novel, *Anastasius, or, Memoirs of a Greek*.[8]

Hope's book was immensely successful in its time, and was falsely ascribed by one critic to the pen of Lord Byron. Hope, a noted furniture designer, was a typical specimen of the wealthy traveler and aesthete of his age, and had journeyed extensively in the Islamic world. The seizure of Mecca by the Wahhabis, and their clearance from Arabia by Muhammad Ali Pasha of Egypt, then had loud and wide echoes across the globe. *Anastasius* includes an exceptionally detailed account of Wahhabism, including its redoubt in Diriyah, that is chilling in its parallels with the phenomenon of al-Qaida. Like its contemporary acolytes, the Wahhabi movement of two centuries ago practiced assassination and other forms of terror, and "in the very midst of Baghdad, in the broad face of day, Wahhabis had been seen—scarcely disguised—taking note of the individuals and marking the houses, which their vengeance or their avarice had devoted to destruction." Similarly, William Brown Hodgson, a writer from Savannah, Georgia, wrote accurately of the Wahhabis in 1835, as "formidable enemies of the Muslim faith . . . an heretical sect which for so many years had defied [the Sultan's] authority, desecrated the holy places of the Prophet, and interrupted the annual pilgrimages."[9]

The warnings of Islamic scholars and European travelers about the dangers of Wahhabism were ignored for generations, especially after oil made the Wahhabi/Saudi alliance a valuable partner of the Western powers. In addition, Western elites simply considered intra-Islamic issues irrelevant to them. Nevertheless, it has long been known that in the histories of absolutist regimes, monarchies as well as dictatorships, there always comes an event or events in which the mask of accommodation to injustice is torn away. The main question is whether that time has arrived in Saudi Arabia, or is fast approaching. For the movement toward American independence from Britain, the moment of truth was seen in the Boston tea party. In the annals of the old order in France, it was marked by the fall of the Bastille; in the long chronicle of tsarist oppression, by the Bloody Sunday massacre of 1905.

In most such incidents, the impunity of armed brutes actively supporting the regime exposes the depth of the social crisis, when violence by the state is, simply, carried too far. Was that the meaning of the Riyadh bombings? Did the Wahhabis, concerned to maintain their power, finally provoke their ultimate self-exposure? It is undeniable that the Saudi monarchs can no longer rule in the old way, and that their subjects increasingly, if not over-whelmingly, refuse to live in the old way. The reform efforts of Crown Prince Abdullah and his supporters may come as too little, too late. It is certain now that the traditional Muslim scholars, who hate Wahhabism, will take to the streets to demand the abolition of its religious dominance. The Shi'as of the south and east will inevitably demonstrate in their masses against the long oppression they have suffered. The oil workers of the Eastern Province will, sooner or later, demand the right to form a trade union—a right that exists in Iran, to cite but one example. The courageous and virtuous women of Arabia will rip off their face coverings and march for their rights.

To summarize, the discontented Saudi generations that wish to live in a normal society will, inexorably and unavoidably, mobilize for the end of the Wahhabi order. A final question thus remains. When the fateful hour has come, will the bodies of armed men that defend the state, that is, the Saudi army, police, and National Guard, obey the orders of the Wahhabi bigots, the hated *mutawiyin*, the patrons and accomplices of bin Laden? Will they serve the forces of darkness, repressing the people, whose demands are just, correct, and eminently Islamic? Will the sons of the people fire on the people? God willing, no blood will flow, and pluralism will be restored peacefully to the Two Holy Places. It would be for the good of Islam, and of the world, and, let me add, for the welfare of the brave traditional scholars, as well as numerous ordinary people, who live under Saudi rule and who have helped me write, and helped their friends and neighbors in the kingdom to read, this book.

Stephen Schwartz
Washington, D.C.
June 2003

ACKNOWLEDGMENTS

Material included in this book first appeared in the *Albanian Catholic Bulletin, San Francisco Faith* (San Francisco), the *Forward, Illyria*, the *New York Post*, the *New Criterion* and *National Review* (New York), the *Weekly Standard* (Washington), the *Spectator* (London), the *Wall Street Journal Europe* (Brussels), *Reforma* (México), *Middle East Quarterly* (Philadelphia), *Partisan Review* (Cambridge, Mass.), and *Anderson Valley Advertiser* (Boonville, Calif.). Citations for most of these publications, some of them republished on the Internet, are included in the Bibliography.

I also published extensively on these topics in Bosnian- and Albanian-language periodicals: *Ljiljan, Oslobodjenje, Valter*, and *Većernje Novine* (Sarajevo), and *Dita, Ekskluzive*, and *Interesi Nacional* (Prishtina). These citations are not included in the Bibliography.

This book would never have appeared without the guidance, even from their graves, of Kenneth Rexroth and Octavio Paz, eternal models of conduct. I could never know Ida M. Tarbell, but her spirit, which is immortal, also aided me.

Paul Nagy, friend and mentor, first invited me to the path of Ibn Arabi. Gjon Sinishta, founder of the Albanian Catholic Institute in San Francisco, taught me about God, the Balkans, and the unity of the monotheistic faiths, may he rest in peace. I owe much to Baba Rexheb Beqiri, founder of the Bektashi *Teqe* in America, whose tears of exile watered the soil of my native land, and whose book opened my eyes, may the blessings of merciful Allah (swt) be upon him on the last day. I owe even more to Shaykh Muhammad Hisham Kabbani of the Most Distinguished Naqshbandi Order of Sufis, very beloved teacher and friend, whose companionship freed my heart, may the blessings of merciful Allah (swt) always be upon him.

I am also grateful for the generosity and hospitality of H.E. Rexhep Boja, Grand *Mufti* of Kosovo, my friend, and his colleagues at the Alauddin *medresa* in Prishtina. The *medresa* fulfilled a noble work throughout the Communist era, when it was the only institution in the world training Albanian Muslim clerics. Wrecked by the forces of Milošević, its reconstruction has been a major task for Kosovo's Islamic community. Finally, I appreciate the personal blessings I have received from H.E. Hafiz Sabri Koci, Grand *Mufti* of Albania, and H.E. Magomed Albogachiev, Grand *Mufti* of Ingushetia. May Allah (swt) reward them all generously.

A Jewish teacher who is an example for the best Muslim and Christian scholars, Professor Moshe Lazar of the University of Southern California, is due all thanks. Gratitude also belongs to David Kamhi, the *chazzan* of Sarajevo, *mi morenu*, beloved teacher and comrade. I owe more than I can express to Professor Muhamed Nezirović of the University of Sarajevo, one of the *awliya*, whose magnificent studies of Sephardic culture brought me back to Sarajevo, and his colleague, Professor Kemal Bakaršić of the University of Sarajevo, also among the *awliya* for his work of preservation, whose companionship kept me in Bosnasaray.

I embrace Memnun Idžaković, who offered me the hand of true friendship, and Alija Behram and Amir Talić, who each survived a different level of hell, and who taught me much. I greet Mehmed Halilović, my second great friend in Sarajevo. Mehmed Husić "opened the way" for me. Kemal Muftić, who also admitted me to the grace of his friendship, Mensur Brdar, a great colleague and mentor in Bosnian journalism, and Enver Ćaušević, whose solidarity was unflinching, are true *mujahidin*.

I salute, from afar, Nedžad Ibrišimović, whose words were eloquent beyond any other in our time, and made me weep with anger; and from nearby, Semezdin Mehmedinović, another mentor and colleague, whose writing comforted me and turned my rage to passion. This book would be inconceivable without Abdulah Sidran, who told me about my past life, and who is also a great *mujahid*; Ademir Kenović, who taught me everything about courage; Hadžem Hajdarević, the model of poetry in our time, and Omer Pobrić, the heart's musician.

To Džemaludin and Nedžad Latić, among the best of the believers — may they be rewarded throughout their lives and afterward. Likewise, Baba Mumin Lama of the Bektashi order, my friend in Kosovo and another of the *awliya*, is always in my thoughts. I offer my gratitude to Sheh Xhemajl Shehu Rifa'i, as well as to my friend and brother Sadik Pelinko Ulqinak, *murid* of Sheh Xhemajl and possessor of the Secret of Secrets.

My friends and colleagues Adem Demaci, Daut Dauti, and Haqif and Shpresa Mulliqi made everything happen for me. Honor belongs to the families of Sheh Myhedin Shehu and Sheh Zejnelabedin Dervishdana, martyrs (*shuhadaa*) of Islam during the Kosovo liberation war, whose tears and devotion inspire me at every moment, and whom I never forget. Honor is also due President Aslan Maskhadov of Chechnya, who provided me with indispensable guidance; Roy Gutman, another "opener of the way"; Adam Bellow, friend and editor; Richard Torre, my best collaborator; and the late Nelson Brown, my colleague at the Voice of America and friend, as well as my meticulous fact-checker.

Finally, however, responsibility for the opinions expressed here rests on me alone.

Although this book focuses on a sequence of events beginning with Ibn Taymiyyah centuries ago, it is based in large part on Internet research. In the 1990s, Islamic fundamentalists took to the Net with the enthusiasm previous totalitarians showed in their use of radio and movies. But Hitler and Stalin did not have to contend with the immediate appearance of countersystems of broadcasting and film production. Vast amounts of information that might otherwise have remained completely obscure to the West, transmitted only in oral or printed form, from mouth to mouth and from hand to hand, by groups of enthusiasts among Muslims, are accessible by the use of a search engine. This does not mean that rare printed and manuscript sources of Islamic history, some of them endangered by the vandalism of Serb and Russian extremists as well as by the Wahhabis, have ceased to be important. But the Internet publication of polemics, and distribution of videocassettes, by Wahhabis, "Salafis," and, more important, their opponents, made the composition of this work easier.

In the information age, no tyranny goes unchallenged. The research interface with the Internet, and the diachronic jumps necessary to understand this history, gave the project the strange feeling of a novel by Philip K. Dick or a motion picture like *The Matrix*—a sense of authentic cyberjournalism. To emphasize, little presented here is based on governmental intelligence or investigative work of the old kind. On the other hand, an insightful man once wrote, "the most merciful thing in the world, I think, is the inability of the human mind to correlate all its contents." There is a paradoxical term used by a certain California author: "public secrets." This book is a compilation of "public secrets"—a concept that remains among the ultimate Sufi mysteries of our time.

Inconsistencies in the transcription of Arabic names in English in this book reflect the diversity of sources.

NOTES

Chapter 1: Snow in the Desert

1. *Hadith* means the whole corpus of lore; the correct plural for citations from *Hadith* is *Ahadith*.
2. This motif seems an archetype for peoples with desert origins; the symbol of the Aztecs, and of modern Mexico, is an eagle with a snake in its claws.
3. Q.: 109.
4. Q.: 96:1–4.
5. Muslims may, however, conceal their faith in the interest of self-preservation or the welfare of Islam in general.
6. Q.: 28:56.
7. Muhammad.
8. Q.: 36:70.
9. *Qur'an.*
10. Q.: 52:32–39. The punishment of "eavesdroppers" on God, in the form of meteors and comets, is one of the most singular and fascinating motifs in *Qur'an*, and seems to originate in Arab mystical conceptions of the night reaching far back into the collective consciousness.
11. Q.: 5:51.
12. Q.: 5:56–67 and 2:62.
13. Q.: 60:8.
14. Q.: 2:256.
15. Q.: 29:46.
16. The faithful.
17. Q.: 5:82.
18. Q.: 17:104.
19. Q.: 9:3–6.
20. Q.: 8:67.
21. Q.: 56:12–39.

CHAPTER 2: FORTRESSES AND MOUNTAIN PATHS

1. These excerpts are based on translations by Annemarie Schimmel.
2. The standard English edition bears the latter title in Arabic: *Tarjuman al-Ashwaq*.
3. Of King Solomon's palace; see Q.: 27:44.

CHAPTER 3: HATERS OF SONG

1. Bukhari and Muslim are the two outstanding compilers of *Hadith*.
2. Wahhabis object to the use of this term by Westerners, and pressure has forced many Western writers and editors to avoid it. In reality, the Islamic *ummah* was known as the Community of Muhammadans or *Jamaat al-Muhammadiyya* for centuries. Such purported concern with Western usages masks the Wahhabi desire to remove the primacy of the Prophet of Islam from the religion.

CHAPTER 5: THE COMING OF THE *IMAM*

1. Q.: 22:39.

CHAPTER 6: PERMANENT *JIHAD*

1. When I returned to the United States from the Balkans, I attempted to call the attention of experts and advocates to the Wahhabi problem, about which I had learned a great deal. I was uniformly treated as an alarmist. A representative of no less a body than the American Israel Public Affairs Committee characterized my comments about the Wahhabi-Saudi danger as "paranoid" and "conspiratorial."
2. Not to be confused with the Saudi Foundation, Benevolence International, that funded terrorism and that was occasionally referred to in the media as "Benevolentia."
3. See, for example, indictments by the International Criminal Tribunal for Former Yugoslavia in The Hague against Enver Hadžihasanović, Mehmed Alagić, and Amir Kubura.

CHAPTER 7: SWORD OF DISHONOR

1. *Dani* is a neo-Communist gutter organ, but in this instance its reportage was seemingly on the mark.
2. In a comical development, *Dani*, which had made a career out of exposing scandals involving Bosnian Muslim and other Islamic figures, suddenly rallied to the cause of the arrested Algerians. Following the deportation, *Dani* published a cover showing Uncle Sam urinating on the Bosnian Constitution. The most outrageous aspect of this sideshow is the fact that *Dani* was completely subsidized by the U.S. government as an "experiment" in "press freedom." An official U.S. investigation of such misadventures and malfeasances was long overdue.
3. Communication with the author.
4. An extraordinary example of this propaganda is the 1996 pamphlet *The American Campaign to Suppress Islam*, published in Britain.

CHAPTER 8: RELIGIOUS COLONIALISM

1. Two other groups, the Arab American Institute (AAI) headed by James Zogby and the American Arab Anti-Discrimination Committee (ADC), whose main spokesman is Hussein Ibish, gained considerable prominence after September 11, during the Afghan war of 2001–2, and while debate over the Israeli West Bank incursion of 2002 raged in the United States. While AAI and ADC stood in for the Wahhabi lobby as defenders of Arab and Muslim extremism, they were not religious organizations and discussion of them is not central to this anaysis.

2. See "Israel won't seek extradition of jailed Hamas leader," April 3, 1997, and "Hamas leader deported to Jordan," May 6, 1997, at www.cnn.com.

3. The so-called "Nation of Islam" has always been repudiated by authentic Muslims for its claims that its founder, Elijah Poole, and his writings were divinely inspired. For Muslims, Muhammad is the last Prophet, and *Qur'an* the final scripture.

CHAPTER 9: WHITHER SAUDI ARABIA?

1. Confidential communication with the author.

AFTERWORD

1. Source: Saudi Institute, Washington, DC.

2. Source: ibid.

3. Al-Saleh, Saeed, "Hatred and Violence Spread at King Saud University," Saudi Information Agency, Washington, DC, May 2, 2003.

4. Al-Ahmed, Ali, "Shia Mosques Torched," May 10, 2003; "Shia Elderly Cleric Kidnapped," May 21, 2003, Saudi Information Agency, Washington, DC.

5. "Editorial: The Enemy Within," *Arab News*, May 14, 2003, published at www.arabnews.com.

6. Weismann, Itzchak, *Taste of Modernity: Sufism, Salafiyya, & Arabism in Late Ottoman Damasacus*, Leiden, E. J. Brill, 2001.

7. See Kabbabi, Shaykh Muhammad Hisham, *Encyclopedia of Islamic Doctrine*, V. 5. Mountain View, Calif., As-Sunna Foundation of America, 1998, p. 125.

8. Baudry's Foreign Library, Paris, 1831.

9. Hodgson, William Brown, "An Edited Biographical Sketch of Mohammed Ali, Pasha of Egypt, Syria, and Arabia, Written at the City of Washington, March 1835." Republished at www.sunnah.org.

BIBLIOGRAPHY

The Koran, Translated with notes by N. J. Dawood. London: Penguin, 1990.

Aburish, Said K. *The Rise, Corruption, and Coming Fall of the House of Saud*, New York, St. Martin's Press, 1995.

[Ajami, Fouad]. Interview cited in Kaiser, Robert G. "U.S. Message Lost Overseas," *Washington Post*. October 15, 2001.

Algar, Hamid. "Biography of the Ayatollah Khomeini (1902–1989) From Birth to Revolution," Summary published on-line.

Algar, Hamid. "The Fusion of the Gnostic and the Political in the Personality and Life of Imam Khomeini," Published at www.khomeini.com.

——. *Wahhabism: A Critical Essay*. Oneonta, NY: Islamic Publications International, 2002.

Ali, Tariq. "Afghanistan: Between Hammer and Anvil," *New Left Review*. London: March–April 2000.

Ali Khan, M. Ghazanfar, and Omar Al-Zobidy. "SAMA denies freezing any bank account," *Arab News*. Jeddah: May 14, 2002.

American Friends Service Committee, et al. "Statement to the Press." March 28, 1996.

Armstrong, Karen. *Islam*. New York: Modern Library, 2000.

Arslanagić, Sead. "Predizborni bin Laden," *Ljiljan*. Sarajevo: May 13–20, 2002.

Avineri, Shlomo. "Saudi Totalitarianism," *Jerusalem Post*. March 19, 2002.

[Azzam, Abdullah, et al.]. *Jihad Stories: Stories of Foreign Mujahideen Killed in Jihad*. Published at www.azzam.com.

——. "Virtues of Shahaadah in the Path of Allah." Published at www.as-sahwah.com.

Bakri, Sheikh Omar Muhammad. "Aal-Saud: Past and Present." London: OBM Network, 1997. Published at www.obm.clara.net.

Balkhi, Fasihuddin. *Wahabi Movement*. New Delhi: Classical Publishing Company, 1983.

Barsky, Yehudit. "Hamas—The Islamic Resistance Movement of Palestine." Published at www.ajc.org.

Benbassa, Esther and Aron Rodrigue. *Jews of the Balkans*. Oxford: Blackwell, 1995.

Bension, Ariel. *The Zohar in Moslem and Christian Spain* (2nd printing). New York: Sepher-Hermon Press, 1974.

[Beqiri], Baba Rexheb. *The Mysticism of Islam and Bektashism* (Vol. I). Naples: Dragoti, 1984.

Bin Laden, Osama. "Declaration of War Against the Americans, etc." Published at www.washingtonpost.com, October 1996.

——. Interview, "The New Powder Keg in the Middle East." Published at www.islam.org, October–November 1996.

Birge, John Kingsley. *The Bektashi Order of Dervishes*. London: Luzac, 1994.

Blanch, Lesley. *The Sabres of Paradise*. New York: Carroll and Graf, 1984.

Boehlert, Eric. "'Betrayed' by Bush," Salon.com, April 2, 2002.

Bolton, John R. "Libya, Syria, Cuba Need Scrutiny for Weapons Programs, U.S. Says." Published at www.state.gov, Washington: May 6, 2002.

Bougarel, Xavier, and Nathalie Clayer. *Le Nouvel Islam balkanique*. Paris: Maisonneuve & Larose, 2001.

Braudel, Fernand. *The Mediterranean and the Mediterranean World in the Age of Philip II*. New York: HarperCollins, 1992.

Callies de Salles, Bruno. "Algeria in the Grip of Terror," *Le Monde Diplomatique*. Paris: October 1997.

Catholic Encyclopedia. New York: Appleton, 1907, on-line edition, 1999.

Cerić, Mustafa ef. *Islam i Državljanstvo u Evropi*. Sarajevo: VKBI, 2000.

Chittick, William C. "Ibn al-Arabi," article from *Encyclopedia Iranica*.

De Corancez, Louis Alexandre Olivier. *The History of the Wahabis*. Reading, UK: Garnet Publishing, 1995.

Crum, Bartley C. *Behind the Silken Curtain*. New York: Simon & Schuster, 1947.

Culi, R. Yaakov, et al. *Yalkut MeAm Lo'ez (The Torah Anthology)*, various vols., Translated by R. Aryeh Kaplan. New York/Jerusalem: Moznaim Publishing Corp., various dates.

Dallin, David J. *Soviet Russia's Foreign Policy, 1939–1942*. New Haven: Yale University Press, 1942.

Damad, Dr. Sayyid Mustafa Muhaqqiq. "Cultural Relations Between Christianity and Shi'i Islam." Translated by Dr. A. N. Baqirshahi, Message of Thaqalayn (Tehran), n.d.

Darwish, M. "The Hidden Face of Extremism—The 'New Wahhabi' Movement," *EastWest Record* (on-line periodical), post October 8, 2001.

Development Reporting Cell. "Number of seminaries grew by 136 percent from 1988 to 2000," *Jang* [Raw-alpindi]: January 17, 2002.

Dungersi, Mohamedraza. *The Commander of the Faithful: Ali Bin Abi Talib*. Published at home.swipnet.se/islam/imams.

Durán, Khalid. *Children of Abraham: An Introduction to Islam for Jews*. New York: Ktav, 2001.

——. "How CAIR Put My Life in Peril," *Middle East Quarterly*. Philadelphia: Summer 2002.

Elazar, Samuel M. *El Romancero Judeo-Español*, 2 vols. Sarajevo: Svjetlost, 1987.

Emerson, Steven. *The American House of Saud*. New York: Franklin Watts, 1985.

——. *American Jihad*. New York: The Free Press, 2002.

Esposito, John. "The Future of Islam," *The Fletcher Forum*, Medford, MA: Summer 2001.

——. *Unholy War*, Oxford University Press, 2002.

Ferani, Kerim. "The *Jihad* of Imam Shamyl." Published at www.naqshbandi.net.

——. "Puncturing the Devil's Dream About the Hadiths of Najd and Tamim." Published at http://66.34.131.5/ISLAM/misc/najd.htm.

Findley, Paul. *Silent No More*. Beltsville, MD: Amana Publications, 2001.

Fischer, David Hackett. *The Great Wave: Price Revolutions and the Rhythm of History*. Oxford University Press, 1996.

Fisk, Robert. "Divided kingdom that became a cradle for determined killers," London: *The Independent*, September 27, 2001.

Foer, Franklin. "Fevered Pitch," Washington: *The New Republic* November 12, 2001.

Gall, Carlotta and Thomas de Waal. *Chechnya*. New York: New York University Press, 1998.

Gammer, Moshe. *Muslim Resistance to the Tsar*. Portland, OR: Frank Cass, 1994.

Goodson, Larry P. *Afghanistan's Endless War*. Seattle: University of Washington Press, 2001.

Gulen, Fethullah. *Prophet Muhammad: Infinite Light*. Published at www.fethullahgulen.org.

Haddad. G. F. "Ibn Hazm." Published at www.sunnah.org.

El-Halaby, Muhammad. "The Role of Sheikh-ul Islam Ibn Taymiyyah in Jihad Against the Tatars." Published at www.as-sahwah.com.

Halsall, Paul, ed. *The Internet Medieval Source Book*. Published at www.fordham.edu.

Hamzaj, Bardh. *A Narrative about War and Freedom: Dialog with Commander Ramush Haradinaj*. Prishtina: Zeri, 2000.

Harris, Paul, Nick Pelham, and Martin Bright. "Expat Brits live in fear as Saudis turn on the West," *The Observer*, London, July 28, 2002.

Hassan, Fayza. "The king of spring," Cairo: *Al-Ahram Weekly*, April 15–21, 1999.

Heiden, Konrad. *Der Fuehrer*. Boston: Houghton Mifflin, 1944.

Hendricks, Shaykh Seraj. "The Prophet Muhammad (s) — Portrait of a Guided Mercy."

[Hizb-ut Tahrir]. *The American Campaign to Suppress Islam*. London: Al-Khilafah Publications, 1996.

Hoffman, Jamal al-Din. "Family of Light: Five Generations of Mujaddidi Shaykhs," Washington: *The Muslim Magazine*, January 1999.

Ibn 'Abd al Wahhab, Muhammad, *Kitab al Tawhid*, Tr. into English by Isma'il Raji al Faruqi, Riyadh, International Islamic Publishing House, 1991.

Ibn Al-Arabi, Muhyi'ddin. *The Tarjuman al-Ashwaq*. Translated by R.A. Nicholson. London: Theosophical Publishing House, 1978.

Ibn Sulaiman, Dawud. *Ashadd al-jihad* (Arabic edition of 1970). English translation at www.ummah.org.uk/ Al_adaab.

Ibrišimović, Nedžad. *El Libro de Adem Kahriman*. Translated into Spanish by Antonio Saborit and Stephen Schwartz, Mexico: Breve Fondo Editorial, 2000.

Idel, Moshe. *Studies in Ecstatic Kabbalah*. Albany: State University of New York Press, 1988.

Idiz, Semih. "A slippery slope for the Saudis," Istanbul: *Star*. English translation published on-line at *Turkistan Newsletter*, January 13, 2002.

International Criminal Tribunal for the Former Yugoslavia. "The Prosecutor of the Tribunal Against Enver Hadžihasanović/Mehmed Alagić/Amir Kubura, Amended Indictment." Case No: IT-01-47-PT, The Hague, 2002.

[Ishik, Hilmi, ed.] *Advice for the Muslim*. Istanbul: Hakikat Kitabevi, 1998.

——. *Islam's Reformers*. Istanbul: Hakikat Kitabevi, 1998.

——. *The Sunni Path*. Istanbul: Hakikat Kitabevi, 1998.

Ismaeel, Saeed. *The Difference Between the Shi'ites and the Majority of Muslim Scholars*. Riyadh/Falls Church, Va.: World Assembly of Muslim Youth, 1988.

Israeli Defence Forces. *Documents Captured by the IDF*. May 2002, published at www.idf.il.

Izetbegović, Alija Ali. *Islam Between East and West*. Plainfield, Indiana: American Trust Publications, 1984.

Jayyusi, Salma Khadra, ed. *The Legacy of Muslim Spain*. Leiden: Brill, n.d.

Jehl, Douglas. "Dinner Guest of bin Laden Identified as Saudi Fighter," *New York Times*, December 16, 2001.

Johnson, Paul. "'Relentlessly and Thoroughly.'" *National Review*, October 15, 2001.

Kabbani, Shaykh Muhammad Hisham. *Encyclopedia of Islamic Doctrine, Vol. I: Beliefs*. Chicago: Kazi Publications, 1998.

——. ibid., *Vol. 4: Intercession*. Chicago: Kazi Publications, 1998.

——. ibid., *Vol. 7: Forgotten Aspects of Islamic Worship, Part 2*. Chicago: Kazi Publications, 1998.

——. *Islamic Beliefs and Doctrine According to Ahl al-Sunna*. Chicago: Kazi Publications, 1996.

——. *The Naqshbandi Sufi Way*. Chicago: Kazi Publications, 1995.

Karsh, Efraim and Inari. *Empires of the Sand*. Cambridge: Harvard University Press, 1999.

Kaviraj, Narahari. *Wahabi and Farazi Rebels of Bengal*. New Delhi: People's Publishing House, 1982.

Kelly, J. B. *Arabia, the Gulf, and the West*. New York: Basic Books, 1980.

Khomeini, Ruhollah al-Musavi. *Islam and Revolution, Vol. I*. Translated and annotated by Hamid Algar. Berkeley: Mizan Press, 1981.

——. "The Last Message: The Political and Divine Will of His Holiness Imam Khomeini." Published at www.irna.com.

Kiser, John W. *The Monks of Tibhirine*. New York: St. Martin's Press, 2002.

Kline, Chris. "The West and Chechnya: The diplomacy of Realpolitik." Published at www.ichkeria.org, February 5, 2002.

Krauthammer, Charles. "Arafat's Harvest of Hate," *The Washington Post*, March 26, 2002.

Kyle, Keith. *Suez*. London: Weidenfeld and Nicolson, 1991.

Laher, Suheil. "Fiqh of Moon Sighting." Published at www.columbia.edu/cu/msa/files/sightingfiqh.html.

Laqueur, Walter. *The Struggle for the Middle East*. London: Routledge & Kegan Paul, 1969.

Lawrence, T. E. *Seven Pillars of Wisdom*. Harmondsworth: Penguin, 1976.

Lebanese political party Web sites: www.ketaeb.com (the Ketaeb/Phalange) and www.psp.org.lb (Progressive Socialist Party).

Legenhausen, Dr. Muhammad. "Islam and Religious Pluralism." Tehran: *al-Tawhid*, n.d.

Lewis, Bernard. *The Jews of Islam*. Princeton: Princeton University Press, 1984.

——. *The Middle East*. New York: Touchstone, 1995.

——. *The Muslim Discovery of Europe*. New York: Norton, 2001.

Lings, Martin. *Muhammad*. Rochester, VT: Inner Traditions International, 1983.

Lippman, Thomas W. *Understanding Islam*. New York: Penguin, 1995.

Llull, Ramon. *The Book of the Lover and the Beloved*. Edited by Mark D. Johnston. Warminster, UK: Aris & Phillips Ltd., 1995.

Lubman, Sarah, and Richard Scheinin. "Muslim leaders debate their response to extremism," *San Jose Mercury News*, October 22, 2001.

Mansel, Philip. *Constantinople*. New York: St. Martin's Press, 1996.

McGeough, Paul. "Saddam stokes war with suicide bomber cash," *Sydney Morning Herald*, March 26, 2002.

Metcalf, Barbara D. "Piety, Persuasion, and Politics: Deoband's Model of Islamic Activism." Published at www.ssrc.org/sept11/essays/metcalf.htm.

Morris, Benny. *Righteous Victims*. New York: Vintage Books, 2001.

Al-Musnad, Muhammed. *Islamic Fatawa Regarding Women*. Dar-us-Salam Publications, offered for sale at www.dar-us-salam.com.

Naegele, Jolyon. "Yugoslavia: Saudi Wahhabi Aid Workers Bulldoze Balkan Monuments." *Radio Free Europe/Radio Liberty*, published at www.rferl.org.

Nassi, Gad, ed. *Jewish Journalism and Printing Houses in the Ottoman Empire and Modern Turkey*. Istanbul: The Isis Press, 2001.

Neff, Donald. *Warriors at Suez*. New York: Simon & Schuster, 1981.

Norris, H.T. *Islam in the Balkans*. London: Hurst and Co., 1993.

Al-Nowaiser, Mowaffaq. "Khattab, the man who died for the cause of Chechnya," Jeddah: *Arab News*, May 4, 2002.

Nu'mani, 'Allama Shibli. "The Battle of Badr." Extract from English translation of *Sirat-un-Nabi*, published at www.geocities.com/badr_313.

O'Beirne, Kate. "One Question for Abdullah," New York: *National Review Online*, April 25, 2002.

Peterson, J.E. *Historical Dictionary of Saudi Arabia*. N.P.: The Scarecrow Press, 1993.

Qutb, Sayyid. *Social Justice in Islam*. Oneonta, NY: Islamic Publications International, 2000.

Rashid, Ahmed. *Jihad*. New Haven: Yale University Press, 2002.

——. *Taliban*. New Haven: Yale University Press, 2000.

Razwy, Syed A. *Khadija tul Kubra*. Elmhurst, NY: Tahrike Tarsile Qur'an, n.d.

Revue des Etudes Islamiques (Paris), vol. LX, fascicule 1, 1992: "Bektachis."

Rexha, Qerim, and Shyhrete Kadriu. "First Illegal Students Against Terrorism," Prishtina, Kosovo: *Epoka e Re*, December 18, 2001.

Ridley, M. R. *Gertrude Bell*. London: Blackie and Son, 1941.

Rizvi, Seyyid Saeed Akhtar. "Martyrdom of Imam Husayn and the Muslim and Jewish Calendars." Tehran: *Al-Serat*, n.d.

Roig-Franzia, Manuel. "Muslim Linked to 'Dirty Bomb' Suspect is Held," *Washington Post*, June 16, 2002.

Rougemont, Denis de. *Love in the Western World*. Princeton: Princeton University Press, 1983.

Rubin, Alyssa J. "In Kosovo, Ethnicity Outranks Faith," *Los Angeles Times*, April 21, 2002.

Russian Information Centre and RIA Novosti. *Chechnya. The White Book*. Published at www.fas.org, 2000.

Sadat, Mir Hekmatullah. "The Dreaded Devil's Spiral," *The Afghan Magazine*, October 1999, at http://afghanmagazine.com.

Safi, Mawlana Ali ibn Husain. *Beads of Dew from the Source of Life*. Translated by Muhtar Holland. Fort Lauderdale: Al-Baz Publications, 2001.

Saidov, S. "Interview with President Aslan Maskhadov." Published at www.chechenpress. info, May 25, 2002.

Samman, Muhammad. "Saudi Yasin al-Qadi, Accused of Funding Al-Qaida: Yes, I Know Bin Laden and U.S. Vice President is My Friend," London: *Al-Asharq Al-Awsat*, October 14, 2001.

Saudi Information Agency. "Saudi Telethon Host Calls for Enslaving Jewish Women," *National Review Online*, April 26, 2002.

Saudi Institute. *Religious Freedom in the Kingdom of Saudi Arabia*. McLean, VA, 2002.

———. *Torture in Saudi Arabia*. McLean, VA, 2002.

Schimmel, Annemarie. "Karbala and the Imam Husayn in Persian and Indo-Muslim Literature." *Al-Serat*, 1986, published at www.al-islam.org.

Scholem, Gershom. *Kabbalah*. New York: Penguin, 1978.

———. *Sabbatai Sevi: The Mystical Messiah*. Princeton: Princeton University Press, 1973.

Schwartz, Stephen. "The Arab Betrayal of Balkan Islam," *Middle East Quarterly*, Spring 2002.

———. "Arabia's Royal Family Must Choose," Brussels: *Wall Street Journal Europe*, October 10, 2001.

———. "A Balkan Poet," *National Review Online*, June 17–18, 2000.

———. "Behind the Balkan Curtain," *San Francisco Faith*, May 2000.

———. "A Blood Brotherhood," *San Francisco Faith*, September 1998.

———. "Catholic Revival in Kosovo?," *San Francisco Faith*, September 1999.

———. "A Certain Exhaustion," New York: *The New Criterion*, October 2000.

———. "The Cybermonk of Kosovo," Washington: *The Weekly Standard*, December 13, 1999.

———. "Despotism in Saudi Arabia," *The Weekly Standard*, February 18, 2002.

———. "A *Dishonest 20th Century Comedy*." Sarajevo: Forum of the Congress of Bosnian Muslim Intellectuals, 2000.

———. "A Distant Mirror," *National Review*, June 17, 2002.

———. "A Fable for Our Time," *The New Criterion*, October 2001.

———. "Fighting to Save 500 Years of Sephardic Culture," New York: *Forward*, August 11, 1995.

———. "Five Yugoslav Classics," *The New Criterion*, May 2000.

———. "Ground Zero and the Saudi Connection," London: *The Spectator*, September 22, 2001.

———. "In Bosnia, Even the Dead End Up as Casualties," *Forward*, January 21, 1994.

———. "In Sarajevo, a Symbol of Survival," *San Francisco Chronicle*, June 13, 1995.

———. "In Search of the Moderate Sheikh," *The Weekly Standard*, November 12, 2001.

——. "Islam's Wrong Turns," *National Review*, February 25, 2002.

——. "Islamic Fundamentalism in the Balkans," Boston: *Partisan Review*, Summer 2000.

——. "Killing the Messenger," *National Review*, September 3, 2001.

——. *Kosovo: Background to a War*. London: Anthem Press, 2000.

——. "Kosovo's a Mess," *The Weekly Standard*, March 27, 2000.

——. "The 'Ladenese Epistle,'" *The Weekly Standard*, October 29, 2001.

——. "Letter from the Balkans," *The Muslim Magazine*, Winter/Spring 2000.

——. "Letter from Kosovo: Interfaith Dialogue Where No Jews Live," *Forward*, November 17, 2000.

——. "Letter from Sarajevo: Cherished Books," *Forward*, March 3, 2000.

——. "Liberation, Not Containment," *National Review*, November 19, 2001.

——. "Marian Muslim," *San Francisco Faith*, March 1999.

——. "Muddling Through in Bosnia," *The New Criterion*, February 2000.

——. "Muslim Holy Leaders Denounce Terrorism," *San Francisco Chronicle*, August 13, 1998.

——. "Muslims Celebrate Mawlid; Festivities this week honor birth of Prophet," *San Francisco Chronicle*, July 6, 1998.

——. "A Note on 17th-Century Albanian Jewry," San Francisco: *Albanian Catholic Bulletin*, 1994.

——. "Not So Holy After All," *The Weekly Standard*, December 17, 2001.

——. "Our Allies in the Balkans," *The Weekly Standard*, June 17, 2002.

——. "Our Uzbek Friends," *The Weekly Standard*, October 22, 2001.

——. "Our Uzbek Friends," *The Weekly Standard*, March 18, 2002 (the same title used for a different article).

——. "Readings from the Sephardic Diaspora," *Forward*, October 9, 1992.

——. "Recruiters for Jihad," *The Weekly Standard*, January 28, 2002.

——. "Report from Stolac, Hercegovina: The Jewish Cemetery and the Grave of Rabbi Moshe Danon." Sarajevo: Jewish Community of Bosnia-Hercegovina, 1999. Published at www.haverford.edu.

——. "Safe Haven," *The Muslim Magazine*, Summer 1999.

——. "Sarajevo Memories," *The Muslim Magazine*, July 1998.

——. "Sarajevo Serenaders," *Forward*, August 21, 1992.

——. "Saudi Friends, Saudi Foes," *The Weekly Standard*, October 8, 2001.

——. "The Second Betrayal of the Balkans," Budapest: *Soros Local Government Brief*, June 2000.

——. "Seeking Moderation," *National Review Online*, October 25, 2001.

——. "Sheep vs. Goats," *San Francisco Faith*, July 1999.

——. "Sketches of War," *San Francisco Chronicle*, January 10, 1999.

——. "Some Notes on Albanian Jewry," *Albanian Catholic Bulletin*, 1991.

——. "A Sufi Poet Whose Time Has Come—Again," *San Francisco Chronicle*, October 25, 1998.

——. "Trust but Verify," *The Weekly Standard*, November 26, 2001.

——. "Two Books on Bektashi Islam in Albania," *Albanian Catholic Bulletin*, 1991.

——. "The Varieties of Muslim Experience," *The Weekly Standard*, October 15, 2001.

——. "Wahhabis in America," *The Weekly Standard*, November 5, 2001.

——. "Wahhabis in the Old Dominion," *The Weekly Standard*, April 8, 2002.

——. "War Crimes and Punishment," *The Weekly Standard*, August 6, 2001.

——. "Yo soy una rosa," Mexico: *Vuelta*, May 1994.

Scott, Ernest. *The People of the Secret*. London: The Octagon Press, 1983.

Sennott, Charles M. "Before oath to jihad, drifting and boredom," *Boston Globe*, March 3, 2002.

——. "Doubts are cast on the viability of Saudi monarchy for long term," *Boston Globe*, March 5, 2002.

——. "Saudi schools fuel anti-US anger," *Boston Globe*, March 4, 2002.

——. "Why bin Laden plot relied on Saudi hijackers," *Boston Globe*, March 3, 2002.

Shams al-Din, Shaykh Muhammad Mahdi. *The Revolution of al-Husayn [a]: Its Impact on the Consciousness of Muslim Society*. Translated by I. K. A. Howard, Muhammadi Trust of Great Britain and Northern Ireland, 1985.

Sharaf al-Din, Khalid. "Fundamentalists' Leaders Formed Bogus Organizations to Confuse the Security Organs," London: *Al-Asharq al-Awsat*, March 7, 1999.

Siddique, Kaukab. "ISNA's Campaign Against Shaikh Kabbani." Kingsville, MD: *New Trend*.

Siddiqui, Mateen. "Mujahid Saints of the Caucasus." Published at www.islamicsupreme-council.org.

Sulaiman, Abu. "Exposing Al-Tijani's Lies in His Book *Then I Was Guided*." Published at www.ansar.org.

Sulaiman, Amir. "The Battlefield: The Safest Place on Earth." Published at www.as-sahwah.com.

Supreme Council for Islamic Affairs, Cairo, Egypt. *Why the Prophet Muhammad (pbuh) Married More Than One*. Published at www.islamicmessage.net.

Timmerman, Kenneth R. "Sneak Preview." "Saudis Buy Friends, Influence in Washington," Washington: *Insight*, June 3, 2002.

Trotsky, Leon. *The Struggle Against Fascism in Germany*. Harmondsworth: Penguin, 1975.

Tutuncu, Mehmet, ed. *Turkish Jewish Encounters*. Haarlem (Netherlands): SOTA, 2001.

U.S. Department of Justice, International Crime Alert, Re: Khalid Bin Hamad Al Gheshiyan.

Unsigned. "Arafat says foreign powers support suicide bombers." Reuters news service, May 13, 2002.

Unsigned. "The Battle of Badr." Published at www.islaam.com.

Unsigned. "The Battle of Uhud." Published at www.al-islam.org.

Unsigned. "The Battle of Uhud." Published at www.prophetmuhammad.org.

Unsigned. "The Historic Afghan Jihad (1979–1989)." Published at www.azzam.com.

Unsigned. "History of the Cemetery of Jannat al-Baqi." Published at www.al-islam.org.

Unsigned. "History of the Shrine at Kerbala." Published at www.al-islam.org.

Unsigned. *How the Khilafah Was Destroyed*. London: Al-Khilafah Publications, n.d., published at www.khilafah.com.

Unsigned. "Influential American Muslims Temper Their Tone." October 19, 2001, published at http://senrs.com.

Unsigned. Press Releases. Saudi Embassy, Washington, D.C., 1997–2001, published at www.saudiembassy.net.

Unsigned. *Religion in Kosovo*. Brussels: International Crisis Group, 2001.

Unsigned. "Saudi Government Paper: 'Billions Spent by Saudi Royal Family to Spread Islam to Every Corner of the World.'" Washington: Middle East Media Research Institute, translated from *Ain Al-Yaqeen* of March 1, 2002.

Unsigned. "Saudi monarchy faces religious dilemma." February 2, 2002, published at www.sauditimes.com.

Unsigned. "Saudis Seek U.S. Muslims for Their Sect." n.d., published at http://senrs.com.

Unsigned. *Stories of the Shuhadaa' of Sheeshaan and Frequently Asked Questions about the Jihad in Chechnya*. Azzam Publications, 2000, published at www.qoqaz.net.

Unsigned. "Two People in Kosovo Arrested for Terrorism are from Iraq," Prishtina, Kosovo: *Bota Sot*, December 17, 2001.

Unsigned. *Uzbekistan: Class Dismissed: Discriminatory Expulsions of Muslim Students*. New York: Human Rights Watch, 1999.

Valensi, Lucette. *The Birth of the Despot*. Ithaca: Cornell University Press, 1993.

Various. "Muslim Soldiers in the U.S. Armed Forces in Afghanistan: To Fight or Not to Fight?" Middle East Media Research Institute, November 6, 2001.

Vassiliev, Alexei. *The History of Saudi Arabia*. London: Saqi Publications, 2000.

Weismann, Itzchak, *Taste of Modernity*. Leiden: Brill, 2001.

Wihbey, Paul Michael. "Succession in Saudi Arabia: The not so Silent Struggle." Institute for Advanced Strategic and Political Studies, 1997.

Williams, Daniel. "Bomber Unleashed Secret Rage," *Washington Post*, April 14, 2002.

Yergin, Daniel. *The Prize*. New York: Simon & Schuster, 1992.

Al-Zahawi, Jamal Effendi al-'Iraqi al-Sidqi. *The Doctrine of Ahl al-Sunna Versus the 'Salafi' Movement*. Chicago: Kazi Publications, 1996. (Translation of *The True Dawn in Refuting Those Who Deny the Seeking of Intercession and the Miracles of Saints*.)

Zahoor, Dr. A. and Dr. Z. Haq. Various articles on Islamic history. 1998, published at http://users.erols.com/zenithco/muhammad.html.

[Al-Zawahiri, Ayman]. "*Al-Asharq Al-Awsat* Publishes Extracts From Al-Jihad Leader Al-Zawahiri's Book." London: *Al-Asharq Al-Awsat*, December 2, 2001.

Zogiani, Avni. "Who Are bin Laden's People in Kosovo?," Prishtina, Kosovo: *Koha Ditore*, December 18, 2001.

INDEX